COLONIALISM *and* INDIAN ECONOMY

COLONIALISM *and* INDIAN ECONOMY

Amiya Kumar Bagchi

OXFORD
UNIVERSITY PRESS

OXFORD
UNIVERSITY PRESS

Oxford University Press is a department of the University of Oxford.
It furthers the University's objective of excellence in research, scholarship,
and education by publishing worldwide. Oxford is a registered trademark of
Oxford University Press in the UK and in certain other countries

Published in India by
Oxford University Press
2/11 Ground Floor, Ansari Road, Daryaganj, New Delhi 110 002, India

First Edition published in 2010

ISBN-13: 978-0-19-806644-6
ISBN-10: 0-19-806644-9

Typeset in 10.5/12.5 Adobe Garamond Pro
by Excellent Laser Typesetters, Pitampura, Delhi 110 034
Printed in India by Replika Press Pvt. Ltd

In grateful memory of Maurice Herbert Dobb (1900–76)
and Joan Violet Robinson (1903–83)

Contents

Tables

Preface

From the time I began to examine the phenomenon of the low standard of living of the vast majority of the Indian people, I was repeatedly forced to ask questions about how it came about. The answers almost always required delving into history. Very often that delving required me to throw away the false arguments that covered up the real reasons. Most of the papers that have been collected in this volume arose out of that quest for the basic reasons for the emergence and perdurance of low human development in a country that gave rise to one of the ancient civilizations of the world.

The papers have been written over a period covering a quarter of a century. Naturally, their writing has involved incurring a debt to very large numbers of economists and historians. Some of that debt has been acknowledged in specific cases. But I should record my debt to those institutions in particular which facilitated my researches. They include the Centre for Social Sciences, Calcutta; the State Bank of India and especially the team of researchers in the History Cell of the bank, ably led by Abhik Ray; the Maison des Sciences de l'Homme, Paris; and the Institute of Development Studies Kolkata (IDSK). Many friends helped stimulate my thinking and dispel cobwebs of confusion. They include Samir Amin, Maurice Aymard, Debdas Banerjee, Himani Bannerji, Sabyasachi Bhattacharya, Terry Byres, Nirmal Chandra, the late Pramit Chaudhuri, Amalendu Guha, Irfan Habib, John McGuire, the late John Martinussen, Saugata Mukherji, Prabhat Patnaik, Utsa Patnaik, Peter Reeves, Manoj Sanyal, Mark Selden, Amartya Sen, Sunanda Sen, Marika Vicziany, Immanuel Wallerstein, and David Washbrook.

I am lucky that practically all the members of my immediate family, Barnita Bagchi, Jasodhara Bagchi, Tista Bagchi, and Aditya Bhattacharjea have, at various times, acted as sounding boards for my ideas. At the IDSK, Ramkrishna Chatterjee, Madhusri Ghosh, Sanchari Guha (Samanta) and Kakoli Banerjee and all members of the devoted non-academic staff have helped in the production of the book. Juliet Yee of Monash Asia Institute helped find a critical reference. At the Oxford University Press, I would like to thank the team for their untiring effort to produce a presentable volume. Their perseverance in the belief that this selection would become an independent book was critical in producing it.

None of the above-mentioned persons bear any responsibility for the blemishes of this offering.

AMIYA KUMAR BAGCHI

Acknowledgments

I join the publisher to gratefully acknowledge the publishers of the journals and publications cited below for permission to publish the following articles in part or in full:

BIBLIOGRAPHICAL RESEARCH CENTRE
'An Estimate of the Gross Domestic Material Product of Bengal and Bihar in 1794 from Colebrooke's data', *Nineteenth Century Studies*, No. 3, *Indian Peasants,* (Calcutta, 1973).

BENGAL PAST AND PRESENT
'Reflections on Patterns of Regional Growth in India under the British Rule', *Bengal Past and Present*, XCV (1), January–June, pp. 247–89 (Calcutta, 1976).

ROUTLEDGE
'De-industrialization in India in the Nineteenth Century: Some Theoretical Implications', *Journal of Development Studies*, Vol. 12, No. 2, pp. 135–64, (January, 1976).
'Land Tax, Property Rights, and Peasant Insecurity in Colonial India' *Journal of Peasant Studies*, Vol. 20, No. 1, pp. 1–50, (October, 1992).

PEOPLE'S PUBLISHING HOUSE
'De-industrialization Gangetic Bihar 1809–1901' in B. De *et al. Essays in Honour of Professor S.C. Sarkar* (New Delhi, 1976).

SAGE PUBLICATIONS
'A Reply (to Dr Marika Vicziany)', originally published in *The Indian Economic and Social History Review*, Vol. 16, No. 2, [Copyright © The Indian Economic and Social History Association, New Delhi. 1988,

all rights reserved]. Reproduced with the permission of the copyright holders and the publishers, Sage Publications India Pvt. Ltd. (New Delhi, 1979).

FRONTIER
'Relation of Agriculture to Industry in the Context of South Asia', *Frontier*, Vol. 8, Nos 22–4, pp. 12–27 (Calcutta, 1975).

Introduction

Colonial Rule as Structural Adjustment: Expropriation, Agency, and Survival*[1]

Global Competition for Empire and the Perspective of Imperialism

How did the British create an empire in India (today's South Asia)? The idea that the British empire in India was created in a fit of absent-mindedness has been perhaps buried. But the idea that it was really the unforeseen result of British, and more generally European, intervention in local conflicts is still floating around. Marxists and world-system theorists have long claimed that imperialism was a driving force from the time Europeans 'discovered' the Americas and an oceanic route to Asia (Dobb 1946; Baran 1957; Bagchi 1972a, 1972b; Wallerstein 1980), and that furthermore, it had generally had a negative impact on the fortunes of the conquered people.

Only recently, historians have recognized the creation of the empire as the outcome of a series of deliberate acts and 'empire' has become a respectable category again. The Oxford University Press has come out with a five-volume history of the British empire (Canny 1998; Marshall 1998; Porter 1999). From the late fifteenth century, there was active competition among major European powers such as Spain, France, and England, and even smaller powers such as the Netherlands and Sweden

*Non-incriminating thanks are due to Jasodhara Bagchi, Arun Bandopadhyay, Himani Bannerji, and David Washbrook for their searching comments on earlier versions of this essay.

for carving out an empire, especially in lands overseas (Pagden 1995; Armitage 1998, 2000; Bagchi 2006[2005]. Harvey (2005) has distinguished between territorial and capitalist logics of power. However, in the history of actually existing capitalism and imperialism since the late fifteenth century, the two logics were inextricably intertwined. If Portugal and Spain seemed to be keen on territorial expansion, search for bullion as the main item of trade with Asia was a driving force in their case. On the other side, the Dutch fought successfully to take over the major trading posts in the Indonesian archipelago from the Portuguese and proceeded to impose a coercive monopsony on the spice trade of Indonesia.

Even some analysts claiming to be Marxists, Bill Warren (1980) being a notorious example, have lauded imperialism as a progressive force. They regard any growth of large-scale industry or trade or what they regard as capitalist enterprises as positive for a territory without inquiring into their relative magnitudes in relation to other activities such as last-resource or subsistence farming and their actual impact on the social structures and the standards of living of the people concerned. They also ignore the phenomenon of primitive accumulation (Marx 1886[1887]: Chapters 26–32; Dobb 1946), which has been styled by David Harvey (2003) as 'accumulation by dispossession'. Under that process, while the peasants of pioneering capitalist countries suffered greatly, the non-white colonies of Europe suffered demographic and economic disasters extending from the early sixteenth to the middle of the twentieth century (Bagchi [2006[2005]: Chapters 13–18).

The British empire was the largest territorial empire ever known in history and the British Indian empire was its most important component in terms of the number of colonial subjects and in terms of the resources extracted from it, from at least the beginning of the eighteenth century to the First World War. So Indian colonial history is an integral part of global history in the age of imperialism; conversely, global history has to be an overarching framework for writing Indian history. There has, therefore, been a strenuous attempt on the part of pro-imperialist historians and publicists to portray British rule in India as an unmixed or at least strongly positive blessing for India. On the other side were Indian nationalist historians, among whom R.C. Dutt wrote the most systematic discourse (Dutt 1963a[1906], 1963b[1906]), who challenged the view of British rule as a benign presence in India.

The pro-imperialist discourse re-surfaced in Indian historiography with a paper by Morris David Morris (1963), who argued that India had clearly benefited under British rule and most arguments contradicting that view were both theoretically and empirically unsound.[2] Many of the contributions in *The Cambridge History of India*, vol. 2, on the period of British rule (Kumar and Desai 1983) have followed Morris's lead in this respect, with utter disregard for some of the basic facts of economic development in that period.

The Oxford History of the British Empire includes the writings of historians who have found that many phases of British rule in India were attended with enormous dislocation and decline (for example, Ray 1998; Washbrook 1999). In the first volume of the *New Cambridge History of India*, Bayly (1990: Chapter 5) recognized that there were phases of absolute economic decline in India and that the establishment of the British empire led to a greater degree of authoritarianism and the exalting of the (alien) 'executive over local liberties' (Bayly 1989: 8), and the downgrading or decimation of local elites with the metropolitan officials lording over them. Nonetheless, recently, there has been a gloating celebration of imperialism by many publicists (for example, Ferguson 2004). Others, while admitting that Britain possessed an empire, have denied that it benefited Britain in any fashion (for example, O'Brien 1982, 1988) or that it could have harmful effects on India or other non-white colonies.

In my own work, I have been concerned to analyse (a) the rise of capitalist imperialism as an inevitable outcome of competition among capitalists and the states backing them with arms (Bagchi 2006[2005]; (b) the mechanism generating and sustaining the resource flows that catapulted Britain and other capitalist powers to global dominance (Bagchi 1972a, 1972b, 1982a, and 2006[2005]); and (c) the economic and social consequences of colonial rule in India. Some of the articles collected here shed light particularly on this last area of operation of British imperialism.[3]

The Mirage of Emergence of a Civil Society under Colonialism

It is necessary first to be clear about some of the terms used in discourses on economic development and underdevelopment. Celebrants of capitalism and capitalist colonialism claim that Western powers introduced the notion of equality before law and introduced and protected the right of private persons to possess productive assets, including land. These measures are alleged to have laid the foundations of a civil society in India.

In the pre-colonial era, however, in both India and China, private property in land and its heritability and transferability were legally protected. Ironically, in British India and other colonies, the British (and the French) deliberately made such property insecure for the non-white peoples, for the sake of extraction of a surplus, and in order to provide the white settlers both practically free land and command over the labour power of the dispossessed people (Chapter 8 in this volume and Bagchi 1982: Chapter 4; Bagchi 2006[2005]: Chapters 9–10; Bagchi 2009). In these countries, land was the very basis of existence for most people; the deprivation of access to that asset struck at their very survival prospects. This was all done by codifying that deprivation, so that racialism became part of the fabric of colonial rule.

A civil society as conceived by theorists of the bourgeois or capitalist order should have a clear separation between private and public spaces. The latter should not be differentiated between different groups on the basis of religion, ethnicity, or gender, and no person should be prevented from using the public space because of non-market coercion. The abolition of private coercive power, which was bound up with feudal institutions, was a precondition for the creation of a civil society in Europe. In continental Western Europe, it required the onslaught of the French revolutionary and Napoleonic armies for the grossest forms of feudal privileges to be exorcized.

A civil society could not emerge under colonialism because the rulers used various forms of ethnic discrimination, often deliberately encouraged patriarchy in property rights, routinely practised non-market coercion, and discriminated between the rulers and the ruled on a racial basis. On the other side, the colonialized people routinely used various forms of patriarchy and ethnic or religious ascription to strengthen or invent their own identities. That does not mean that particular groups of the ruled did not try and create their own civil organizations that tried to do away with the ascriptive gender, ethnic, or religiously sanctioned hierarchies. But the repressive nature of the colonial order ensured that such organizations could never become dominant.

To illustrate the problems of creating a truly civil society, let me start with the case of the civil freedom enjoyed by labour under colonialism. Pre-colonial India did not have the chattel slavery used by the European capitalists in the tropical plantations and mines. When south Indian kings still had independent power in their territories, they disapproved of the kind of chattel slavery the Dutch tried to introduce there (Raychaudhuri 1962; Washbrook 1993a). Except in some pockets of south India and Bihar, 'slaves' were rarely used for productive purposes (Dhar 1973; Washbrook 1993a). In Thanjavur and some other regions of wet paddy cultivation, the bonded 'slaves' often belonged to a community rather than to individuals; they were often sold with the land and could not be sold otherwise (Hjejle 1967). This was really akin to servitude of the East European variety than to plantation slavery of the Caribbean or Mauritius in the eighteenth century. As in the case of the servitude imposed by the Romanovs on the Russian peasantry, this was an indication of the scarcity of labour (Kliuchevsky 1960[1906]; Domar 1970; Bagchi 2007). Such bonded workers could often turn an increased scarcity to their own advantage, until the East India Company could use its power to exclude all competitors to impose a condition of monopsony, or throw the bonded labourers, who had enjoyed the right to subsistence, on to the labour market in the name of freeing them (Washbrook 1993a). There is a mistaken notion that the British abolished slavery in India in 1843 (Hjejle 1967). Actually, what they did was to legislate that a slave could attain freedom by appealing to a court: it is this device of non-recognition of slavery that they also used in their African colonies such as Nigeria (Lovejoy and Hogendorn 1993; Bagchi 1999). Agrestic serfs were essential for the cultivation by landholding groups in many parts of south India (Sarkar 1985; Washbrook 1993a), and the colonial rulers could not afford to abolish that kind of bondage for fear of provoking a drastic decline in land revenue.

Moreover, the British state repeatedly intervened in order to restrict the freedom of weavers working for the East India Company, to recruit forced labour for public works, to allow plantation owners to indenture labour, and to criminalize the breach of contract on the part of workers and give the planters the power of arresting workers who were supposedly guilty of a breach of contract (Sarkar 1985; Ahuja 1999, 2002; Bagchi 1999). The British rulers continued to use the coercive provisions of the Masters and Servants Act for a long time after they had been given a quietus in Britain (Bagchi 2009).

When an absolute compression of incomes from both agriculture and industry led to the rise of vast masses of people living on the verge of subsistence and underemployment and became an endemic phenomenon, it led often to the strengthening of old ties of bondage or emergence of new ties of casual bondage (Bagchi 1973b; Breman 1974). Of course, very often landlords faced with falling incomes and the burden of maintaining agrestic serfs sought to get rid of them. These freed serfs often then became victims of indenture in distant lands (Baak 1999).

Several myths were constructed by the ruling power in order to sustain the ideology of continued occupation. One was that there was no private property in land in pre-British India, and all land belonged to the sovereign. The right of the sovereign to claim a portion of the produce of the land was converted into the proposition that land belonged solely to the sovereign. Another presumption that justified usurpation of all land outside the cultivated areas was that if there was no documentary evidence of occupation of land by any group, such as forest-dwellers or pastoralists who moved regularly from one ecological niche to another, depending on the availability of pasture and shelter, then that could be treated as waste land or disposable public domain. Except for the areas that European planters or railway companies were interested in, the British did not allow land to be held under fee simple tenure or even under long leases. What they did was to create property rights in land revenues to be paid to the state, and rendered landed property highly insecure for actual cultivators of land (Bagchi 1982a: Chapter 4).

Take two other aspects of reform the British rulers sought to introduce. The attempt of the British to disallow distinctions of caste and community in courts of criminal justice and to give some recognition to women's autonomy within the family, certainly resonated with the awakening of people of the so-called lower castes such as Jotirao Phule (2002) and the fighters for women's rights such as Pandita Ramabai (2000) and Rokeya Sakhawat Hossain (Barnita Bagchi 2009). But in their attempt to find the least-cost structure of administration and justice, the British in fact accepted many of the caste taboos and the basic laws and customs sustaining the subordination of women. Hence the fighters for women's freedom and the rights of Dalits and other lower castes had to fight both the conservative nationalists and the colonial government. In south India and elsewhere, the colonial courts often delivered judgements that recognized the rights of particular castes, excluding others from the enjoyment of what should have been in the public domain (Appadurai 1981; Susan Bayly 1999).

Of course, the colonial interaction with the local people was not a one-way affair. In parts of Kerala, a tradition of matriliny had prevailed among the Nairs from pre-colonial days. This appeared to be anomalous to the colonial rulers with their strong traditions of patriarchy, who smelled polyandry and worse, in this system. They were joined by Nair men who felt oppressed by the power of the older people over the disposition of the property and other rights. The colonial authorities elevated the *karanavan*, an elder man of the household, who acted as the intermediary between the property-owning collective and the outside world, to the position of the head of the household, and eventually took away the rights of the elder women, including their property rights (Arunima 2003).

Similar transformations through the interactions of the changes brought about by colonial rule and the response and resistance of different sections of the community can be traced in both Hindu and Muslim revivalism, especially from the late nineteenth century. There were two different paths to Muslim revivalism taken in Uttar Pradesh and Bengal. In Uttar Pradesh, while Sir Sayyid Ahmad Khan of the Aligarh movement wanted the Muslims to follow Western education and gain equality in that sphere with the Hindus, the founders of the Deoband school wanted Islam to be purged of its supposedly impure accretions from local practices, and thereby resist the cultural onslaught of colonialism (Metcalf 2002). Both cases were *ashraf* initiatives, but they were able to convince many poorer Muslims of the need to forge a separate Muslim identity. In Bengal, the movement for purifying Islam and properly Islamicizing the illiterate Muslim masses in the difficult terrain of the Brahmaputra Gangetic delta was conducted by itinerant preachers moving among the peasantry. It is only from the early twentieth century that the elite, often Urdu-speaking Muslims, recognized the political utility of these reformist movements and incorporated them in their own agenda. Faced with the rise of a Congress-led nationalism under mostly Hindu leadership, the colonial rulers began to favour the Muslim separatist tendencies (Ahmed 1981). In the case of Bengal, the background of the later success of the movement for partition of the country owed much to the discontent of the impoverished Muslim peasantry who saw the mostly Hindu zamindars as their main enemy (Bagchi 1972a: Chapter 14). The rise of Hindu fundamentalism, for example, as expressed in the so-called cow-protection movement, had as its background similar interactions between the dominant Hindu landlord groups and their professional spokesmen and a Hindu peasantry suffering multiple deprivations and oppressions (Sarkar 1983: Chapter 3; Pandey 2006).

Some of the Enlightenment theorists of civil society and their latter-day followers had claimed that the spread of the market and the rule of law would lead to the emergence of a civil society, in which distinctions of religion or ascribed status would not matter in determining the contours of human existence. In all the cases sketched above, colonialism—by imposing its impoverishing and degrading rule, by codifying caste and community distinctions that had been much more fluid in pre-colonial days, and circumscribing many of the property rights of women among the Nairs and Muslims—precluded the emergence of a secular, civil society, let alone a human society, in which everybody would enjoy both formal and substantive freedom. Apart from these macrosocial departures from the ideal of a homogenized civil society under colonial rule, the cellular relations between labour and capital remained very different from owners of the means of production facing a mass of free workers. The latter remained semi-servile even in many apparently 'capitalist' enterprises and racism remained the norm rather than the exception in enterprises controlled by Europeans (Bagchi 1988b).

Washbrook (1993b) has rightly associated the 'traditionalization' of south Indian society under colonial rule with the long depression extending from 1820 to 1855 (Raghavaiyangar 1893; Thomas and Natarajan 1936; Mukherjee 1962; Bandopadhyay 1992). The price depression from the 1820s to the 1840s affected practically all of India, and led to major structural changes that tended to increase the power of the local landlords and their castes (Narain 1929; Siddiqi 1973).

However, we must remember that India underwent the equivalent of a two-century long IMF-style structural adjustment programme (SAP) in major parts of India. There could be price depressions and on some occasions price inflations, such as the periods of the American Civil War, two World Wars, and the years between 1896 and 1913, superimposed on the long-term downward trend in income and living standards. Under the impact of the colonial SAP, hundreds of thousands of artisans lost their livelihood, productivity-increasing investment in agriculture shrank, and business communities in many parts of colonial India were pushed out of the most profitable avenues of trade or became subordinate collaborators of European businessmen. India witnessed some of the biggest famines in history, in Bengal from 1769, in south India from the 1780s down to the 1830s, and again between the 1870s and early 1900s in western and southern India, apart from many smaller famines that were not officially recognized (Arnold 1999; Klein 2001; Bagchi 2006[2005]: Chapter 18).

The phenomenon of de-industrialization, to which I have paid considerable attention, is only one component of this depression of the long-term trends of the economy. 'De-industrialization' of a country in current usage, and as used in my essays included here, means a decline in the proportion of workers deriving their income from secondary industry, and also a decline in the proportion of GDP derived from secondary industry. A stronger definition, appropriate for the major time period of colonial rule in India, would also include a fall or stagnation of income per head.

Capitalism and its constant companion, colonialism or imperialism, have always been riven with contradictions, as has been argued most canonically by Marx and Engels and their eminent followers. The gap between the promise and the reality has shown up in the strengthening and the global spread of slavery just as capitalist industrialization was maturing; the strengthening of male-centred property rights even as equality between sexes was proclaimed; and the use of racist laws and conventions to consolidate European hegemony even as Enlightenment thinkers such as Rousseau and Condorcet were attacking the phenomenon of human inequality sanctioned by social and political institutions. Thus the creation of 'civil society' which lies at the heart of the professed ideology of capitalism remained an ever-receding dream, especially in the non-white colonies. As Marx (1976[1845]: 617) proclaimed in his tenth thesis on Feuerbach: 'The standpoint of the old materialism is civil society; the standpoint of the new is human society, or social humanity'. The celebrants of capitalist colonialism have failed to recognize that the material and legal conditions for attaining a semblance of a civil society were totally lacking in the colonial societies.

While the colonialized peoples' response or resistance often led to the strengthening of patriarchy, caste, or religious divisions, the search for 'social humanity' was also led by some of the great thinkers searching for models transcending the boundaries of colonial culture. Mahatma Gandhi's rejection of the kind of modernity preached by the Westernizers is well known. To my mind, the much more interesting case is that of Rabindranath Tagore, who accepted many aspects of that kind of modernity, but sought to decolonize the whole culture of Indians. He rejected a narrow form of political nationalism, because he found that its incarnation in the imperialist countries led inevitably to a struggle for mastery over others and generated genocidal wars. But his creative energy was directed towards educational projects teaching the equality of all human beings, releasing their imaginative energies and getting rid of the stigmas of gender and communal discrimination. That creative urge of the ruled for decolonizing and secularizing the Indian society was incompatible with the colonial political order (Jasodhara Bagchi 1996; Bannerji 2008).

The Spoils of Monopoly: East India Trade from the 1690s to the 1750s

We will see later that the tribute extracted from India was a crucial support for the British victory against the French in their century-long competition for acquiring a hegemonic position in Europe and the world, especially in the critical phase of war against first Revolutionary, and then Napoleonic, France. In the meantime, let me briefly glance at the relation of the emergence of the cotton textile industry, the leading industry of the Industrial Revolution in Britain, and the fortunes of the Indian cotton textile industry during that period. Trade with the 'East' and 'West Indies' proved to be increasingly profitable over the seventeenth century for the East India Company (EIC) and the interlopers who traded from England in breach of the monopoly of trade granted to the EIC and the Royal Africa Company. While the main 'commodity' traded by the Africa Company was enslaved Africans, manufactures, particularly textiles, were the main staple of the import trade of the EIC. Contemporaries such as Charles Davenant (1696/1771) and Henry Martyn (1701) argued in favour of continuing to engage in the East India trade, contradicting the arguments of those who saw it as a threat to the woollen manufactures of England, on the ground that the re-export of Indian textiles was highly profitable, that it promoted shipping and ship-building, thereby benefiting the naval strength of the British and speeding Britain towards the lordship of all the oceans. Most of the pamphleteers of the time also agreed that the EIC should enjoy a monopoly of the East India trade because only then would it be able to maintain expensive factories and troops to defend them and ships that could defend themselves against competitors. Thus they had no doubt that the trade would be defended and expanded with arms, whenever the occasion demanded.

Between 1660 and 1700, while the imports and exports of England grew fast, re-exports of the imports from the Americas and Asia constituted 30 per cent of the total imports (Davis 1954). Further, re-exports of Indian textiles in the years 1699–1701 probably formed 40 per cent of the corresponding imports into England. Indian imports grew in spite of a continual increase in the duties on Indian textiles from the 1660s, as P.J. Thomas in his strangely neglected classic documented (1926: 65–6). Then in 1700, the import of all Indian textiles, except for purposes of re-export was banned (Ibid.: Chapter 5).

However, in the meanwhile, the English, the French, and other Europeans had become used to wearing Indian and Chinese textiles, which were much lighter than the heavy English woollens (Thomas 1926: Chapter 2; Tilly 1994). An active process of import substitution, with imitations of Indian printing and dyeing methods and the invention of new designs to suit the changing European tastes, was in operation. In 1720, in response to an agitation by weavers of woollens, even the wearing of locally printed 'calicoes' was banned in England. There is little doubt that imitation and emulation of Indian textiles greatly stimulated the eventual rise of the mechanized cotton spinning industry as the leading sector of the English Industrial Revolution.

Colonial Rule as Structural Adjustment: The First Phase

The economy that EIC conquered was not a barter or so-called natural economy, but was a thriving exchange economy with strong links of trade amongst different regions and with the rest of the world. The majority of the people eked a livelihood from agriculture, but it was also a manufacturing economy. It has been estimated that in 1750, India accounted for almost a quarter of the manufactures—products of handicraft industries and China for another third of the manufactures—products of the world (Simmons 1985). The political economists of seventeenth-century England referred to their own country as a trading, manufacturing country. India and China were also trading, manufacturing countries until the British conquest of Bengal and the defeat of the Chinese in the first Opium War. They were following a pattern of growth, which, following Bin Wong (1997), I have characterized as Smithian growth. The difference between that pattern and capitalist growth was that while in China and India, private property in movables and in land was recognized, the transfers, sales, and inheritance of land were regulated by state laws or local usage that had the force of law; in Britain and the Netherlands, such restrictions were done away with. Moreover, in Britain as in the Netherlands, state power came to be concentrated in the hands of a property-owning oligarchy, whereas in China, property-holders as such never acquired that kind of power (Bagchi 2006[2005]).

India, then the second largest manufacturing nation in the world, was seen by the emerging capitalist powers first as a region whose trade was to be monopolized by a particular nation, and then as a rich country to be conquered for the sake of profit and glory. In the competition between the French and the English for obtaining control over the subcontinent, the latter won. As we will see, the tribute extracted from India played a critical part in sustaining the British war against the French, and in facilitating the building up of the overseas settlements of the Europeans through the process of European migration and British foreign investment from the 1870s to the First World War. Moreover, the migration of indentured Indian labourers to European-controlled plantations stretching from the Caribbean to Malaysia provided sugar, tea, and other plantation products much needed by the global capitalist economy. Thus Indian history is a critical part of global history, as indeed, conversely, global history is a part of Indian history.

Within sixty years of the defeat of the last independent Nawab of Bengal by the British, India was reduced to the status of an agrarian and underdeveloped economy. This was noted by contemporary British observers themselves, and evoked protests against the policy that led to this retrogression from some of the top colonial administrators such as Henry St George Tucker.[4] The process of colonialization of the Indian economy involved the extraction of a tribute from the economy at an unprecedented rate. That extraction, in turn, required the structural adjustment of the economy in the sense that the domestic absorption of commodities produced by India had to be continually squeezed so as to yield an exportable surplus that would be remitted to the ruling country. That structural adjustment involved the severe depression of investment in both agriculture and industry and also required radical alteration of the modes of extraction of the tribute. De-industrialization in India was accompanied not by reallocation of normally growing resources to agriculture but the depression of growth rates of both industry and agriculture.[5] Structural adjustment also, of course, required some basic changes in property rights and legal institutions.

This continual drain of resources acted as an endemic, relentless depressant on both the demand and supply sides of the economy, and involved massive market failures all over India (See Chapter 9 in this volume). People survived by sheer determination to negotiate the hazards posed by oppression and deprivation. Many artisans became cultivators or landless labourers, or simply starved to death in famines, while some others shifted to coarser varieties of products meant for an impoverished domestic market. Forest-dwellers were uprooted to become plantation labourers in India and abroad, or became the advance army for opening up land. Free peasants with secure occupancy rights to their land became dependent on landlords in semi-servile bondage. Business communities were decimated; some adapted to the colonial conditions, and even prospered in regions in which British domination came later. But all this enormous human energy could not stop Indians from becoming impoverished in most regions. Human agency was not enough to stop India from sliding into the status of one of the poorest societies under imperial rule, with very high mortality rates, almost universal illiteracy, and with various ties of bondage often becoming tighter even after 'enlightened' legislation sought to free Indians from the extreme oppressions of patriarchy, casteism, and religious bigotry.[6]

During the days of the Company Raj, the EIC realized the dividends by exacting a tribute in the form of land tax and erecting a coercive monopoly of trade (and production in the case of opium and salt) for the Company or, after the abolition of the Parliament-sanctioned monopoly of external trade, through the intermediary of the so-called agency houses controlled by a clique of British businessmen.

The conquest and 'pacification' of India between 1757 and 1818 involved a long-drawn out depression, effective de-monetization of large parts of the economy in the interior, and repeated famines and emergence of new types of bondage around the production of indigo, sugar, and—from the 1840s—tea and coffee plantations.

Pre-British India had a thriving exchange economy moving along the path of Smithian growth. Under such a regime, markets in commodities, as pointed out above, labour and land functioned, but the activities of capital and the exchangeability of land were strictly regulated by the state. These markets co-existed with many varieties of non-market coercion exercised by the ruling classes. But the British did not free markets—apart from the dependence that is often induced by endemic unemployment and insecurity of subsistence, the British rulers curbed the freedom of workers by specific legislation. In place of a free market of land, they made landholding conditional on the prompt payment of an often-exorbitant land tax. At most, they created a market in revenue farming rights. Avenues for the advance of the emerging capitalist strata were blocked by explicit and implicit racial discrimination.

The resurgence of a neocolonial view that somehow India thrived under British rule is based on wilful illiteracy and total insensitivity to the deaths of tens of millions of Indians in famines and indirectly, of several hundred millions in avoidable malnutrition and epidemic diseases and a structural retrogression of the economy that squeezed both the base of and incentives for domestic investment in industry and even more, in agriculture. The neocolonial, largely phantasmagoric, perspective utilizes the supposed lack of systematized data on the Indian subcontinent for most of the period and picks out some features that seem to favour their view.[7]

The complex of causes and effects of this colonial mechanism, working through the economy and society, can be summarized in the following sketch: From the 1820s there was a massive decline in the exports and domestic demand for Indian textiles, both spun and woven; conquest led to a decline in demand for services and domestically produced commodities; rigorous collection of a land tax only in high-powered and remittable money led to further depression of demand and investment in agriculture and non-agricultural sectors (and in neoclassical language, a continual pushing of the production frontier inward). Demonetization of all earlier media of exchange, including those circulating in local exchanges and often accepted earlier for public payments, turned the terms of exchange savagely against poorer people. Apart from the bondage that was induced by this complex of insecurity of life and employment, various non-market restraints were imposed both by the state and the superior power-holders of Indian society and led to the fixation of the production basket further away from the shrinking production frontier, and choice of unproductive assets by the Indian wealth-holders. Colonialism started with the market failure that has been the birthmark of capitalism emanating from Europe, namely, the use of arms to grab what could not be earned in peaceful trade. The colonial order continued with both induced and state-imposed market failures.

Until 1756, the EIC had to import several hundred thousand pounds of silver into India in order to finance their trade in the country, because the balance of trade was always in favour of India. (In the year 1716, the value of silver imported amounted to as much as £746,890. UK Parliamentary Papers, House of Commons 1812–13, vol. 8, as quoted in Ray 2008: Annexure 1). But there was no import of silver into Bengal at all from 1757 to 1797. Moreover, the import of silver into Bombay and Madras also never reached a six-figure amount between 1758 and 1796, except in 1790 and 1791. There was a sudden jump in imports into the three presidencies together between 1797 and 1805, and that was almost certainly for financing Wellesley's wars against Tipu Sultan and the Marathas.

From 1757 to 1764, the EIC's 'investment' was financed entirely by the funds extracted from the collaborators, including the generals and their kin who had betrayed Sirajuddaulla in the battle of Plassey.

From 1765, the EIC obtained the Dewani of Bengal and Bihar from the Mughal emperor in Delhi, and the land revenues of Bengal financed not only the EIC's 'investment' but also the wars of conquest that the EIC officials waged. Table 1 shows that when Cornwallis and Wellesley were waging war against Tipu Sultan and the Marathas, it was Bengal's revenues that supported those assaults.

Table 1 Land Revenue of Different Presidencies of British India (in £s), 1792–1811

Year	Bengal	Madras	Bombay
1792–3	3,091,616	742,760	79,025
1800–01	3,218,766	957,799	45,130
1810–11	3,295,382	1,071,666	437,108

Source: Banerjea (1928: 187).

Many neo-imperialist historians have claimed that the so-called Plassey Revolution was not a revolution at all, but the continuation of the same social and governance structure with the British, rather than the Mughals, as the suzerain of India. It is true that despite their various experiments, the British relied, as had the Mughals and post-Mughal nawabs, on land revenue as the major fiscal resource. But the British replaced all senior administrators and judges with their own men, thus blocking all official avenues of advancement for the Indians, as many British observers themselves noted (Colebrooke and Lambert 1795). Even more damagingly, they remitted most of the land revenue as an 'investment' of the EIC.

In 1973 (Chapter 1 in this volume), I had estimated the gross domestic material product (GDMP) of Bengal and Bihar as Rs 474,250,000 or £47,425,000. Cuenca Esteban (2007: Table 3) gives an annual average of net inflows from India to Britain over 1793–1807 to be £3,354,000. This does not take into account another million or two pounds the British were spending every year to conquer other parts of India, using the Bengal–Bihar revenues for the purpose (for an alternative estimate of the gains made by Britain from its empire, see Patnaik 2006). This meant that 7.07 per cent of the gross domestic product of Bengal and Bihar was sent out of the country without any return. We should remember that the industrializing economy of England was not investing much more than 7 per cent of its GDP during precisely the decades that India was fast changing from an economy with a substantial share (ranging from 15 to 20 per cent) of the manufacturing sector in the

GDP and employment of the economy to one in which that share fell well below 10 per cent over the course of the nineteenth century. The continual disinvestments or drain, to use a word that both early British observers and nationalists used, meant that the production function was being continually pushed inward, and people survived, when they did, by mining the land without replacement of its nutrients, by adapting to lower value-added products that had a domestic but no international market, and in some favourable situations and conjunctures, competing successfully with the privileged Europeans.

Colebrooke and Lambert (1795) pointed out that the drain of sixty millions sterling in forty years (a figure which falls only a few millions short of the estimate by Cuenca Esteban [2007]), had greatly impoverished the inhabitants of Bengal and Bihar. After noting that Sayers,[8] which used to be collected by the earlier zamindars, who regulated and protected the markets from which the tolls were realized, had been abolished, they continued:

> Numerous[9] markets by promoting intercourse, contributed to general prosperity. The discontinuance of many markets in the short space of four years, and the decline of the existing marts, is an alarming circumstance. (Colebrooke and Lambert 1795: 48)

Recent work by Patnaik (2006) and Cuenca Esteban (2001, 2007) has shown that the drain from India to Britain was very large in absolute values. Further, Cuenca Esteban also underscores the extremely critical role the Indian tribute played in sustaining the British in their final tussle with the French for acquiring European and global hegemony. As Bayly (1989: 2–3) has pointed out:

> '... the 1770s and 1780s were a British recessional ... In 1783, the First British Empire of American settlement and oriental trade seemed to have foundered into ruin. Worse, it seemed to attract resources and energy away from the more pressing problems of domestic development. Fresh military and diplomatic disasters dogged the years of war against revolutionary France.
>
> By 1815 the nation could celebrate an astonishing, indeed providential recovery of fortunes. Great Britain had finally managed to engineer a coalition of European powers to oppose French power within Europe.'

That providential recovery was largely financed by the Caribbean and Indian surpluses extracted by British rulers. From Cuenca Esteban's (2007) Table 3 we get an estimate of the cumulative surplus transferred from India to Britain over the years 1765–1812 that comes to £122.8 million. Using a methodology that admittedly underestimates the transferred surplus, Patnaik (2006) gets a figure of £87 million over the years

1765–1814 transferred from Asia to Britain.[10] Patnaik's figures are in constant official values and so do not take account of the price inflation from the 1790s reflected in Cuenca Esteban (2007).[11]

Structural Adjustment: The Phase of Direct Parliamentary Rule

It has sometimes been argued (for example, by Washbrook 1981) that the change-over from the rule by EIC to direct rule by the Parliament led to the replacement of the British state by European capital as the main exploiter of India, and that required legal changes facilitating the growth of a more civil society. It is true that private European capital played a more important part in the economy of India after 1858. But the major source of the surplus earned by the metropolis still remained the tribute extracted by the state. To land revenue was now added a debt process as loans were raised for exacting the self-ransoming payment for the cost of suppressing the Indian revolt of 1857, as loans were raised in London on India's behalf for financing railway construction, irrigation works, ports, and meeting any emerging deficits in the budget. As before, the Indian army, whose cost was paid by the Indian people, was deployed all over Asia and beyond, not only to defend the British empire in India but to extend that empire elsewhere (Washbrook forthcoming).

Marx (1853) had pointed out that the East India Company had imitated the earlier rulers of India in extracting a tribute from the people and engaging in wars, but unlike the earlier governments, it had spent very little on public works (see also Washbrook, forthcoming). From the early 1850s, this deficiency was repaired by the British Indian government, but the cost—both financial and, of course, ecological—was borne by the Indian people.

It is useful to figure out how much tribute was transferred from India in this phase of colonialism. In Bagchi (2002b and 2006[2005]: Chapter 17), I provided alternative estimates of the tribute and profits transferred from India and Burma from the 1870s to 1915–16. According to those estimates, the annual surplus extracted from India and Burma by the British state and European businessmen rose from a minimum of £21.4 million and a maximum of £28.9 million in the 1870s to a minimum of £52.9 million and a maximum of £65.3 million on the eve of the First World War.

The usually accepted figure of total British investment worldwide in 1913–14, namely, about £4000 million, is composed very largely of the reinvestment of returns on accumulating balances of those investments and compounding them at the normal rate of interest or profit (Pollard 1985). For comparing that total to the accumulating balances of Indian surpluses, for which the Indians received no recompense, we have also applied compound interest rates to the accumulating surpluses up to the year 1914. Compounding the Indian surpluses at 4 per cent, we obtain figures from £3,199,320 to £3,779,264 as the value of the surpluses taken by the British from South Asia, including Burma. Thus those surpluses alone would have financed anywhere between 75 per cent and 95 per cent of the total British foreign investment worldwide. That foreign investment was absolutely critical in financing the massive European migration during the period in question and in building up the prosperity of especially the English-speaking overseas settlements in the USA, Canada, Australia, and New Zealand. Moreover, the despoliation of the native peoples of those countries also contributed to the prosperity of the immigrants (Bagchi 2006[2005]:, Chapters 13–17).

In this phase also, market failures occurred not just because of the unemployment caused by leakage for tribute to the metropolitan country and the endemic depression resulting from it, but also from deliberate suppression of free markets for the workers and artisans that were growing up in the highly commercialized economy of those regions of India involved in long-distance trade, inland and abroad. Most administrators professed tenets of political economy with property rights vested in individuals, but they regularly violated those tenets under the imperative of revenue collection at low cost. For example, in many parts of Punjab and the North-West Frontier Provinces, the administrators conjured up a village community where none had existed and made it responsible for collection of the land tax (Van den Dungen 1972; Chapter 9 in this volume).[12]

In all the regions of India, from the beginning of British rule to its end, peasants were highly indebted to moneylenders, were on insecure tenure, with little support of public expenditure on irrigation or other growth-enhancing investments. They were continually subject to the threat of crop failure through drought or floods or of price depression, because of troughs of domestic demand or international trade cycles. Most attempts to show that peasants prospered, except for a small section and brief periods in the Krishna–Godavari delta and in Punjab and Sind after 'productive' irrigation works were opened up in those areas (Chapter 2 in this volume), have proved to be futile.[13]

Agricultural Productivity and Agrarian Change

George Blyn's detailed work on Indian agricultural growth posed a problem because if his data were to be believed—and they were all official—then during the last fifty-five years of colonial rule, Indian agriculture had stagnated and foodgrain output growth had fallen clearly behind even the moderate population growth of those years. Then began an assault on the reliability of the official data by Clive Dewey and Alan Heston, whose objections were blown away by the critiques of Ashok Desai, Satish Mishra, and Sumit Guha. When the dust settled, it was found that given all their limitations, the data culled by Glyn from 1891–2 to 1945–6 are the best we have (for a selection of the articles, see Guha 1992a; for a summary of the arguments, see Guha 1992b).

The neocolonialist writers could not seriously impugn the findings of Blyn and Sivasubramonian (2000) about the stagnation, or worse, of per capita incomes of Indians during the last forty-six years of British rule. They then turned to proving that India had after all done well in the nineteenth century. Alan Heston, after a laborious scrutiny of available data, decided to make the assumption that 'yields of principal crops did not change' over the last half of the nineteenth century (Heston 1983: 390). I will presently scrutinize the validity of the assumption of constant yields. The quality of Heston's estimate of income from manufacturing can be judged by comparing it with Sivasubramonian (2000). The two estimates agree closely when it comes to the growth of large-scale industry: Heston (1983: Table 4.3B) gets the value of output (at constant prices) of 1946–7 as 7.29 times that of 1900–01, while from Sivasubramonian (2000: Table 6.4) we obtain a figure of 7.28. But when we come to the ratios of the value of output (at constant prices) of cottage and small-scale industries in the two years, Heston's Table yields a figure of 1.55 as against Sivasubramonian's of 1.24. This apparently small difference makes a large difference to the estimate of growth, because the value of the output of cottage and small-scale industries exceeded that of large-scale industry in 1900–01, and continued to do so almost until the beginning of the Second World War.

In the case of yields, Heston's assumption flouts not only Blyn's figures of productivity growth of foodgrains from 1891–2 to 1945–6 but also the few we have for the nineteenth century. These few estimates are decisive in refuting Heston's ungrounded claim of a growth in agricultural production per capita. Ashwani Saith had shown in his doctoral thesis submitted in the 1970s that in the two districts of Muzaffarnagar and Bareilly, the intrinsic yields of wheat per acre both on irrigated and unirrigated lands were lower at the end of the nineteenth century than in the 1830s and 1840s, and even with extension of irrigation, the average yield in Bareilly fell by 11.3 per cent in 1878 compared with 1828–31 (Saith 1992: Table 16). We have to bear in mind that population growth was slow but positive between those years.

Currently, the understanding of Indian economic change during colonial times is being damaged, especially among scholars with no first-hand knowledge of Indian data, by the apparently authoritative estimates of growth of GDP and per capita GDP produced by Maddison (1995, 2003). Maddison (2003: Table A3-c.) puts the per capita income of India (in 1990 Geary-Khamis dollars) as 533 in 1820, 533 in 1870, and 673 in 1913. The implied growth in the estimated per capita income between 1870 and 1913 is totally without any basis. Agricultural productivity per capita in most regions of India stagnated or declined as did real wages of labour;[14] hundreds of thousands of artisans became unemployed and had to shift to either low-paying employment in agriculture or produce coarser varieties of their products with lower value added. Plantation workers, miners, and Indians employed in the few large-scale industrial units that came up earned pitiful wages, with little growth. Of course, when we shift to estimates of per capita incomes of *Indians* from GDP per capita, the picture was even more bleak, since all the better-paying jobs in the public sector were virtually closed to the 'natives'; implicit and explicit racial discrimination barred the entry of Indians as owners or managers into large-scale industry and foreign trade, with the partial exception of western India and some sectors of trade with Ceylon, Burma, and Malaya.

On the basis of the Colebrooke and Lambert (1795) data referred to earlier, I had estimated the per capita GDMP of Bengal and Bihar as Rs 47.4 in 1794 in 1900 prices; using similar methods I calculated the per capita GDMP of British India as Rs 33.2, at the same prices (Chapter 1 in this volume). From Sivasubramonian (2000: Table 6.1), we get an estimate of net value added generated in India by the primary and secondary sectors, in 1900–01, at current prices as Rs 9,679 million. With a total Indian population of 284 million in 1901, this works out as a per capita income of Rs 33.7. Thus there is a close correspondence of this figure with that of the figure in Chapter 1 of this volume. We must remember that by 1794, Bengal and Bihar had already suffered the impoverishing tributary extraction for almost forty years. Even then we get a decline of more than 25 per cent in per capita income over the next century of British rule.

Many of the 'optimists' about Indian productivity or income growth tend to be casual about the processes that would sustain their optimism. How would productivity growth have taken place? As I had argued more than thirty years ago (Chapters 2, 3, 5, and 6 in this volume), an increase in population dependent on agriculture, whether it occurs through a natural growth or through a shift from industry or some other non-agricultural occupation to agriculture, would require some investment in agriculture. In pre-British times, the peasants could maintain productivity by utilizing the manure of the cattle because pasture was either not taxed at all or taxed very lightly; often the cultivators would regularly invite shepherds to graze their livestock on their land and fertilize it. Second, many cultivated two or three crops, one of them a leguminous one, in the same plot, with a slight spacing according to the season of growth. Third, they were given liberal tax concessions for opening up new land. Fourth, they would be given large taccavi advances for cultivation, especially for valuable crops. After the British take-over of south Indian districts, collectors were apparently horrified by the amount of taccavi loans that earlier tax farmers or renters had given to the farmers (Washbrook, 1993b: 75). Finally, either the peasants themselves or the local political authorities or superior right-holders to the land constructed and maintained local irrigation works.

Under British rule, all land that anybody claimed as his own paid a tax, whether he cultivated it or not. Second, huge territories were declared waste land because nobody could produce written documents of possession. Forest-dwellers lost their rights and so did peasants who had used forests for grazing livestock and foraging that added to their real income and often to land productivity. Third, in Permanent Settlement areas the tax-farmers, the new zamindars, had no longer any authority over the peasants' work and had no incentive to maintain old irrigation channels, which silted up and became malarial swamps or dried out altogether (Mukherjee 2009[1938]; Chapter 2 in this volume; Gupta 1984). In *raiyatwari* areas, the colonial government did not assume any responsibility for maintaining old channels or giving adequate advances to peasants for capital formation. The assessments of land tax were generally too high to leave the peasants any surplus to spend on capital formation (Chapter 8 in this volume). Large-scale irrigation, except for the Cauvery and part of the Godavari works, were not undertaken until the 1860s, and they were meant to yield profits to the government after paying for their construction.

Most of the so-called Ceded Districts in south India, that is, those ceded by the Nizam as well as the districts of Bombay Deccan, which were conquered from the Peshwa in 1818, were extremely drought-prone and subject to frequent famines. S. Srinivasa Raghavaiyangar (1893), one of the shrewdest defenders of British rule—who did not try to defend every act or phase of British rule but relied on trashing the record of pre-British rulers and attempted to show that the record of British rule had been far better after 1854 or so—had to report that British assessments of land tax in the raiyatwari districts of south India continued to impoverish peasants for most of the first half of the nineteenth century (Ibid.: 26–33). In 1807, Thomas Munro, the supposed father of the raiyatwari settlement, had recommended that in order to encourage cultivation and give land a positive sale value, the government demand should be reduced from half of the gross produce to 25 per cent on dry and wet lands and to one-third on the so-called garden lands. But the Madras government could not accept the recommendation because orders were 'received from England for the remittance of an additional sum of a million sterling annually, accompanied by a threat from the Court of Directors, that unless this were done they would take the question of reducing the establishments in their own hands' (Ibid.: 27).

Raghavaiyangar noticed that there was a huge depression of prices in south India and in fact all over India between the 1820s and early 1850s. He attributed this primarily to the decline in the stock and flow of media of exchange because of the drain of coins. A later, more detailed, analysis of the depression in the south Indian context used similarly monetarist language (Thomas and Natarajan 1936), but like Raghavaiyangar (1893), it also took account of the drain of the surplus remitted abroad by the colonial regime as a principal determining element. Drain of bullion was only part of the problem—it was the consequence of tributary demands of the colonial state, but it was also caused by the huge decline in exports of manufactures, especially cotton textiles, and a surge in the imports of machine-made goods that took away the markets of Indian producers. The twin developments naturally reduced the difference of exports and imports, but the colonial policies ensured that in the long run, the export surplus of India needed to finance the tribute would remain positive, however costly that might be for the current incomes and investment potential of ordinary Indians.[15]

The Indian economy was depressed not only in the years from the 1820s to the early 1850s but practically throughout the period of British rule, except for the period 1898–1914, when terms of trade turned in favour of agricultural commodities globally, and during the two World Wars, when inflation of prices resulted from the British extraction of an even larger surplus from India than in other years.

All the official accounts of south Indian districts point to the utter distress of the peasantry under the operation of the colonial regime. Raghavaiyangar (1893: 30), referring to the condition of Bellary district states:

> The incidence of land revenue assessments, notwithstanding Sir Thomas Munro's reductions, continued, owing to the heavy fall in the prices of produce, oppressive, while this district enjoyed no special privileges like Cuddapah in regard to good subsoil water-supply, and extension of indigo cultivation. Mr Mellor, the Collector, reported in 1845: 'The universal complaint and request of the ryots is to be allowed to reduce their farms, a convincing proof that cultivation is not profitable. (p. 30) Land has never been saleable ... were it not for the aid of the Collector through his revenue subordinates, one-half, or at least one-third of the highly assessed lands would ere this have been thrown up .... The number of pattah holders has increased, but they are a poor class who seek a maintenance only husbandry with poor spirit and by no means to be compared with the substantial farmers who have fallen into difficulties and disappeared from the rent roll of the district. With regard to food and raiment the majority of them are poorly clad and ill-fed, and it is impossible to arrive at any other conclusion than that poverty is the cause ...'

According to the report of Pelly, the collector, in 1851, only 17 per cent of the Bellary *raiyat*s were in good circumstances and 49 per cent had to mortgage their crops and 34 per cent had to sell their crops at harvest time in order to pay their *kist*s (Ibid.: 30).

In Rajahmundry, later Godavari district, 'of the ten years between 1831–40, 1831 and 1832 were famine years, in 1835, 1836 and 1837, the season is described as "unfavourable", and in 1838, 1839 and 1840 as "calamitous". The population which in 1830 had been 695,016 had decreased in 1840 to 533,836' Raghavaiyangar (1893: 30). This shows that the usual accounts of famine years vastly understate the desperate condition of a large part of the peasantry in most years. Further, 'the closing of the Government weaving factories in consequence of the abrogation of the Company's trading privileges had thrown large numbers of weavers out of employment, and money to the extent of 7 lakhs of rupees per annum, which was in circulation in connection with the maintenance of the factories, was withdrawn' (Ibid.).

The tendency towards equalization of patta-holding (I do not call it proper landholding) was caused not by the prosperity of the smaller peasants, but the distress of the peasantry in general. A similar situation of a trend towards equality in oppression was also observed in Java after the re-introduction of Dutch rule in the Indonesian archipelago when the British handed the islands back to the Dutch after their victory in the Anglo-French war in 1815. This tendency towards equalization of patta-holding in Bellary was arrested in two periods: first, when the American Civil War raised cotton prices and made it profitable for the bigger farmers to diversify into cotton production, and secondly, when between 1905 and 1915, cotton prices rose relatively to those of foodgrains (Washbrook 1994: 133–41). In the black soil of Bellary or Cuddapah, cotton cultivation required deep ploughing with large numbers of bullocks and watering to produce a good crop and only large farmers could make a profit even when prices ruled high (Ibid.: 137; Rao 1999: 27). It was also labour-intensive, so the big farmers would hire more full-time farm servants. But when cotton prices were bad or the short-staple cotton fell out of favour as it increasingly did after the First World War, they hired less labour and these landless labourers took up the pattas for land that the bigger farmers gave up. These poor farmers in turn became bonded to locally monopolistic purchasing houses and were forced into cultivation of a cash crop, often at the expense of their subsistence. This subsistence was particularly endangered as with the loosening of older ties of dependence and protection, and opening up of facilities for selling grain in distant markets, the bigger farmers ceased to keep large stocks of grain (Washbrook 1994: 141–4).

The analysis for Bellary indicates that there are no easy ways of generalizing about the impact of penetration of markets or extension of railways in the late colonial period on the conditions of living of the people. On the one hand, from the 1880s, the growth of agricultural trade led to more diversified cropping patterns in many regions of India: this has often been regarded as a positive development, especially by economists (cf. Rao 1999). On the other hand, it also meant lower security for the poor in most regions, because scarcity not only raised prices for them but also diminished their employment and earnings. It is not accidental that the period witnessed some of the biggest famines in Indian history. Moreover, these developments may also have increased the power of merchants and moneylenders, especially since the state removed many of the earlier prohibitions against dispossession. Of course, in Bombay and Punjab, the state tried, rather ineffectually, to restrict the alienation of land to what it styled as ineffectual classes. In the United Provinces and Oudh, it bolstered the power of the taluqdars at the cost of most peasants, as a way of ensuring the loyalty of the big men in the countryside. So grand narratives of expansion of markets and the upward movement of indices of economic development, let alone human development, are out of place in India's colonial history, in any macro-region or in any phase.

Living Standards and Survival

One of the ways in which we can try and gauge how people's incomes and productivity fared in an era in which prophylactic measures or improvement in sanitation as such did not save lives is their record of survival. We do not yet have good assessments of population changes in different regions of India before 1872, when the first comprehensive census was carried out in British India. Bhattacharya (1987: 67–72) has compared the population figures given by Hamilton (1815) for districts adjacent to Muzaffarnagar and Bareilly, what Bhattacharya calls the Agra and the Allahabad Provinces. As in most other early accounts, the populations of these territories were almost certainly underestimated. Over a period of almost sixty years (1815–72), the populations of these districts increased by 63.38 per cent (in the case of Agra Province) and 67.60 per cent (in the case of Allahabad Province). That Hamilton's figures of 6 million and 7 million were almost certainly underestimates is indicated by the fact that during the next fifty years (1872–1921), the population of Agra Province increased only by 8.29 per cent and that of Allahabad Province actually declined by 3.16 per cent. How reliable are these figures of population growth over 1815–72? According to Visaria and Visaria (1983: Appendix 5.2) in the North-West Provinces (as most of the areas covered by Agra and Allahabad Provinces of Hamilton were known officially), there were famines in 1819–20, 1833–4, 1837–8, 1860–1, and 1868–70. We must remember also that many districts suffered from famines, but the British administrators styled them as seasons of scarcity or used some such dismissive phrase. Among ten districts of the North-West Provinces and Oudh, for example, between the years 1864–5 and 1873–4, there was no district that did not have very poor harvests (meaning harvests that were 6:16, or even a lower ratio to the normal) running for two crop seasons (kharif and rabi) or more. Benaras, for example, had poor harvests every season from kharif (1872–3) to rabi (1873–4), Sitapur reaped poor harvests from kharif (1870–1) to rabi (1871–2) (Whitcombe 1972: Figure 1). But the North-

West Provinces do not figure in Visaria and Visaria's list of famines for these years.[16] Hence almost certainly, the pre-census population growth figures derived from Hamilton (1815) and Bhattacharya (1987) are gross overestimates.

The only major region of India to have experienced sustained growth of population over the period 1872 to 1946 was the eastern region, consisting primarily of Bengal, Bihar, and Assam. This growth was, however, based largely on the clearing of new land in the lower Gangetic delta and the Brahmaputra valley to which people migrated as the older parts of the delta became moribund. The decreasing productivity of the older delta was caused by the shifting of the branches and tributaries of the Ganga and the Brahmaputra, and the ecological damage and spread of malarial swamps resulting from construction of railways that paid scant attention either to ecology or public health (Mukherjee 2009[1938]; Zachariah 1964). Moreover, in the wake of the Permanent Settlement, the zamindars were absolved of all responsibility for maintaining irrigation and drainage channels or temporary embankments for holding flood waters. This had a particularly damaging effect on the districts of Gangetic Bihar, which were also badly affected by the process of de-industrialization set in motion by British rule (Chapters 2–5 in this volume). The agrarian relations under which peasants had little incentive or resources to invest in land and proprietors, or rather, rent farmers became thoroughly impoverished, also render incredible any narrative of improvement over the period of colonial rule (Chapter 6 in this volume).

De-industrialization

The early imperialist administrators as well as the nationalists recognized that British imports of machine-made goods had severely damaged the Indian handicrafts, decimating their output and impoverishing the artisans who clung to their occupations. Although the word 'de-industrialization' was not used by them, Charles Metcalfe much later alongwith Romesh Dutt (1963a[1906]: Chapters 14–15; 1963b[1906]: Book I, Chapter 7, Book II, Chapter 8) both argued that India was de-industrialized under colonial rule. However, two economic historians with two very different ideological bents launched an assault on this view. The first was Morris David Morris (1963), who stands at the fountainhead of neocolonial history in the post-independence period. The second was Daniel Thorner, who was more of an Indian nationalist than many Indian economists and economic historians.

Thorner argued that despite colonial rule, India had been undergoing a process of industrialization in the late colonial period. In extension of this argument, he also argued that if de-industrialization occurred in India, it had happened before the 1880s (Thorner 1962/2005).

All the available evidence points conclusively to the de-industrialization of India on a massive scale over the course of the nineteenth century (Habib 1975a; Bagchi 1976, 1989: Chapter 1; Clingingsmith and Williamson 2004, 2008). In Gangetic Bihar, for example, the proportion of population engaged in industry declined from18.6 per cent in 1809–13 to 8.5 per cent in 1901 (Chapters 3–5 and 7 in this volume). The officially commissioned surveys of Francis Buchanan Hamilton (BH, from now), provide the data for Chapters 3 and 4 of this volume, relating to the districts of Gangetic Bihar. If it is assumed that BH overestimated the total population of those districts, we obtain an even higher figure, namely, 21 per cent for the proportion of population dependent on secondary industry in the early nineteenth century (Chapter 5 in this volume). We must remember, in this context, that the Bihar districts in question, and Bengal had already suffered a decline both in export sales and domestic demand at the time BH had conducted his survey, and as BH and Dutt (1963a[1906]) had noted.

It has been argued (for instance, by J. Krishnamurty 1985), that Gangetic Bihar or Bengal proper may have been exceptional in suffering de-industrialization over the nineteenth century and that regions in the interior regions, not so closely connected with export trade, did not suffer it. But this argument does not bear up to serious scrutiny. To take an example at random, in the districts that the Nizam of Hyderabad ceded to the British in 1800, all of which were in the interior with low rainfall and little irrigation, the proportion of craft workers to the total population in 1810 was estimated as 19 per cent (Ludden 2005: 24). In four districts, namely, Cuddapah, Kurnool, Bellary, and Anantapur, which were included in that ceded territory, the proportions of the population dependent on secondary industry had been halved over the nineteenth century even if we count 'partially agriculturists' among the secondary sector workers, as Table 2 would indicate.[17]

In every case, soon after the British occupation of a province or region in India, the proportion engaged in secondary industry declined, the reason being not just the abolition of restrictions on the entry of foreign goods, but also the decline in local demand for products of secondary industry. This is what happened in the Bombay Deccan after the conquest of the Peshwa's territories by the British. The whole of the

Table 2 Proportion of Population Dependent on Secondary Industry in Four Districts of the Madras Presidency, in 1901

District	Percentage of actual workers to total population	Percentage of workers, including partially agriculturists, to total population
Cuddapah	7.81	8.58
Kurnool	7.85	8.80
Bellary	8.90	9.48
Anantapur	9.02	9.51

Source: Table XV, 'Occupations', *Census of India 1901, Vol. XVA, Madras, Part II, Imperial Tables*, by W. Francis, Madras: Superintendent, Government Press, 1902.
Note: The figures of secondary sector workers have been taken as those pertaining to Class D, 'Preparation and supply of material substances'.

Bombay Deccan was seized by depression, which was reflected in the increased unemployment of the people, the figures of which were not recorded. Agricultural prices began falling from 1822 and except for the years of high prices such as 1824–5, 1833–4, and 1845–6, caused by acute harvest failures, they continued falling till 1853–4. The disbanding of the Peshwa's army and retainers, and import of British manufactures led to de-industrialization as well as distress of farmers (Guha 1985: Chapter 2).

Three and a half decades on, in 1856 the British occupation of Oudh (which was one of the proximate causes of the great revolt of 1857), led to a drastic decline in the population of Lucknow (Table 3), primarily because of the decline of craft industries catering to the court of the erstwhile Nawabs of Oudh.

Table 3 Population of Lucknow (1857–81)

1857	530,670
1869	357,712
1881	261,303

Source: Taban (1995).

In the mainstream literature as flagged by Clingingsmith and Williamson (2004 and 2008), it is now accepted that there was massive de-industrialization of India between 1760 and 1860. However, the implicit assumption that de-industrialization ceased in the 1860s repeats the fallacy of Daniel Thorner's assertion that by 1881, India's de-industrialization story was over. As Chattopadhyay (1975) demonstrated, the decline in the proportion of industrial workers to the total workforce continued down to 1931, even after the growth of large-scale industries such as cotton and jute mills (Chattopadhyay 1975); the data given in J. Krishnamurty (1983) also lead to the same conclusion (see also Bagchi 2006 [2005]: 153–4).

Large-scale production units, using mechanical means for processing agricultural products such as cotton and jute, grew up from the 1850s in India. Mining enterprises for extracting coal and other minerals also grew, but slowly. Many of the enterprises depended on export markets, and except in Bombay, until 1914, the major modern firms were controlled by Europeans (Bagchi 1972a; Chapter 7 in this volume; Ray 1979; Tyabji 1995; Chakrabarti 2003; Mukherji 2005). But even though the value of output of large-scale units in the secondary sector grew much faster than that of the cottage and small-scale industries over 1900–40, the latter exceeded the former (Sivasubramonian 2000: Table 4.43). The large-scale units were much more capital-intensive than the cottage and small-scale units, moreover, the former grew partly by displacing the latter. Hence the growth in employment in large-scale units was not enough to compensate for the slow growth of employment in the cottage and small-scale units even in the late colonial period.

Even when mainstream economists and economic historians recognize the fact of de-industrialization, they factor out the endemic depression caused by colonial exploitation when analysing its causes. Both unjustified assumptions about income growth and the inability to get out of the maintained assumption of all neoclassical economics, namely, that the economy always works with full capacity and full employment, are responsible for such elimination of the most important causal chains in the process. The leading unjustified assumption is that somehow or other, Indians experienced a growth in real incomes under British rule. That assumption has a long genealogy, starting explicitly with F.J. Atkinson, and then percolating through the efforts of Alan Heston to the seemingly authoritative estimates of Angus Maddison (Bagchi 2006 [2005]: Chapter 17; Chapter 7 in this volume).

The depressing effects of de-industrialization on the incomes of women of all classes were already noted by BH (Chapter 5 in this volume; see also Gupta 1984: Chapter 5). As Tilly (1994) suggests, since spinning was the most important source of earnings of many women, especially for those who for social reasons could not work outside their homes, the effect of the drastic decline of spinners' numbers had a deleterious effect on the women's autonomy within the family and society.[18] Many weavers adjusted to the situation by weaving coarser varieties of cloth. But the net earnings from such work fell, and a declining market made them more indebted to the merchants and moneylenders. When the weaver happened to be a Muslim and the moneylender was (typically) a Hindu, weavers' rebellions appeared to outsiders to have a religious tinge and gave rise to the British official stereotype of the 'bigoted julaha' (Pandey 2006).

Clingingsmith and Williamson (2008) attribute India's de-industrialization to a rise in the prices of non-tradables and agricultural goods, relative to those of Indian manufactures.[19] The most severe process of de-industrialization probably occurred in the long period of falling agricultural prices lasting from 1821 to 1854. Moreover, they also implicitly attribute it to the growth of agricultural output exceeding the growth of the workforce. As usual with such analysts, they totally ignore the virtual cessation of investment under the demand-depressing regime maintained by colonialism (Chapters 2–5 in this volume; Habib 1975a).

In Bagchi (1972a: Chapter 6), I had discussed how the survival of a strong Indian business community in western India as against its virtual decimation in the Bengal and Madras Presidencies was greatly facilitated by the fact that the British did not manage to finally conquer the Peshwa territories until 1818. It was also facilitated by the cessation of the EIC's monopoly of trade with India in 1813, a date at which western Indian merchants had still retained contact with oceanic trade. In Bagchi (2006[1987]), I discussed the legal and situational reasons for the decimation of the Bengali business community in the three capitalist crises from 1825–6 to 1847–8 and the different fate of the Parsi and Gujarati business communities in the crisis following the cotton boom caused by the US Civil War. Paradoxically enough, the gradual marginalizing of the Indian business community in foreign trade in cotton induced them to invest in the cotton mills more intensively from the 1870s (Vicziany 1979a).

Within the limited choices offered by imperial rule, in some situations, the strategies and attitudes of Indian and European businessmen could be surprisingly similar. For example, the Ahmedabad cotton mill industry, controlled almost exclusively by Indians was primarily oriented towards the domestic market. In Kanpur, most of the cotton mills and big leather goods factories were controlled by European businessmen. The latter depended primarily on government patronage and the domestic market, and their attitudes towards the economic policies pursued by the colonial government were surprisingly similar (Manali Chakrabarti 2003).

When south India recovered from the terrible famines that devastated it in the nineteenth century, and the colonial government constructed the irrigation works in the Krishna–Godavari delta, an Indian industrialists' group grew up in Andhra Pradesh and Tamil Nadu and began investing in oil mills, cotton gins, leather-processing units, and cotton mills. The relative lack of business opportunities in the export sector also induced European businessmen to invest in industrial enterprises with the domestic market as its main target. A more positive Madras government policy for fostering some economic enterprises in leather and textiles also helped in this matter, even though that policy had to be reversed soon under the pressure of the local European business community (Bagchi 1972a: Chapters 6 and 8; Tyabji 1995).

Fortunately, the raiyatwari system that had earlier devastated much of south India through the extortions of the government proved to be conducive to this development, because big farmers, especially in the irrigated regions, aided in the process of capital accumulation. Moreover, the capital accumulation of south Indian business communities such as the Nattukottai Chettiars was facilitated by their extensive trading and moneylending activities in Sri Lanka, Burma, and South-east Asia.

South India also underwent a fertility transition from the end of the nineteenth century, much earlier than the rest of India. But not all regions of the peninsula participated in this. Class structures and prospects of rural growth influenced the patterns of family limitation. During 1891–1931, the proportion of single women to women of reproductive age was 15 per cent in the Madras Presidency, and was the highest such figure in British India. On top of that, marital fertility was lower than in the rest of India. Both these factors caused a lower total fertility in the Madras Presidency than in the rest of India (Gopinath 2005: 79–81). Ecological conditions such as high or low land productivity influenced fertility but other—socially conditioned—factors influenced choice and fertility outcomes. The districts of Cuddapah, Kurnool, Bellary, and Anantapur had high mortality and moderate fertility, whereas the more fertile districts in the Krishna–Godavari delta had a high fertility and high demographic growth. On the other hand, 'The agriculturally secure west coast and the dearth-prone Deccan both had the lowest proportion of married women, while north and south Madras had much higher proportions' (Gopinath 2005: 81). In drought-prone areas, a low rate of nuptiality was chosen as a strategy of risk aversion, whereas on the west coast, it seems to have been influenced by considerations of social status. Thus peasants exercised choice as mediated by custom, but there is no reason to believe that those customs were invariant relatively to changes in material conditions.

Conclusion: Agency and Survival

One peculiar argument of neocolonial historians is that Indian artisans and peasants did not lose their agency under colonialism and, therefore, colonialism is an irrelevant category in economic or social history. This is based on the presupposition that human beings en masse can lose the will to act independently for long periods. They never do so—even as slaves in the Roman Empire or as chattel slaves in the islands and the seaboard of the Atlantic Ocean—as the record of repeated slave revolts in both settings demonstrates. We need to pinpoint the constraints under which human beings exercise their agency, and delineate the structures that grow up as a result of the interaction of different agents, including, of course, the superior power-holders. The question of agency cannot be confined only to actions of individuals or particular firms as economic agents. Their acts as political animals have also to be considered.

The chronology of imperial rule and its fiscal compulsions strongly influenced patterns of land relations throughout the subcontinent. Since the Bengal Presidency was the main source of the tribute and the sinews of war for the colonial state, the British, in their anxiety to stabilize that source, introduced the so-called Permanent Settlement of land revenues in that region. This quickly led, through successive processes and layers of subcontracting, to a primarily rentier landlordism, with little responsibility for productivity-enhancing investment in agriculture (Chapters 2 and 6 in this volume).

Usurious moneylenders prospered when the colonial regime reduced most cultivators to the status of insecure tenants; and in most regions of India, the residual surplus (after the colonial state had extracted its pound of flesh) was concentrated in a few hands, even if the nominal title remained with the cultivator (Whitcombe 1972; Rothermund 1992; Bose 1993; Sanyal 2004). This happened even in the so-called areas of land abundance such as Assam (Mukherjee 1979). The conditions of the indebted peasantry in East Bengal deteriorated further in the depression of the 1930s, and the Hindu zamindars and professionals refused to alter the oppressive tenure conditions of the peasants. These factors, along with the propaganda of fundamentalist preachers supported by the Muslim elite, pushed them towards the Muslim League and the political partition of Bengal in 1947.

Within raiyatwari regions, different patterns of landlord–tenant relations grew up in different parts of the Madras Presidency, depending on ecological conditions, which were themselves partly shaped by state policies regarding irrigation and the use of forests and so-called waste lands (Baker 1984; Bandopadhyay 1992). Peasants with different degrees of control over land grew up in different parts of the Presidency, but the prosperity of the superior layers of peasantry could be observed only in late colonial times, and only in the few pockets in which the colonial state had invested in 'productive' irrigation projects.[20]

The different degrees of presence that the Europeans had in industry and business in Bombay and Calcutta also shaped labour relations. In Bombay, they came to approximate the bargaining relations between capitalists and workers in typical capitalist enterprises. In Calcutta, on the other hand, they approximated the coercive relations between a racist oppressor and a worker without any rights in the presence of the employer. Of course, the semi-feudal relations created under British rule in typical regions from which labour was recruited also partly influenced both capital-labour and worker-worker relations (Bagchi 1972a: Chapter 4; Bagchi 1999; Ghosh 2005). While Indian capital gradually grew in the interstices of the colonial regime, it had always to reckon with the hostility of a state that was unwilling to allow the competition of Indian manufactures to eat away a niche market for British manufactures (Bagchi 1972a: Chapters 2 and 7). In fact, the policies of the colonial government also proved to be unpalatable to those European capitalists who were dependent on the domestic market for their business, such as owners of cotton weaving mills in Bombay or Kanpur (Chakrabarti 2003: Chapter 7).

The colonial order in India was a very complex system and changed over the 190 years from its beginning. It tried to dominate the social system it found—but it had also to adapt to that system for securing low-cost governance and revenue extraction. Both the rulers and the ruled in their different ways invented traditions, which were in turn used to re-define their mutual relations. There was a churning of class positions, with some business communities coming up as others declined, or—as in the irrigated areas in the late colonial period—rich farmers sought to advance their own interests by using both economic and political tools of the major raiyatwari regions in south, west, and north-west India. New energies for social activism were released among the women or

Dalits or people belonging to so-called backward castes who came in touch with new ideas of civil freedom as well as gender equality and human equality in general. But in none of these cases did the activists begin from scratch nor did the rulers bring those gifts freely or ultimately deliver them to the oppressed, because the imperatives of a tributary regime constrained their choice. The papers in this selection seek to shed light on the tributary compulsions of the colonial state and their outcomes.

How constraining the colonial incubus was for the outcomes is indicated by the fact that in spite of all the obstacles posed by a highly inegalitarian social system, growth in Indian national and per capita incomes underwent a structural break almost immediately after independence, even though the population grew at much faster rates than under the colonial regime (Sivasubramonian 2000; Hatekar and Dongre 2005). Recognizing the role of agency at different levels does not mean that we reduce it to a voluntaristic romanticism and in the process exculpate colonialism in all its unappealing manifestations.

In analysing the outcomes of economic and human development and processes shaping them, it is always necessary to link the processes to the overarching political structure and the class relations shaped by it, and the way those class and political relations might influence the processes and the outcomes. This applies to colonial India as much as to the outcomes in any other society. This might be illustrated by a proposition put forward by David Ludden, one of the more careful students of Indian economic history. In a recent paper, Ludden (2010), arguing that Curzon, after all, wanted the good of the people of East Bengal and Assam, when he effected the partition of Bengal, writes:

> In 1911, Calcutta lost its status as India's capital but returned to its former supremacy as capital of Bengal. Along with this came renewed underdevelopment in the east, which appeared in dark form in 1943–44, after which the Famine Commission lamented that the Bengal government was uniquely unable to protect food security in rural areas. After 1911, Dhaka lapsed back into relative stagnation, until it revived in 1947 and then more so in 1971. (p. 20)

It takes a very bold historian indeed, a new Oswald Spengler or Arnold Toynbee, to predict that there would have been no famine in Bengal in 1943 if the province had been partitioned on Curzonian lines in 1905.[21] Let us look at the more serious parts of Ludden's proposition. In what sense was East Bengal more underdeveloped than West Bengal? By 1905 all of Bengal had become an agrarianized economy, with more than 65 per cent people dependent on agriculture. So agricultural growth was the base of whatever incomes ordinary people enjoyed. According to the work of George Blyn (1966: Chapters V–VII) supported by the later work of Sugata Bose (1986, 1993), Manoj Sanyal (2004) and others, the central and southern West Bengal districts witnessed stagnation or decline in absolute agricultural output between 1901 and 1931 whereas the deltaic region of East Bengal continued to display a growth in acreage which was the main source of growth during the period. The internal migration figures also show that throughout the early part of the twentieth century, it was East Bengal and Assam that witnessed the largest flow of immigrants, who mostly cleared land and set up as landholding, though poor and indebted, peasants (Davis 1951: Chapter 14; Zachariah 1964). Landlessness was virtually absent among the cultivating peasantry in deltaic East Bengal (Bose 1986: Chapter 7, this chapter has been included in Ludden 1994).

Both in West Bengal and in East Pakistan, after independence, power passed into the hands of a conglomerate class of landlords, merchants, lawyers and other professionals, and economic and human development suffered in both parts of Bengal. East Bengal developed a high degree of landlessness and no attempt was made to carry out pro-peasant land reforms (Khan 1972b; Bose 1983; Bagchi 1998; Sanyal *et al.*, 1998). Boyce (1987) famously characterized the situation on both sides of the border as an agrarian impasse. So fascinated is Ludden by the Curzonian rhetoric that he pays no attention to the developing class relations in Bengal after 1905—relations that no imperially initiated administrative tinkering would have corrected. Those class relations defeated A.K. Fazlul Huq's attempts from 1937 to reduce the indebtedness of the peasantry or reduce the power of the landlords (see Ahsan 2002). But even without enquiring more closely into what happened in East and West Bengal after the revocation of the Bengal partition in 1911, we can ask what happens in Bihar and Orissa which became a separate province from 1912, with Patna as the capital. The condition of Bihar agriculture did not improve after that (Blyn 1966), nor did Patna become a major centre of trade and investment (Bagchi 2006[1987], 1997).

Apart from the question of whether the establishment of large-scale industry by the British offered to the Indian worker more choices than dying from overwork or from starvation (Bagchi 1990; Ghosh 2000), it is clear that establishing an administrative capital at a place as such did not promote investment, and especially Indian investment centered on that city. To take a striking example, the Bank of Bengal branch at Lahore, the capital of Punjab, remained valuable to the bank not as a focus of investment but as a centre for deposit mobilization, and those deposits were primarily used to finance the British companies operating from Calcutta or London and increased the flow of remittances of European profit overseas (Bagchi 2006[1987], 1997).

I have made these brief observations to show that assigning causes of development of underdevelopment in colonial India requires a careful tracing out of the processes of that underdevelopment rather than making startling ex cathedra revisionist pronouncements.

Notes

1. When a chapter is mentioned, without giving any further reference, it refers to a chapter in this book (for example, Chapter 2, to differentiate references to chapters in other books). It may also be mentioned that, in the case of Chapters 4, 5, 6, and 7, several pages have been omitted in order to eliminate facts and analyses that are included in other chapters.

2. The acme of neocolonial historiography is reached with Tirthankar Roy (2000), who with no new evidence and no new arguments, simply denies that deindustrialization or stagnation characterized the colonial economy. For a thorough critique of this brand of Indian historiography, see Mukherjee (2007).

3. I have not asked or answered the question whether pre-colonial India had the potentiality to develop into a capitalist economy. This issue was addressed in a canonical paper by Habib (1969). My own view is that pre-colonial China and India were undergoing a Smithian growth in which markets had a big role to play, but the capitalists did not control the state apparatus (Bagchi 2006[2005]). This was also the situation in most of the European countries until the beginning of the nineteenth century, and without the crippling impact of the French Revolution on Western European feudalism and the spread effects of British industrialization on the closely linked but formally independent states, most of these other countries would also have found it difficult to industrialize.

4. For example, Henry St George Tucker—who was effectively the finance minister of the East India Company's government in India in the early 1800s, and rose to be the Chairman of the Company—wrote in his *Memorials of the Indian Government* (1853: 494) that because of the commercial policy followed by the British government, 'India is ... reduced from the state of a manufacturing to that of an agricultural country' (quoted by Dutt 1963a[1906]: 180). See also H.H. Wilson's trenchant comment on the British in his edition of James Mill's *History of India* (as quoted by Dutt 1963a[1906]: 180–1).

5. Samir Amin in his doctoral thesis (1957: 615) had written: '(Le sous développement) c'est le mécanisme de l'ajustement structurel des pays sous développés aux besoins des économies développées dominantes', that is, 'Underdevelopment is the mechanism of the structural adjustment of underdeveloped countries according to the needs of the developed and dominant countries'.

6. W.W. Peter, a US public health expert, compared the Indian health care situation unfavourably with the Philippines, Malaya, and Singapore. A major problem

was the meagreness of government expenditure on health and education. Moreover, the officials in charge of health complained about the paucity of funds. The outcome was that, according to the report of the Public Health Commissioner of Bombay Presidency, for example, for 1920 (even in the city of Bombay, among Parsis, by no means a poor community), the infant mortality rate (IMR) was 199, and the average IMR for the city was as high as 500 (Peter 1923: 630).

7. The beginning of the neocolonial historiography can be dated to Morris (1963); it was continued in several essays of Kumar and Desai (1983) and has reached its acme (or nadir) in Roy (2000). For a thorough critique of this brand of Indian historiography, see Mukherjee (2007).

8. As mentioned in *Hobson-Jobson*, 'The term Sayer in the eighteenth century was applied to a variety of inland imposts, but especially to local and arbitrary charges levied by zamindars and other individuals, with a show of authority, on all goods passing through their estates' (Yule and Burnell 1903: 799).

9. In a footnote Colebrooke and Lambert (1795) add: 'Not fewer than 12,000 in Bengal and Behar, but now greatly reduced in number'.

10. During these years, the surplus from the West Indies, as estimated by Patnaik (2006) came to £104 million, so that during these years the Caribbean plunder was even more important than the Indian tribute for the preservation of the British empire. On the other hand, a significant part of the Indian plunder was used to finance further expansion of the empire in India and protect it from the French.

11. The British Governors-General of India, especially Cornwallis and Wellesley, were fully aware of the importance of preventing the effective linking up of the French revolutionary regime with that of Tipu Sultan, who with his effective absolutism posed a serious alternative to British misrule in Madras Presidency (Stein 1989: Chapter 2).

12. Many varieties of apparently ancient institutions, such as the jajmani system, were largely adaptations to changes brought about by British rule (Mayer 1993).

13. See, for an analysis of the conditions of the peasantry in Bengal, Bose (1993) and Sanyal (2004); for Maharashtra, see Mishra (1985); for Tamil Nadu, Baker (1984); and for Andhra Pradesh, Washbrook (1994).

14. To take two examples from two regions at random, the wages of labour, including those of artisans, fell in the district of Bareilly in today's Uttar Pradesh between the 1820s and 1870s (Bagchi 1976b: 145). In the Bombay Deccan districts, in the period 1874–1922, Sunanda Krishnamurty (1987) found little growth in irrigation, a stagnant cultivated area continuation of the trends from the 1820s to the 1870s recorded in Bagchi (1992), a sharp rise in the share of uneconomic holdings and declining real wages of labour. Guha (1985: 141–2) found stagnant wages of field labourers in the Bombay Deccan districts in the twentieth century. See also the wage data from villages, regions and industries given in Sivasubramonian (2000: Tables 4.29–4.40).

15. For data on the exports and imports of Tamil Nadu and a critique of the monetarist argument explaining the price depression of the 1820s–1850s, see Bandopadhyay (1992: Chapter 5).

16. That the officially cognized incidence of famines is smaller than the actual visitation is indicated further by the fact that Raghavaiyangar (1893: 27) claims that 'from 1834 down to 1854 there was no famine of a severe type', and Visaria and Visaria (1983) seems to concur in this as far as south India was concerned, except for signalling a famine in Madras in 1853–5. But Thomas and Natarajan (1936: 67), pointing to a spike in prices in 1838–9, tag it as a year of famine.

17. I am indebted to Subhanil Banerjee for computing the figures. The method followed in re-classifying and aggregating the census categories is the one I had indicated in Bagchi (1976a).

18. In the poor agrarian society that India was reduced to, the earning opportunities of women confined to the domestic sphere or working as pluckers of tea leaves or at other menial tasks, continued to be further constricted by technical or legal changes. For an insightful discussion in the context of Bengal, see Bose (1993: 99–103).

19. Income compression resulting from the factors mentioned earlier would also mean that there would be not only an absolute decline in demand for manufactures along with that for foodstuff and services, but also that the demand for manufactures would fall relatively to those of agricultural goods at the income levels we are talking about. So even a rise in the prices of agricultural goods relatively to those of manufactures and non-tradables would only indicate impoverishment rather than a movement along a pre-colonial production frontier. Many weavers shifted to the production of coarse goods, especially when cheap yarn of low counts produced by British mills flooded the market. But this would not have protected the earnings of the skilled weavers, since value added per rupee of gross output would be lower. It would not also protect employment since the labour-intensity of coarse manufactures was much lower than that of finer textiles.

20. These projects were meant to yield surplus revenue after meeting the cost of the imputed or actual charges for servicing the debt or the opportunity cost of the public expenditure.

21. See Sen (1981) for a cogent analysis of the causes of the Bengal Famine of 1943 and numerous studies preceding and succeeding that.

1

An Estimate of the Gross Domestic Material Product of Bengal and Bihar in 1794 from Colebrooke's Data*

Introduction

H.T. Colebrooke wrote, at the end of the eighteenth century, one of the most interesting books ever written on the economy of Bengal and Bihar.[1] It is no exaggeration to say that for clarity, and sense of organization and relevance, this work is still unrivalled in its field. It computes the population of Bengal and checks it by various alternative methods; it gives the output of the important agricultural products; it calculates in detail the cost of production of various agricultural products (including sugar, indigo, opium, and hides); it gives estimates of the consumption of cotton cloth, and of salt; it gives figures of prices of various products, and of wages of labour. It compares the situation of a wage-labourer with that of a share-cropper, finding the latter worse off than the former. It refutes the canard that Indians are not suited by their social organization or values to the conduct of commerce, and so on. After reading Colebrooke, one begins to wonder whether the eighteenth-century British buccaneer or civil servant was not altogether a more honest and straightforward person than his nineteenth-century successor, trying desperately to rationalize the naked exploitation of the country by an alien power and an alien class.[2]

*Reprinted from 1973, *Nineteenth Century Studies*, No. 3, *Indian Peasants*. Calcutta: Bibliographical Research Centre, pp. 398–412.

Colebrooke was, of course, not above his times or his group ethos as a middle-class Briton; while wanting free trade in those Indian products which his country did not produce, he could not deplore the growth of cotton manufactures in Britain behind high tariffs and other restrictions against import of foreign—particularly Indian—cotton goods (Apparently, the British manufactures could not even then rival the finer products of the Indian cotton industry). He passes without comment the very high rates of profit on turnover realized by European private traders, and even more, by the East India Company, when the Indian producers of these products could barely survive on their earnings. He also does not touch on the widespread chicanery and oppression in the name of commerce practised by the servants of the East India Company and by private European traders (one reason being perhaps that the fruits of oppression had been legitimized in the form of fantastically high salaries and commissions through the reforms of Governor-General of India, Lord Cornwallis). But one can form a rough idea of the total material output of Bengal and Bihar and of some mechanism of its expropriation by Indian landlords and the Europeans from the concise descriptions of Colebrooke.

In the sequel, we shall confine ourselves to the estimation of the gross domestic material product (GDMP) of Bengal and Bihar. There are two different reasons for this. First, the data provided by Colebrooke on internal trade and commerce is more incomplete than the data on the output of tangible products. He provides an estimate of the long-distance grain trade of the area (not less than two crores of rupees[3]), and of the cost of transport over land or water, but this does not add up to an estimate of income from what is now called the tertiary sector. The second reason for omitting the income from the tertiary sector is more fundamental. It is difficult to separate the earnings of the banker, middleman, or trader for services rendered from his earnings through exploitation because of his class position vis-à-vis the peasant or the artisan. Increase in 'trade' often means increased payments to a parasitic class with no genuine economic function: this is reflected in an inflation in the price of the final product, of which the real producer gets a smaller fraction than before. Hence, if we cannot form an idea of the degree of inflation of earnings of the tertiary sector through an increased degree of exploitation while we suspect that such change has taken place, we shall be in danger of overestimating any increase in real national income over time. Since I shall compare the estimate of material output derived from Colebrooke with estimates relating to the period 1895–1900, I thought it better to leave out trade altogether (It is to be noted that in the estimates of British-Indian national income by later authors also, the figure for income from trade is far more conjectural than the figures for output of agriculture or industry).

Colebrooke's Estimate of the Produce of the Land

In para 20, Colebrooke gives the value of the gross produce of the land in the form of crops as Rs 329,130,000 and after making an allowance for seed for the following season, he obtains Rs 300,750,000 as the income earned from the land in the form of foodgrains and other crops.[4] He estimates the cultivated area of Bengal and Bihar to be 95 million standard *bighas* or about 32 million acres. As the physical base of his value estimate, he assumes the output of rice, wheat, and barley to be 150 million maunds, of millets and other foodgrains to be 90 million maunds and that of pulses to be 60 million maunds. Taking the net cropped area devoted to these crops to be about 30 million acres (the other crops are sugarcane, indigo, opium, and so on), this works out to an average total cereal yield of about 10 maunds per acre or a little more (after taking account of multiple cropping), which does not seem to be excessive (particularly if we remember that Bengal and Bihar had a much lower population than now, and hence the proportion of submarginal land in the total cropped area was much lower).

Land also adds to the income of the people in the form of livestock. Colebrooke estimates the number of cattle (including buffaloes) as 50 million.[5] Part of the services of these cattle is already included in the gross value of agricultural produce (excluding their services in the form of carriage of goods overland, which we will not discuss here). But it is still necessary to separate the working animals from milch animals and young stock. *The Indian Livestock Census, 1956*, volume 1 (issued by the Economic and Statistical Adviser, Directorate of Economic and Statistics, Ministry of Food and Agriculture, Delhi, 1956),[6] gives the proportion of working animals in the population of kine and buffaloes as 35.6 per cent in Assam, 40.7 per cent in Bihar, and 41.2 per cent in West Bengal; the proportions of breeding cows as 25.8 per cent in Assam, 21.5 per cent in Bihar, and 29 per cent in West Bengal; and the proportions of breeding buffaloes as 2.9 per cent in Assam, 8.3 per cent in Bihar, and 1.1 per cent in West Bengal. In 1794, there were large uncultivated areas which could be used as pasture for cattle—this would mean that the proportion of working animals to the total stock would tend to be lower. Furthermore, with more abundant pastures, female buffaloes would be kept in larger numbers because of their higher milk-yielding capacity. But on the other side, one might contend, transport would absorb a very large number of animals, since roads were bad, mechanical transport of any kind was unknown, and wheeled carriages could travel only on some roads and during some seasons. Balancing this drawback, the rivers of Bengal were far more navigable and in fact for long-distance transport, water carriage was the dominant means.[7]

We assume, in the tradition of guessers of such numbers, that in 1794 the proportion of working animals was 40 per cent of the total, and that the proportion of milch-cows to milch-buffaloes for Bengal and Bihar was close to the Bihar situation of 1956 (that is, eight milch-buffaloes and twenty-two milch-cows for a hundred of kine and buffaloes). In fact, while the numbers of adult male and female buffaloes in 1956 were about equal in Bihar, and males far outnumbered females in West Bengal, Colebrooke assumed fully two-thirds of a typical herd of buffaloes to consist of milch-animals. So we may be underestimating the number of female buffaloes, and thus, as we shall see, underestimating the contribution of livestock to GDMP in 1794.

Colebrooke estimated the profit per female buffalo to be Rs 7.[8] We take the profit per cow to be half of that per female buffalo. Thus we have:

	Number	Contribution to output (Rs)
Milch-buffaloes	4,000,000	28,000,000
Milch-cows	11,000,000	38,500,000
		66,500,000

Livestock added to the national product also in the form of an increase in the stock of animals every year. Colebrooke estimates it at 30 per cent of the value of the herd. To keep our estimate on the low side, we take only the value of the adult livestock and assume that additions to the stock account for only 10 per cent of that value. The value of a milch-buffalo is given as Rs 20: we take the value of a cow to be half of that. The price of a working animal is taken to be Rs 5;[9] this gives Rs (20 × 5 + 4 × 20 + 11 × 10) million = Rs 290 million as the value of the adult livestock. Hence the income through the increase of livestock is Rs 29,000,000.[10]

Thus a very conservative estimate (conservative, because we exclude all livestock other than cattle and buffaloes, the value of fish, the value of hides, skins, and so on) of the income generated by the primary sector is Rs (300,750,000 + 66,500,000 + 29,000,000) = Rs 396,250,000.

This income was, of course, not all appropriated by the people of Bengal, rich or poor, for the East India Company in its dual role as trader and ruler appropriated a large chunk of it and another large share went to private European traders. But still, in order to get an idea of what might be called the *potential income* per head of the ordinary people of Bengal and Bihar, one needs an idea of the total population. Colebrooke himself took 27 million as the probable population of Bengal and Bihar.[11] But in the next paragraph, on the basis of a survey in the district of Purniya, he arrived at an estimate of abut 30 million. While one cannot be dogmatic about either figure in the absence of more comprehensive data, there are reasons to believe that the early enumerators in India—particularly those who took large regions as their units—tended to underestimate the human population.[12] Hence we have used the larger figure. In order to compare the potential level of living of the people of Bengal and Bihar in 1794 with that of their descendants after a century of British rule, I have used Atkinson's estimate for 1895[13] and Sivasubramonian's estimate for 1900–10.[14]

Prices changed greatly between Colebrooke's time and 1900. Colebrooke does not specify the exact area in which the prices given by him (rice at 12 annas per maund, pulses at 10 annas per maund, and so on) prevailed. We assume that since he had an intimate knowledge of the Purniya district, he used the prices of that district. The cereal prices in Purniya, Kishanganj, and Araria in 1900–01 were at least three times as high as those given in Colebrooke.[15] If, however, Colebrooke had actually used the general average of prices in Bengal and Bihar (in particular, giving proper weight to the prices in Calcutta and the neighbouring districts) our assumption will lead to a downward bias in the estimate of the rise in prices.

The potential income per capita derived from agriculture and allied activities by the people of Bengal and Bihar in 1794 in the prices of that year comes to Rs 13.1; in the prices of 1900 it comes to Rs 39.3 approximately. In 1900–01, the population of India was 284.5 million, and according to Sivasubramonian, the total agricultural income in that year at current prices was Rs 7,822 million;[16] hence the income per capita derived by the Indian people from the primary sector was Rs 27.5.

There are some points to be noticed about this comparison. First, assuming that the value of agricultural produce is correctly stated by Colebrooke, our estimate of income from livestock in 1794 is almost certainly an underestimate, for it bears about the same proportion to income from agriculture as the corresponding income from animal husbandry (Rs 1,832 million) bore to the income from agriculture (Rs 5,873 million) in 1900–01,[17] which flies against our general observation that with population growth; (a) the number of working animals to the total livestock population probably increased, (b) the proportion of farm animals to human population declined,[18] and (c) the milk-producing capacity of cows declined over time.[19]

Second, the two figures are not exactly comparable since Colebrooke's figure relates to Bengal and Bihar, whereas Sivasubramonian's relates to the whole of India. In 1900, Bengal must have been among the highest-income regions in India; but to counterbalance this, Bihar, which has failed to secure even some of the marginal improvements of the British period, was a ruralized province, with most of its industry gone, and with its traditional irrigation system in a state of decay. Whether the Bengal–Bihar average income in 1900 would approximate to the Indian average remains conjectural at this stage of the enquiry. But one can say that the average Indian of 1900 had not come up to the standard of the average inhabitant of Bengal and Bihar in respect of his potential income after a century of British rule.

Estimate of the GDMP of Bengal and Bihar

In order to compute the GDMP of Bihar and Bengal, we can take the consumption of agricultural goods (including products of animal husbandry) and manufactured goods, add domestic investment and throw in the current balance of trade to obtain the gross national material product. Unfortunately, Colebrooke's data do not permit us to construct this estimate in a pure form. He gives the data for the consumption of the most important manufactured goods, namely, cotton cloth (Rs 60 million[20]), but does not provide data on the consumption of other locally manufactured goods (a figure for the consumption of salt is given but a large amount of this commodity was imported). Further, he does not separate the exports of agricultural produce from local consumption—so we make an estimate of the following composition:

(Exports + consumption) of products of the primary sector + consumption of cloth + an unknown figure for consumption of other locally manufactured goods + (exports of products of the primary sector) + exports of manufactured goods – total imports of goods.

Now obviously there is double counting of exports of the products of the primary sector in the above formula. But if we assume that exports of products of the primary sector at least equalled the consumption of manufactured goods other than cloth (including consumption of processed agricultural produce after deducting the value of the raw material), for which we have made no allowance, then our estimate comes very close to the gross national material product (we neglected domestic investment other than additions to livestock because we have no information about it). However, in 1794, Bengal and Bihar had a surplus of exports over imports and this surplus was not appropriated by inhabitants of this country but by foreigners. Hence, departing slightly from standard usage, we call this figure a minimum estimate of the GDMPof Bengal and Bihar. The objection might be raised that our net export figures include some invisible services, and we thereby get figures of income from trade mixed up with the figures of our material output. In actual fact, since export figures were on a free on board (f.o.b.) and import figures on a cost including freight (c.i.f.) basis, and since practically all shipping was foreign-owned, our way of measuring it would again under- rather than over-estimate GDMP.

We have taken this GDMP rather than the minimum estimate of actual Indian consumption for later comparisons, for neither Sivasubramonian nor Atkinson deducts the full incomes of Europeans resident in India. Atkinson does not seem to make any deductions at all and Sivasubramonian takes account only of actual remittances made by foreigners, with some adjustment for interest on foreign investment. Atkinson, for example, includes Rs 81 million as the income of civil and military officers, and a scrutiny of the detailed figures reveals that at least Rs 64,855,200 (being the sum of the pay of covenanted civil officers, staff corps, the British army and marine services, plus the exchange compensation allowance) must have been primarily the income of Europeans in India.[21]

For the sake of comparability, we add to Sivasubramonian's estimate of the total income derived from the primary and secondary sectors, his estimate of the income sent abroad and obtain the sum of Rs 7,822 + 1,438 + 191 million = Rs 9,451 million as the GDMP produced by Indians in 1900–01 from the primary and secondary sectors together. This gives an Indian GDMP of Rs 33.2 per capita at 1900–01 prices.

Atkinson divided the population into three groups for the purpose of computation of national income of British India. In the first group (Section I) he included the population dependent on agriculture. He divided the people who were dependent on occupations other than agriculture into ordinary people (Section II) and people of ample means

(Section III). We have taken the whole income of Section I, the incomes of labourers and industrial population included in Section II. and the incomes of agents, managers, and others included in Section III, to represent the gross national output. (This is, in fact, likely to exaggerate such output through the inclusion of some incomes derived from trade, commerce, and transport). Thus we have the GDMP of British India (excluding native states) in 1895, according to Atkinson:

	(Figures in Rs)
Income from agriculture	5,014,694,470
Income of labourers	416,288,400
Income of the industrial population	1,504,364,480
Income of agents, managers, and others	206,400,000
	7,141,750,350

With a population of 222 million in British India in 1895 (according to Atkinson), the GDMP per capita comes to about Rs 32.2. Even if we throw in the 'Miscellaneous' group in Atkinson's Section II, this raises the GDMP per head to Rs 33.2 only. There is thus a remarkable closeness in the estimates of GDMP per head derived from Atkinson and Sivasubramonian although neither the year nor the area was exactly the same in the two cases.

We now turn back to the derivation of GDMP in Colebrooke's time. For this we need an estimate of the export–import gap around 1794. According to Lambert, the total exports of Bengal (meaning Bengal and Bihar) to other parts of India and to foreign countries in 1794 was Current Rupees[22] 4,07,50,000.[23] The total imports into Bengal from different parts in the same year came to sicca Rs 2,03,37,615.[24] We shall take the difference between exports and imports to be roughly Rs 20 million.

We have a rough idea of the composition of the East India Company's 'investments' during the 1790s. The Company kept up an annual average 'investment' of current Rs 66 lakhs in the piece-goods of Bengal. 'In 1795 investment allotment was to amount to Rs 92.68,770—cotton piece-goods Rs 47,74,591, raw silk Rs 17,24,137, sugar Rs 19,41,213, saltpetre Rs 3,37,875 being the principal items. In 1799 investment amounted to Rs 90,51,324—piece-goods Rs 59,59,724 and raw silk Rs 17,25,000.'[25]

The composition of major private exports from Calcutta to the rest of the world in 1795–6 and 1801–02 was as follows (in sicca Rs):[26]

	1795–6	1801–02
Indigo	62,51,424	38,48,139
Grain	9,11,365	22,59,618
Sugar	8,20,186	12,01,798
Silk	5,81,183	13,65,882
Piece-goods	94,83,284	1,65,91,309
Opium	13,08,360	27,51,915

Although our list is incomplete, it seems clear that the major part of exports—whether on the East India Company's account or on private account—consisted of either manufactured or semi-manufactured goods, and that raw agricultural produce formed only a minor part of total exports (In the case of products such as sugar, silk, indigo, or opium, the processing cost accounted for a major fraction of the total value). Moreover, there were many locally manufactured goods, for example, wild silk of various kinds[27] which entered international trade only marginally, but which were consumed in Bengal in vast quantities. Hence we are probably on safe ground in assuming that the value of the locally manufactured products retained in Bengal and Bihar for consumption (or investment) was greater than the value of the raw agricultural produce exported. Since the Current *Rupiya*s used by Lambert in estimating export values might be less valuable than *Sicca* Rupiyas, we take the export-import balance to lie between (Sicca) Rs 18 million and Rs 20 million.

We get the minimum figure of Rs 18 million by adding the totals of net private remittances of European traders and 'investments' by the East India Company, and thereby estimating the annual drain of wealth from Bengal and Bihar in the 1790s.[28]

Thus, we get as the minimum estimate of the GDMP of Bengal and Bihar in 1794:

	(Figures in Rs)
Agriculture and animal husbandry	396,250,000
Consumption of cotton cloth	60,000,000
Export-import balance	20,000,000
	or (18,000,000)
	476,250,000
	or (474,250,000)

Taking the figure of Rs 474,250,000 as the basis of our calculations we get Rs 15.8 as the GDMP per capita of Bengal and Bihar in 1794.

Again, multiplying the figure by three to approximate the price-level of 1895 or 1900, we have Rs 47.4 as the GDMP per head in 1794 at the prices of the year 1900.

The objection might be raised here that prices of manufactured goods did not rise as much as the prices of grains and hence we might over-estimate the general rise in prices if we take the index of grain prices as the general index number. On the other side lie the following facts and suppositions: (a) prices of many agricultural goods—such as pulses and oil seeds—and of products of animal husbandry probably rose more than prices of grains; (b) foodgrains and agricultural products in general continued to dominate both output and consumption in India; (c) many varieties of manufactured goods, which were earlier produced and consumed in India, practically vanished and became unattainable to Indians between 1794 and 1895, and conversely, many new types of manufactured goods remained beyond the buying power of the vast majority of Indians, and (d) Atkinson's and Sivasubramonian's figures include trade margins to a greater extent than Colebrooke's, since we took prices of an interior district for 1794 whereas the later figures are probably regional averages or figures at ports.

Thus making the most conservative assumptions possible, which impart a strong downward bias to our 1794 figures, we find that an average Indian in 1895 or 1900 was *producing* less than an average inhabitant of Bengal and Bihar in 1794. If the average income of Bengal and Bihar together at all approximated the average income of India in 1895 or 1900, a century of British rule had impaired the productive capacity of the country. Such a conclusion would knock the bottom out of most colonialist apologetics—in however attenuated a form (since 1794 had seen the end of the Bolts, Barwells, and Grants and Cornwallis[29] had just brought in 'order')—and would also make nonsense of those development theories which see the history of under-developed countries as a slow progression from medieval poverty to modern prosperity.

Notes

1. Henry Thomas Colebrooke, 1795, *Remarks on the Husbandry and Internal Commerce of Bengal*, first edn, Calcutta; second edn, London, 1804; reprinted, from the edition published by Robert Knight in 1884, in *Census of India, 1951, vol. VI, West Bengal, Sikkim and Chandernagore, Part I c—Report* by A. Mitra (Delhi, 1953, pp. 180–231). All references are to this last reprint. It appears from the 'Advertisement' by the author that most of the calculations relate to 1794; hence that has been taken as the base date throughout.

2. Of course, the successful debasement of the Indian businessman to a subordinate position or to the life of an idle *rentier* helped this rationalization enormously.

3. See Colebrooke, para 200.

4. Ibid.: para 20.

5. Ibid.: para 232.

6. The relevant data have been reproduced in A.V. Desai (1965: 329–38).

7. See Colebrooke, para 190–3.

8. Colebrooke, para 131.

9. Ibid.: para 113.

10. While it is impossible, without some independent evidence relating to Colebrooke's time, to check the reasonableness or otherwise of our assumptions, we shall compare the number of working animals as estimated by us—20 millions—with (a) the total number of working animals in Bihar in 1966 and (b) the total number derived from another part of Colebrooke's book. In 1966, the total number of working animals in Bihar alone (data for West Bengal for 1966 are not available) was 7.6 million (see Table 20 in *Statistical abstract of the Indian Union*, 1967, 1968, Delhi). Assuming that the total number of working animals in the area comprising Bengal proper (before 1947) was at most twice this number, the total could come to 22.8 millions for a cultivated area, which was at least double the area (95 million bighas) given by Colebrooke. Hence our estimate of 20 million would appear to be on the higher side. But presumably, the working animals were used to a greater extent for transport in Colebrooke's days. On the other side, Colebrooke states: 'A plough, with the usual yoke of two or three pairs of oxen assigned to it, is equal in common management to the full cultivation of fifteen bighas of land.' Thus according to this estimate, at least 25 million animals would be required to work 95 million bighas. But working animals owned by a large farmer would also be used by the farm servants, who would usually be given 2 or 3 bighas of land to cultivate as a tenant. This would bring down the figure nearer to our estimate, making our crude estimate not outrageously improbable.

11. See para 15.

12. I have discussed the early population figures of Bengal in greater detail in Bagchi (1976a). Also see Chapter 4 in this volume.

13. F.J. Atkinson (1902: 209–83).

14. Sivasubramonian (1965)

15. See Colebrooke, para 26.

16. See Sivasubramonian (1965) Tables 2.10 and 3.24.

17. Ibid.: Table 3.24.

18. For observation from another part of India corroborating this, see Catanach (1970: 16).

19. As the *Report on the Marketing of Milk in India and Burma* (1941) put it,

> '... the general consensus of opinion seems to be that the milking capacity of Indian cattle has deteriorated in as much as it is not easy now-a-days to obtain good quality cows and she-buffaloes as was the case some twenty or thirty years ago. The opinion is also strongly held that the deterioration in cows has been generally greater than in she-buffaloes'. (Quoted in Sivasubramonian[1965: 118])

20. See para 201.

21. See F.J. Atkinson (1902: 236–7).

22. Current Rupees were an accountant's fiction worth 2 shillings; because of exchange fluctuations they could be either more or less valuable than Sicca Rupiyas. We shall treat them generally as equivalent to Sicca Rupiyas.

23. Tripathi (1956: 36–7).

24. This figure is obtained by adding values of imports from various ports given by Lambert and reproduced in (Ibid.: 37–8).

25. Sinha (1970: 1).

26. Tripathi (1956: 79n).

27. See Colebrooke, para 178.

28. The average annual total balance (exports–imports) of private remittances from Calcutta to Copenhagen, Lisbon, Hamburg, America, and London over the years 1795–6 to 1797–8 amounted to Sicca Rs 78,73,073. Adding the annual average balance for the private trade from Calcutta to China, Penang, the Gulfs and so on, amounting to roughly Rs 400,000 over the years 1796–7 to 1798–9, the private drain amounted to Sicca Rs 82,73,000 (see Tripathi 1956: 44n and 77n). If the 'investment' out of the surplus revenue by the East India Company amounted to even Rs 10 million, we get a minimum estimate of the drain as Rs 18.3 million annually. See Tripathi (1956: 256n) for an estimate of the drain by other authorities; and for an account of 'investments' by the East India Company up to 1793, see Sinha (1961: 230–1).

29. William Bolts was a Dutchman who came as a factor of the East India Company in the 1760s and was expelled from the Company's territory for engaging in private trade, against the condition of his employment (a practice in which many other factors also indulged). After going back to England, he wrote a blistering attack on the malpractices of the Company and its covenanted servants. Richard Barwell was a member of the Governor's Council when Warren Hastings was the Governor and supported Hastings in his squabble with Philip Francis. Charles Grant was an influential member of the Governor's Council in the 1780s and wanted Protestant missionaries to be allowed to proselytize in India.

2

Reflections on Patterns of Regional Growth in India under British Rule*

Introduction

Although there exist several regional or subregional histories of India during the British period, there has been little systematic attempt to compare growth patterns as between different regions. Such an attempt is worthwhile for several reasons. We are interested in the dynamics of the regional societies on their own, but it is not possible to get a perspective on such dynamics if we do not have some standard of comparison. That standard of comparison normally makes much better sense if it comes from India than if it is derived from a German palatinate or a Turkish satrapy. Secondly, the macroeconomic constraints can be better understood when we can see their impact on smaller entities. In particular, regional stratification can be an aspect of the general processes of uneven development under colonialism. In fact, region-specific predictions can provide a test for transregional or supraregional hypotheses.

At the moment, the most thorough account of the location of large-scale industries before independence starts explicitly with a Weberian perspective.[1] That account, however, does not even begin to explain the *rate* of growth of different industries or the *timing* of their establishment

*Originally published as 'Reflections on Patterns of Regional Growth in India during the Period of British Rule' in, 1976, *Bengal Past and Present*, XCV(1), January–June, pp. 247–89.

in the different regions of India. The usual Weberian requirements of the availability of raw materials and a market merely provide the *necessary* conditions for the survival of an industry, once established, in a colonial context, but do not at all explain the failure of many industries to be established at all or to grow. The regional dimensions of the Indian market have hardly been explored anyway. The Weberian approach does have the merit of explicitly bringing in the geographical constraints on development. But those constraints are subject to alteration through government policies, behaviour of social classes, and so on.

One question we shall be concerned with in this essay is how the basic mechanism of colonial exploitation of India revealed itself regionally, and how the working of that mechanism was modified by region-specific factors. In particular, how did the colonial set-up facilitate or thwart the survival and growth of capitalist classes in different parts of India?[2] How did land relations conjointly with other colonial policies, in different parts of the country, influence (a) the formation of a capitalist class, (b) the pattern of public investment, (c) the relations between agriculture and industry, and (d) relations between capital and labour? Although we raise these questions, we do not pretend to answer them within the compass of this essay, leaving aside limitations of data. We do not have inter-regionally comparable data on the growth or decline of small-scale industries. We do have Blyn's work on regional growth rates in agriculture from 1891–2 onwards,[3] but these have to be supplemented by detailed analyses of agricultural growth rates. In the latter part of this essay I have used the work of M.M. Islam and Saugata Mukherji on growth rates in agriculture in Bengal. But for other regions, similar work is yet to be accomplished.

These data gaps are evidence of lacunae not only in empirical work, but also in the conceptual apparatus employed—most of the available work concentrated only on large-scale industries.[4] While such work is extremely valuable, it still can depict only the peaks of the structure of domination in the Indian economy: the movements lower down can alter the positions of the peaks and can, so to speak, elevate or depress the whole mountain range. Our partial and impressionistic account of the structure of the capitalist class and of relations between agriculture and industry are to be seen as preliminary sampling work for delineating the dynamics and the structure of economic development in colonial India. This attempt will hopefully provoke others to collect and analyse relevant data bearing on the questions raised.

Differential Rates of Colonial Penetration in Western and Eastern India and their Impact on Export Surpluses: Processes of Export-led Exploitation

Bengal (that is, Bengal, Bihar, and Orissa) was the original stamping ground of British colonialism in India. The resources of eastern India provided the wherewithal to the British for the conquest of the rest of India. From this point of view, it is the aggregate output of the region of exploitation and the part that the government could squeeze out for maintaining an army and engaging in warfare that is crucially important. We do not have comparable data on the outputs of Bengal, Madras, and Bombay Presidencies in the eighteenth century,[5] or, for that matter, for the nineteenth century. But we know that Bengal's surplus revenue was regularly utilized by the British government to meet the deficits of the Presidencies of Bombay and Madras in the late eighteenth and early nineteenth centuries.[6]

The British, however, were not a 'country' power but a transoceanic imperial power. They were not interested in carving out an empire in India simply because they could have a *masnad* in Delhi—they were interested in taking the tribute out of the country. From this point of view also, Bengal provided much the biggest base of exploitation, particularly before the crushing of Tipu Sultan in the south and the Marathas in the west and north of India. Even after the British had established their hegemony over the rest of India, Bengal continued to provide the biggest export base to the British.[7]

We can go a little further and say that even more than the total volume of export, it is the surplus of export over imports, particularly of merchandise, that provided the bacterial culture for the fattening of the colonial interests. When Lambert enquired into the trade and commerce of Bengal, he had no difficulty in arriving at a figure of the drain of the annual product of Bengal.[8] The contemporary observers realized easily that under the general umbrella of protection provided by the East India Company, private European merchants were earning vast profits: whatever quarrel there was, was about the sharing of spoils. Prinsep divided remittable 'private accumulation' (apart from dividends on the securities of the East India Company earned by Europeans, and surplus public revenues) as between Bengal, Madras, and Bombay as follows (figures in Rs lakhs):[9]

Bengal	Civil	21.5
	Military	19.0
	Commercial	33.5
	Law	4.0
	Retail-trade	8.0
	Indigo-workers	4.0
	Mortgage, houses, etc.	5.0
	Total	95.0
Madras and Bombay	Civil	11.0
	Military	19.0
	Commercial, etc.	12.0
	Total	42.0

It is only in days of greater sophistry that the fact of the continual extraction of a political and mercantile tribute from India could be glossed over and denied altogether.[10] It is partly because of this lying sophistry that our use of the export surplus on merchandise account as a first approximation to the degree of exploitation has to be defended.

In ordinary international accounts, if a country shows a persistent surplus of exports over imports, then the balance accumulates as claims against foreign countries plus reserves of gold or of foreign currencies. If we scrutinize the Indian balance of trade accounts (excluding 'invisibles' for the moment) before independence, we find that while India had a persistent balance of trade surplus, Europeans were all the time accumulating claims against India in the forms of ownership of private capital and holdings of public securities of various kinds. How did this happen? The stock answer is to point to the payments for invisible services and to imports of gold and silver as the items that more than counterbalanced the favourable balance of trade accounts. However, as it has been aptly put, payments for invisibles are often difficult to compute because no services were rendered in the first place. In the Indian case, the invisibles would consist of those parts of home charges, military expenditures abroad, and so on, for which no goods were received in India. These were straight political tributes and covered up an unrequited export surplus. Then there were the charges for banking, insurance, and shipping services, and finally, there were the remittances on profits of business and employment. It is difficult to accept these payments also as *quid pro quo* for straight commercial transactions, for the Europeans' position was built up and bolstered by the political arrangements of colonialism: Indians were simply denied entry into most of these profitable fields on one pretext or another.[11] The accumulation of capital by British businesses in India consisted almost entirely of ploughed back profits. The initial base for that capital, as in the case of tea gardens, was generally control over land and labour conferred almost gratuitously on the Europeans by the British government.

It would at first appear that imports of gold and silver are on a different footing altogether. However, most of the imports of silver, at least since 1850 (and probably earlier too), were for the purpose of silver coinage.[12] By refusing to introduce currency notes on a large scale, the Government of India imposed an immense burden on Indians, and this burden increased greatly during the years 1872–92 when silver depreciated continuously.[13] Gold imports were for the most part for hoarding purposes, but in the nineteenth century at least, they accounted for considerably less than half of the total imports of bullion and treasure. The motives for hoarding were connected with the dominance of zamindars and princes among the men of property in India, the unfavourable climate for private industrial investment in India created by British colonialism, and the great uncertainty associated with fluctuations in harvests and agricultural prices in an underdeveloped, and retrogressive, agrarian economy. It would take us too long to analyse these motives in this paper and would amount to a digression from the main theme.

The real argument against the use of export surplus as an index of exploitation is that it is almost certain to underestimate its effects. Among the items of import figure the consumption by Europeans resident in India and the import of military stores for purposes of imperial defence. Furthermore, many of the imports—particularly of government stores and railway engines and material—were virtually tied to Britain as a source, and were overpriced. For similar reasons, there would be a downward bias in the figures of Indian exports. We would have to add the true value of imports springing only from the needs of the colonial rulers to the true value of the export surplus in order to arrive at a proper measure of exploitation.

On the other hand, the use of the export surplus as an approximate index of exploitation has the virtue of emphasizing that in a colonial context, the mechanism for expansion of exports is that of export-led exploitation rather than that of export-led growth. It is the need for remitting the increased spoils earned in the colonized country that provides the drive for increasing exports. In an imperial payments framework within which India had a crucial role to play, the export surplus further provided the wherewithal for balancing accounts within those countries with which Britain happened to run a deficit. Both these objectives were abundantly clear to British policy-makers and merchants when China was 'opened' to trade in opium, but the imperial strategists never lost sight of them when the payments system became more tangled.[14]

Export and import figures are available separately for the major ports of British India: Calcutta, Bombay, Madras, and Rangoon. Figures of total exports and imports of the littoral Presidencies of Bengal, Bombay, and Madras and the province of Sind are also available. We have taken these figures to represent the exports and imports of the hinterlands of the four major ports (excluding Rangoon) and their subsidiary minor ports. Plotted in Tables 2.1 and 2.2 are the five-yearly averages of exports, and of the surplus of merchandise exports over merchandise imports, respectively.

Table 2.1 Five-Yearly Averages of Total Exports of Merchandise from the Four Major Regions of India

(Rs '000)

Period	Bengal	Bombay	Madras	Sind
1871–2 to 1875–6	241,510	220,962	67,230	10,969
1876–7 to 1880–1	301,708	225,443	76,240	13,363
1881–2 to 1885–6	340,591	319,711	83,486	33,244
1886–7 to 1890–1	375,250	369,856	1 02,853	38,118
1891–2 to 1895–6	432,511	384,710	116,311	61,669
1896–7 to 1900–1	484,468	326,220	116,467	54,355
1901–2 to 1905–6	589,400	437,654	141,01 7	119,152
1906–7 to 1910–11	770,956	510,123	190,032	173,445
1911–12 to 1915–16	924,299	580,092	240,502	240,926
1916–17 to 1920–1	1,291,319	879,693	262,711	239,235
1921–2 to 1925–6	1,301,795	1,026,661	347,084	345,260
1926–7 to 1930–1	1,304,679	705,441	412,343	253,722
1931–2 to 1935–6	630,490	313,425	254,045	144,620
1936–7 to 1938–9 (3-yearly averages)	807,199	402,803	367,689	225,283

Sources: *Annual Statements of the Trade and Navigation of British India* (Computed in the Statistical Bureau, Director General of Statistics, Government of India) and *Annual Statements of the Trade and Navigation* of the Bengal, Bombay, and Madras Presidencies and of the province of Sind (separately for each region), and Government of India, Commercial Intelligence and Statistics Department, *Annual Statements of the Seaborne Trade of India,* vol. II.

If there are limitations to the use of aggregate data on export surplus as a rough index of exploitation, there might be even greater reservations

Table 2.2 Five-Yearly Averages of Export Surplus (Export Minus Import of Merchandise) of Different Regions of India

(*Rs '000*)

Period	Bengal	Bombay	Madras	Sind
1871–2 to 1875–6	73,123	101,612	31,568	5,955
1876–7 to 1880–1	109,819	71,302	39,496	2,896
1881–2 to 1885–6	119,106	109,532	36,528	13,033
1886–7 to 1890–1	118,716	95,302	43,308	–3,1 83
1891–2 to 1895–6	155,955	1 02,802	52,775	1,478
1896–7 to 1900–1	166,726	–21 ,470	53,701	1,897
1901–2 to 1905–6	214,400	105,626	60,300	33,433
1906–7 to 1910–11	272,776	82,204	85,520	37,200
1911–12 to 1915–16	303,256	58,120	83,924	82,693
1916–17 to 1920–1	275,331	40,744	1 03,945	37,381
1921–2 to 1925–6	399,914	118,437	143,845	55,221
1926–7 to 1930–1	502,749	–99,691	167,267	–61,224
1931–2 to 1935–6	269,338	–208,923	95,566	17,873
1936–7 to 1938–9 (3-yearly averages)	336,967	–214,488	136,634	45,087

Sources: As in Table 2.1.

against the use of regional data on export surplus as rough indices of the regional burdens of exploitation. First of all, there might be abrupt or long-term changes in the hinterlands of the different ports brought about by changes in communications networks, particularly railways in the case of India. While this danger would be considerable before the 1870s, by the end of the nineteenth century, this had been considerably minimized. Already by 1878, most of the arterial railways connecting the major ports with the hinterland—such as the East Indian, the Great Indian Peninsular, the Madras, the Bombay, Baroda, and Central India, and the Sind, Punjab, and Delhi lines—had been laid down.[15] Between 1878 and 1901, the railway lines had been extended from about 8,500 to about 23,000 miles, but much of the new mileage was in the nature of military lines as in north-west India, or were meant to connect gaps between lines, or connect famine-prone areas with the rest of the country. In the course of these changes, the most important shift probably occurred in the hinterlands of Karachi and Bombay, the former gaining at the cost of the latter. But it is most unlikely that Calcutta and Bombay—the two most important ports—could have gained in relation to each other. By 1914, the hinterlands of the different ports were supposed to have been fixed enough for a government publication to compute Table 2.3:

Table 2.3 Percentages of Provincial Trade Passing Through Different Major Ports

Province	Calcutta	Bombay	Madras	Karachi
Bengal	64	...	...	...
Madras	2	1	70	...
Bombay	...	41	...	
United Provinces	20	10	...	12
Bihar and Orissa	42	1	1	...
Punjab	2	3	...	42
Central Provinces and Berar	5	49		
Assam	35	...	...	
Sind and British Baluchistan	...	...	...	75
Rajputana and Central India	2	16	...	1
Nizam's Territory	...	31	6	
Mysore	...	4	21	

Source: Shirras (1914: 51).

Of course, the hinterlands might be changing continually, and so might the importing population served by the different ports. *A priori,* it would seem that changes in relative freight rates would induce changes in actual flows of goods along different lines. But the Indian railways worked under explicit or implicit collusive arrangements or under government regulations or rates; much of the time there were also shortages of wagons. While the delineation of the effective hinterlands of the different ports should be the subject of detailed research, our guess about relative stability of the outlines of hinterlands of major ports cannot be dismissed out of hand.[16]

A second complication would seem to arise from the fact that the exploitative mechanism of the British government was a supraregional one: while military and civil establishments would be distributed regionally, their expenses would be paid out of a central pool. This would have contradictory effects on the export surplus figures. If the salaries of some government officers stationed in Calcutta were paid out of the revenues of the Central Provinces, and if these officers imported goods for their own consumption, these would swell import figures and understate the export surplus generated in the hinterland of Calcutta. On the other side, if these officers remitted their savings to England, this would have a tendency to swell the export figures. It is difficult to judge *a priori* which would be the dominant pattern. Until 1910, Calcutta was the capital of India. It could be argued that unless the spending-saving patterns of Europeans in eastern India were widely different from the spending-saving patterns of, say, Europeans in Madras or Bombay, and/or unless there were systematic flows of subsidies as between different regional administrations and between the central administration and the regions, the regional export surplus figures could be used as first approximations to the burdens imposed by colonialism on the different regions.[17]

With these preliminary remarks out of the way, we can briefly analyse the figures in Tables 2.1 and 2.2. Between 1871–2 and 1895–6, the rates of growth of exports of Bombay, Bengal, and Madras are remarkably similar, although Sind grows fastest during this period. But if we take the period from 1896–7 up to 1915–16, the rate of growth of exports from Bombay lags considerably behind the rates of growth of exports from Bengal and Madras, and, of course, Sind. After a short flurry of growth between 1916–17 and 1925–6, Bombay again falls behind Calcutta and Madras. Sind's relative rate of growth decelerates after 1915–16. In the agricultural depression, which really started in India after 1925–6, all the regions lose, but Bombay loses most heavily in proportionate terms, followed by Sind, Bengal, and Madras.

The behaviour of export surpluses as between different regions is even more disparate. With the sole exception of the initial five-year period of 1871–2 to 1875–6, Bengal generated the largest export surplus among all the regions in every period. In fact from 1896–7 onwards, Bengal's export surplus exceeded the export surpluses of all the different regions put together. While Bengal and Madras never had an import surplus, Sind and Bombay produced import surpluses in several quinquennia. In fact, Bombay had an import surplus over the whole period from 1926–7 to 1938–9. The origins of the import surpluses in Sind and Bombay are different: in the case of Sind they were caused by heavy public expenditure on railways (in the late nineteenth century), primarily for military purposes and irrigation works. For the period 1896–7 to 1900–01, the import surplus in Bombay was caused by the effects of the famines of 1896–7 and 1899–1900, and of the plague which caused a decline in the exports of cotton yarn from Bombay to China. But the import surpluses of Bombay in other periods are organically connected with the growth of an Indian capitalist class undertaking industrial investment in the western region.

Even during the period when the exports of Bombay were expanding almost as fast as the exports of Bengal, part of the buoyancy was caused by the exports of crude cotton manufactures in the shape of cotton twist and yarn and coarse cotton cloth, particularly to Japan and China, and later on mainly to China. Although Greaves Cotton were large exporters in the field, most of the exports originated from Indian mills. Meanwhile in Ahmedabad, an exclusively Indian-owned cotton mill industry was expanding to supply the home market in cotton cloth. After the plague disaster at the end of the nineteenth century and the beginning of the twentieth century, Bombay mills also began to turn towards the home market, supplying cotton yarn to handloom weavers and weaving coarse cotton cloth themselves.[18]

By contrast, in eastern India, all the major exports were controlled by European businessmen: they invested in tea plantations, jute mills, jute exporting businesses, and controlled the export trade in hides and skins, shellac, and other commodities. Cotton mills in eastern India remained primarily spinning mills, either exporting abroad or catering to the needs of the handloom weavers. While this concentration on exportables would explain the continued buoyancy of exports in eastern India and in Madras after 1895–6, this would not explain why export surpluses expanded as fast as, or even faster than, exports. The hypothesis here is that since business in all parts of India other than western India was dominated by Europeans, as exports rose, overseas remittances also went up, thus widening the gap between exports and imports, *pari passu* with increasing exports. By contrast, in western India, since business was controlled by Indians, the profits would be reinvested in India, thus leading to increases in imports. Furthermore, because of the structure of control of business in European-dominated regions, which precluded the employment of Indians in managerial or supervisory positions and also thwarted the growth of labour organizations, there was no trickling down of increasing incomes to lower-income groups. By contrast, there may have been a greater degree of diffusion of increases in incomes in western India, leading to an increase in importables and contraction in the supply of those exportables which could be consumed at home.

We have already pointed out some of the limitations to the use of the export surplus figures as even rough indices of the regional burdens of colonial exploitation. We should point to another possible reservation. Our interpretation of the origin of the export-import gaps and their movement would be vitiated if it happened that Indian traders or other Indian (or for that matter foreign) capitalists invested their profits from eastern (or southern) India in industries in western India. Although the capital flows within India in the British period have not been analysed, whatever crude evidence is available indicates that this did not happen on any large scale before 1939. If, for example, the Birlas with their trading base in eastern India invested in Gwalior in western India, the Tatas, with their base in western India invested in the iron and steel complex, in and near Jamshedpur; most other capitalists tended to invest in locations near their trading bases.[19]

On Some Characteristics of the Capitalist Classes in Different Regions of India and their History during the British Period

We have postulated that some at least of the difference between the burdens of exploitation as between eastern and western India can be attributed to the fact that the dominant capitalist class in western India had a very large Indian component, whereas the capitalist strata dominating manufacturing, plantations and mining, and large-scale banking and external trade in eastern India was almost entirely European, particularly before the First World War. I have analysed elsewhere the behaviour patterns of European capitalists, and of the Parsi capitalists in western India and the reasons for their success.[20] There is besides a large literature on the Parsis.[21] There are also books on Ahmedabad[22] and valuable articles on the industrial growth of Ahmedabad and the socio-cultural influences on such growth.[23]

But these studies are still incomplete because they do not delineate the structure of the Gujarati capitalist class nor do they indicate the links of the big Gujarati capitalists to the Gujarat region as a whole. The different volumes of the *Gazetteers* of the Bombay Presidency contain materials which throw interesting light on the composition of the capitalist class in Gujarat at the beginning of British rule (that is, in the beginning of the nineteenth century) and help to establish that there was already a capitalist class in Gujarat in a discernible sense at that time. Furthermore, this class managed to survive into the third quarter of the nineteenth century when modern, large-scale, cotton mills began to grow up in Bombay and Ahmedabad.

In the latter part of this section I shall turn to a detailed analysis of the functional composition of the Gujarati capitalist class. Before I do that, I mention some of the important contrasts between the histories of the capitalist classes in eastern and western India. In Bengal, just prior to the British conquest, the external trade and shipping were controlled by Gujarati merchants and shipowners, and much of the wholesale trade and organized banking were in the hands of upcountry traders and financiers, such as the house of Jagat Seth.[24] With the British conquest, Indian merchants and shipowners were quickly eliminated from external trade, and more slowly but no less surely, from wholesale trade as well.[25] Some Indian merchants thrived as collaborators of the British but in this game in which Europeans held all the political cards, the Indians were quickly worsted. The failure of the Agency Houses in 1830s sealed the fate of most of the big Indian merchants and financiers as businessmen; the failure of the Union Bank and the winding up of the business enterprises of Dwarakanath Tagore marked the end of large-scale Indian business in eastern India for quite some time. It has been hypothesized that the elimination of Indian business from eastern India was not difficult, because big Marwari or Gujarati merchants had other areas of India to fall back upon. However, this hypothesis does not explain why Bengali merchants who had nowhere else to go also failed to put up much resistance. Political control by the British seems to be the decisive factor in this phase of struggle of Indian capitalists to keep themselves alive as capitalists.

In Ahmedabad and Gujarat a local business class, some of whom may have been immigrants from Rajasthan, had developed and came to dominate the Gujarat economy and much of the external trade of Gujarat by the end of the seventeenth and the beginning of eighteenth century.[26] While Asian shipping was virtually eliminated from the Bay of Bengal even before the formal conquest of Bengal by the British, Indian and Arab shipowners continued to control the shipping and much of the external trade in Gujarat even up to the end of the eighteenth century. In fact, Indian traders were in control of a considerable part of the external trade in western India, including Gujarat, throughout the nineteenth century, although both Indian shipping and shipbuilding declined under the impact of colonialism. The ability of Indian capitalists to survive in western India is to be ascribed to several factors: the continued need of the British for collaborators until the first quarter of the nineteenth century,[27] the resistance of the Marathas until 1818, the survival of some principalities like Baroda, Gwalior, and Indore, and perhaps the relative smallness of the export base of Bombay and Gujarat compared with that of Bengal.

Along with the capitalist strata, handicrafts also survived to a greater extent in Gujarat and western India than in Bengal: in Bengal, handloom production had become very greatly dependent on external trade and on organization by the East India Company. When the external trade in handlooms collapsed, and the internal market was invaded by British manufactures, handloom weavers had no alternative but to cut their prices in a desperate attempt to survive, and when that failed to work, to fall back upon agriculture. There were no indigenous capitalist strata who in their own interest might have tried to put up some resistance against this process of de-industrialization.[28] We shall see later that the survival of some of the artisan groups in Ahmedabad into the late nineteenth century had important implications for the growth of industry and labour relations in Ahmedabad.

By the time the *Gazetteers* of the Bombay Presidency came to be written, many of the features of the Gujarati capitalist class had been eroded or obliterated by the action of colonialism, so that we have to resort to a kind of 'commercial archaeology' in order to decipher the distinguishing marks of the surviving elements. The *Gazetteers* are themselves eloquent on the decline of the capitalist strata. We learn, for instance, that in the Navsari division of the Baroda state, the bankers (were) a declining class.[29] Many of the old banking houses of Baroda city also had declined, partly owing to the cessation of the practice of bankers lending to the state in anticipation of revenue.[30]

In Surat, bankers had declined from the position of discounting and cashing bills of exchange, and acting as deposit banks for small savers, to that of having to invest their funds in money lending or, much more rarely, in the few joint-stock companies that had sprung up.[31] In Broach, fifty years ago (1820), savings were to a large extent placed in the hands of private bankers, who allowed interest at the rate of three per cent on such deposits. Since that time the practice would seem to have fallen into disuse. Even with the Bank of Bombay the amount of deposits was small, while the credit of the native bankers had not recovered from the shock of the failures that took place between 1864 and 1867.[32] The *Broach Gazetteer* also records how the operations of the Bank of Bombay, which was subsidized by the interest-free deposit of the treasury balances, had favoured the Europeans and Eurasians at the expense of the Indian dealers in cotton, so that 'the greater part of the cotton trade is now [1875] carried on by Europeans and Eurasians, only about one-eighth remaining in the hands of the local capitalists.'[33] However, in Ahmedabad, and to a lesser extent, in Surat and Broach, and even in the rural Kaira district, functional specialization among bankers and financiers survived to a remarkable degree.

First of all, bankers were distinguished from money-changers. Then the bankers themselves were divided into several classes, the clearest demarcation being perhaps observed in Ahmedabad:

At present, it may be said, that the first class banking firms of the district employ their capital chiefly in loans, but also in buying and selling bills of exchange in insurance, and in gambling. They also act as agents in the purchase of cotton for firms in Bombay and elsewhere, and at times speculate in that article on their own account. A few in Viramgam and Dholera make advances on cotton to large landholders, and even keep agents, *gumastas,* to tour through the villages of their connection to collect outstanding debts and obtain new constituents. The majority, however, chiefly confine their loan transactions to a second class of bankers such as are to be found in all the towns and many of the larger villages, men who work beyond the limits of their own capital and who, to money lending and a small exchange business, add an export trade in produce for which their intimate business relations with the agriculturalists afford especial facility. They advance money on cotton crops and at the same time buy for forward delivery. Large sums are withdrawn by these persons, when the Government assessments are falling due, from the first-class banking houses in Ahmedabad with which they have credit. Lowest of all in the ladder of professional moneylender is the village shopkeeper, who is generally a vania but sometimes a Bohora, a Brahman, a Bhatia, a Luhana, or a Kanbi.'[34]

Along with the functional specialization of bankers went the generally thrifty habits of the rich people, and a low level of interest rates at least for the more 'creditworthy' class of borrowers. The rates of interest may, of course, have been pulled down by the closing of opportunities of investments: the compilers of the *Gazetteers* vacillate between attributing it to a low marginal return on investment and to the supposed improvement in 'law and order' brought about by British rule.

Owing to the contraction of former outlets for capital and the conservative disinclination of old houses to turn their money into new channels, a resident merchant or banker of unblemished repute can raise a loan in the city of Ahmedabad for a short period at four and sometimes as low as two per cent per annum. That is the rate he would also allow for deposits. The second class banker or merchant can obtain advance from one of the first class at from three to six per cent if he is a known and approved client ...[35]

As for rural clients,

the most substantial of the rural classes borrow, not from their village shopkeeper, but from the banker in the neighbouring town. From such clients no mortgage or even bond or security is ordinarily required. A sufficient guarantee is to the honourable position in his village which has been transmitted to him by generations of ancestors. Small advances are merely entered in his current account like an ordinary shop debt, and even if the sum be large, the only additional precaution is to cast up the account and take an admission of the correctness of the balance upon a receipt stamp. The average rate of interest is 7½ per cent but occasionally it runs as high as nine or as low as six percent. The great mass of Kanbi cultivators and others on a similar footing, being already encumbered with debt up to, though not, as a rule, beyond their assets, are not considered so perfectly trustworthy .... Generally it may be said that this class can only obtain loans on stamped bonds with or without securities, but that they are left free to realize the produce of their fields as they please. The rate of interest they pay varies from twelve to eighteen per cent exclusive of a premium .... Finally we come to the lowest order of landholders, including notoriously insolvent Kanbis and the great majority of Kolis, who fail to get more favourable treatment, not only because of their almost invariable poverty, but because of the stigma which still attaches to them as a caste. Such persons at the opening of the cultivating season (June–July), if the rains are favorable, obtain grain for seed and subsistence, repayable when the crop is reaped at an enhancement of twenty five to fifty, and in extreme cases even 100 per cent of the quantity advanced.[36]

Thus we have crossed the whole terrain from the gentle slopes of credit relations among the upper income groups to the steep gradient of extreme exploitation; the extreme is not really reached with the poor peasants, but with the landless, who were not terribly indebted since nobody, except perhaps their employers, would lend to them.

Naturally too much should not be made of the capitalist relations prevailing in the Gujarat towns and villages, certainly not relations that are supposed to conform to the absurdly simple axiom of competitive capitalism. Although credit relations were well-developed, capital markets were grossly imperfect; although labour had become a commodity, the 'supplier' could not sell as much as he liked in any market he liked. Various forms of debt bondage, and nearly servile relationships, bound the landless labourers or artisans to traders, moneylenders, and landlords.[37]

With these qualifications out of the way, we can concentrate on some of the more interesting features of the capitalist class. The functions of banker, trader, and landlord were still sufficiently distinct for them to have group specialization. The fusion into an unholy exploitative trinity burdening the cultivator was extremely incomplete, if the process had begun at all. The wealthiest bankers were still powerful enough in many regions to offer effective competition even to the state-backed Bank of Bombay. Artisans, in many cases, were still considered sufficiently creditworthy to be charged moderate rates of interest, and land certainly was not the predominant asset of interest to the wealthy.[38]

The functional differentiation between the different classes of village moneylenders, town *sowcars*, and rich bankers in Ahmedabad or Broach was preserved during the period of Maratha rule by the severe restrictions that were placed on the acquisition of land by outsiders and by anybody at all without the consent of the village panchayat and the *patil.* With the imposition of British rule, the authority of the village panchayat was gradually undermined, individual ownership of land became the norm even when, formally, revenue assessments might be made on a collective basis, and moneylenders or bankers found it much easier than before to acquire land. The abolition of laws against usury and the gradual disintegration of handicrafts in towns and villages hastened this process of greater involvement of bankers and moneylenders with landownership at various levels and the blurring of the distinction between the village *vania* and the town sowcar.[39]

But this distinction did survive to a greater extent in Gujarat than in most other parts of India. This may be attributed to the greater degree of development of capitalist strata in that region. In the next section, we take a look at the land relations in different parts of India in order to see whether a significant role can be attributed to them in explaining the development of capitalist classes in different regions, and ultimately, in explaining the differences in regional patterns of economic growth.

Production Relations in Agriculture in Different Regions of India and their Bearing on the Development of Capitalist Strata

The bearing of production relations in agriculture on capitalist (or any other kind of) growth in India is a vast and complicated subject. We need to know the relations of the state to the revenue-payers; the relations of the revenue payers to other superior right-holders (if any) and to cultivators exercising some ownership rights; the distribution of ownership of land where such ownership is unambiguously determined; the distribution of operational holdings of land; the relations of owners to tenants with various degrees of security of tenure; the conditions of agricultural labourers and their relations to their employers or *malik*s. We need to know the relations of landlords, cultivating owners, tenants with superior rights, and tenants-at-will, and agricultural or other kinds of labourers, bonded or free, to moneylenders, traders, and bankers. We need to determine the proportions of the outputs of land and village industries going to the different classes of people. We need to determine the access to information, markets, and channels of investment open to classes with some investable surplus at their command and the alternative rates of return to be obtained from ownership of land, its operation, moneylending, trading, and real capital formation, or any combination of these activities. We have to know the relation between agricultural development and industrial growth, both regionally and over India as a whole.[40] And we have to be constantly aware of the way the colonial system and its changes affect the different components of this network of relations.

Here what we shall do, in conformity with the perspective in the rest of this essay, is to concentrate on the contrast between histories of land tenure and revenue in eastern and western India. Hunter could write as late as in 1881: 'As the land furnishes the main source of Indian revenue, so the assessment of the land tax is the main work of Indian administration.'[41] The obsession of the British with land revenue settlements started with their conquest of Bengal. It was from the proceeds of the plunder of Bengal that they derived the wherewithal for the conquest of the rest of India, besides sending anywhere between £1.5 million and over £4.70 million annually abroad as the political booty in the last quarter of the eighteenth century.[42] Lambert had already exposed the pretence that this was simply a redirection of the tribute that had been sent to Delhi.[43] The amount of the tribute was more than doubled by the British and no part of it came back to stimulate internal trade or economic activity. In achieving their ends, of course, the British turned the whole system of land relations several times over: the Permanent Settlement of Cornwallis was merely setting the seal of approval on a system which promised in perpetuity a much higher level of revenue than had ever been extracted by the Mughal emperors or the nawabs of Bengal. By the *haptam* and *pancham* laws of 1799 and 1812, the East India Company gave almost unlimited powers to the zamindars. But since there was no restriction on the subleasing of the rights of zamindars, intermediary rights between the cultivating peasantry and the zamindars grew apace. By the Bengal tenancy laws of 1859 and 1885, the hands of the so-called occupancy ryots (who might or might not be actual cultivators or even supervisors of cultivation) were strengthened. But the lot of the poor peasantry and the agricultural labourers was not improved by such legislation.

The legal forms of land tenure arrangements in Gujarat were very different.[44] The East India Company classified Gujarat villages into three classes, *talukdari* or landlord villages 'owned' by *girasia*s or landlords, sharehold villages where land was held jointly by *bhagdar*s, *narwadar*s, or *patidar*s, and peasant or 'simple' (*senja*) villages, where a co-sharing community did not exist. In all the cases, the line of least resistance was adopted and older types of rights were respected as far as practicable. The all-consuming drive that the Company in Bengal displayed towards raising land revenues at all costs, partly because of the need for finding revenue to conquer other parts of India, no longer existed. This does not mean that the government let go any opportunity of increasing revenue on any pretext. As the land settlement chapters of R.C. Dutt's *Economic History* make abundantly clear, the drive was always towards more revenue: the government recoiled only when this drive miscarried, and total collection fell or a disastrous famine occurred. But this recoiling was also a temporary affair.

Whatever the intentions of the government may have been in preserving old forms of village management, whether in Gujarat or in Madras, the insistence of the government on realizing revenue even at the cost of depriving owners of their land, the increased power of the moneylenders and traders over the peasantry, and the revocation of ancient rights of pasture on communal or semi-communal land or on waste land, resulted in the breakdown of communal authority in the villages.[45]

Several features continued, however, to distinguish the ryotwari areas from zamindari areas. Since the state had to realize revenues from individual owners, and assessments had to be based on some principle (however arbitrarily it was applied in practice), cultivators generally possessed some record of rights so that intermediaries could not aggrandize themselves arbitrarily. In some native states such as Baroda, the cultivator was protected to a considerable extent against dispossession of land or eviction for failure to repay a moneylender's debt.[46] Probably the older structure of authority in Gujarat or the ryotwari areas of Madras survived to a greater extent than in Bengal, although such authority was now derived from connection with the central or provincial government administration rather than with the hereditary or semi-hereditary headship of a village or a clan.[47]

The rise of a rich peasant class in some pockets at least of ryotwari areas has probably something to do with the lack of a stratum of pure rentiers lording it over them. Large parts of the ryotwari area became subject also to legislation against transfer of land to non-agriculturists and tended to limit the power of pure moneylenders over both landlords and cultivators.[48] This also probably strengthened the position of rich peasants and landlords vis-à-vis moneylenders. Some of the men from a rich peasant background entered Indian industry at a later stage. However, no direct connection can be established between the survival and growth of the rich peasant class in a region and growth of large-scale or even small-scale industry in that region. How much of a mark such a class could make in modern industry depended on several factors: the degree of dominance of the region by European businessmen, the position of the Indian economy in the international capitalist-colonial framework, the strength of competing indigenous capitalist groups in a particular region, and the size of the internal market as determined by the productivity of the land, the degree of colonial exploitation and the degree of poverty or degradation of the lower income groups. While it will not be possible here to delineate the interconnections between all these factors, we shall provide some examples to show the kinds of influence we have in mind.

In both Gujarat and Madras, some people with a peasant background entered the cotton mill industry. But in Gujarat this was already happening in the third quarter of the nineteenth century, when Rao Bahadur Becherdas Ambaidas, who was a Patel, set up the second cotton mill. By 1920, four out of 51 cotton mills in Ahmedabad were owned by Patels.[49] In the Kistna and Guntur districts in the north and in Coimbatore in the south of Madras, by the First World War, rich farmers who also often controlled local trade were wanting to invest in industry.[50] But their entry was restricted to rice mills (which were partly financed by the Bank of Madras), cotton gins and presses, and such other small-scale industries. It was only in the 1930s that local businessmen, among whom figured persons with backgrounds in farming, made an entry into the cotton mill industry which was the major large-scale industry of the region.

It is not unreasonable to suggest that this variance is due to the basic difference between the timing and the intensity of colonial penetration into the two regions of India and the degree of survival of earlier capitalist strata in the two regions. Some connection with trade and markets and some command over capital were essential for entry into modern industry: the later the date of entry, other things remaining equal, the larger would be the degree of command over capital needed. Since the British businessmen dominated the Madras economy to a much greater extent than the Gujarat economy, the barriers against the entry of native businessmen into large-scale industry would be greater. Even within the Madras Presidency, Indian businessmen from the so-called dry areas would enjoy a slight advantage over businessmen from irrigated districts, for the latter were penetrated to a greater extent by British businessmen with their concentration on exportable crops.[51] But this advantage would be partly counterbalanced by the lower base of accumulation in the dry districts.

After we have analysed all the factors and weighed them properly it may turn out that the history of European domination of the permanently settled areas of Bengal is the crucial variable explaining the failure of a peasant proprietor class to emerge strongly and to enter large-scale business. Any surplus of the peasantry would be skimmed off by traders, moneylenders, and zamindars. The rich peasantry could not make its entry into trade on a large scale in the nineteenth century because the European businessmen were always there either to beat them off or subordinate them. It had to be an external trading class, such as the Marwaris, who could gradually creep up on the Europeans, beat them at their game of vertical control of channels of trade, and challenge them in modern industry.

But for this challenge to materialize, the position of the Indian economy had to shift in the mesh of capitalist-colonial relations. I have pointed out elsewhere[52] that over the period 1900–39, there were always some groups of capitalists, either British or Indian, who had capital to invest whenever opportunities for investment were opened up. A scrutiny of the evidence presented by R.S. Rungta[53] leads to a similar conclusion for much of the nineteenth century, particularly in the case of eastern India before 1830 and western India after 1860 or so. Taking only one field of investment, the cotton mill industry, the opportunities at different stages and in different regions, were presented in the form of a residual internal market for cotton cloth or yarn (by 1870, such a market had disappeared in eastern India to a much greater extent than in western India or in the interior parts of southern India), an external market opened up by relative movements of international costs, or access to a new country which imperialist countries could not entirely monopolize (as in the case of China) or, finally, in the granting of tariff protection.

Apart from the overall constraints imposed by the colonial regime, there were the other ubiquitous features of the Indian economy in the shape of a universal degradation of small peasants, agricultural labourers, and artisans. In southern India, there was widespread agrestic slavery or serfdom at the time of British conquest.[54] In eastern India, there was agrestic serfdom or slavery, although on a small scale, in the beginning of the nineteenth century when Buchanan Hamilton conducted his surveys. In Gujarat, too, there were agrestic serfs called *hali*s in the southern districts.[55]

The formal abolition of slavery by the British cannot be credited with much improvement in the position of the labourers. A law of 1859 enacted in the interest of European tea planters, more or less made employees indentured serfs of the masters. With the increase in the power of the moneylender (who might be the employer), debt bondage often replaced formal serfdom. In the traditional structure of exploitation, there was often discrimination against particular communities, particularly from tribal backgrounds: for instance, the so-called *kali paraj* communities, such as the Bhils in Gujarat, were typically charged higher rates of interest than the *ujli paraj* communities. This discrimination survived at least until 1929–30.[56] In eastern India, the process of de-industrialization and population growth threw literally millions of artisans on to the mercy of the landlords, and various forms of agrestic serfdom survived unabated.[57]

In these forms of degradation, it is difficult to know how important the relative roles played by tradition, illiteracy, structure of land control, and the threat of unemployment were. But I suspect that the last threat both aggravated the dependence of formally free labourers on their employers and emphasized the servile nature of bonded labour. In the case of south Gujarat, there is some evidence that increased opportunities of employment in the cities of Surat and Navsari after the end of the nineteenth century and seasonal migration to the environs of Bombay were partially responsible for the decline of the hali system.[58]

In Gujarat, in spite of the processes of de-industrialization, the artisan strata had survived to a greater extent up to the last quarter of the nineteenth century. These provided a pool of skilled labour to the cotton mills of Ahmedabad. Some of the handicraft processes, such as bleaching or dyeing of cloth, were directly integrated with the cotton mill industry. The linguistic homogeneity of the labour force among themselves and with the owners and managers also contributed to the establishment of industrial labour relations along capitalistic lines. Further, Spodek has attributed a special role to the traditional guild system in making possible a situation in which real wages of mill workers in Ahmedabad increased at a faster rate than in Calcutta from 1900 to 1939, and than in Bombay after the First World War, without the workers actually resorting to a strike. The traditional financing system of Ahmedabad, including the practice of the public entrusting bankers with their funds at low rates of interest, also served the Ahmedabad industry well.

By contrast, capital-labour relations in the more intensely colonized parts of India were characterized by the degradation of the labour force to semi-servile status, with little prospect of increases in wages. There may have been a period in the history of Bengal jute mills (in the last half of the nineteenth century) when European owners had to woo labourers.[59] But in the twentieth century, the relations between European managers and supervisors and Indian workers were strongly tinged with racialism: the failure to appoint Indians in supervisory posts was often rationalized by the claim that Indian workers would not respect a black or brown supervisor.[60] The working force was fragmented by the ability of the British Managing Agency houses to draw labour from the poorest parts of India, far from tea plantations, coal mines, or jute mills. This labour force was again differentiated from the local population by linguistic, and sometimes religious, barriers. Altogether colonialism perfected the arrangements for keeping a subjugated people as divided as possible.

We have found it difficult enough to summarize the problems of agricultural labour, insofar as they had an impact on production relations, even as 'stylized' facts. It is practically impossible to attempt such a summary in the case of the middle peasantry, because no comprehensive work on the stratification of the landowning peasantry is available. Instead I shall here mention a trans- or supraregional factor which affected both the productivity of the land and the standards of living of the peasantry: this is the depletion of the livestock wealth of the peasantry in relation to the total amounts of land cultivated and in relation to the human population. This depletion in turn constricted the internal market.

Under the British land tenure system, all land that a person claimed as his own, and not just the cultivated portion of it, became subject to taxation by the state. The cultivators were forced to raise crops that would enable them to pay rent in money and they could no longer afford to treat pasture as an untaxed capital asset. Furthermore, the ordinary cultivators were left with very little surplus to maintain their livestock properly. Livestock formed both their major consumer durables and their main capital goods (in the form of draught buffaloes and oxen). As far back as 1875 the Deccan Riots Commission had noted: 'A consequence of the payment of assessment by registered holdings instead of by actual cultivation is the discouragement of fallows. The ryot having nothing to pay for his wastes could well afford to let his land rest and cultivated portions in rotation. During the early period of our administration, the lands of this region [the Bombay Deccan] were largely devoted to grazing purposes, and there was no direct Government demand upon the wastes so used. The encouragement given to cultivation by the survey was accompanied by a discouragement to grazing, through the right of pasture being made subject to purchase from Government. The supply of manure from flocks and herds, the demand for which should have increased with this increase in cultivation, diminished, and doubtless with it must have diminished the fertility of the soil.'[61] The evidence on this is not only inferential. There is direct evidence of decline in the quality of the cattle in most parts of India and of a drastic decline in the proportion of cattle to human beings.[62]

There were certain additional features which were exaggerated, particularly in the Permanently Settled areas of eastern India, that tended to lower the productivity of the peasant-cultivated land. Initially there were many minor irrigation works in eastern India, which it was the responsibility of the zamindars to maintain. As the superior government lost all interest in the management of the land and as the zamindars were stripped of most of their earlier functions (such as those of maintaining a police force and administering justice in small local matters), the latter began to neglect their duties, particularly since they could coerce the peasantry directly to pay their rent. After an attempt to maintain these irrigation works through contractors, they were allowed to be neglected in many places (the systems of share rents were maintained in some places partly as a device to hold the landlords to their parts of the bargain).[63] This neglect of irrigation works, starting from the beginning of the Permanent Settlement, was going on into the twentieth century. The irrigated area in Bihar and Orissa was declining even in the twentieth century; the same thing probably happened also in the western parts of Bengal proper.[64] We shall take up the other causes of decline in agricultural productivity later on.

The Government of India and European businessmen, and along with them, Indian zamindars, treated the peasant-cultivated land of eastern India as a kind at exhaustible resource. Peasant agriculture with traditional techniques had already reached a high level in most parts of India; there were no obvious ways of raising productivity without putting in a good deal of industrial and research inputs, in the form of state-sponsored agricultural research, and chemical fertilizers. The only type of agricultural investment the government was willing to execute was large-scale irrigation works; until almost the end of the nineteenth century such works had to be 'productive', that is, commercially profitable. Even then the government generally passed the unintended and harmful side-effects of irrigation on to the defenceless peasantry.[65] In any case, neither large-scale nor small-scale irrigation works were on the cards as far as eastern India was concerned. Instead, the change in the traditional cropping pattern, decay of minor irrigation and flood control works, swamps created partly by unplanned railway construction, and soil erosion brought down the productivity of the land.

The government found that since its revenue did not depend directly or indirectly on the prosperity of the peasantry in the Permanently Settled areas, it was not interested in investing in these areas in any form; not only irrigation works but also *takkavi* loans for agricultural improvement were conspicuous by their scarcity or total absence.[66] The European planters and Indian landlords found that, given the structure of exploitation, it was more profitable to control the land and let the peasant carry out cultivation under some kind of *metayage* (*bargadari*) system, than to invest in land directly as a capitalist farmer.[67]

For all practical purposes, the landlords or businessmen of eastern India became completely divorced from any interest in the improvement of agricultural productivity or of the conditions of peasantry in their region of operation. This would again seem to be in contrast with the structure in western India, where at least as far as the rural cooperative movement is concerned, businessmen and industrialists of the stature of Vithaldas Thackersey and Lalubhai Samaldas (Mehta) took an active part in founding and running the provincial co-operative bank.[68] However, while this kind of enterprise may have helped in the growth of a rural oligarchy of substantial farmers, this in itself did not lead to a high rate of growth in agricultural output in western India, particularly in Maharashtra; for while many administrators such as Keatinge thought that the lack of 'capital' was the real bottleneck on agricultural growth in western India, agronomists of the calibre of Voelcker pointed out that without the provision of controlled supply of water private investment in agriculture could not be profitable.[69]

The differences in the social structures, patterns of domination, and composition of economic activities as between eastern and western India were significant enough to produce the differences in the degrees of external exploitation that are displayed in Tables 2.1 and 2.2. It might be supposed that the fact that the Indian zamindars took a larger share of the land revenue in eastern India than the British government did in western India would tilt the balance of burden of exploitation towards western India. But this was massively counterbalanced by the ability of British businessmen in eastern India to force larger export surpluses out of the peasantry,[70] and by the inability of the Indian businessmen to penetrate the fields of external trade or industry until after the First

World War. Even after that date, the basically export-oriented nature of the output of eastern India, combined with a massive presence of foreign businessmen, continued to drain resources out of the country. One effect of this can be seen in the export surplus figures for the 1930s: unlike in most other countries of the world, where the Depression coincided with large balance of payments deficits, India and particularly eastern India and Madras, produced export surpluses which financed a massive repatriation of British-owned capital. Much of this debt had been incurred during and after the First World War in the interests of defence of the British imperial system.

However significant the differences in the processes of formation of capitalist classes in eastern and western India, they are not enough to make any tall claims for industrial growth in western India, for the colonial regime shaped the growth patterns of all regions in certain fundamental ways. Out of all the possible tableaux that are conjured up by the constellation of class forces in British Gujarat, for instance, the colonial constraints ultimately allowed only one to surface: many of the important bankers and traders emerged to form the core of a tightly knit industrial bourgeois class in Ahmedabad (and Gujarat in general), either directly as pioneers or in collaboration. But their growth was limited by the low level of development of productive forces in agriculture, by the low level of innovative ability built into the industrial organization, and by the overall lack of dynamism of the home market.

Agricultural Growth in Madras, Punjab, and the Rest of India and Lack of Articulation of Agricultural and Industrial Growth

We have already indicated that the impact of capitalist colonialism was adverse on most regions of India: under its impact all regions of India were underdeveloped, but some more than others. After the destruction of handicrafts in India, the stance of many spokesmen of the British government was that they were promoting agricultural development so as to fit India better into the pattern of international specialization which sprang up in the wake of the Industrial Revolution in Britain. But in fact, practically the only instrument wielded by the government for promotion of agricultural growth was the promotion of large-scale irrigation works which were directly revenue-yielding. Its record in the field of agricultural research was anything but brilliant.[71] The total accumulated amount spent on all 'productive' irrigation works in

British India up to 1938–9 was Rs 114 crores. This was less than the accumulated export surpluses of India for even five years in the first decade of the twentieth century. The annual expenditure on irrigation was a minute fraction of what was spent on defence or on railways. Naturally, if one or two provinces of India, such as Punjab or the Madras Presidency, received substantial amounts for irrigation, the rest of India went without any expenditure. Whatever the limitations of irrigation as carried out on a large scale by the British, an assured supply of water was a *sine qua non* for agricultural growth. So we look at the same factors of the relations between agricultural growth, industrial change, and irrigation in the best-irrigated regions and in the rest of India.

Our comparisons and contrasts will, however, remain impressionistic only since our information remains very sketchy. For the comparison in respect of agricultural growth, we rely largely on Blyn's work, supplemented by Islam's and Mukherji's on Bengal. Blyn provides figures for Bombay–Sind, which is a composite of the hinterlands of the ports of Bombay and Karachi, so for our purpose these figures are not directly useful. Hence, even in the case of comparisons of agricultural development, we are limited to Bengal, Madras, and Punjab.

There are similarities as well as important differences between the two regions of Punjab and Madras in respect of the characteristics we are interested in. Punjab came under British rule relatively late in the day, whereas parts of Madras had been occupied by the British even before they had conquered Bengal. Foreign trade, organized banking, and much of the internal wholesale trade in both Punjab and Madras were effectively monopolized by the British before the First World War. Both Punjab and Madras had other traditional trading groups and handicraft industries, but the handicrafts were probably better developed in at least some parts of Madras than in Punjab. The Madras trading groups, particularly the Chettiars, had overseas connections and were prominent in the trade of Burma, Indonesia, and Indo-China.[72] There were more cotton mills in Madras than in Punjab by 1939, but both were industrially backward by the standards of Calcutta or Bombay.

The two provinces resembled each other in one important respect: they, along with the United Provinces, witnessed the most intense development of large-scale irrigation in British India. Madras already had an extensive network of irrigation based on the Cauvery (Kaveri), going back at least a thousand years, and Punjab had some inundation canals. But the British improved and extended the Cauvery network and created new irrigation systems based on the Godavari and the

Krishna rivers further north. In Punjab they created one of the most extensive perennial irrigation systems in the world. In neither case can the whole of the apparent addition to the irrigated area by the large-scale government canals be regarded as a net addition to the effectively irrigated acreage. For, apart from problems of water-logging and salinity brought in by neglect of drainage requirements and the almost universal practice of flow irrigation, the new canals often replaced older minor irrigation works, such as tanks and wells in south India and inundation canals in Punjab. Hence, one must be cautious in interpreting the public outlay on irrigation works as an index of irrigation capacity created by the government, and in interpreting the increase in the apparent area commanded as a net addition to the effectively irrigated area. With these caveats we present the figures in Table 2.4 to illustrate the relative magnitudes of irrigation work carried out in Punjab, Madras, and the United Provinces.

Table 2.4 Area Irrigated in Madras, Punjab, and the United Provinces by Government Works, Annual Averages

(figures in acres)

	Madras	Punjab	United Provinces	India (excluding Burma)
1915–18	7,339,008	8,646,495	3,121,834	24,415,215
1918–21	7,276,257	9,273,009	3,501,848	25,305,835
1921–4	7,151,988	10,465,404	2,433,595	25,842,501
1924–7	7,178,457	10,349,121	2,678,178	25,962,751
1927–30	7,277,967	11,200,550	3,639,867	27,959,738
1930–3	7,484,466	10,995,258	3,805,205	28,052,645
1933–6	7,448,100	11,007,800	3,977,400	28,868,800
1936–9	7,396,100	12,195,800	4,769,200	31,648,500

Sources: Government of India (GOI), Public Works Department, *Triennial Review of Irrigation in India,* 1918–21 (Calcutta, 1922); GOI, Department of Industries and Labour, *Triennial Reviews of Irrigation in India,* 1921–4, 1924–7, and 1930–3 (Calcutta, 1925, 1928; and Delhi, 1935, respectively); and GOI, Department of Labour, *Triennial Review of Irrigation in India,* 1936–9 (Delhi, 1942).

Further, Madras and Punjab both threw up substantial farmers. My hunch is, however, that whereas in Punjab the farmers were throughout dominated by trading castes in all the regions, in Madras the farmers in some areas could control much of the trade themselves. But for a successful entry into industry they had to become camp followers of the big traders who emerged as industrialists in the 1930s.

The figures in Table 2.4 show first that out of the total area irrigated in India by government works, more than three-quarters were accounted for by the three provinces of Punjab, Madras, and the United Provinces, and more than three-fifths were accounted for by the two provinces of Punjab and Madras. They also show that while the area irrigated by government works in Madras had become stagnant from the First World War onwards, it continued to increase in Punjab in the inter-war period. The total capital expenditures made by the government on 'productive' irrigation works in the three provinces by the end of 1938–9 are as follows

(*figures in Rs*)

Madras	Punjab	United Provinces	India (excluding Burma)
155,571,994	366,662,679	259,344,66	1,140,049,650

It is obvious that there is no one-to-one relationship between the total areas irrigated and the total capital expenditures made (this would remain true even if we deducted the figures for areas irrigated by the so-called 'unproductive works' from the figures in Table 2.4). The irrigated acreage in Madras was created considerably more 'cheaply' than either in the United Provinces or in Punjab, probably because Madras had started with a more extensive irrigation network, and partly, of course, because the bulk of the Madras works was carried out in the nineteenth century when costs were lower. The irrigation works of the United Provinces seem to have been more 'expensive' than the average for India as a whole. All these statements are, of course, only approximate, and they have to be qualified by detailed information on the true productivity of the different irrigation systems.

Coming back to our specific problem—that of comparing patterns and rates of growth of Madras and Punjab—it is interesting to see how far the extension of irrigation works was reflected in the growth in acreage and yields per acre of these provinces, as measured by Blyn (Table 2.5).[73] Comparing the figures for Greater Punjab and Madras, we find that while the extension of acreage was far higher in Greater Punjab than in Madras, the growth in productivity per acre is far higher in Madras than in Greater Punjab. But in Madras. most of the gain in acreage and in productivity had been made over the first thirty-year period with both the productivity per acre and acreage of foodgrains registering a decline between the quin-quennium 1921–6 and the quin-quennium 1941–6. This was also the period when irrigated acreage in Madras was expanding, especially in the areas which had been prone to drought earlier on.[74] Furthermore, we notice that Greater Punjab is very much of an exception among the regions as far as the rates of growth of productivity and acreage of foodgrains between 1921–6 and 1941–6 are concerned: for British India as a whole, and for Greater Bengal, Madras, and the United Provinces, the productivity per acre of foodgrains declined; there was a small rise in the acreage under foodgrains in Madras, but declines in Greater Bengal, the United Provinces and British India as a whole. But Greater Bengal differed again from all the other regions included in Table 2.5 (but probably not from the Central Provinces, which is not included in our Table) in that the decline in acreage under foodgrains and in the productivity of foodgrains per acre had been going on also over the first thirty-year period, whereas for the others some gains at least had been registered for the earlier period, which were often more than offset by the decline over the later twenty-year period.

We shall pause here to look a little more closely at the record of Greater Bengal in respect of agricultural growth.[75] It was suspected

Table 2.5 Percentage Change in Acreage and Yield per Acre in Different Regions of India

	Acreage			Yield per acre		
	All crops (1)	Food-grains (2)	Non-food grains	All crops (1)	Food-grains (2)	Non-food grains
A. Total change between 1891–5 and 1941–6						
1. British India	+16.27	+25.55	+19.84	+6.45	–7.3	+52.96
2. Greater Bengal	–3.37	+0.79	–29.54	–12.85	–22.17	+54.55
3. Madras	+16.45	+3.89	+82.95	+46.02	+30.35	+79.84
4. Greater Punjab*	+51.69	+46.42	+94.38	+35.60	+19.24	+74.20
5. United Provinces	+28.18	+27.93	+29.12	+2.62	–8.63	+29.32
B. Total change between 1921–6 and 1941–6						
1. British India	+5.54	+7.08	–.87	–1.45	–9.69	+25.24
2. Greater Bengal	+4.87	+6.47	–9.71	–7.86	–12.96	+24.45
3. Madras	+3.51	–1.66	+23.61	+.92	–4.99	+9.45
4. Greater Punjab*	+7.25	+7.09	+8.48	+13.58	+4.91	+39.64
5. United Provinces	+5.00	+4.39	+7.41	–2.10	–14.47	+28.88

Source: Computed from Blyn (1966: Appendix Table 4C).

Note: *Greater Punjab includes Punjab and North-West Frontier Province.

earlier, from qualitative evidence on the eastward shift of the rivers of the Gangetic delta, the extensive soil erosion through deforestation in the Chotanagpur plateau of Bihar and Orissa, and other indications that most of the decline in productivity of crops—particularly field-crops—in Greater Bengal occurred in Bihar, Orissa, and the western part of present West Bengal.[76]

Recent studies by Saugata Mukherji covering the period 1900–01 to 1920–1, and by M.M. Islam covering the period 1920–46, confirm most of the earlier hunches and provide firm quantitative bases for the qualitative hypotheses.[77] Mukherji analysed the trade flows, outputs, and yields per acre in the four trade blocks of Bengal proper—the Dacca, northern Bengal, western Bengal, and eastern Bengal blocks. He found that yields per acre declined in all the blocks over the twenty-year period, except for the eastern Bengal block, consisting of 24-Parganas, eastern Nadia, Jessore, Khulna, and Barisal and thus including the major part of the 'active' delta of the Ganges. Islam found that the annual rate of growth of all crops taken together for Bengal proper between 1920 and 1946 was 0.3 per cent per year; whereas the rate of growth for Greater Bengal as estimated by Blyn was –0.2 per cent.[78]

If we assume that the total output of Bengal proper formed 60 per cent of the output of Greater Bengal, then we get the rate of change of output of all crops in Bihar and Orissa from the following equation:

$$100 - .2 = 60 \times 1.003 + 40\,(1+r),$$
$$\text{or}\quad 99.8 = 60.18 + 40\,(1+r),$$

where r, the annual rate of change of output of all crops in Bihar and Orissa, turns out to be –.95 per cent per year. How this is divided between the rate of change of acreage and the rate of change of productivity per acre, of course, cannot be found until one knows one of the two rates. If acreage remained stagnant or declined slightly, then productivity per acre would have declined a little less than 1 per cent per year: if acreage increased by a significant percentage, then productivity per acre would have declined even more drastically.[79]

Whatever may be the final outcome of rigorous calculations of output growth in the agriculture of eastern India, there is little doubt that peasants in eastern India suffered a drastic decline in their real incomes during the last fifty years of British rule. This conclusion follows from the statistics of agricultural change quoted above and from the fact that the population of Bengal, Bihar, and Orissa increased from about 77 million in 1901 to about 97.5 million in 1941, while the proportion of population depending on agriculture did not decline. The conclusion is reinforced when we remember that in Bengal proper a very significant percentage of the rise in the yield per acre of non-foodgrains was accounted for by the phenomenal rise in productivity per acre of tea, which was entirely a plantation crop.

Table 2.6 reveals that there was a substantial fall in the acreage under non-foodgrains in Greater Bengal in both the sub-periods 1891–6 to 1921–6 to 1921–6 to 1941–6 (compare columns 7 and 9), and that tea accounted for a significant fraction of the measured growth in yield per acre of crops other than foodgrains (although tea acreage formed only about 1.2 per cent of acreage under crops other than foodgrains to begin with, it rose to form more than 3.5 per cent of the acreage under non-foodgrains, and its productivity rose much faster than that of other crops). Furthermore, Table 2.6 also shows that the productivity per acre of foodgrains in Greater Bengal fell in both the sub-periods. The most important cash crop raised by peasants—jute—experienced a mild growth in the area sown, but a decline in productivity in the last sub-period.

Taking all these indicators together, it is safe to conclude that the last fifty years of British rule were attended by a steady deterioration in the peasant agriculture of eastern India, whose effects on industrial growth were masked by the growing protectionism of the inter-war years and by the general crisis in the primary sector during the late 1920s and practically the whole of the 1930s. It was only after independence that the full impact of the agricultural crisis was felt on industrial growth in eastern India.

Going back to Punjab and Madras, we find in the agricultural development of these provinces a contrast not only with Greater Bengal but also with most parts of the rest of India. In both Madras and Punjab, apart from execution of large-scale irrigation works, the government also encouraged the use of modern or improved implements in agriculture. In Madras, Alfred Chatterton, with the cooperation of the Public Works Department (around 1903–04) tried to popularize the use of oil-engines and pumps for the purposes of lift-irrigation; this work was facilitated by government loans under the Land Improvements Act for the purchase of oil-engines and pumps. It was soon accompanied by the boring of wells with the help of tools and mechanisms maintained by the Government of Madras. The Industries Department of the Government of Madras helped also in the installation of rice mills. The Department

Table 2.6 Acreage and Yield of Crops in Greater Bengal

	1891–2 to 1895–6		1921–2 to 1925–6		1941 to 1945–6		Percentage change between 1891–6 to 1941–6		Percentage change between 1921–6 to 1941–6	
	Acreage (thousand acres) (1)	Yield per acre (2)	Acreage (thousand acres) (3)	Yield per acre (4)	Acreage (thousand acres) (5)	Yield per acre (6)	Acreage (thousand acres) (7)	Yield per acre (8)	Acreage (thousand acres) (9)	Yield per acre (10)
Greater Bengal										
All crops	267,400	371.2	246,400	351.1	258,400	323.5	–3.37	–12.85	+4.87	–7.86
Foodgrains	227,000	353.7	214,900	316.3	228,800	275.3	+0.79	–22.17	+6.47	–12.96
Non-foodgrains	40,380	470.0	31,500	583.7	28,450	726.4	–29.54	+54.5	–9.71	+24.45
Tea	497	1,571.0	918	2,127	1,024	3,638.0	+106.04	+131.57	+11.54	+71.04
Sugarcane	5,173	9,666.0	2,547	11,592.0	3,632	13,689	–29.79	+41.62	+42.60	+18.09
British India										
Jute	10.211	4,885.0	11,853	5,784.0	12,435	5,664.0	+21.78	+15.95	+4.91	–2.08

Source: Computed from Blyn, (1966: Appendix Tables 3A and 4C).

Notes: (a) The rupee values are at constant prices.

(b) Blyn gives figures only for jute acreage and output for whole of British India, and not separately for Greater Bengal. However, Greater Bengal accounted for 80 to 90 per cent of the area under jute in British India.

of Agriculture also tried to push iron ploughs and iron cane mills as part of the regular propaganda work. By the late 1920s, 1,600 to 1,800 iron ploughs were being sold in the Madras Presidency, which of course, is not a large figure for a province with a population of more than 42 million in 1921.[80]

In Punjab, the governmental efforts towards the introduction of improved machinery began in some earnest in 1907, when Mr Milligan, the first Deputy Director of Agriculture, in collaboration with a firm of agricultural implement manufactures in Scotland, evolved the Raja (furrow-turning) plough, which became very popular and served as a model for later improvements. The variety of more modern implements introduced into Punjab was apparently greater than in Madras and in other provinces of India: apart from Raja and Meston ploughs, reapers, fodder-cutters, harrows (presumably British types), and cultivators were also manufactured, often by local blacksmiths.

In 1924–5, according to the statistics of the Agriculture Department, 832 furrow-turning ploughs (Raja ploughs and others), 1,234 imported Meston ploughs, 3,263 locally manufactured Meston ploughs, four reapers, 65 hoes, harrows and cultivators, 941 fodder-cutters and 3,549 miscellaneous implements (including 3,311 cane-crushers) were sold in Punjab. In fact, it was by then 'becoming increasingly difficult to keep in touch with the sales of modern implements that [were] finding their way into the Province through various agencies and local manufacturers, Therefore, it [was] probable that far more [had] been purchased of late by farmers than the departmental records [showed]'.[81]

One can legitimately dispute that the use of modern, capital-intensive implements in Punjab necessarily indicated a higher potential for agricultural growth than in other parts of India. But it certainly indicated the existence of farmers with relatively large amounts of capital and land at their command, and the emergence of capitalist farmers, though *capitalist relations* may not have become general yet in the Punjab countryside. In fact, some policies of the government strongly favoured the emergence of relatively rich farmers. From the 1880s onwards, the government planned canal colonies in the areas which were rendered cultivable through the introduction of large-scale, perennial irrigation. In these colonies, plots of land with minimum sizes varying from 22½ to 27½ acres were distributed to colonists (usually 'people of substance' who wanted to move to better lands). By the beginning of the 1930s, over a sixth (about 5½ million acres) of the total cultivated area of Punjab was in the canal colonies.[82]

One other measure of the British government—the enactment of the Punjab Land Alienation Act—was also meant to encourage the growth of prosperous peasant farming and diminish the power of moneylenders; but since the root of the problem lay in the inequality of distribution of income and a fiscal system which demanded the regular payment of a rent calculated in money, the place of professional moneylenders was soon taken by 'agriculturist' moneylenders. This happened in both the more prosperous western Punjab districts and in a district such as Gurgaon, which had little irrigation but the advantage of administration by F.L. Brayne, the civil servant turned missionary.[83] However, along with growth in irrigated acreage and area under cash crops in Punjab, tenancy also grew both in absolute and relative terms. Furthermore, in many cases there was a shift from cash rents to share rents.[84]

But in spite of counteracting forces, breeding usury, and impoverishment of the smaller peasantry, the growth in agricultural output in Punjab and its concentration in the hands of relatively prosperous farmers did stimulate the growth of a small-scale industry producing agricultural implements, in the 1920s and 1930s.[85]

Some of this was reflected in the comparatively large fraction (66 earners and dependants in every 1000 of population) of the labour force engaged in industry (including small-scale and cottage industries) in Punjab; this fraction was apparently greater than in Bengal (25 in 1000), and Bombay (46 in 1000). Of course, the initial complement of people occupied in cottage industries probably accounted for the majority of the industrial population.[86] But in 1930 the number of workers employed in the factories of Punjab was 44,724 as against 381,349 in Bombay and 480,349 in Bengal (the populations of (a) Punjab, (b) Bombay (including Aden) and (c) Bengal in 1931 were (a) 23,581,000, (b) 21,931,000 and (c) 50,114,000 respectively.[87]

This preponderance of small-scale enterprise in manufacturing industry in Punjab continued even after independence, when Punjab was divided into West and East Punjab. But that story falls outside our chosen period.

To turn back to the problem of relative stagnation of agriculture particularly peasant agriculture in eastern India, we have stressed mainly the agrarian relations inhibiting real investment in land. The most important single item of capital formation in agriculture in the more dynamic regions of Punjab and Madras was the extension of public irrigation works. For various reasons, which we have discussed above, the state found it unprofitable to invest in large-scale irrigation works on a large scale in eastern India. It may also be speculated that in the predominantly rain-fed agriculture of eastern India, large-scale irrigation works with little control over fieldwise distribution of the flow of water, on the pattern of Punjab and Sind, could not be terribly productive. This may account for the predominance of unproductive works in Bihar and Orissa when the construction of such works was permitted under revised Government of India fiscal regulations. The 'unproductiveness' of such works was, however, more a function of the kind of excessive centralization practised by the colonial government than of any inherent nature of the hydrological system. The inefficiency of the colonial system in controlling water systems of monsoon agriculture in eastern India is also revealed by the decay of the indigenous systems of minor irrigation, drainage, and flood control. However, it must be emphasized that formal freedom from colonialism does not in itself remove the basic curse of the malady, which is the attempt to control micro-hydrological systems by methods of remote control when such control is unsuitable. The formal end of colonialism does not also terminate the factors that deprive the peasant of both the means and the incentive to improve the productivity of the soil.

It is obvious that some growth of large-scale industry in eastern India or Bombay did not stimulate the growth of agriculture as a whole in these regions.[88] On the other side, growth of agricultural output as a whole did not lead to any substantial growth of large-scale industry in Punjab before independence. Thus the colonial economy imposed a dual disjunction between the growth of agriculture and the growth of industry. In this situation, with some exceptions, the industrial entrepreneurs of note emerged neither from the ranks of large farmers nor from the ranks of artisans, but from those of traders, who seized upon various opportunities for import substitution and exploited them up to the limit imposed by a rather stagnant home market. In some ways, the easy mobility of trading capital as between different fields of profitable investment was also translated into a mobility between different regions of India. This interregional mobility of capital in a situation of abundance of labour in most parts of India thwarted the emergence of sub-economics in which agricultural and industrial growth stimulated each other.[89] This also partly explains the failure of the surplus-producing regions to act as nodes of cumulative industrial growth in the period after 1939.

Population Growth and Productivity Growth

In this essay, I have neglected that hardy perennial of conventional development economics—the influence of population growth on changes in output and productivity. The reasons are, first, that in general the relations between population growth and output change have proved to be much too complex for the skill of demographers and demographic historians,[90] and secondly, that in the Indian context, the hypotheses that are formulated on the basis of conventional economic theory and aggregative data (including provisional data) turn out to be quite unhelpful in explaining the facts.

On an earlier occasion I had discussed the connection between population growth and growth of yields per acre during the period 1901–41,[91] primarily concentrating on the hypothesis that an increase in the ratio of rural population to land cultivated would lead to a rise in the amount of labour applied to a given area of land, and thus an increased level of productivity per acre. A crude analysis of the provincial population changes in the relevant period failed to reveal any systematic relation between growth in population and growth in productivity, but a crude hypothesis of 'diminishing returns' following from population growth was not confirmed either.

The crucial hypothesis can be formulated as follows: Traditional techniques of production had reached their highest level of development in the different parts of India, and population growth could not in fact affect actual labour-intensity on land already cultivated. However, population growth, by eating into the surplus available to peasants, could force them to effectively decumulate the capital applied to land, thus leading to a fall in productivity per acre. A subsidiary factor working in the same direction would be an increase of acreage under foodgrains, thus lowering the effective quality of land under cereals and pulses and decreasing the average productivity of foodgrains per acre. A full-scale test of such a hypothesis is beyond the scope of this paper. We here concentrate on a pair-wise comparison of population growth, changes in acreage (total and under foodgrains), and productivity growth in Greater Bengal, Greater Punjab, and Madras in the sub-periods 1891–1921 and 1921–46 (see Table 2.7).[92]

A rough comparison between the figures of Tables 2.5 and 2.7 fails to reveal a one-to-one correspondence between the rates of population growth and changes in acreage (total or under foodgrains only), or between rates of population growth and rates of change in yield per acre. In Greater Bengal, while population increased by about an eighth between 1891 and 1921, acreage under foodgrains and total cultivated acreage actually declined. Since acreage declined, no simple hypothesis of too many people working on the same land would explain the decline in yield. It is possible to argue that acreage declined because some land became submarginal through soil erosion, and other factors. But then we come back to questions of exploitation of the peasantry, spoliation of forests, protecting the land, silting up of rivers, of malarial swamps created by unplanned railway extension, and so on.[93]

Table 2.7 Total Growth of Population in Three Provinces

	Figures in Percentage	
	1921(between 1891 and 1921)	1941 (between 1921 and 1941)
Greater Bengal (comprising Bengal, Bihar, and Orissa)	12.1	27.3
Greater Punjab (comprising Punjab and North-West Frontier Province)	11.8	37.1
Madras	18.7	23.0

Sources: For comparisons between 1891 and 1921, Census of India, 1931, vol. I, *India*, part II *Imperial Tables* by J.H. Hutton (Delhi, 1931), and for comparisons between 1921 and 1941, Census of India, 1941, vol. I, *India,* part I, Tables by M.W.M. Yeatts (Delhi, 1943), pp. 6–4.

Notes: For Greater Bengal, the figures for the two periods are not exactly comparable since the areas covered were slightly different. Native states are excluded from the respective provinces.

In fact, we can turn the hypothesis round and look at the influences on population growth itself, and then look at the consequential effects on acreage, taking the yield per acre to be determined by an overlapping but not identical, set of influences. For instance, the population in Greater Bengal increased very slowly over the period 1900–21, and acreage under foodgrains declined; population growth speeded up over the period 1921–41, and acreage under foodgrains also increased. For determining the influences on population growth, economic historians such as Ira Klein and Elizabeth Whitcombe are beginning to look at data on mobility, epidemics, frequency of natural calamities, and so on.[94] These, along with more quantitatively specified work on the growth or erosion of private or public capital stock in agriculture, and on changes in techniques and crop patterns, should illuminate the interactions between population growth and economic change in India: imperialist abstractions on this subject are a definite stumbling block against such work.

Coming to pair-wise comparisons among the three regions, we observe that during the period 1891–1921, Madras experienced the highest rate of population growth, but the rates of growth of productivity of foodgrains and of all crops together were also the highest there. The positions of Madras and Punjab were reversed in the period 1921–46, when the rates of population growth, growth in crop acreage and growth in yields per acre were the highest in Punjab. However, as we have indicated earlier, the explanation for these changes is not to be sought in terms of increase in man–land ratio on the basis of traditional techniques, but in terms of growth of public irrigation supporting more private capital formation on land.

If naive hypotheses relating to population growth and productivity growth perform so badly in the field of agriculture, there is no sensible way of even formulating similar hypotheses relating regional population growth to regional industrial growth. We conclude then that any attempt at a rigorous explanation of differences in regional growth patterns must take into account the production relations and the behaviour of the colonial state apparatus in determining the levels of public and private investment, and the disjunction or disarticulation of growth of industry and agriculture created by the integration of the Indian economy in the international colonial system of inter-dependence. This may be seen as a tentative attempt at indicating what factors are relevant in beginning such an analysis.

Concluding Remarks

To repeat, this paper has been a strictly exploratory enterprise. There are some areas, such as the differential rates of growth of large-scale or small-scale industries, which we have hardly touched at all. We have attempted to show that the determinants of growth are complex, but in spite of that complexity, some tentative conclusions are possible, through a process of elimination. The supply-demand or saving-investment categories of economists can be helpful in eliminating nonsensical formulations, but we have to go behind these apparatuses and explore the processes of formation and behaviour of classes under colonialism in order to get at a really causal explanation. Such explanations will also destroy the purely idealistic (and very often, racialist) formulations, by showing up their superficiality and a temporality. It is hoped that this essay can serve at least as a tentative research programme in laying bare the differences and similarities of regional growth patterns in colonial, or even politically independent, India.

Notes

1. See 'Introduction' in Sharma (1946). Even such a sophisticated book as Spate (1957), employs a Weberian framework.

2. I explored this problem in Chapter 6 of my book, Bagchi (1972a, Indian edition, 1975). This essay is partly a continuation of that work.

3. Blyn (1966).

4. See, for example, Sastry (1947) and M.M. Mehta (1955).

5. I have attempted to compute the gross domestic material product of Bengal in 1794 from H.T. Colebrooke's data in *Nineteenth Century Studies*, 1973.

6. See C. Northcote Parkinson (1966 [1937]: 86–7), and Furber (1951: Chapters VI and VII).

7. G.A. Prinsep (1823) in the Appendix, gives figures of exports from Bengal, Bombay, and Madras over the years 1813–14 to 1822–3. For Bombay and Madras, the figures were not as complete or detailed as for Bengal; furthermore, we do not know exactly how the discrepancies between custom house returns and true values of exports and imports would affect comparability between the different regions. But still, one can assert that merchandise exports from Bengal during this period probably equalled or even exceeded the merchandise exports from Madras and Bombay together. This situation does not seem to have changed until raw cotton exports from Bombay and Madras boosted the export figures after the middle of the century. For regional export figures between 1834–55 and 1849–50, see R.C. Dutt (1963b[1906]: 114).

8. Colebrooke and Lambert (1795) especially, pp. 221–2.

9. Prinsep (1823: 63n).

10. Alfred Marshall, who may be considered the real begetter of English neo-classicism, formulated the sophists' argument with unconscious humour, incidentally anticipating the latter-day ideology of the 'human capital approach': 'England exports to India a good many able young men: they do not enter in India's list of imports; but it is claimed that they render to her services whose value exceeds that of her total payments to them. They return to England (if they come back at all) after their best strength has been spent: they are unreckoned exports from England. But that part of their incomes, which they have saved, is likely to come sooner or later in the form of material goods which enter into her imports. On the other hand, India counts these material goods among her exports to England: but of course she makes no entry among her imports for the expensive young men who have been sent to her.' A. Marshall (1923: 134–5).

11. For evidence of political and racial discrimination against Indians, see Bagchi (1972a: Chapters 5 and 6).

12. For figures of imports of silver and silver coinage in India, see Gold and Silver Commission, 1888, *Final Report of the Royal Commission Appointed to Inquire into the Recent Changes in the Relative Values of the Precious Metals; with Minutes of Evidence and Appendixes*. Eyre and Spottiswoode for Her Majesty's Stationery Office, pp. 4–6; and Reserve Bank of India (1954: 673 and 940).

13. For an incisive analysis of the issues, see De Cecco (1974: Chapter 4).

14. On the China–Britain–India triangle, see Greenberg (1951); Singh (1966: Chapter 3); and Chung (1973). For the later period, see Saul (1960: Chapter 14). See also K. N. Chaudhuri (1971).

15. *Encyclopaedia Britannica,* ninth edition, 1881, vol. XII, p. 755.

16. We have neglected coastal shipping as a means of interregional trade; in my full analysis, changes in the tonnage, network, and freight rate of coastal shipping must be taken into account.

17. We have not tried to allocate imports or exports of treasure as between regions, because Bombay was the bullion market of India, and Bombay imported treasure on behalf of all the different regions.

18. For a short account of the cotton mill development in Bombay and Ahmedabad between 1900 and 1939, see Bagchi (1972a: Chapter 7).

19. See Ibid.: Chapters 6 and 14.

20. Ibid.: Chapter 6.

21. See, for example, A. Guha (1970a) and (1970b). See also A.V. Desai (1968) and Kulke (1974).

22. See, for example, Gillion (1968). See also Pavlov (1964).

23. See Spodek (1965) and (1969).

24. On the domination of external trade and shipping by Gujarati merchants in the early eighteenth century, see Prakash (1967)quoted in A. Guha (1969). See also Little (1967); Sinha (1961) and (1970: Chapter 5).

25. Trade in foodgrains seems to have been an exception. See Colebrooke (1804: 169) .

26. See Gokhale (1969: 187–97); Spodek (1969). The Gujarati Muslims had come to dominate much of the trade of the Indian Ocean when Vasco da Gama arrived in India, and Gujarati sailors and merchants remained indispensable to European traders for a long time. See Boxer (1973: 45, 57, 73–4).

27. The British utilized Indian financiers for attaining political and commercial hegemony in western India. See Nightingale (1970: Chapter 2).

28. A detailed analysis of the magnitude of the process of de-industrialization in eastern India will be found in Bagchi (1976a).

29. *Gazetteers of the Bombay Presidency* (*GBP*), (1883: 109).

30. Ibid.: 125.

31. *GBP* (1877: 187).

32. Ibid.: 448.

33. Ibid.: 446.

34. *GBP* (1879b: 64); on functional specialization among Surat bankers and moneylenders, see *GBP* (1887: 185–90); for Broach, see Ibid., for Kaira, see *GBP* (1879a: 57–60).

35. *GBP* (1879b: p. 68).

36. Ibid.: 69–70.

37. See, for example, *GBP* (1879a: 58–60); *GBP* (1887: 185–202) for Surat and (1887: 449–52) for Broach, especially p. 452 (on 'mortgage of labour').

38. *GBP* (1879b: 68–9).

39. See Ravinder Kumar (1968: Chapters 1 and 5) for an analysis of the relationship of moneylenders to landholding in Maharashtra in 1818 and in 1875, at

the time of the Deccan riots. Qualitatively, the same kind of analysis could apply to Gujarat, although it is probable that the process of disintegration of the older structure proceeded much further in Maharashtra than in Gujarat.

40. I have essayed a very brief analysis of some of these problems in Bagchi (1975b).

41. *Encyclopaedia Britannica,* ninth edition, vol. XII, p. 769.

42. Irfan Habib has estimated the 'drain' at this higher figure in Habib (1975a).

43. Colebrooke and Lambert (1795: 232, 218–19).

44. This very brief sketch is based on the following, Dutt (1963a[1906]: Chapters 20–1); Dutt (1963b[1906]: Book I, Chapter 4, Book II, Chapter 6, Book III, Chapter 6); *GBP* (1879b: 126–33); *Imperial Gazetteer of India*; Provincial Series, 1909, *Bombay Presidency,* vol. I, Calcutta: Superintendent of Government Printing, pp. 259–60; Nanavati and Anjaria (1951: part II, Chapter 8); Fukazawa (1974); and Breman (1974).

45. Cf. Dutt (1963a[1906]: 35).

> It is a lamentable fact that both these ancient institutions, the Village Community and the Mirasi tenure, virtually ceased to exist before the first generation of British administrators had closed their labours in the conquered territories [belonging earlier to the Marathas—A.B.]. A fixed resolve to make direct arrangements with every separate cultivator, and to impose upon him a tax to be raised at each recurring settlement, necessarily weakened village communities and extinguished Mirasi rights. See also Fukazawa (1974).

46. See *GBP* (1883: 127–8, 133).

47. On the character of social change in the ryotwari areas in Madras, see Frykenberg and Mukherjee (1969); and Washbrook (1973).

48. See Nanavati and Anjaria (1951: part II, Chapter 12), for a summary of anti-moneylender legislation enacted during the British period.

49. Spodek (1969: M-28).

50. See the evidence of Kopalle Hanumantha Rao, Headmaster, Andhra Jatheya Kalasala, Masulipatam in Indian Industrial Commission, *Evidence,* vol. III, *Madras and Bangalore*, UK Parliamentary Papers, 1919, vol. XIX), pp. 78–88; Washbrook (1973: 162–9).

51. Washbrook in his otherwise incisive analysis in (Ibid.) seems to overlook this point.

52. Bagchi (1972a: Chapters 1–3 and 6). Besides the evidence cited in this book, the curious reader may also refer to Jacomb-Hood (1929: vol. II, 'History of the Jute Mills Department'). In a letter dated 7 September 1903, Ernest Cable, who controlled Bird & Co. in its most prosperous and dynamic years, wrote, after floating the Dalhousie Jute Co. with money 'from a small group' of wealthy friends of Bird & Co. and their auditors and from Bird & Co. itself:

> I could do the Clive Mill extension through the Allahabad Bank at once, but to do so would be to break faith with the Alliance Bank who have taken up the whole of the debentures and preference shares of the 'Dalhousie', and they would strongly object to a rival bank offering similar stock on the market at

the same time, therefore, the Clive extension should be done in London. (Ibid.: 193)

Again, Ernest Cable's policy with regard to the capital component for the companies he floated later was to have a preponderance of debentures and preference shares with a small ordinary share issue, and it was these latter which both he, and Messrs. Bird & Co., took up, on their own account, leaving the former for the banks and the investment companies (Ibid.: 198). On the same page, Cable is quoted as writing in 1903: 'In the prosperous times of a boom, we can, "off our own bat", float a jute mill in three hours'. All this throws interesting light on the supposed scarcity of capital for industrial investment in India and on the supposed unwillingness of banks to finance fixed capital. But, of course, you had to have the right connections and your skin the right colour.

53. Rungta (1970) especially Chapters 2, 5, 7, and 9.

54. See Hjejle (1967).

55. Breman (1974: parts 1 and 2).

56. See the evidence of B.D. Patel, Deputy Director of Agriculture, Gujarat, before the Banking Enquiry Committee, quoted by Choksey (1968: 105–06n).

57. See *Census of India, 1901,* 1902, vol. VI. *Bengal,* Part I, p. 475; *Bengal District Gazetteers,* 1906, *Gaya,* pp. 153–4; and *Bengal District Gazetteers,* 1909, *Monghyr,* pp. 129–30.

58. Breman (1974: 75–6).

59. I am indebted for this point to Dipesh Chakravarty.

60. See the evidence included in De *et al.* (1912).

61. Extract from the *Report of the Deccan Riots Commission,* 1875, reprinted in S.C. Ray (1915: 9).

62. Colebrooke in 1795 estimated that while the human population of Bengal (including Bihar and Orissa) was about 30 million, the cattle population (including buffaloes) was about 50 million. The total number of bovine stock (including cattle, buffaloes, and yaks) in Assam, Bihar, Orissa, and West Bengal together was 50 million in 1961 which was much less than half the population of the area in that year. See *Indian Livestock Census,* 1966, *Summary Tables,* 1971. Data on cattle population provided in the *Gazetteers of the Bombay Presidency* referred to already, generally indicate a declining or a slowly growing cattle population between the 1850s and 1870s. There is no reason to believe that the trends were very different in other decades in these or in most other regions of India. Deterioration in the milk-yielding capacity of cows is alleged in the authoritative *Report on the Marketing of Milk in India and Burma* (1941).

63. For accounts of the deterioration of the indigenous system of irrigation, see *Bengal District Gazetteers,* 1906, *Shahabad,* Chapter 6; *Bihar and Orissa District Gazetteers,* 1942, *Shahabad*; *Bengal District Gazetteers, Monghyr,* Chapter 5.

64. See Narain (1965: 128–31).

65. For a brilliant analysis of the government's irrigation policy and its effects on the productivity of the land and on the social structure, see Whitcombe (1972: Chapter 2).

66. European (and Indian) traders had a definite interest in keeping the peasantry weak financially. See evidence cited in Bagchi (1972a: 269).

67. On rural credit relations and debt bondage, see B.B. Chaudhuri (1969), (1970a) and (1970b). The survey and settlement Reports of the indigo-growing districts describe the methods by which indigo-growers were bound to the planters. On European planters and businessmen as landlords, see the references cited in Bagchi (1972a: 200 and 363). Our formulation is a partial answer to the puzzle (about why the zamindars did so badly in terms of productive investment) posed by Ray Chaudhuri (1969).

68. See Catanach (1970: 78–87). See also the evidence of Lalubhai Samaldas Mehta in *Bombay Provincial Banking Enquiry Committee, 1929–30*, vol. III. *Evidence*, 1930, pp. 1–32.

69. See Keatinge (1913: 267–73); and comment by Dr J.A. Voelcker, p. 276.

70. Saugata Mukherji (1970: Chapter 2, Tables 2, 8) has shown that the British jute mill owners and jute exporters got much the larger share of the surplus extracted from the ultimate producer.

71. See Bagchi (1972a: Chapter 4).

72. Mackenzie (1954).

73. 'Greater Punjab' in Table 2.5 includes the North-West Frontier Province, but this will not affect the main points of the comparison.

74. The irrigated acreage in the Madras Presidency was about 6.35 million acres in 1898. See *Encyclopaedia Britannica,* tenth edition, 1906, article on 'Irrigation', p. 599.

75. In 1901 the population of Bengal, Bihar, and Orissa, roughly coterminous with Blyn's 'Greater Bengal', was about 77 million out of an all-India population of 285 million. See Bagchi (1972a: 113, 118).

76. See Dharm Narain (1965: 128–32); Narain (1967); Blyn (1966: 138–41, 197–200); and Bagchi (1972a: 107–8), and the works cited therein.

77. Mukherji (1970: vol. I, Chapter 4); and M.M. Islam (1972: Chapters 1–3).

78. M.M. Islam (1972: Table 2.1).

79. It is interesting to note that our guess about the annual rate of change of crop output in Bihar and Orissa is very nearly the same as Islam's estimate of the annual rate of change of crop output (–1 per cent) in the Burdwan division, the westernmost division of Bengal proper.

80. See the evidence of R.D. Anstead, Director of Agriculture, Madras, and of M. Bazlullah Sahib Bahadur, Director of Industries, Madras, in the Royal Commission on Agriculture in India, vol. III, 1927, *Evidence taken in the Madras Presidency*, London, pp. 48 and 446–7, respectively.

81. See the evidence of D. Milne, Director of Agriculture, Punjab, in Royal Commission on Agriculture in India, vol. VIII, 1927, *Evidence Taken in the Punjab*, Calcutta, pp. 191–4 on p. 194.

82. Darling (1932: 119).

83. On the failure of the Land Alienation Act to effect its desired purpose, see *The Punjab Provincial Banking Enquiry Committee,* 1929–30, vol. I, 1930, Calcutta:

Government of India, Central Publications Branch. Note H: 'Punjab Village Surveys: Borrowing and Debt', (pp. 221–34); and Barrier (1965: 144–5), especially p. 161.

84. See Calvert (1936).

85. See Census of India, vol. XV, *Punjab and Delhi,* part I, *Report,* 1923, Lahore, pp. 78, 352–5; Census of India, 1931, vol. XVII, *Punjab,* part I, *Report,* 1933, Lahore, pp. 41–2.

86. See Census of India, 1931, vol. I, part I, *Report,* 1933, Delhi, p. 307.

87. Ibid.: 35; and Government of India, Commercial Intelligence and Statistics Department, *Statistical Abstracts for British India from 1922–23 to 1931–32,* 1933, Calcutta, pp. 812–13.

88. The growth of large-scale industry was preceded and accompanied by massive destruction of traditional handicrafts. For those regions for which reasonable quantitative data are available, there is a clear trend of de-industrialization throughout the nineteenth century. See Bagchi (1976a).

89. In the international context, Ricardo, the most effective advocate of free trade among economists, had welcomed international immobility of capital as conducive towards the prosperity of nation-states. 'Experience, however, shews [shows] that the fancied or real insecurity of capital. when not under the immediate control of its owner, together with the natural disinclination which every man has to quit the country of his birth and connexions, and intrust himself with all his habits fixed, to a strange government and new laws, check the emigration of capital. These feelings, which I should be sorry to see weakened, induce most men of property to be satisfied with a low rate of profits in their own country, rather than seek a more advantageous employment for their wealth in foreign nations.' Ricardo (1966: 136–7).

90. For a convenient selection of views on the relation between population growth and economic change, see Drake (1969).

91. Bagchi (1972a: section 4.4).

92. There is a slight hiatus in the terminal dates for population and output estimates: we use the population of 1941, but output during the period 1941–6 as estimated by Blyn.

93. Besides the references cited in note 76 above, on soil erosion see Gorrie (1938) and (1953).

94. See Klein (1972, 1974), and Whitcombe (1972).

3

De-industrialization in India in the Nineteenth Century

Some Theoretical Implications*[1]

The 'naïve' idea current among many of the older nationalists of the Third World regarding the de-industrializing effect of Western capitalism on their countries is confirmed by the analysis of occupational data relating to the state of Bihar in India. Similar evidence is also available for Egypt and China. If we shift from models of what can ideally happen under capitalism in its international aspects and look at what actually happened until, say, 1914, we find that it often had opposite effects on the advanced capitalist countries and their overseas offshoots, and on the colonial or semi-colonial economies of the Third World in respect of industrial employment, investment in productive assets, and distribution of income. Technological change, even today, often carries highly disruptive and inegalitarian consequences for Third World countries. In the light of such experience with market-orientated growth, an alternative model is suggested in which development proceeds by localized economic activities, distributing incomes and opportunities equally and keeping out 'backwash' effects on other regions. One major task of the economist in the future will be to explore the inner logic of such a 'paradigm', suggest the means of implementing the model, and ferret out possible contradictions. The Chinese (and perhaps Vietnamese) experience may serve as an example or laboratory for such explorations.

*Reprinted from, 1976, *Journal of Development Studies*, 12(2), January, pp. 135–64.

Introduction

Although the Indian nationalists of the nineteenth century counted among the evil effects of British rule the complete or partial destruction of many of the indigenous industries in India[2] neither the facts of the case nor their import for economic development have been thoroughly investigated yet. Either evocative descriptions or mere assertions serve as surrogates for a systematic analysis of the existing data.[3]

Daniel Thorner was one of the first scholars to investigate the alleged phenomenon of the de-industrialization of India.[4] He implicitly defined de-industrialization as a decline in the proportion of the working population engaged in secondary industry, or a decline in the proportion of the total population dependent on secondary industry, and we shall also adopt this definition. (The two versions of the definition will yield different results if the proportions of workers to the total population behave differently over time in the case of secondary industry and in the case of the economy as a whole). Thorner comes to the conclusion that a meticulous analysis of the *census data alone* provides no ground for believing that de-industrialization occurred in India over the period 1881–1931. But even such a careful investigator suffers from preconceptions regarding the process of de-industrialization. He says: 'There can be no dispute with a flat statement that India's national handicrafts have declined sadly from their pristine glory. This falling-off, however, was not a phenomenon peculiar to India but a world-wide development affecting different countries at different times. The ruin, sooner or later, of the old-style craftsmen was as integral a part of the Industrial Revolution as the coming of the factory system'.[5]

The statement ignores the difference in the impact of the Industrial Revolution of the metropolitan and the colonial countries, pushes aside questions of relative numbers of men and lengths of time involved in the two cases, and assumes a peculiar doctrine of historical inevitability—a doctrine it is fair to say, which has embedded itself in orthodox textbooks, and in some so-called Marxist works—on economic development. In Britain and Germany it was their own industrial revolution which led to the destruction of handicrafts so that employment was being created in one branch of secondary industry while it was declining in another; after a point, the rate of creation of employment in the new branch of secondary industry was far higher than the rate of loss in the older branch. By contrast, for a very long time, the impact of the industrial revolution of other countries on the employment and income in the secondary industry of today's underdeveloped countries was almost entirely destructive.

It is pertinent to quote here the remark of Sir John Hicks:

> The English handloom weavers, who were displaced by textile machinery, could (in the end and after much travail) find re-employment in England; but what of the Indian weavers who were displaced by the same improvement? Even in their case there would be a favourable effect, somewhere, but it might be anywhere; there would be no particular reason why it should be in India. The poorer the country, the narrower will be its range of opportunities; the more likely, therefore, it is that it will suffer long-lasting damage, now and then, from a backlash of improvements that have occurred elsewhere.[6]

This essay may be seen as partly an empirical commentary on, and partly an attempt at the extension of, the arguments of Hicks and Ricardo to the case of the underdeveloped countries.

Second, even in England, the first industrializing country of the world, the *initial* effect of the technological revolution, in the cotton spinning industry (that is, until the powerloom was introduced on an extensive scale) was to *increase* the employment and wages of the handloom weavers. Further, it took a long time for the woollen industry—the traditional staple industry of England—to feel the impact of the technological revolution in other spheres of the economy. The destructive effects of the Industrial Revolution were considerably cushioned by absolute growth in demand and by various protective devices fashioned in the mercantile era (the protective devices in England were not effectively dismantled after all until the middle of the 1840s, eighty long years after the conventional dating of the beginning of the Industrial Revolution). The use of protective measures was even more general in other European countries than in England. By contrast, protective devices were used—perversely—to further cripple the indigenous industries of India, and practically no state help was rendered to the modern Indian industries until the end of the First World War.[7] Third, in the British case the most important carrier of the Industrial Revolution—the cotton mill industry—was a relatively *new* growth, and the destructive effects were not felt by a very large section of the industry. In the Indian case, handloom weaving and hand-spinning constituted the largest traditional industry and the numbers involved were enormous, both absolutely and in relation to the rest of the population. Hence destructive effects on this sector had a generally depressive effect on the rest of the economy.

Finally, the doctrine of the inevitability of the ruin of traditional handicrafts was born out of the experience of capitalist expansion. In a situation in which other types of social order have come into existence, and in which the largest socialist country of the world has adopted the policy of 'walking on two legs', there is plenty of room for envisaging other types of development which keep traditional industries alive until *society as a whole* (and not just the private businessman—at home or abroad) finds it rational to replace them by other methods or products.

It may be considered unfair to read so much into a single statement of Thorner, but a very extended meaning is often given to even such an innocuous-looking proposition, which is why I have analysed the possible interpretations in such detail.

For the purposes of this essay, we have used a decline in the proportion of the population dependent on secondary industry as evidence of de-industrialization. Such a criterion is used in order to contrast it with the requirements of a positive process of industrialization. Speaking in terms of national economic arithmetic, capitalist industrialization up to at least the phase of maturity is attended by three developments: (a) an increase in the proportion of national income generated by the secondary sector; (b) an increase in the proportion of the population engaged in secondary industry; and (c) a continual rise in the degree of mechanization in industry (and to a lesser extent in agriculture).[8] For the fulfilment of the third condition, it is not necessary that the degree of mechanization of new techniques should rise all the time; it is only necessary that the degree of mechanization of new techniques be higher than that of old techniques on an average. While these changes are going on, *per capita* income must be rising. But *per capita* income may rise even without industrialization, so that a rise in income per head is only a necessary condition for a positive process of industrialization and by no means a sufficient one.

The mere lack of fulfilment of any of the three conditions can be characterized as non-industrialization (if income *per capita* is also stagnant) or stagnation. The reversal of any of the first three conditions over the long period is here characterized as de-industrialization. India witnessed the reversal of the first two conditions for most of the nineteenth century.

In the next section, direct evidence bearing out the case for the reversal of the first condition is presented. What happens to the second condition then depends on the productivity of the relatively declining labour force engaged in secondary industry, and on the behaviour of the income generated by the primary and tertiary sectors together. We know that in India, until the end of the nineteenth century, the cottage industrial production made up the bulk of the income generated by the secondary sector.[9] We know further that there were few innovations of any importance within the cottage industries until the gradual introduction of fly-shuttle looms starting about the end of the nineteenth century.[10] So with the major component of industrial production declining and the growing component remaining very small in relation to the total, there is a presumption that total industrial production could have grown, if at all, only very slowly and may actually have registered a declining trend, for most of the nineteenth century. If we assume then that the income generated by the primary and tertiary sectors together grew faster, or declined more slowly, than the income generated by the secondary sector, the reversal of the second condition associated with industrialization also follows. If it in fact turns out that the primary and tertiary sectors grew even more slowly, or declined faster, than the secondary sector (from the point of view of income generated), then the second condition will not be reversed. But then we can legitimately characterize the whole process as one of absolute economic retardation with de-industrialization in the sense of a decline in the proportion of the population dependent on secondary industry being one aspect—though a very important aspect—of such a process of economic retardation or stagnation.

The Proportion of the Population Dependent on Secondary Industry in Gangetic Bihar in 1809–13 and in 1901

Until now most of the discussions on the extent or reality of de-industrialization in India in the nineteenth century have been based either on impressionistic observations or on *aprioristic* arguments alone. However, there is a unique set of observations by Francis Buchanan Hamilton, who was specifically commissioned by the East India Company to make a survey of the resources of south India, and then of a major portion of eastern and northeastern India. From the data compiled by him, after making certain obvious adjustments, it is possible to compute the total population dependent on secondary industry and also the share of the population dependent on secondary industry around the years 1809–13 in the tracts designated as Bhagalpur, Patna-Gaya, Purnea, and Shahabad by Buchanan Hamilton, making up what may be called Gangetic Bihar in modern India.[11]

In arriving at the total population dependent on industry, the assumption was made that spinners of cotton or silk yarn supported only themselves (since their earnings per head were low) whereas other artisans working full time supported normal-sized families (of five). Table 3.1 summarizes the results of the computations.

Table 3.1 Population Dependent on Secondary Industry in Gangetic Bihar around 1809–13

District	Number of spinners	Number of industrial workers or artisans other than spinners	Total population dependent on secondary industry	Percentage of industrial to total population
Patna-Gaya	330,396	65,031	655,551	19.5
Bhagalpur	168,975	23,403	286,080	14.2
Purniya	287,000	60,172	587,860	20.2
Shahabad	159,500	25,557	287,285	20.2
Total	945,871	174,163	1,816,776	18.6

Source: Buchanan (Hamilton) F., 1809–1813, *Statistical Tables for Reports on Bhagalpur, Patna and Gaya (Bihar) Purnea and Shahabad.* London: India Office Library, Mss. Eur. G.14, 15, 17, 18, 19, and 20.

We took 1901 as another benchmark date to compare with the situation at the beginning of the twentieth century. It was a census year, and the census was methodologically as sound as an Indian census ever was.[12] But in arriving at the total number of people dependent on industry, I deducted from the number of people dependent on the provision of food, drink, and stimulants, the number of pure sellers, and from the population dependent on the making and selling of cloth, the number of piece-goods sellers, for their occupations obviously belonged to the tertiary sector. But sellers of many other goods are still included in the category of secondary industry and to that extent, the figures for population dependent on secondary industry in 1901 are likely to be inflated. We have chosen the districts of Patna, Gaya, Shahabad, Monghyr, Bhagalpur, and Purnea as corresponding most closely to the tracts included in Table 3.1. Any slight discrepancies between the two regions would not matter since there are no reasons to believe that the relevant tendencies in the contiguous tracts were widely dissimilar.

Comparing Tables 3.1 and 3.2, it can be seen that there was a drastic fall in the percentage of population dependent on secondary industry between around 1809–13 and 1901. In fact, the percentage at the later date was less than half of what it had been at the earlier date. If we take absolute numbers, it turns out that while the total population was larger in 1901 (the total population in the tracts included in Table 3.1 was 9.7 million), the *absolute* number of the population dependent on industry had come down by almost 50 per cent between the two dates. The major component of this decline was, of course, the decline in the largest traditional industry, the textile industry. It had declined not only absolutely and in relation to the primary and tertiary sectors together but also in relation to other types of secondary industry: whereas around 1809–13 the percentage of the population dependent on cotton weaving and spinning to the total industrial population in Gangetic Bihar had been 62.3, by 1901, the percentage of population dependent on spinning of cotton yarn, the weaving, sizing, and so on, of cotton cloth to the total industrial population had come down to 15.1.

Table 3.2 Population Dependent on Secondary Industry in 1901

Districts	Total population	Industrial population	Percentage of industrial to total population
Patna	1,624,985	179,695	11.1
Gaya	2,059,933	187,016	9.1
Shahabad	1,962,696	228,051	11.6
Monghyr	2,068,804	155,439	7.5
Bhagalpur	2,088,953	115,618	5.5
Purnea	1,874,794	121,933	6.5
Total	11,680,165	987,752	8.5

Source: Census, 1902, (Census, 1901b) *Census of India,* Parts I, II, and III, *Report and Tables,* Calcutta: Superintendent, Government Printing.

These quantitative results are supported by qualitative accounts contained in the *Statistical Accounts* of the Bengal District published in the 1870s and in *the Gazetteers* of the districts concerned, which were published in the first decade of the twentieth century.[13] In the districts of Patna, Gaya, Purnea, Shahabad, and Monghyr, we meet very similar stories of a decline in cotton and silk manufacture. The manufacture of certain coarser varieties of cloth catering to the needs of the poorest people survived. The condition of weavers deteriorated very greatly both absolutely and in relation to other skilled workers. Most of the displaced were probably absorbed in agriculture, but vast numbers migrated towards Calcutta and the industrial centres on the Hooghly in search of employment.

There is a continuity between the stories told by the *Statistical Accounts* and the *District Gazetteers*: what had already been a well-established trend towards decline in the 1870s had been consummated by virtual extinction by the beginning of the twentieth century. This was true, for example, for the hand-made paper industry and, again, for *bidri*ware in Purnea.

Thus there is reason to believe that the results obtained from a comparison of the data on employment in secondary industry in Buchanan Hamilton's time and in 1901 are not freaks but reflect certain deep-seated processes of change—processes that we have characterized as de-industrialization.

De-industrialization in the All-India Context

To what extent was the de-industrialization a phenomenon peculiar to central Bihar? Were there any special reasons favouring the concentration of traditional industry there in the first place, so that de-industrialization occurred in an exaggerated form? Were the effects of the death of the old industry in respect of employment more than made up by the growth of modern industry?

To begin with we shall answer the first two questions. It has been claimed that the degree of concentration of traditional industry was unusually high in the districts south of the Ganges because a large number of Muslim nobles with an essentially urban culture settled there during the disturbed years off the eighteenth century. It must be noted, however, that (a) the Gangetic Bihar districts in Buchanan Hamilton's survey also included Purnea, which lies wholly north of the Ganges; and (b) that Buchanan Hamilton's observations came fully fifty years after the effective displacement of the Indian rulers by the British: thus the degree of de-industrialization as measured between 1809 and 1901 was additional to rather than the immediate result of the elimination or impoverishment of traditional patrons of luxury manufactures through the coming of British rule. Turning to another possible reason for the concentration of manufactures in Gangetic Bihar, we note that this area was also not a major seat of manufacture for export. It was situated too far inland, and although the East India Company had a 'factory' in Patna, its 'investments' in (purchases of) local manufactures formed only a small fraction of both the total cloth 'investments' of the company and of the total output of the districts themselves. Thus it cannot be claimed that the de-industrialization was merely a decline from a development which had been specially stimulated by the activities of the European merchants themselves in buying Indian cloth for export to other countries. Hence the major part of the de-industrialization must be attributed to the displacement of traditional manufacturers as suppliers of consumption goods to the internal Indian market. This makes the case of the Gangetic Bihar perhaps typical of the major cotton goods manufacturing districts of India.

Turning to the question of whether the growth of modern industry resulted in providing employment in lieu of traditional industries, we notice first that within the Gangetic Bihar districts, in 1901, only at Jamalpur in the Monghyr district was there a railway workshop which could be termed a modern large-scale manufacturing establishment in any sense at all. But the employment generated there was totally inadequate even to make up for the loss of employment in the traditional industry of the Monghyr district, let alone the traditional industries of the other districts of Gangetic Bihar.[14]

As far as other parts of India were concerned, by 1900 some modern industry had grown up around Calcutta and Bombay: but even if we include mines and plantations along with factories, in 1901 the total employment in 'modern enterprise' would not exceed one million. The annual addition to this total was generally inadequate to absorb even the growth in the labour force of India. On the other side, agriculture proved to be a diminishingly profitable activity in much of eastern India.[15] This was revealed at the source in a tremendous pressure for migration in the districts surveyed, and in a practically unlimited supply of labour for jute mills, coal mines, and even tea plantations. Thus, for many workers who could neither ply their old trades nor make a living out of agricultural labour, nor find employment in the distant factories, mines, or plantations, the process of de-industrialization must have been a process of pure immiserization.[16]

What was the situation in the other parts of eastern India, and in other parts of India as a whole? For eastern India, excluding Assam (Bengal, until the creation of the province of Bihar and Orissa) the phenomenon of de-industrialization must have been a pretty general one for at least the first fifty years of the period we are studying. (The first jute mill did not come up until 1855 and the growth of jute mills was quite slow until the 1870s). The East India Company had come to monopolize the export trade in cotton piece-goods, but between 1813 and 1830, 'Bengal piece-goods practically disappeared from the investment list (of the East India Company). Private trade followed the same trend'.[17] N.K. Sinha estimated that taking cotton weavers, cotton growers, spinners, dressers, embroiderers, and so on, together, one million people of Bengal (including Bihar and Orissa) were thrown out of employment by 1828.[18] In the light of our computations for the districts of Gangetic Bihar, this appears to be rather a low estimate in fact. Sinha provides a Table of centres of production and procurement of cotton piece-goods with the respective values of the output procured there in 1793.[19] From that Table we find that Patna (the chief city of Gangetic, and in fact, of the whole of Bihar) accounted for current Rs 414,287 and Benares for current Rs 448,866 out of the total 'investment' of current Rs 6,553,753. Thus these western centres of Bengal accounted for at most 12 per cent of the total cloth export on the East India Company's account. Assuming that Patna alone was the centre of collection for the Gangetic Bihar districts and that production for export formed roughly the same proportion of total output everywhere, and the extent of the fall of cloth export provides a rough index of the degree of de-industrialization, then the fall in employment in traditional industry for Bengal as a whole was about sixteen times that for the districts of Gangetic Bihar. But, of course, the exact extent of the estimated fall by 1828 would depend on how the total displacement from traditional industries was distributed over the major part of the nineteenth century.

The disproportion between the employment creation in Britain and the destruction of employment in the rest of the world is shown by the fact that while in Bengal alone, as early as 1828, at least a million persons employed in cotton trades lost their jobs, the total number of cotton workers of every kind together in Britain in 1851 was 527,000.[20] And in 1851, Britain was indisputably the leading industrial nation, and may have alone accounted for something like half of the cotton textile production of the countries for which there is data available.[21] It is this kind of global balance as well as adjustments within the underdeveloped countries that I want to draw attention to in this essay.

The results obtained for these districts of Bihar cannot, of course, be generalized for the whole of India without similarly intensive enquiries for each tract taken separately. We are not equally fortunate in respect of usable data for other parts. But extensive data can be culled from other surveys by Buchanan Hamilton and from the proceedings of the Government of India whose officials collected enormous quantities of statistics and other types of data in the course of their routine work. These data can be pieced together to provide at least a general picture of the state of employment and wages of weavers, spinners, and other artisans in different parts of India on different dates of the nineteenth century.

To illustrate this last point, I now cite some data on the North-Western Provinces (the United Provinces of Agra and Oudh in the later British period and the Uttar Pradesh of today). In the early 1860s at the time of the American Civil War, the Bengal Chamber of Commerce complained to the Government of India that the demand for English cotton goods in the North-Western Provinces had fallen off and that this was due to the revival of handloom-weaving. The government had an intensive enquiry instituted into the facts of the case and their probable causes in every district and the results of these enquiries were published.[22] The Secretary to the Sudder Board of Revenue summarized the most important finding in the following words:

> First, then, it may be stated decidedly that the diminished demand for English cotton has not been caused by increased Native manufacture. With few exceptions, there has been nowhere any such increase. On the contrary, there has, speaking generally, been a marked and distressing contraction of local manufacture. This ... is less observable in the western districts, where perhaps from a sixth to a fourth of the looms in the cities and towns (though not in the outlying villages) have stopped working. But in the eastern districts the trade has altogether decayed, and within two or three years the falling-off is shown to have reached a third, and in some districts, a half of the looms; and even of the remainder a large portion is only worked occasionally. The weavers have be-taken themselves to agricultural or other menial labour, to menial service, emigration to the Mauritius and elsewhere, and even to begging.[23]

In most cases, the published extracts from the officers' reports contain only comparisons for the years 1860 to 1863, and as such it is not possible either to form an idea of what went before 1860 or what came after 1863–4 or thereabouts. But from the nature of the damage caused to weavers—loss of capital for the purchase of cotton, abandonment of looms, loss of usual trade connections—it is not unreasonable to infer that part of the loss of employment by weavers and spinners was permanent. In fact, the further spread of railways probably accentuated that aspect of the de-industrialization process, for even in the case of some of the western districts which contained several thousand looms each in 1860, the official *Accounts of the North Western Provinces*,[24] written barely thirteen or fourteen years later, record contemptuously that the districts contained very few industries worth mentioning.

Some, however, of the reports made at the time of the 'slackness of demand for European goods' enquiry specifically compared the situation in the 1860s with earlier years.[25] After recording a large increase in the percentage of people wearing Manchester cloth over a period of twenty-five years, Colonel Baird Smith comments: 'I am inclined to believe that less than one-third of the field open to its operations (i.e., to Manchester trade) has as yet been taken possession of; and I am confident that, when the comparative plenty of ordinary seasons is restored, and the march of internal improvement can be resumed, there lies before the trade a growth as steady and perhaps even more rapid than it has previously known'.[26] Colonel Baird Smith's prediction came to be largely true, and the import of English cotton piece-goods into India increased steadily until the beginning of the First World War, when India was importing 3,104 million yards of cloth from the UK.[27]

There is little doubt whatsoever that the number of cotton spinners declined drastically all over India.[28] and as we have seen above, cotton spinners far outnumbered the cotton weavers in the traditional industry, and whatever evidence exists points to either stagnation or decline in the numbers of handloom weavers at least until the last decade of the nineteenth century. The overall effect on employment in rural areas cannot be judged in aggregate terms: the impression of excessive pressure on the land by the end of the nineteenth century is widespread among government officials in many parts of India. One index of a gradually worsening employment situation would be a downward trend in real wages. Where part of the wage was paid in kind, it is difficult to assess the trend of real wage without knowing both the trend of the cost of living index and the way in which the real part of the wage was changing. Where wages could not be reduced any further, all the pressure would take the form of open or hidden unemployment, and the real wage would show no trend. But again, there are some indications that in pars of India real wages fell over much of the nineteenth century. Thus the compiler of the first *District Gazetteer* of the Bareilly district in the then North-Western Provinces noted that while the wages of various classes of workers (such as field labourers, herdsmen, tailors, masons, and others) were very nearly the same as they were in 1826, prices had risen substantially between the two dates.[29]

Turning now to another kind of evidence, we find that whereas at the time of Buchanan Hamilton's survey, weavers belonged to the aristocracy of artisans, by the end of the century, in many areas of Bengal, Bihar, and the United Provinces, their wages were even lower than those of the agricultural labourers.[30] (Economic distress had often converted many a master artisan into a mere wage-earner working for a merchant). Although this evidence admittedly relates to sectional wage movements, on the basis of plausible assumptions one can conclude that the downward drift of the wages of weavers reflected a persistent gap between the supply of and demand for hand-weaving labour.

There may have been some areas in India, such as much of the Deccan, which were partly protected against the erosion of the indigenous hand-weaving industry by: (a) their relative inaccessibility at the time when coarse cloth predominated in the Manchester exports and the indigenous handlooms producing coarse cloth would have been most vulnerable; (b) their relative lack of exportable products which would otherwise have created strong trade channels bearing cotton piece-goods up from the ports; and (c) their lack of 'westernization' which kept the upper classes also attached to Indian modes of clothing.[31] But such areas did not account for the major part of cloth consumption: in 1900–01, out of a total Indian consumption of about 2,830 million yards of cloth, net imports accounted for fully 1,875 million yards.[32] Easy communications seem to have been the greatest friend of foreign cloth—even in Kathiawar, which is associated with the survival of a strong mercantile conservatism, but is easily accessible from the sea. As early as 1842, Captain Le Grand Jacob, political agent of Kathiawar, wrote 'that the local arts and manufactures had been early annihilated by the united power of English capital and steam machinery'. The compiler of the *Gazetteer* (published 1884) continued: 'Since 1842 these forces have been still more actively at work'.[33]

Thus the fragmentary evidence does suggest the working of a general process of de-industrialization in India over much of the nineteenth century, caused mainly by the decline of the traditional cotton weaving and spinning but not confined to such decline. Pending further enquiry, it is useful to see whether this is a peculiarly Indian phenomenon or whether analogous experience is recorded in the history of other under-developed countries; and, if so, what lessons this would have for our understanding of the process of what Kuznets has called 'modern economic growth'.[34]

Technological Changes in the Nineteenth Century Viewed from the Underdeveloped Countries

Although it is now generally agreed that some of the 'backwash effects' (to use a phrase popularized by Gunnar Myrdal) of the industrialization of advanced capitalist countries may have retarded the industrialization of the underdeveloped countries of today, there is no general agreement either about the extent of this retardation or on the implications of such retardation for growth of incomes. Connected with such divergence of views (some of which are only vaguely articulated and are therefore difficult to pin down) about the interaction between advanced and underdeveloped countries, there are also disagreements about the nature of the development process. The conventional picture is best summarized in the Clark–Fisher scheme of the pattern of industrialization,[35] economic development proceeds from a situation where a very large part (say between 60 and 80 per cent or even more) of the population is dependent on agriculture towards a situation in which the agricultural population has fallen to, say, 20 per cent or even less of the total. There is now a general recognition that many underdeveloped countries may be in a situation where the perspective in the foreseeable future is only a very slow change or no change at all in the proportion of population dependent on agriculture.[36] But apart from economists of a radical or Marxist persuasion, very few investigators have been prepared to accept that the Industrial Revolution in the advanced capitalist countries may have meant systematic de-industrialization of large regions of the world, which may, in fact, account for the majority of the population of the underdeveloped countries and, very nearly the majority of the population of the world as a whole.

However, there does exist some work by economists and economic historians that points in this direction. Albert Feuerwerker has argued in a recent paper that in China between 1871–80 and 1901–10, while the output of handlooms increased, the yarn spun by handicraft methods drastically declined.[37] He estimates that while the increase in handloom output may have meant an increase of 200,000 man-years per year employed, the decline in yarn output meant a fall in employment by two million man-years per year.[38] In Burma, the Philippines, and Thailand rural industry also gave way on a large scale to production for exports—mainly of food—under the impact of colonialism and expanding world trade in the nineteenth century.[39] Egypt under Mohammed Ali presents a dramatic example of an attempt at industrialization through deliberate state patronage of industry and deliberate de-industrialization under the pressure of Western powers, particularly Britain, in forcing free trade on her. More generally, enforcement of the Anglo-Turkish Commercial Convention of 1838 led to a massive destruction of handicrafts throughout the Ottoman Empire, and the diversion of the employed population to agriculture. Of course, handicrafts in the Ottoman Empire had begun to suffer already under the impact of competition of European manufactures during and after the end of the Napoleonic Wars.[40]

Thus although the quantitative structure for the world as a whole is still to be built up, a long phase in the history of the major countries of Asia (excluding Japan, the USSR, or the Middle East) of a process of de-industrialization (as defined in the beginning of this paper) can be sketched in outline. This process was not compensated for by the simultaneous rise of modern manufacturing industry offering an equal amount of employment. The theoretical possibility of a fall in employment as a result of the introduction of more capital-intensive technology has been realized at least since the time of David Ricardo[41] and Hicks has revitalized this possibility through his recent writing.[42] But neither its global nature nor its possible significance in changing the development perspective of the underdeveloped countries of today has been even considered by the vast majority of economists.

To be more specific, I have argued elsewhere[43]—largely on the basis of the work on capital flows and international migration done by Kuznets, Thomas, Easterlin, Williamson, Deane and Cole, and Imlah—but partly also on the basis of some rough computations of the magnitude of the capital outflows from India over the nineteenth century—that in the century and a half before 1914, the movement of capital and labour was essentially a one-way traffic. Real capital moved mainly from the colonial or semi-colonial economies of India, Indonesia, China, and most economies of Africa and Latin America to the metropolitan countries of Europe and hence to the 'new' colonies, settled mainly by migrants from Europe, and European labour moved to take advantage of the economic opportunities opened up through the investment of capital in virgin (or, in areas populated by American Indians, not-so-virgin) land. The new technology enabled the European nations to use the new capital more fruitfully than the colonial and semi-colonial countries could have done. But the process of mopping-up of that capital destroyed many traditional technological complexes in the underdeveloped countries of today, without bringing in new industrial technologies on an adequate scale.

The mechanisms of transfer of surplus can be broken down into several components. There was firstly the straightforward political device, which took the form of charging to the colonies the 'costs' of conquering them and keeping them under subjugation. It also generally meant the exclusion of all 'natives' from the superior administrative posts. Then there was interest on the public debt floated by the colonial governments. Along with it went the profit made on public utilities financed by private capitalists. Then there were the profits made on the mines and processing industries and plantations selling their products mainly to the advanced capitalist countries. (The cultivation of opium in British India for sale to China was an exception). Finally there were the profits made on the sales of mass manufactures of the metropolitan countries to the colonies, which generally expanded simply by taking over new territories or displacing yet another branch of traditional manufacture. The 'expansion' of the market in the fast-growing European-settled areas and in the non-European colonies have very different meanings, and the problem of finding markets for manufactured products can be seen as only part of the problem of transferring surpluses from underdeveloped to advanced capitalist economies. Looking at the world economy as a whole, one can say that a significant part of the 'saving' (generally involuntary) of the colonies was invested overseas.[44]

Similarly, many economists just assume that the process of 'modernization' would take place along a smoothly curving frontier of production opportunities without any permanent loss to the invaded economies of the Third World. Even those economists who did not start with a neoclassical bias towards the assumption of continuous full employment and smooth transition to any new equalizers generated by changes in data, assumed that a surplus existed in the countries of the Third World which could be tapped without any loss to anybody and with, in fact, a tremendous gain to the indigenous people through the opening of these countries to the expanding trade drive of the Europeans.[45] It was not realized that the surplus had generally to be created by destroying the earlier economic structure, which often included a large amount of artisan production for the market, and that this destruction was not automatically compensated.

When the creation of markets overseas for the manufactures of Europe led to a contraction in employment and incomes of the artisans in the underdeveloped countries, the losses in employment suffered by the latter were not fully compensated by the gains made in the advanced countries either. The artisans in underdeveloped countries had been working with techniques which were much less mechanized than the techniques that came to be used in the advanced countries. So, arguing in a rough and ready fashion, if a given amount of investable resources had to be transferred from the underdeveloped to the advanced countries, then the gain in employment would be much smaller than the loss that led to the release of those resources in the first place. In fact, the purely technological unemployment (assuming the same level of effective demand in the situation before and after the change) was probably aggravated by a fall in total effective demand. This may well have lasted in underdeveloped countries such as India until the expansion of trade in primary commodities in the 1870s: even then, we must remember, the expansion was in quantities rather than in prices. The general problem of depression in prices of primary products was aggravated in the case of India and China by the demonetization of silver.

The above sketch is still a conjecture in parts; but it is still a concrete, and to my mind, plausible, alternative to the Panglossian syllogism which works as follows: It is *possible* to think of a sequence in which technological change in the advanced countries leads to a smooth transition in underdeveloped countries characterized by full employment throughout, but with the gradual adoption of superior techniques both in agriculture and industry, and an attendant shift of the working population towards agriculture (in order to exploit the new comparative advantage thrown up by the changes in the advanced capitalist countries) and therefore, this is what happened in the case of the underdeveloped countries.[46] In such a syllogism there is no place for such questions as, where did the capital for employing the workers in underdeveloped countries displaced by technological change come from? Who actually carried out the needed investment? How long did the adjustment process take? In the absence of a government with a fully fledged planning apparatus, who ensured that there was no unnecessary deflation of effective demand and that investment in the needed directions and quantities at the right times was carried out? But these are precisely the questions that must be raised both for understanding actual processes of history and for moving towards a socially acceptable solution of the employment problem in today's underdeveloped world.

It can easily be seen that we are suggesting that although Ricardo and Hicks have considered some aspects of technological change, they are not the aspects that interest us most. Among the economists of the nineteenth century, Marx was aware of both the effective demand and the labour reallocation aspects of technological change; furthermore, he explicitly mentioned the international repercussions of the introduction of modern machinery into industry.[47] It would, however, be easier for me here to try to bring out the differences between the Ricardo-Hicks framework and the problems I have in mind than to develop a fully articulated model of technological change for a group of interdependent economies along Marxian lines.

First, in the Ricardian case, the root of the problem is an increase in the degree of mechanization in the sense of a rise in the proportion of fixed to working capital (the latter is supposed to consist mainly of wages) and the failure of the rate of actual saving (=*ex ante* saving=investment) to rise sufficiently to compensate for the fall in employment in the consumer goods industries. In the case we have been considering, the problem arises because of technological changes occurring abroad and causing a drastic fall in the prices of the basic manufactures of the country. Whether the technical change occurring abroad also involves a rise in the degree of mechanization is not very important, except when we consider problems of the import of the more mechanized technology into the underdeveloped country.

Associated with the assumption that planned savings are invested and the problem is essentially one of inadequacy of saving rather than of incentive for investment, there is the assumption, in the Ricardo–Hicks model, that a fall in the incomes of the wage-earners in the consumer goods industry in the wake of technological change does not lead to any contraction in the market for consumer goods.[48] Whether this assumption was really valid in the case of the British home demand for British consumer goods, say around 1830, has not been, as far as I know, rigorously tested. Certainly, many of the economists of the utilitarian school—particularly those, of whom J.S. Mill was the outstanding example, who were influenced by E.G. Wakefield—thought that colonies served an extremely useful purpose in postponing the decline of profitability of investment and improving the working conditions and employment prospects of the British working class.[49] In any case, because of the simultaneous development of other modern industries (and railways) and because of the fact that cotton textiles never occupied the dominating position among the manufacturing industries of Britain that they did (together with silk textiles) among the traditional industries of India, the Ricardian assumption could be maintained as a first approximation without arousing total incredulity.[50] In the Indian case, a drastic decline in cotton manufactures could not be treated as a marginal change and since the decline of cotton manufactures involved interests other than those of the artisans (such as the local producers of raw cotton, and traders and merchants in cotton and cotton goods) the income effects of such a change cannot be ignored.

Finally, in the case of India and other Third World countries, the technological change could not simply be taken as a factor complicating a transition to a predetermined equilibrium, with the distribution of employment between different sectors remaining more or less unchanged in the new position. The Third World countries did not have any machine-making industry nor did their governments have any programme for developing such industries within the country. So no new skills or capacity in machine-making replaced the skills and the capacity for building the traditional capital goods. The merchant or trading class which might have gone in for investment in the new types of machinery and which might have exerted political pressure for changing government policy had either dwindled greatly in power or numbers as a result of the operations of the European rulers and traders (the East India Company and private European traders in India) or had not developed sufficiently at the time when these economies were exposed to penetration by European machine-made goods. (Ironically enough, the monopoly of trade organized by Mohammed Ali in Egypt had also the effect of thwarting the growth of a capitalist class; thus when de-industrialization came, no internal resistance was offered to the process). So there was not much pressure on the state apparatus to fill any gaps in information, coordination, or investment except in areas where the interests of European businessmen were directly or indirectly involved, and there was hardly any pressure to counteract or cushion the consequences of destruction of traditional handicrafts. In this situation, there was no obvious stopping point before the nearly complete elimination of major branches of traditional industries, and the new 'normal' pattern of activities of the economy came to acquire a completely different character. The absence of conscious action by the State also made the re-employment of the displaced workers a needlessly long-drawn-out process, and rendered the average income of a cultivator much lower and much more precarious than could be justified even on the basis of a crude doctrine of comparative advantage. I shall return to this point a little later.

Let me note here that even if the Ricardo–Hicks approach neglects the problems of effective demand and incentives, for, and agents of, necessary investment, it does have the advantage of making our attention rivet on what happens to employment as a *direct* result of technological change. This is in contrast with the usual neoclassical approach, which tends to ask much too refined questions before even the crude facts of the case have been established. For example, take the question of improvement in consumer 'welfare' as a result of cheapening of goods made by machines or by new techniques in general. Before such questions can be answered in the aggregate, surely some estimate must be formed of the total money income and the total employment level before and after the change. And that in its turn must involve questions of balance between output flows and expenditure flows, and over a longer period, the amount and the pattern of investment in the economy. Only after such broad questions have been answered can we ask questions involving the slope of the demand curve or the elasticity of demand for the commodity which has become cheaper as a result of technological change. In fact, as is well known, price elasticities are notoriously difficult to measure, even when some agreement has been reached about the specification of the model for estimating the demand functions. In the Indian case, for example, Meghnad Desai, after examining the usual *a priori* arguments about the elasticity of demand for cotton cloth in the nineteenth century in conjunction with the available data on cloth imports and their prices, concluded: '... it is difficult to say much about the elasticity of the demand curve for cotton cloth in India ... In fact, the elasticity of the demand curve is a function of the elasticity of the domestic supply curve and not the other way round'.[51] In a way, our argument centres precisely on the necessity of looking at the parameters other than price on which the demand curve depends and at the total balance of income and expenditure which determines the levels of demand curves for individuals. In other contexts, econometricians have noted the relative insignificance of price elasticities in comparison with total income (expenditure) in explaining demand for consumer goods.[52] If the analysis starts from the presupposition that cheapening of cotton cloth led to large increase in the *actual* real income of consumers in the Third World, then it really is begging the basic question. Even if *total* purchases of cloth could be shown to have gone up much more than the increase in population and income per head could account for, reasonable social welfare judgements would have to be based on judgements about changes in the distribution of incomes. There is considerable evidence that in India at least the poorer people stuck to the products of local handlooms much longer than the rich did. This evidence would have to be accommodated in any comprehensive explanation or judgement.

Apart from measurement of improvements in consumer welfare, neoclassical theorists (and others) are also likely to raise questions about increases in real income resulting from reallocation of resources in favour of agriculture. If the technological change occurring abroad leads to the shift of the artisans from the making of cotton goods to the production of agricultural commodities, will that not lead to an improvement in the productive capacity of the economy? Let us assume heroically that resources had earlier on been allocated so as to achieve roughly

Pareto-efficient distribution of economic activities (an assumption which is no more and no less absurd about India in 1815 than about India in 1855). Let us further assume that prices of agricultural goods do not change, there is no augmentation of the productive capital stock in agriculture either through investment or through technical progress, and that the quality of the new land opened up is on an average worse than that of the land already cultivated; then the physical output per head of the new cultivators will be lower than average. If an average artisan was as well off as an average cultivator before the change, then the position of an artisan newly employed in agriculture will deteriorate, except insofar as he gains through a cheapening of some of the consumer goods he buys. Since at that stage of development in India there were no intermediate industrial inputs into agriculture, there is no question of a gain through the cheapening of such inputs.

However, even with existing techniques the massive transfer of artisans from textiles to agriculture in India, say in the 1820s and 1830s, would require a massive investment effort. There was certainly no governmental planning for this at the time. What I suspect happened was that landlords were able to get the displaced artisans or new entrants into the labour force to clear land largely at the expense of their own work, and then use their control of rights over land to depress the effective earnings of the actual cultivators very greatly. By the time the export boom in agricultural commodities started in earnest as a result of the construction of railways and of the Suez Canal and expansion in world trade, much of the process of de-industrialization had already been completed. The Government of India began to invest massively in irrigation works only from the 1860s onwards. That investment too was largely localized in a part of northwestern India and a small part of southern India, and did not add substantially to the irrigated acreage per head of the cultivating population. Furthermore, there was little investment in research into new types of seeds, new techniques of cultivation, or in the spread of fertilizers. Actual shifts in production patterns on a large scale generally involve massive investment if such shifts are to actually improve the productive efficiency of the economy: the neoclassical parable of movements along a given production frontier obscures rather than illuminates the process by which transition is achieved.

For the particular tract of northern India for which I have analysed the occupational data at the beginning and the end of the nineteenth century, there is plenty of evidence that agriculture did not experience much public investment in the nineteenth century; that on the contrary, traditional systems of irrigation and drainage with decentralized control decayed as a result of the particular type of land tenure system introduced by the British, and that agricultural productivity *per acre* (and *a fortiori*, with an increase in the total population and in the population dependent on agriculture, *per cultivator*) tended to decline at least from the last part of the nineteenth century onwards.[53] There is also plenty of evidence that traditional handloom workers had to migrate to other parts of India, mostly to mines, plantations, and factory areas, in search of work.[54] But, of course, a secure judgement on welfare gains and losses cannot be passed without more intensive work on the facts of the case.

Conclusions and Implications for Development Theory

At the risk of some repetition I shall try to summarize my discussion and draw out the general relevance of nineteenth-century experience in the field of technical change and employment in the following paragraphs.

First, quite a part of the adjustments to technological change in the advanced capitalist countries took place overseas and, therefore, tended to remain hidden from the view of most economists. One major 'frontier' for both the digestion of the essentially labour-saving technological changes and the creation of markets for the industries using the new techniques was provided by the Third World countries.

Second, these processes and other market and non-market processes set into operation by formal and informal empires had the result of transferring investable surpluses from Third World countries to Western Europe and its offshoots overseas. This made the transition easier in Western Europe but much more difficult in underdeveloped countries.

The technological changes and other effects of colonial economic regimes in the Third World countries may or may not have led to contraction in the *potential* income and saving of these countries. But the absorption of the displaced workers in agriculture, in old industries with new techniques, or in new industries would have required massive investment; and there was neither a government nor a business class willing and able to carry out that investment. The neoclassical habit of picturing reallocation of resources after technological change as costless movements along the old production frontier or a new production frontier (for many underdeveloped countries the frontier stayed put where it was, because of lack of information or organization, except that a part of it simply became unviable owing to foreign competition) dies hard, and conceals this simple point. The physically massive irrigation works of Egypt and India have obscured the smallness of the total agricultural investment in relation to the incomes or the populations of the Third World countries as a group.

Furthermore, the processes we are concerned with may have set into operation certain changes in income distribution, which probably had opposite tendencies in the advanced and in the underdeveloped countries. Labour-saving technical change, under competitive conditions, or more generally, wherever workers' organizations are not strong, will tend to depress real wages of labour and depress the share of wages in value added. An increased degree of urbanization with an increase in the share of industries with below average share of wages in value-added might have the same effect. It has been recently argued that the condition of European workers was ameliorated through their migration to empty lands (this also had beneficial effects on the workers remaining at home).[55] In most Asian countries, there simply was not much land to colonize. Most of the migration of workers from India to other countries in the nineteenth century took place under the indenture system, and the wages of such workers remained very low. (It has been argued that such immigration in fact led to a worsening of the condition of free peasants in the Caribbean, and thus of the general distribution of income). Within India itself, when de-industrialization drove labourers to seek their living in agriculture, they faced a highly imperfect market, the most important complementary asset, land, being already concentrated in the hands of landlords (contrast the situation in the USA, Australia, or New Zealand). So it is very likely that whereas the distribution of incomes in advanced capitalist countries tended to grow better[56] in the Third World countries they tended to grow worse.[57] In addition to the effect of slow growth of incomes per head, the markets for mass consumer goods in the Third World countries thus tended to remain constricted because of the high degree of skewness of income distribution which may have got worse over time. We shall come back to this point later on.

This admittedly brief analysis has thrown up certain important types of asymmetry between the growth process in advanced capitalist countries and the process of change in the underdeveloped countries from about 1820 to 1914. What is more, these types of asymmetry appear to be interconnected. They may not be logically necessary in some ideal world of continually fully employed, efficiently functioning economies, adjusting instantaneously in an optimal fashion to changes in data. But they were strongly present in the only kind of capitalism we have so far known.

Those theories of development, which picture underdeveloped countries as evolving, like Leibnitz's monads, separately but very similarly to the advanced capitalist countries through some inner dynamics given by their constitution,[58] miss, among other things, the asymmetrical—if not downright antagonistic—nature of the interconnections between the developed and the underdeveloped countries before at least 1914 (and possibly continuing thereafter). They not only misinterpret the past but fail also to grasp the full implications of capitalist-style development in the underdeveloped countries today. To go over the ground covered from the point of view of immediate prospects, let us take some of the likely effects of a major labour-saving technological change on a typical underdeveloped country.

First, practically all the adjustment to such changes will be internal (unlike in the case of European countries in the nineteenth century): there are no colonies to which the people displaced from traditional occupations, including agriculture and handicrafts, can turn. In many of the underdeveloped countries the wages of labour have tended to remain stagnant even though average *per capita* incomes may have risen over the same period. In Argentina, for example, since the Second World War, after some rise in the late 1940s, real wages tended to remain surprisingly stagnant up to 1963 or 1964 and actually fell in the 1950s.[59] At the other end of the spectrum of underdevelopment, in India also, the stagnant or even falling trend of real wages of factory workers and the worsening and deterioration in the conditions of agricultural labourers in the 1960s have been brought out in numerous studies.[60]

A highly skewed initial distribution of incomes and a rising or unchanging degree of inequality of incomes create serious problems of narrowness of markets for both mass consumer goods and goods characterized by a high degree of static and dynamic economies of scale. Some of these problems have already been discussed in the context of underdeveloped countries such as Argentina and India.[61] Of course, as has been stated already, capital-intensive techniques are not the sole cause of unequal distribution of incomes. But they become a powerful supporting factor when the product composition is already geared to the needs of the upper income groups, who in turn derive too large a share of income because of the highly skewed distribution of ownership of productive assets and extreme degrees of imperfection in product markets and the markets for land, capital, and labour.

Second and much more directly, more mechanized techniques will tend to limit growth of employment in industry and agriculture. This is now generally considered an undesirable effect even apart from its impact on income distribution. Employment may, for example, be viewed as a positive good because of the dignity it confers on the employed person.[62] It has been observed, moreover, that in underdeveloped countries the existing measures of social insurance generally benefit the well-off and the already employed,[63] so that the only effective means of improving the position of the poor is to see that they find employment. On the other hand, in most underdeveloped countries, capitalist modes of distribution of incomes and accumulation, combined with a high rate of population growth, are leading to the creation of a reserve army of labour.[64]

It has been argued that the 'services' or 'informal' sector can and does take care of employment while production takes place in capital-intensive enterprises. But in the Third World countries, outside the organized sector, employment in services is very badly remunerated and is often not better than disguised unemployment. The prospect of likely technological changes in the market-oriented economies does not offer any comfort. A very large component of technological change that has taken place in the advanced economies has taken the form of innovations in products.[65] In the advanced capitalist countries, most of these have ultimately filtered down to the level of the very poor, but in the underdeveloped countries they remain the luxuries of the rich. The prospect in the future is the further expenditure of scarce resources including foreign exchange for the production or import of these luxury goods, creating very little additional employment, but generating a pattern of growth of incomes, such that output grows mainly to satisfy the requirements of the rich. When we turn to innovations in method the picture is no less gloomy. In the advanced capitalist countries, the rise in real wages has been a potent goad for more and more mechanized and relatively labour-saving innovations.[66] For a variety of reasons, very little endogenous technological change takes place in the underdeveloped countries.[67] The techniques they import come from the advanced capitalist countries and use more and more capital, whereas for creating more employment they need more labour-using innovations and products that generally do not involve a high degree of mechanization but cater to the needs of the poor people. The market does not seem to provide much of a link between the existence of cheap labour and the generation of labour-using techniques and products.

A development strategy for the underdeveloped countries taken as a group then ought to spell out how it would reverse the manifold antinomies of market-oriented development so far mentioned: the asymmetry between employment expansion in advanced countries and destruction of employment in the underdeveloped ones, the utilization of the surplus for colonization of empty lands and its removal from the populated regions of Asia and the Third World in general, the raising of the position of the lowest-income groups in the advanced economies, and the further worsening or at least lack of improvement, of income distribution in countries where agriculture is the predominant occupation and land is privately owned,[68] and finally, the creation of goods and techniques to suit capitalist affluence and their transmission to countries where they cater to the rich and further worsen the condition of the poor. It may be that some of these antinomies are less stark today than they were in the nineteenth century. But their presence in some form can hardly be conjured away. And any strategy that is proposed must show itself free from any of these antinomies at the moment of its conception.

Many commentators have referred to the Chinese experience as proof that a development strategy *can* be conceived on entirely different principles. Stress on the development of the countryside, stress on the use of any available surplus for the betterment of people employed in agriculture, refusal to produce luxury goods before necessities have been produced in abundance, the widespread use of techniques with deep roots in ordinary people's experience, the spread of social services so as not only to make them available to ordinary people but also controllable by them (witness the institution of 'barefoot' doctors) and the prevention of a high degree of inequality of income distribution by linking production and distribution as closely as possible—all these do suggest that a whole new programme with an inner consistency of its own is not only possible but is eminently practicable.[69]

Pondering on the difficulties and contradictions that underdeveloped countries must face if they follow an essentially market-oriented path (whether the particular strategy adopted along that path is that of import-substituting industrialization or that of export-oriented development of agriculture and manufactures), Professor Lefeber has called for a new 'paradigm' for economic development.[70] He has emphasized the success of China in organizing the rural manpower for development and in utilizing communes 'as an effective means for decentralized planning and for implementing broad social and economic policies'. By these means China 'could locally redistribute income and, at the same time, generate savings or food surpluses for maintaining labour engaged in rural capital formation'.[71]

It would be useful to enquire exactly which of the three groups of meaning that Kuhn attaches to the word 'paradigm' Professor Lefeber has in mind in this context. Is it a paradigm in the sense of an organizing principle, or a mode of perception in which old facts take on a new perspective? Or is it a paradigm in a sociological sense in that the scientific community has accepted it as a concrete scientific achievement? Or is it an artefact or a tool-box which gives us new tools for research?[72] It is perhaps most useful from a scientific point of view to adopt it as a paradigm in the first and third senses, for the character of the Chinese achievement is certainly not agreed to even by a majority of academic economists. Our enquiry neatly fits into the attempt to set before economists a new organizing principle for viewing future development, for we have tried to bring out certain characteristics of market-oriented development such as its effects on international capital transfers, on international transmission of technological unemployment, and on internationally disparate changes in the pattern of income distribution, which have tended to lie dormant so far.

The exploration of the corollaries of the adoption of the new paradigm has hardly begun yet. Can a Chinese-style development in one locality be grafted on to the market-oriented development for the nation as a whole? Is there a gradualist path from the unbalanced development of income distribution, product composition, and production techniques under market forces in less developed countries to a balanced development with an egalitarian distribution of incomes in widely, dispersed locations, healthy product composition, and techniques that utilize the full potential of human labour? A thorough-going Marxist might answer, 'No'. But a thorough-going Marxist has the duty to specify exactly what kinds of contradictions he expects if the paradigm is tried out partially and locally. After all, there was a path from the NEP to the first Five Year Plan of the Soviet Union, and in the Chinese case, the economic and social organization has certainly evolved through many phases, and if the perspective of Cultural Revolution is to be continued, this evolution has no end. Social scientists might yet have a role in exploring the various ways in which the different elements of the new paradigm would mesh together, in finding out what adaptations the paradigm would need in the context of different nations and in suggesting the evolution of the paradigm itself. They will also continue to have to analyse the results of the alternative paradigm of market-oriented development. But the exploration of the Chinese-style paradigm need not be a mere utopian quest. Prices and markets constitute the controlling panel for market-oriented economies. What instruments can a society choosing an egalitarian path of development use to carry out the functions that markets perform in capitalist economies? How does the society prevent any temporary maladjustment from creating tendencies towards cumulative inequality? What incentives can such a society provide for inducing relevant technological change? Such questions provide a crowded agenda for research. But I suspect that economists will have to use rather unfamiliar tools and resort to far more 'participant observation' with a far greater degree of commitment towards egalitarian social change than they have been used to in the past.[73]

Notes

1. The author is grateful to Tony Brewer, Pramit Chaudhuri, Barun De, Louis Lefeber, and in particular, to Prabhat Patnaik and Michael Lipton for their helpful comments. Any errors in the same remain the author's own.

2. Dutt (1963a[1906]: Chapters XIV–XV).

3. M.D. Morris presented aprioristic arguments to support the view that Indians had gained enormously from British rule in India (1963). This led to a debate between him and three other historians, Toru Matsui, Bipan Chandra, and Tapan Ray Chaudhuri, presented in *The Indian Economic and Social History Review* (1968: 319–88).

4. Thorner (1962).

5. Ibid.: 70.

6. Hicks (1969: 165).

7. For data on employment and wages in old and new branches of the textile industries of England, see Mantoux (1961: 432–4); Deane (1965: 156); and Hobsbawm (1968: 47, 73).

8. Joan Robinson defines the degree of mechanization in such a way that an admissible technique with a higher investment per man than before must produce larger output per man (otherwise, the technique would not have been admissible in the first place, on efficiency grounds). See Robinson (1956: 124–31). However, the more mechanized technique may also embody superior technical knowledge.

9. Sivasubramonian has estimated that even in 1900–01, the small-scale industries in India generated Rs 1,165 million of income, whereas manufacturing industries generated only Rs 220 million, and mining generated only Rs 53 million. See Sivasubramonian (1965: Table 4.19).

10. See Bagchi (1972a: 221–4), for a brief account of the spread of fly-shuttle looms in India until the beginning of the Second World War.

11. The methods and sources used to get these estimates from Buchanan Hamilton's surveys have been more extensively described in Bagchi (1976a: Sections II–V). Apart from published works of Buchanan Hamilton, the unpublished Statistical Tables, F. Buchanan (Hamilton), 1809–1813, Statistical Tables for Reports on Bhagalpur, Patna and Gaya (Bihar) Purnea and Shahabad, London: India Office Library, Mss. Eur. G. 14, 15, 17, 18, 19, and 20, were also used.

12. See Census, 1902, (Census 1901b) Part I, pp. 461–2, 466–9, and 477 on the methodology of occupational groupings and their limitations.

13. See, for example, Hunter (1877a); O'Malley (1906a). The other volumes used are listed in my paper in Bagchi (1976a).

14. The total number of persons dependent on cotton spinning and weaving, and so on, in the two modern districts of Bhagalpur and Monghyr (which accounted for practically the whole industrial population of the 'Bhagalpur' district of Buchanan Hamilton's survey) was 46,627 in 1901 as against 200,035 in Buchanan's time, even though the population was larger in 1901. So we should not go far wrong is assuming that the population dependent on this—the most important—branch of traditional industry in Gangetic Bihar had gone down by 150,000 between the two dates. The workers in the railway workshop formed only a part of the workers in 'railways' for which census figures are given: the total population dependent on railways altogether in 1901 was only 10,516. See Census 1902, (Census, 1901b) Table XV. This number was smaller even than the population dependent on the rump industry of cotton spinning and weaving in the Monghyr of 1901, which came to 23,493.

15. Sivasubramonian (1965: Table 4.2) gives the figure of 584,000 for employment in factories in 1900–01. An analysis of Blyn's figures for productivity changes in Greater Bengal reveals that for Bihar and Orissa alone, productivity per acre of food crops (mainly rice) must have gone down by more than a third between 1891–2 and 1945–6 and the total acreage also went down substantially in spite of a sizeable growth of population between the two dates. See Blyn (1966) and Bagchi (1972a: Chapter 4). This analysis is borne out by some later work done by M.M. Islam and Saugata Mukherji.

16. It is often assumed that an unlimited supply of labour automatically produces an infinitely elastic labour supply with no shifts over time. However, as the experience of many African countries demonstrates, the existence of a large 'reserve army of labour' is not incompatible with rising real wages. See Turner and Jackson (1970). Conversely, even in a situation of scarcity of labour, deliberate action can be taken by employers to keep wages depressed. The black labour market in South Africa is an extreme example of this situation (Wilson 1972). In the Indian case, there is definite evidence that on the one hand, European employers in mines, factories, and plantations were far more active in searching out new sources of labour than their Indian counterparts and that relative absence of trade union activity in European-dominated regions helped keep wages depressed compared with western India where India businessmen were the most dominant element. See Bagchi (1972a: Chapter 5) and the reference cited in it.

17. Sinha (1970: 4).

18. Ibid.

19. Sinha (1965: 178–9).

20. Mathias (1972: 260).

21. Hobsbawm (1968: 295, diagram 24).

22. See Information Regarding the Slackness of Demand for European Cotton Goods in Selections (1864).

23. Ibid.: 116.

24. See, for example, E.T. Atkinson (1874) and (1879).

25. See, 'Comparative Pressure on the Same Classes of society at Different Periods' in Geddes (1874: 389–92).

26. Geddes (1874: 391–2).

27. Bagchi (1972a: Table 7.5)

28. Ibid.: 220

29. E.T. Atkinson (1874: 633–4).

30. Bagchi (1972a: 221).

31. As far as the technological complexes represented by the Indian handlooms and the Manchester cotton mills are concerned, a phenomenon akin to 'reswitching' occurred over the period, say, 1790–1900. In the very beginning of this period, in spite of a tremendous improvement in spinning technology, the Manchester mills found it difficult to compete with the Indian handlooms on equal terms, particularly in the case of finer varieties of cloth. As is well known, discriminatory internal and external customs and sumptuary regulations were used by the British rulers, initially to protect the British-made cotton goods not only at home but also in India. Soon, however, the cotton mills proved more than a match for the handlooms of India even without any unfair tariff advantages. By the beginning of the twentieth century, again, Indian handlooms may have found themselves at a comparative advantage in respect of the coarser varieties of cloth. In this they were aided by several changes. First, the wages of the mill workers of Britain increased steadily whereas the wages of Indian handloom weavers reached an absolute rock-bottom; second, British cotton mills wove progressively finer varieties of cloth over time, exporting to India and other poor countries on an average coarser cloth; but by 1900, even their exports to India excluded the coarsest varieties, in which they had lost their competitiveness. These varieties would then be taken up by Indian handlooms, and cotton mills. As far as spinning is concerned, no reswitching occurred, and Indian handlooms were supplied by spinning mills in Britain or India. However, the Indian handlooms soon found themselves losing out to their new enemy, the Indian cotton mills.

32. Bagchi (1972a: Table 7.1).

33. *GBP* (1884a: 199).

34. Kuznets (1966).

35. Fisher (1935), (1939); *GBP* (1884a); Clark (1940).

36. Khusro (1962); Turner and Jackson (1970)

37. Feuerwerker (1970: 338–78); also see Feuerwerker (1968).

38. The reasons for the survival of handloom production seem to have been: a) genuine competitiveness with British imports (the dates may be important here: by the 1870s, the British producers were producing increasingly higher-quality cloth, and rising wages were pushing up the costs of coarser goods; b) adherence of both the upper and the lower income groups to traditional styles of clothing; and c) lack of development of transport. Comparing the Indian and Chinese cases, one feels that the railway system and xenophilia of the Indian upper classes (the poorer people stuck to the coarse but durable, indigenous cloth with remarkable stubbornness) may have been the decisive factors making for the downfall of the Indian handloom industry.

39. For references see, Resnick (1970).

40. Hershlag (1964).

41. Ricardo (1966).

42. Hicks (1969), (1971), and (1973).

43. Bagchi (1972b).

44. A dramatic modern analogy of the hiatus between the source of saving and location of investment can be found in the case of East and West Pakistan before the break-up of Pakistan.

45. See, for example, Myint (1958: 317–37).

46. Cf. Kalecki (1971: 147):

> 'The theory of Tugan-Baranovski is in fact very simple: the author maintains that with "appropriate proportions" of use made of national product the problem of effective demand does not arise. This argument, illustrated numerically by means of Marxian schemes of reproduction, is in fact tantamount to the statement that at any level of consumption of workers and capitalists the national product may be sold provided investment is sufficiently large ... Thus the fundamental idea of Tugan rests on an error that what *may* happen is actually happening, because he does not show at all why capitalists in the long-run are to invest to the extent which is necessary to contribute to full utilization of productive equipment'.

See also Robinson (1959).

47. Marx (1886[1867]: parts IV and VII).

48. cf. Beach (1971: 920).

49. Cf. Wakefield (1967); Mill (1967: 26–35); Semmel (1970: 77–92).

50. cf. Hicks (1971) .

51. M. Desai (1971: 359).

52. cf. Houthakker and Taylor (1966).

53. For a summary of productivity trends in Indian agriculture see Blyn (1966) and Bagchi (1972a: Chapter 4). We are assuming that the trends evident since 1891–2 could be extrapolated backwards, at least for one or two decades, in the case of Bihar. The assumption can be justified with harder historical data.

54. On the employment prospects of weavers and spinners, it is instructive to quote O'Malley (1906a: 159–60):

> ... if all the members of the Jolaha case had to depend on the produce of their looms, they would have disappeared long ago. Many of them have now forsaken their hereditary calling for more profitable occupations, and others who still work their looms eke out their slender earnings by agriculture and labour of various kinds. Every year large numbers of them seek service in the jute mills on the Hooghly or work as menials in Calcutta, and those that still ply the trade have seldom more than one loom at work at a time, whereas formerly the number was only limited by that of the members of the family who could work.

55. Lefeber (1974).

56. See Kuznets (1966: Chapter 4); Soltow (1965, 1968).

57. It is possible that the root of the problem posed by Emmanuel (1972), may lie in the process described here.

58. Rostow's theory of stages in Rostow (1960), is perhaps the most quixotic example of this genre.

59. Zuvekas (1966).

60. Bardhan (1970a), (1970b); Sau (1973: 26).

61. Felix (1968); Bagchi (1970).

62. Stewart and Streeten (1973).

63. Paukert (1968).

64. For a short survey of the unemployment problem in India see Sen (1973); for a summary of the easily available facts about unemployment in underdeveloped countries see Turnham (1970). Even a country such as Argentina, which cannot be considered 'overpopulated' by any standards, and where the average income per head has recently grown at a respectable rate, faces problems of increasing urban unemployment. See UN (1973).

65. Kennedy and Thirlwall (1972)

66. Among the notable studies of technological change in advanced capitalist countries are Rosenberg (1971); Saul (1970); and Schmookler (1966).

67. For a recent survey of the problems and prospects of technical change in underdeveloped countries, see *The Journal of Development Studies*, 1972.

68. The changes in the production pattern within agriculture in response to the expansion of world trade in the nineteenth century also often went against the interests of the poor people. Thus good land was diverted from the production of so-called inferior food grains to the raising of superior food grains and exportable crops precisely when the income of the poor people remained stagnant.

69. For a discussion of various aspects of choice of techniques and methods of industrial organization in China see Riskin (1969); for further discussions of technology and technical change in China see the articles by S. Ishikawa and G. Dean in *The Journal of Development Studies* (1972). The Chinese seem also to have succeeded in avoiding what has been termed the 'double development squeeze' on agriculture (Owen [1966]) that has characterized both the capitalist and the Soviet models of development of large-scale industry. They have been able, through the development of rural industries and a generally favourable rate of exchange between farm and industrial products, to plough back the benefits of industrial growth to peasants directly. Of course, the peasants have to contribute to the cost of maintenance of collective goods and of capital accumulation for the future, but the ratio of costs to benefits seems to be far more favourable for rural areas than has been the case in most countries that have achieved sustained economic growth in the past. The economy of North Vietnam also shares many of the characteristics of the Chinese style of development.

70. Lefeber (1974).

71. Ibid.: 176.

72. This classification is adopted from Masterman (1972: 65). See also the articles of P.K. Feyerabend, I. Lakatos, and T.S. Kuhn in the same volume.

73. Gurley (1971), is an early attempt to contrast capitalist and Chinese style development. It is interesting to contrast both Gurley's attitude and the Maoist attitude against that of Tobin (1973) who was baffled by what he considered an obvious lack of rationality in the refusal of the Chinese people to exploit the possibility of output-raising reallocation of resources between regions and sectors for the sake of local development or fighting the tendency towards inequality.

4

De-industrialization in Gangetic Bihar 1809–1901*

Buchanan Hamilton's Survey and Population Estimates

Under the order of the East India Company, Dr Francis Buchanan (later Buchanan Hamilton—we shall use BH to denote his name) surveyed a large part of Bihar and north Bengal over the years 1809–13, recording their population, their agricultural and mineral resources, giving details of flora and fauna, the means of livelihood of the people, and the land tenure systems, and going into the history of these regions. He packed an incredible amount of information in his survey reports. It may be objected that such a quick survey is not likely to be very accurate, in all its details.

But BH's methods were apparently very thorough. He covered most of the area by road, halting at the important marts and towns, and keeping notes all the while. As an authorized agent of the East India Company, he had the assistance of local officials. Besides he was accompanied by his own assistants who acted as interpreters. He kept elaborate journals of his travels, which are separate from his official reports, and we are thus acquainted with his methods of work. The journals 'are of the nature of official diaries kept by Buchanan, recording his movements from day today, with the distance travelled, the features of the country passed through the sites and objects of interest examined, the

*Reprinted from, B. De *et al.* 1976, *Essays in Honour of Professor S.C. Sarkar*, New Delhi: People's Publishing House. In the present version some portions have been removed. For complete text see the original version.

inquiries: made on subjects of archaeological, historical, ethnological, geological, etc. interest. The statistical information collected, e.g. as to population, castes, professions, numbers of towns and villages, education, soils and methods of cultivation, livestock, manufactures, exports and imports, etc., all of which are dealt with at length in the Reports and appendices thereto, is not referred to in the Journals. All this information was doubtless recorded by his Indian assistants; while the drawings and copies of inscriptions, and so on. were made by a draftsman who accompanied him.'[1]

Thus BH's survey was thorough enough for those days, and all economic historians and statisticians coming after him have used his data as benchmarks. Hunter's *Statistical Accounts of Bengal* always compared the current data with BH's whenever such a comparison could be made. R.C. Dutt used BH's evidence extensively in his volume on the *Economic History of India under Early British Rule.* Hence my use of the early nineteenth-century data will have the added advantage of establishing a link with the investigation of the stalwarts mentioned.[2]

Since I shall try to determine the proportions of the industrial population to the total population in the districts of Bihar surveyed by BH, it is necessary to say something about the quality of the population data given in his survey reports. BH's estimate of the total population for Patna and Gaya (or according to the nomenclature of the time, Patna and Behar), Bhagalpur, Purniya: (Purnea, Puraniya) comes to 9,707,620. There are no independent estimates of about the same date. But in 1822, in a 'census' of the Bengal population,[3] for roughly the same area (Bihar, Shahabad, and Patna in the Patna division and Bhagulpore and Purnea in the Moorshedabad division) the total population was found to be 4,595,120 (this 'census' was contained in the police report of Henry Shakespeare, superintendent of police in the lower provinces in 1822). Again, in 1824, a 'census' of houses of the lower provinces of Bengal was taken, and reproduced in Martin (1839).[4] Martin estimated the population by allowing five persons to a house; but from the detailed tables of family sizes given by BH we find the mean family size to be about six (this will be discussed later). Assuming that there was one family to a house on an average, and using six for the size of the family, the total population of about the same area as was surveyed by BH comes to 4,698,244. Since this figure tallies with the figure of 1822, it would appear that even assuming zero population growth between 1809–12 and 1822. BH overestimated the population by almost 100 per cent!

Further there is one district at least—Purnea—for which the *Statistical Account of Bengal* considered BH's estimate a gross overestimate.[5] However the reason given for such a judgement was no more than that, if BH's figure were correct, then the population would appear to have decreased between BH's survey year and 1872, which was thought to be improbable. Now Purnea was a singularly unhealthy district, where malaria was endemic. The local proverb was: '*Na zahar khao, na mahur khao. Marna hai to Purnia jao*'[6] ('Don't take poison. If you have to die, go to Purnea'). The population of Purnea increased very slowly from 1872 to 1891 and actually declined between 1891 and 1901. Thus *a priori* there is nothing outrageous in the suggestion that the population of Purnea may have declined or at most, increased very slowly between 1809–10 and 1872. Hence BH's estimate for Purnea might not be as gross an overestimate as Hunter and his assistants supposed.

For the other districts, actually, the *Statistical Account* tended to accept BH's estimates, with only minor reservations. In the case of Monghyr, it specifically mentioned that 'Dr Buchanan Hamilton's estimate was, at the time it was made, at least approximately correct.'[7] The volume for Patna, after discussing the faultiness of BH's method, had to admit: 'but the remarkable agreement between Dr Buchanan Hamilton's figures and those obtained in 1872, compels us to pay more weight to his estimate than to the other early enumerations, which have been proved to be very far from accurate.'[8] In the case of Gaya and Shahabad, the *Statistical Account* reproduced BH's estimates for relevant areas without any comment.[9] In the case of Bhagalpur, the *Statistical Account* comments: 'Viewed by the light of the recent census of 1872, his (i.e. BH's) own estimates made about 1811 possess statistical value, only on the assumption that since his day the population has more than doubled.'[10] The same volume however dismisses BH's estimate of the population of Rajmahal as useless, 'owing to the difficulty of identifying the area to which his return refers, and the doubtful evidence on which he bases his estimate of the numbers of the hill-men.'[11]

Thus the *Statistical Account* compilers did not consider BH's estimate always to err on the high side. If their judgement was correct, how do we then reconcile BH's estimate with the estimates of 1822 and 1824 (for the elimination of any excess in the estimate of the population of Purnea alone will not bring BH's figure down to their level)? A small part of the gap might be covered by including areas covered by BH's reports but not included in the districts of the lower provinces which we have taken. But this would still leave a large discrepancy. A possible answer is that we do not have to reconcile the two. For it is not BH who erred too much on the high side; it was the censuses of 1822 and 1824 which erred too much on the low side. The reason for the remarkable agreement of the two latter figures may be simply that they were based on similar, but erroneous, methods.

There are in fact some reasons, *a priori*, for considering the population estimates of 1822 and 1824 to be on the low side. The estimates of 1822 put the population of the lower provinces of Bengal at 37.5 million persons for Bengal, Bihar, and Orissa, the census of 1872 puts it at 64 million. The population of Bengal, Bihar, and Orissa in 1921 was 85.6 million.[12] Making deductions from the area of Bengal, Bihar, and Orissa in 1872 of areas (mostly hilly, sparsely populated districts or states in Orissa) not included in the lower provinces might be a little less than 60 million. The implicit total growth of the fifty-year period 1822–72 comes to about a little less than 60 per cent on a base of 37.5 million. On the other hand, the total growth in the forty-nine-year period 1872–1921 for Bengal, Bihar, and Orissa comes to 40 per cent. There is no good reason for expecting the rate of population growth to be higher in the earlier period. On the contrary, this was a period of extensive de-urbanization and, as we shall see, over a large part of the provinces at least, of de-industrialization.[13] The terrible Orissa famine which claimed several million lives occurred within this period. The population of Bengal had by 1822 fully recovered from the famine of 1770 and was apparently pressing against the margin of cultivation.[14] The period did not witness any great upsurge in peasant exports, which might support a teeming population at however low a level of living.

Although, until firm data are adduced, our hypotheses about the population of Bengal before 1872 must remain mere hunches, the following tableau seems to be consistent with the better known facts. The period from 1770 up to, say, the end of the 1780s was one of rather slow recovery from the famine because of continued oppression by revenue farmers, uncertainty about the whole land tenure system involving both the old zamindars and the peasants, and lack of any strong incentive on the part of large zamindars to have the margin of cultivation extended.

The population estimate by Colebrooke at 27 or 30 million around 1794 marks the end of this period.[15] Then followed a period of rapid growth of population when a strong incentive was given to the landlords to extend the margin of cultivation within the old system because of the peculiar provisions of the permanent settlement. We might take 1825 as marking the end of this period. The population of Bengal and Bihar might easily have increased during these twenty years by almost 50 per cent (from 30 million to somewhere near 45 million). Then came the final onslaught of the process of de-industrialization and the superimposition of an oppressive plantation agriculture (in the form of indigo, sugarcane, and opium cultivation by the European planters and the British government) on peasant agriculture, when the population grew slowly, from, say, 45 million in 1824 or 1825 to 60 million or so in 1872.

If we compare this tableau with BH's population estimates the latter appear to be distinctly on the high side. But the degree of exaggeration might not be as much as a straight comparison with the data of 1822 or 1824 might suggest; for (a) as we have argued, the totals in the latter have to be revised upwards and (b) the figures of the districts originally covered by BH may have been more grossly underestimated by the censuses of 1822 and 1824, because the areas happened to be remote from Calcutta, the headquarters of the reporting authorities. To the extent, however, that the total population was exaggerated by BH, the proportion of the industrial population (the figure for which was apparently more firmly based than that for total population) to the total, would seem to have been even larger in BH's time: than are indicated by our calculations.

Buchanan Hamilton's Estimates of the Population Dependent on Industry

For obtaining the number of people dependent on industry, I have relied on the detailed Tables of the numbers of common artists, supplemented by their description in the text of BH's reports, rather than on the numbers of 'artificers' or artisans in the general population Tables. These latter figures were obviously only approximate, and cannot be taken to be very precise. But BH took great pains to ascertain the numbers of artisans and traders in all the important towns. It was his procedure to directly enumerate the numbers of petty dealers, merchants, and artificers at every important town or large village he passed through, and put down these numbers under each thana in the 'Index to the Map' of each district.[16] Further, as regards the most important groups of artisans, that is, weavers and spinners in cotton (and silk), BH went to considerable trouble in getting their numbers right by comparing the results of direct enumeration with indirect estimates from figures of production, the district imports and exports of the output, and the material inputs.

There are major inconsistencies between the numbers of 'common artists' thus arrived at and the numbers of artificers given in the general population Tables. One important source of discrepancy was the fact that when it came to stratifying the general population, BH did not stick to an occupational grouping but shifted to a 'status' or 'class' categorization. His 'gentry' (or 'idlers', in, Montgomery Martin's evaluative terminology) must have included a vast number of spinning women who worked at home, and also owners of 'factories' (that is, manufactories) or other artisans who were regarded as 'gentle folk' by the enumerators. In view of this, it was decided to use only the detailed figures given in the Tables of common artists.

In order to arrive at the number of artisans proper, the figures for 'personal artists' (people who rendered personal service and did not produce commodities) were deducted from the total number of artists. Thus painters, dancers, barbers, singers, clowns, butchers, and others were all excluded. In general, shops were also excluded; but in some cases, for instance, 'distillers shops' in the case of the Patna-Gaya report, it was clear that the manufacturing establishment and the shop were one and the same and so their number was included.[17] There were some borderline cases in which it was not easy to decide whether to include their numbers or not. Many of the washermen, for example, worked as bleachers of cloth,[18] and were thus no less involved than weavers and spinners in the making of cloth. But in order to keep our estimate on the conservative side, the number of washermen was excluded altogether from the number of persons working in secondary industry. Again, in order to make our estimates comparable with those of the census of 1901, in which indigo factories were included under agriculture, we decided to omit indigo factories, although strictly speaking, the making of indigo from the plant is an industrial process.

Table 4.1 shows the total population, and the numbers engaged in spinning and in other industrial occupations, according to BH's survey, after the adjustments indicated in the preceding paragraph have been made.

Since spinners had generally lower earnings than other artisans and were often upper-caste women whose families did not depend solely on their earnings, we treated them differently from other artisans. In arriving at the total number of persons dependent on secondary industry, we made two alternative assumptions about the earning status

Table 4.1 Numbers of Population, Spinners and Industrial Workers Other Than Spinners, Buchanan's Survey Districts 1809–13

District	Total population	No. of spinners	No of industrial workers or artisans other than spinners
Patna-Gaya	3,364,420	330,396	65,031
Bhagalpur	2,019,900	168,975	23,403
Purniya	2,904,380	287,000	60,172
Shahabad	1,419,520	159,500*	25,557
Total	9,707,620	945,871	174,164

Source: Buchanan [BH] (1811–12), Vols I and II; and Martin (1838), Vols I, 2 and 3.
Note: BH does not include the number of spinners in the table of the number of common artists for Shahabad; the figure has been taken from the text.

of spinners, Assumption (a) was that an average spinner supported one other person besides himself or herself; assumption (b) was that every spinner supported himself or herself only.

Regarding the others, we assumed that an industrial worker supported an average-sized family. It might be argued that in a society where production was mostly carried on at home, this was unlikely to be true, since a worker would generally be assisted by other members of his family. This would not affect the validity of our estimates unless it could be shown that the numbers of these other members are already included in the total number of artists enumerated by BH. As far as weavers are concerned, BH enters only the numbers of their houses or their homes in the Tables for numbers of artists; similarly, in the case of the oil pressers, he enters only the numbers of their houses or mills in the statistical Tables.[19] The numbers of houses of weavers, or oilmen were smaller than the numbers of looms or mills respectively. In summarizing BH's tables, Montgomery Martin does not always reproduce the number of looms or mills, but he does reproduce the numbers of houses of weavers or oilmen.[20] For keeping our estimate on the low side, I used the numbers of *houses* of weavers and oil pressers for our calculations.

In the case of paper-makers also BH gives the numbers of their houses in the text and in the Tables.[21] In Shahabad there were kasis makers,[22] and every kasis furnace employed several adult persons, but we have included the number of furnaces alone. Again in the case of saltpetre manufacture in the Patna-Gaya district, instead of giving the number of persons engaged in saltpetre manufacture, BH gives only the number of 'furnaces for making nitre'.[23] Thus while our estimates are crude and contain an unknown margin of error, they are likely rather to err on the low side than otherwise.

The modal and mean family sizes in Purnea, Patna-Gaya, and Shahabad were computed from either the Bihar and Orissa Research Society reprints of the BH reports[24] or from Montgomery Martin's summaries and are given in Table 4.2. The relevant data for Bhagalpur were not available from these sources.

Table 4.2 Family Size in the Survey Districts of Buchanan 1809–13

	Mode	Mean*
Patna-Gaya	5	5.9
Purnea	6	6.8
Shahabad	5	6.5

Source: Same as Table 4.1.
Note: *The class limits were variable in the case of different size-classes of families. In computing the mean, the arithmetic mean of the class limits was taken for weighing the number of families belonging to a particular size-class. A geometric mean would in some respects be superior, but the variation of the geometric from the arithmetic mean is unlikely to be large.

We have taken a conservative estimate for the family size of artisans other than spinners and put it at five. Table 4.3 gives the estimates of the population dependent on industry, on the assumption (a) that every spinner supports one person besides himself (herself) and on the assumption (b) that every spinner supports only himself (herself).

Table 4.3 Industrial Population in Selected Bihar Districts around 1809–13

District	Absolute no. of the population dependent on industry		Percentages of the industrial to total population	
	Assumption (a)	Assumption (b)	Assumption (a)	Assumption (b)
Patna-Gaya	985,947	655,551	29.3	19.5
Bhagalpur	454,965	286,080	22.5	14.2
Purniya	874,860	587,860	30.1	20.2
Shahabad	446,775	287,285	31.5	20.2
Total	2,762,457	1,816,776	28.5	18.6

Source: Same as Table 4.1.

We now assess the effect of almost a century of British rule on the proportions of population engaged in secondary industry in the districts which were surveyed by BH. We chose Patna-Gaya, Shahabad, Monghyr, Bhagalpur, and Purnea because these districts were almost wholly included in the area surveyed by BH, and barring some thanas, practically all areas covered in the Patna-Gaya, Purnea, Bhagalpur, and Shahabad reports of BH are covered by the districts included for the 1901 calculations. (The Rajmahal area which was surveyed by BH in his Bhagalpur report was in 1901 included in the Santal Parganas, but since that district had very little secondary industry in 1901, our conclusions would not be upset by its omission).

We decided to deduct (a) the number of pure sellers from the number of makers, and makers and sellers, in class D, order VII, which gives the number of persons dependent on the provision of food, drink, and stimulants, and (b) the number of piece-goods dealers in class D, order XII. It would seem at first blush, in view of the caution sounded by Gait, that I have thereby underestimated the industrial population. But in the first place, I left the numbers in other classes within the general occupation of 'industry' intact, and thereby many pure sellers in other categories were included. Thus sellers of lime, chunam and shell, stationers, sellers of bangles of glass and of other materials, sellers of raw silk, silk cloth, braid, and thread, saltpetre sellers, and sellers of hides, horns, bristles, and bones are still included in the 'industrial' population. In the second place, many of the 'makers and sellers' must have been primarily sellers, and we could not make any adjustment for that; and in the third place, many of the actual cultivators still returned their caste occupations, which were non-agricultural, as their actual occupations, thus inflating the number by about a million, but with people such as these the traditional occupation dies hard and many of the so-called weavers are in reality mainly cultivators.[25]

Table 4.4 gives both the raw census figures and the adjusted figures of the population dependent on industry in 1901 for the Bihar districts that were covered by BH's survey.

A comparison of Tables 4.3 and 4.4 shows that even the more conservative estimate (by assumption b) of the proportion of industrial to total population in BH's time is considerably larger than the most inflated estimate (that is, the unadjusted census estimate) of the same magnitude in 1901. Taking the more conservative estimate of the proportion of the industrial to the total population around 1809–13 and comparing it with the more realistic (adjusted census) estimate of the same magnitude

Table 4.4 Population Dependent on Industry in 1901 in Selected Bihar Districts

District	Total population	Industrial population		Percentage of industrial to total population	
		Unadjusted	Adjusted	Unadjusted	Adjusted
Patna	1,624,985	279,093	179,695	17.1	11.1
Gaya	2,059,933	287,732	187,016	14.0	9.1
Shahabad	1,962,696	346,400	228,051	17.7	11.6
Monghyr	2,068,804	281,325	155,439	13.6	7.5
Bhagalpur	2,088,953	222,796	115,618	10.7	5.5
Purnea	1,874,794	220,506	121,933	11.8	6.5
Total	11,680,165	1,638,662	987,752	14.3	8.5

Source: Census of India, 1901, VI, VIA, VIB, *Bengal,* parts; I, II, and III (Calcutta, 1902).

in 1901 we find that the weight of industry in the livelihood pattern of the people was more than double at the earlier date. It has been claimed that the districts south of the Ganges in Bihar had a larger development of industry than those north of the river, because at the time of the dissolution of the Mughal empire, many Muslim nobles settled in these districts, bringing with them a large number of artisans and a basically urban pattern of living.[26] This might perhaps explain the surprisingly large development of industry in the districts surveyed by BH in his time (particularly if we remember that BH had underestimated the total population) but this does not account for their later decline. There is no reason to believe that the artisans dispersed to other neighbouring districts and set up their manufactures there. For we find that the unadjusted 1901 census figures showing the weight of industry in the total population in districts such as Saran, Champaran, Muzaffarpur, Darbhanga, and Santal Parganas was considerably lower than the corresponding figures for the districts covered by BH. It is possible that these north Bihar districts had been even more rural in BH's time, and their gain in industry through the dispersal of artisans from the south Bihar districts failed to bring them up to the level of the latter—but this appears to be highly unlikely in view of the orders of magnitude involved, the fact that Patna and Gaya are both included in the districts covered by BH, and finally, in view of our general understanding of the processes of agglomeration and deglomeration involved.

In the de-industrialization process, the destruction of the handloom industry played a considerable part. Table 4.5 shows the absolute numbers of cotton weavers, spinners, and the weight of the population dependent on weaving and spinning in the total industrial population (using assumption b in both cases).

Table 4.5 Industrial Population Dependent on Cotton Weaving and Spinning 1809–13

District	Number of weavers	Cotton spinners	Total number dependent on cotton weaving and spinning	Percentage of (3) to total industrial population
	1	2	3	4
Patna-Gaya	19,900	330,396	379,896	58.0
Shahabad	7,025	159,500	194,625	67.7
Purnea	13,555	287,000	354,775	60.3
Bhagalpur	6,212	168,975	200,035	69.9
Total	46,692	945,871	1,124,331	62.3

Source: Same as Table 4.1.
Note: Assumption b of Table 4.3 was used for estimating the population dependent on industry, and on cotton weaving and spinning.

Table 4.5 might give an exaggerated idea of the number of people engaged in cotton weaving and cotton spinning alone, for many of the spinners must have been engaged in spinning thread for silk, or mixed cotton-and-silk, cloth. But there is no way of separating them from the rest. It seems to be clear that about 60 per cent of the industrial population was engaged in the spinning of cotton yarn and weaving of cotton cloth.

Although the figures of Table 4.5 and Table 4.6 are not exactly comparable, it seems to be clear that both the absolute numbers of persons dependent on the cotton industry and the relative weight of the cotton industry in the secondary sector declined considerably. Thus the main factor behind the de-industrialization process *was* the decline of the handloom and hand-spinning industries, as it has been traditionally supposed. But it was not only the handloom industry that was involved in this cataclysm; many other traditional industries also suffered a catastrophic decline in their output and employment. This is borne out by the verbal descriptions contained in the *Statistical Accounts of Bengal* (relating to the 1870s) and the *Bengal District Gazeteers* (relating to the first decade of the twentieth century).

Table 4.6 Relative Weight of the Cotton Industry in the Total Industrial Population in Selected Bihar Districts, 1901

District	No. of persons dependent on spinning of cotton yarn and weaving, sizing etc. of cotton cloth 1	Percentage of (1) to total adjusted industrial population of 1901 2
Patna	22,318	12.4
Gaya	41,836	22.4
Shahabad	25,258	11.1
Monghyr	23,493	15.1
Bhagalpur	19,034	16.5
Purnea	16,777	13.8
Total	148,716	15.1

Source: Census of India, 1901, vol. VI A, *Bengal*; part II, *Tables* (Calcutta, 1902).
Note: The figures relate to class D, order XII, suborder 40 in the occupational Table.

The Evidence of the Statistical Accounts of Bengal and the *Bengal District Gazetteers*

The *Statistical Account* (*SA*, in brief) volume on Patna[27] records that up to 1835 the East India Company maintained a central factory for handloom cloth there. Besides there were large numbers of tussar silk weavers, and dyers who made a large profit from the dyeing of cloth. By 1877 all these industries had declined: 'the greater part of the cotton weavers (were) employed in making coarse cloths for country use'. The *District' Gazetteer* (*DG*, in brief) volume on Patna continues the same story of decline, but records that cotton weaving was still carried on to a small extent in nearly every village (this must be an exaggeration in view of the census figures) and more extensively in the Patna city: 'The chief article manufactured is a coarse cotton cloth called *motia* or *gazi* which is chiefly used by the poorer classes in the cold weather.'[28] Silk weaving was by then 'almost confined to the Bihar subdivision, where it (was) reported that about 200 looms (were) at work.'[29] (BH had estimated the number of looms for weaving silk and tussar at 1250.)

The story recorded by the *SA* and *DG* volumes on other districts is similar: finer varieties of cotton cloth had practically ceased to be woven, except when specially ordered; silk weaving had contracted considerably (it survived in Gaya to a large extent because of the demand for it for religious purposes). The weaving of coarse cloth survived, because it was durable and cheap. The common people must have been prepared to pay a higher price for certain varieties of coarse cloth than for similar imported varieties, because the greater durability and warmth of the former were believed to compensate for the higher price. For example, the *SA* volume on Shahabad records: 'country Cloth cannot be made for less than 3¾d to 4½d per yard, but Imported sells for 3¼d a yard, and consequently the home manufacture has fallen off.'[30] It is possible that the cost disadvantage of the home-made article increased even within the thirty-year period between the *SA* and *DG* volumes. The *DG* of Gaya records, for example: 'The preference, for *markin,* as the Manchester article is called, can be readily understood, as a piece of country-cloth costs Re 1–4 and will last 8 or 9 months, whereas a piece of *markin* of the same size will last only 6 months, but will be only half the price.'[31]

The decline of the handloom industry also naturally brought down the dyeing industry which had been in a flourishing condition in BH's time. It also led to an enormous contraction in the cultivation of cotton in Bihar. Certain specialized branches of the textile industry, such as satranji-making and carpet-weaving, survived, though none was in a flourishing state. The faint survival of the cotton cloth industry can be accounted for by mainly three factors: (a) the continued attachment of the poorer people to coarse cloth (called *gazi* or *motia* in Patna and Gaya and *photas* and *bukis* in Purnea); (b) the depression of weavers' wages to the level of those of unskilled labourers or even lower;[32] and (c) the taking up of weaving as a part-time occupation by persons or descendants of persons who had earlier been full-time weavers. Agriculture in the districts concerned was generally an extremely seasonal occupation, proper multiple cropping being very rare (the intensity of cropping may even have declined over time). Thus people with looms and with some inherited skills found it worthwhile—and sometimes necessary for survival—to turn from cultivation to weaving in the slack season of the agricultural year. Thus the *DG* of Gaya records: '... if all the members of the Jolaha caste had to depend on the produce of their looms, they would have disappeared long ago. Many of them have now forsaken the hereditary calling for more profitable occupations, and others who still work their looms eke out their slender earnings by agriculture and labour of various kinds. Every year large numbers of them seek service in the jute mills on the Hooghly or work as menials in Calcutta, and those that still ply the trade have seldom more than one loom at work at a time, whereas formerly the number was only limited by that of the members of the family who could work.'[33]

Thus the survival of the handloom industry is more an index of the poverty of agriculture to which the policies pursued by the British government pushed the weavers and of the generally low level of living of ordinary Indians than of any innate 'strength' of the handloom industry under conditions of capitalist colonialism. Furthermore, the mixing of different occupations which is often supposed to be the hallmark of traditional Indian society (cf. the remarks of various census commissioners) may merely have been the result of the de-industrialization process; the 'preindustrial' Indian society in many cases probably had more clearly defined and specialized occupations.

It was not only the handloom industry of Bihar which declined during the nineteenth century. There were other important industries which contracted to the point of extinction. Such, for example, was the paper industry of Gaya and Shahabad.[34] The refined sugar industry went through a cycle: it rose in the first half of the nineteenth century, it flourished in Shahabad particularly up to the 1870s and then went into a decline.[35] But again the making of *gur* or raw sugar, which was primarily a peasant manufacture, continued to be carried on an extensive scale: it may even have been stimulated by the introduction and popularization of a simple iron mill by Messrs Thomson and Mylne of Bihiya.[36] But the increasing imports of cheap sugar from Java and Mauritius must have set back this branch of the sugar industry also.

The de-industrialization process completely changed the character of certain districts. Purnea, for example, appears to have had a considerable variety of manufactures, based on the military and consumption needs of the Muslim nobles, when BH surveyed that district. Tent-making, the making of ornaments of lac, *bidri*ware, glasswork, the making of tooth-powder, the manufacture of *sindur,* blanket-weaving, not to speak of weaving of cotton cloth (and to a minor extent, of silk cloth), flourished in BH's time. By the time the *SA* came to be written, most of these industries had contracted considerably, and some had practically disappeared.[37] The *DG* of Purnea about thirty years later records the complete disappearance of paper-making, the virtual extinction of bidriware (with only one skilled practitioner in the art of finishing the product surviving). Hence it appears that most of the damage had already been done by the 1870s, but the process of destruction continued so long as there was any industry (other than the weaving of coarse textiles and making of some other articles of use by the poorer people) to destroy. It is possible that this residual destruction was more than made up by the growth of agriculture-based industries such as oil mills, but we cannot test that hypothesis without much finer analysis of the data.

We have so far listed mainly consumer goods industries. At the time of BH's survey there was a flourishing ironware and small arms industry in Monghyr.[38] In Hunter's time, the great variety of products produced earlier was already a memory.[39] But guns and pistols of an inferior quality continued to be manufactured. The requirement for licensing of gun manufacturers seems to have further crippled the industry later on. Thus what the lack of demand had begun was consummated by deliberate government interference.

Notes

1. *Journal of Francis Buchanan Kept during the Survey of the District of Bhagalpur in 1810–1811,* edited with notes and introduction by C.E.A.W. Oldham (Superintendent, Government Printing, Bihar and Orissa, Patna, 1930), pp. ii-iii ('Introduction').

2. These data were compiled from (a) Francis Buchanan (BH) 1811–12 (*c.* 1926); and (b) Martin (1838). The Bihar and Orissa Research Society reprinted three other volumes of BH's survey covering the Bihar districts, but they regrettably decided not to reproduce the tables which had been already printed or summarized by Montgomery Martin; and these included the tables of the number of 'common artists' prepared by BH.

3. See Bhattacharya and Bhattacharya (1963); 'Bengal Presidency Lower Provinces: 1822', 1832, U.K. House of Commons, *Appendices to the Third Report of the Select Committee of the House of Commons and the Minutes of Evidence on the affairs of the East India Company,* 17th February to 6th October 1831, London; reprinted in Bhattacharya and Bhattacharya (1963: 71–3).

4. Ibid.: 117–23.

5. Hunter (1877d: 241).

6. O'Malley (1911: 72). See also Hunter (1877d: 432–9.

7. Ibid.: 46.

8. Hunter (1877a: 32).

9. Hunter (1877b: 28 and 180).

10. Hunter (1877c: 45).

11. Ibid.: 273.

12. Census of India, 1921, vol. I, *India,* part 1. *Report* by J.T. Martin, vol. 24, Chapter 1, Calcutta.

13. Cf. Habib (1972).

14. See, for example, O'Malley (1907: 60).

15. See H.T. Colebrooke, *Remarks on the Husbandry and Internal Commerce of Bengal* (originally published, Calcutta, 1795), reprinted in Census of India 1951, vol. VI, *West Bengal, Sikkim and Chandernagore,* part IC,. Report by A. Mitra, 1953, Delhi.

16. See *Journal of Francis Buchanan (afterwards Hamilton) Kept during the Survey of the Districts of Patna and Gaya in 1811–1812,* edited with notes and introduction by V.H. Jackson, 1925, Patna, pp. xvi–xvii.

17. See, BH (1911–12: 630).

18. Ibid.: 616; BH (1939: 582).

19. See, for example, Buchanan, *An Account of the Districts of Bihar* as 782, and the number of their looms as 1622, and finally, the number of houses of oil-makers or *telis* as 5132 and the total number of oil mills as 5466, the number of houses of weavers who work in tussar silk as 782, and the number of their looms as 1622, and finally, the number of houses of weavers of cotton cloth as 19,900 and the number of their looms as 24,352.

20. See, for example, Martin (1838: vol II, Appendix of Statistical Tables, Book I, Bhagalpur, Table K), where the numbers of weavers who work in tussar and silk, and of weavers of cotton cloth were given as 1138 and 6212, respectively. From the text of BH (1810–11: 612 and 616), we learn that the number of tussar silk looms was 3275, the number of houses of weavers of cotton cloth was 6212, and their looms numbered 7279.

21. In Martin (1838: vol. I, p. 56 of the Statistical Tables) the number of paper-makers in Shahabad is given as 60. In the text of BH (1812–13: 398–9) we read: 'In Sahar opposite to Arwal, 60 beaters belonging to 40 houses were acknowledged; and 30 beaters in 20 houses are admitted to be in the Baraong division …'. This obviously shows that BH took the number of houses and not that of beaters, which was considerably larger.

22. See Martin (1838: vol. I, p. 56 of the Statistical Tables). Kasis was 'an impure sulphate of iron, used as medicine, and by tanners and calico printers. Each furnace had as managers two partners, who were bound to merchants by advances. See BH (1812–13: 416–18).

23. BH (1811–12: 773). Every furnace was apparently worked by a whole family.

24. Besides the Bihar–Patna (or Patna–Gaya), Shahabad, and Bhagalpur reports referred to earlier, there remains BH (1809).

25. See the Remarks of E.A. Gait, Superintendent of Census Operations, Bengal, in Census of India, 1901, vol. VI, *Bengal, Part I-Report*, 1902, Calcutta, p. 477. Cf also the remarks in (Ibid.: 470), in connection with artisan groups in general.

26. See, for example, O'Malley (1906b: 92).

27. Hunter (1877a: 137–46).

28. O'Malley (1907: 138–9).

29. Ibid.: 139.

30. Hunter (1877b: 260).

31. O'Malley (1906b: 159).

32. I have discussed this particular factor in the context of India as a whole in Bagchi (1972a: Chapter 7, section 7.1).

33. O'Malley (1906a: 159–60).

34. Hunter (1877b: 113–17 and 258–9); and O'Malley (1906b: 93).

35. See the references in the preceding footnote.

36. Hunter (1877b: 257–8).

37. Hunter (1877d: 354–60).
38. See BH (1810–11: 604–7).
39. Hunter (1877d: 137–42).

5

A Reply (to Dr Marika Vicziany)*[1]

Any serious argument about the degree of de-industrialization can be engaged in, in the particular context analysed in my papers only by admitting the possibility of comparison of data obtained from Buchanan Hamilton's (BH's)[2] survey and from the Census of India, 1901. The case or admission of such a possibility is unwittingly strengthened by Dr Vicziany. For, all that she says in criticism of BH's surveys is really said by the surveyor himself, who comes out as an extremely self-critical investigator. I should have thought that, if anything, this should inspire more, rather than less, confidence in BH's data. An attempted critique of BH's data must confront them with some independent contemporary evidence culled from different sources. This is what I tried to do as regards the population estimates of BH and Dr Vicziany has nowhere attempted to do so in her lengthy citations and paraphrases of BH's comments on his own difficulties.

When I said, by the way, 'As an authorized agent of the East India Company, he had the assistance of local officials',[3] there was no implication that every official *loved* him. And Dr Vicziany has now shown that many of the 'volunteers' for the census work of 1901 were conscripts and were not very fond of their officially imposed chores either. The arguments Dr Vicziany puts forward to suggest that BH was not a free agent or that the local people, officials, and ruling families 'feared the political consequences of any further intervention by the East India Company in local affairs',[4] I must politely decline to consider as being

*Reprinted from, 1979, *Indian Economic and Social History Review*, 16(2), April–June, pp. 144–62. In the present version some portions have been removed. For complete text see the original version.

seriously meant. The reason for Dr Vicziany's suggestion that BH might not have been a fully free agent was that the choice of his exact route was often influenced by the advice of his guides or of local people. If freedom is impaired by listening to the advice of guides or local people who have some knowledge of local conditions and topography, then every research worker in the field is an unfree agent. And with the East India Company entrenched in the Bihar districts for more than forty years, to suggest that any kind of serious 'political consequences' of further intervention by the Company could have occurred consciously as an additional threat to the local people is also far-fetched. A natural suspicion of any white-skinned man acting as an official enquirer would be adequate explanation for not everybody courting that enquirer's company.

Apart from the alleged unreliability of the BH data, the other major (and more fundamental) reason which might have been advanced for refusing to admit the comparability of BH's survey results with the data of the Census of 1901 as regards occupational distribution could have been that, in basic respects, the degree or quality of differentiation as between occupations was seriously changed in the concerned districts between the time of BH's survey and the Census of 1901. The doctrine of the lack of social division of labour in British India is rather fashionable in certain circles. As far as major handicraft industries such as cotton or silk weaving or associated processes were concerned, however, there is plenty of evidence that many weavers or dyers or bleachers in India, at least from the seventeenth century onwards, were full-time workers.[5] Buchanan Hamilton's chapters on the 'artists' contain detailed discussions of the earnings of various classes of artisans whose full-time occupation was the pursuit of particular professions. In the earlier periods as in BH's time, when for some reason it was not possible for the artisans to pursue their usual occupation, they would adopt some other means of livelihood. Agriculture, being the occupation of the largest number of people, and promising some approach to subsistence in difficult times, was then naturally embraced by the artisans for want of anything else. Such desertion of traditional occupations in times of economic difficulty does not bespeak the lack of a clear social division of labour but the contrary. I have argued that in fact, it was the destruction of handicrafts under British rule which resulted in the mingling of different occupations, so that if anything, professions were *more* undifferentiated at the end of the nineteenth century than in the beginning.

Once we have established comparability of the data gathered by BH's survey and those of the Census of India, 1901, the only question that remains for some serious discussion is that of the position of spinners, who occupy such an important place among the ranks of artisans and the probable limits of the proportion of population at the two dates.[6]

Before I take this question up, it is necessary to clear up a point about the proper criterion to use to measure the degree of de-industrialization or industrialization. While I found that the proportion of population dependent on secondary industry in the six Bihar districts declined between 1809–13 and 1901 and argued that de-industrialization occurred in those districts, I used *this* information in conjunction with another criterion—that the *proportion* of income generated by secondary industry to total income also declined. As far as the Bihar districts are concerned, the second inference is direct, seeing that there is no evidence of an increase in productivity in secondary industry, while the numbers engaged declined both relatively and absolutely. For India as a whole I have argued[7] the available evidence suggests a process of de-industrialization according to the two-fold criterion used above. So whether an increase in the proportion of national income generated by secondary industry alone is a suitable criterion of industrialization is irrelevant for our debate.[8] For a number of reasons I need not go into here, I would regard such a criterion as particularly opaque in understanding the issues of economic development in Third World countries. I am, therefore, glad to find that Dr Vicziany endorses changes in the proportion of the population engaged in secondary industry as the more basic criterion for judging whether de-industrialization occurred or not.[9]

We turn now to the question of 'dependence' on secondary industry (or agriculture or trade for that matter). By drawing our attention to the limitations of the data thrown up by the BH survey, Dr Vicziany has, paradoxically enough, called into question the meaningfulness of the census definition of occupation of a person: the instructions for the Census of 1901 laid down: 'Column 9 (*Principal occupation of actual workers*). Enter the principal occupation or means of livelihood of all persons who actually do work or carry on business, whether personally or by means of servants, or who live on private property such as house rent, pension, etc.'[10]

It will be noticed that no income or time criterion is provided for determining 'the principal occupation or means of livelihood', either absolutely or relatively. That is to say, it depends on the respondent's subjective assessment (on a particular day) of what his principal means of livelihood is as against his subsidiary occupation. There is no implication that the principal means of livelihood actually provided a subsistence, or that it occupied the worker full-time. There is no implication even that the principal means of livelihood along with the subsidiary occupation either provided a subsistence or anything like full employment. If anybody argues that surely the worker must have gained a subsistence, since he and his family survived, he is unaware of the vast literature on people living continually below the poverty line and continuing to survive (the price is often paid in terms of shorter stature, thinner bones, and lower levels of intelligence, since children's growth is particularly affected by malnutrition). Furthermore, vast numbers of people in India and among them, vast numbers of artisans, had been dying in famines in the forty years preceding the Census of 1901.

If we now turn our attention to the data thrown up by BH's surveys, there is no difficulty in identifying spinning as the principal means of livelihood or principal occupation of the spinners. Since the work of a housewife is not recognized as an 'occupation' either in BH's survey or in the Census of 1901 (or in modern censuses for that matter), spinning is the only recognizable means of livelihood with a commercial value that the spinners had. It is true that not all the spinners in BH's surveys worked full-time. But did the 86,020 persons (male and female) working in cotton (Class D, Order XII, Sub-order 40, in Census 1901c) in the six Bihar districts really work full-time in the occupations of weaving, sizing, spinning, and so on in 1901? Moreover, BH records in various places that many spinners worked full-time at their occupation.[11] (Ironically enough, Dr Vicziany is more severe on the BH data than on the data of Census 1901, precisely because BH provides a lot more information on the earnings and degree of employment of the workers of various categories than the census does).

Abstracting from the problem of whether the earnings of spinners in BH's time can be regarded as 'normal' or should be regarded as already showing the signs of a process of decline of the handicrafts, particularly textiles, let us compare the spinners' earnings with say, the earnings of farm labourers or ploughmen.

In Purnea, for example, an average spinner earned Rs 10 2/5 per month.[12] In the same district, a ploughman who was hired by the month or the season, was supposed to make over the year Rs 4½ in money wages, Rs 1½ in the form of food or grain allowances and another Rs 4¾ at harvest time.[13] Thus altogether he made Rs 10¾ a year, only about 30 per cent more than an average spinner. Buchanan Hamilton accepts a norm of Rs 24 for maintenance of a ploughman's family, attributes a considerable earning to the ploughman's wife, and still ends up with a deficit of Rs 3¾. For a labourer on daily hire, he estimates an earning of Rs 12 and for his wife also he estimates the same earning. However, these must be overestimates because BH stated that these labourers were 'usually extremely necessitous', and were often bonded to the indigo works for months in advance.

Seeing that the spinner earns two thirds of the wages of ploughmen or daily labourers and that spinning is a sedentary occupation which requires considerably less calories for maintenance than ploughing or field labour, our assumption that spinners support themselves is not so unreasonable after all. Even if the spinners earned one-third the amount of an able-bodied person engaged in hard labour, to take spinners as self-maintaining would not be unreasonable. The standard of living of neither the spinners nor of many of the other artisans might have been ample, but that was the usual lot of artisans in an extremely unequal society ruled by alien rulers.

Buchanan Hamilton took up expenditure norms for the maintenance of families and found again and again that not only farm labourers or ploughmen but also artisans such as weavers often failed to earn a subsistence. Then he sometimes brought in other factors, more or less arbitrarily, so as to balance their budget. But, as I have already noted, living below a subsistence level was probably the lot of a large number of workers, including spinners. Moreover, in order to regard the spinners as dependent on spinning, it is not necessary to show that their earnings from spinning alone could have supported them fully (here my original phrasing is probably open to question). It is only necessary to show that earnings from spinning were the main cash income they had, and they were an essential supplement to the family incomes. Moreover, the artisans' occupations were the repositories of the skill in traditional industry. Hence counting the possessors of such skills as integral numbers, which indicated the industrial potential of the society of the time, is the only natural procedure under the circumstances.

There is no logical compulsion, therefore, not to regard the spinners as dependent on their spinning. But there is probably an element of double counting in the original estimate of artisans in the Bihar districts in my papers. I should have deducted the number of weavers' houses from the total number of spinners, assuming that every weaver's home housed at least one spinner. But as against that, as I pointed out, there were many cases where the number of other artisans was underestimated. However, if I had to re-estimate the percentage of population dependent on secondary industry (including construction as in the case of the census data), I would bring down the populations by 25 per cent, reduce the numbers of spinners by equal percentages, and deduct from that number the number of weavers' houses or weavers (where the estimated number of weavers' houses is not available) and add to that the number obtained by multiplying the total number of artisans other than spinners by the average number of members in a family.[14] In the case of spinners, I follow the assumption of BH that the number was roughly related to the total population. But if we take the exports from these districts to others in the same region, to other parts of India and abroad as given, reducing the estimated number of spinners in population to the estimated population might lead to an underestimation of the number of spinners.[15] The revised estimates of the population dependent on secondary industry in the four districts surveyed by BH are given in Table 5.1.

Table 5.1 Estimated Population and Population Dependent on Secondary Industry in Gangetic Bihar, 1809–19

	Estimated total population (1)	Population dependent on secondary industry (2)	Percentage of (2) to (1) (3)
Patna-Gaya	2,533,315	552,257	21.8
Bhagalpur	1,514,925	234,383	15.5
Purnea	2,178,285	505,865	23.2
Shahabad	1,064,640	238,763	22.4
Total	7,291,165	1,531,268	21.0

Sources: BH (1809–10, 1810–11, 1811–12, and 1812–13).

As I pointed out earlier, I also reclassified the census population of 1901 with occupations in class D so as to make it conform more closely to the concept of secondary industry (including construction). I included all categories where some processing was involved, but excluded pure sellers (except in one or two cases where it seemed probable that many of the sellers were also processing the goods sold and where no category of sellers as such was listed by the census). None of the categories excluded here has been included in the calculation of industrial population from BH's survey. I verified by direct computation that the population supported by industry as given in Subsidiary Table II of Chapter 12 in Census 1901b, is indeed obtained by summing up the figures for the suborders included in class D. The groups excluded are 76, 79–80, 99A,

101, 104–05, 123–4, 128, 130, 132, 134, 149, 182, 209, 211, 261, 289, 304, 323, 329, 337, 358, 360, 366, 389, and 390.[16] But firewood, charcoal, and cowdung sellers (group 150), lime, chunam and shell sellers (group 158) are included. So are cow and buffalo keepers and milk and butter sellers (group 78) and ghee preparers and sellers (group 82).

The logic of inclusion of these categories is that some processing seemed to be involved in selling these commodities and no separate categories of makers or makers and sellers are given. The exclusion of milk and butter sellers and ghee preparers and sellers from the data of the Census of 1901 and correspondingly, of Dahiyar Goyalas, or preparers of milk and butter from the BH survey data would make a much larger proportionate and absolute difference to the population dependent on industry in 1901 than on the population dependent on industry in 1809–13. With these comments, I present in Table 5.2 a slightly revised estimate of the population dependent on secondary industry in 1901.

Table 5.2 Total Population and Population Dependent on Secondary Industry (Including Construction) in 1901 in Six Bihar Districts

District	Total population (1)	Population dependent on industry (2)	Percentage of (2) to (1) (3)
Patna	1,624,985	197,758	12.2
Gaya	2,059,933	211,489	10.3
Shahabad	1,962,696	268,879	13.7
Monghyr	2,068,804	183,817	8.9
Bhagalpur	2,088,953	232,199	11.1
Purnea	1,874,794	137,330	7.3
Total	11,680,165	1,231,472	10.5

Sources: Same as Table 5.1.

While this is as close as we can probably get to an estimate of the population dependent on secondary industry on the basis of the data of the Census of 1901, we should heed the warnings scattered in various places of the census report[17] that many so-called artisans listed by the census were really agriculturalists. Moreover, there is a specific warning about such inflation of the figures of artisans—in particular weavers—in Orissa and south Bihar.[18] And in the census classification of natural divisions, south Bihar consists of the districts of Patna, Gaya, Shahabad, and Monghyr! (It is strange that with all her detailed scrutiny of the census report, Dr Vicziany should have overlooked this very specific warning!)

If we compare Tables 5.1 and 5.2 now, we notice that the population dependent on secondary industry as a percentage of total population, even according to the revised estimates, was exactly halved between 1809–13 and 1901. I do not want to claim that these figures are sacrosanct in any sense. Slightly different assumptions might produce different figures. But on any reasonable assumption applied impartially to the BH figures and to the figures of Census 1901, a conclusion supporting a massive decline in the population dependent on secondary industry between the two dates is inescapable.

Notes

1. This was written as a reply to Vicziany (1979b: 105–43).
2. Francis Buchanan, later Buchanan Hamilton, i.e., BH.
3. Bagchi (1976a: 502).
4. Vicziany (1979b: 9).
5. See, for example, K.N. Chaudhuri (1978: Chapter 11).
6. Professor Nirmal Chandra had pointed out the problem of the treatment of spinners soon after my papers were published.
7. Bagchi (1976b: 141–6).
8. There is not enough space for dealing with the question as to whether Thorner's or Dr J. Krishnamurty's methods for analysing the census data give a proper picture of the post-1881 changes in occupational structure and employment. For a critique of their methods and a conclusion considerably different from theirs see Chattopadhyay, 1975.
9. Vicziany (1979b: fn 2).
10. Census, 1901a, *Census of India, 1901.* vol. I. *India,* Part I, *Report* by H.H. Risley and E.A. Gait, 1903, p. 185.
11. See, for example, BH (1809–10: 537); BH (1810–11: 607–08); BH (1811–12: 647–8).
12. BH (1809–10), p. 537.
13. Ibid.: 444.
14. The footnote added by Dr Vicziany in order to challenge the multiplication of the number of artisans by the average size of a family assumes that in every case the number of actual workers was counted. But we know that in the case of looms, for example, more than one worker worked on one loom (BH [1811–12*:* 652]), and the number of weavers' houses in turn fell short of the number of looms. And we have taken only the numbers of weavers' houses wherever these numbers are given. Similar comments apply to kasis workers, iron smelters, and others. Finally, it is to be noted that the average size of a family has been conservatively estimated.
15. Dr Vicziany tries to show that exports of textile products were more important than I had implied. However, she omits to mention that the major part of exports of all the regions was to the neighbouring districts or other parts of India. From Shahabad, for example, only about Rs 30,000 worth of cotton cloth was consigned to the Company's factory in Patna, part of the total textile exports of Rs 2,09,000

(BH [1812–13: 425] and Vicziany [1979a: Appendix Table I]). From Patna-Gaya, out of total exports of more than Rs 545,000, the Company took about Rs 200,000 worth (BH [1811–12: 677]). As regards Purnea, where 'exports' apparently are so important (Vicziany 1979b: Appendix Table I), BH comments: 'The only external commerce which this country possesses, is with the territories of Gorkha or Nepal' (BH [1809–10: 573]). Then he estimates the *total* exports to Nepal at only Rs 71,000. What all these figures and the detailed discussions of BH prove is that there was a flourishing interdistrict trade in all kinds of commodities—cotton yarn, cloth and carpets, silk yarn and silk cloth, woollen blankets, paper, dyes, salts, and so on. As in an industrially active region, one district might export one variety of cloth to a neighbouring district, importing another variety from the other. Such trade did not impoverish the home market but enriched it.

16. Census, 1901c, vol. VIA. *The Lower Provinces of Bengal and their Feudatories,* Part II, The Imperial Tables, 1902, Table XV, Part B.

17. cf. Census 1901b, vol. VI. *Bengal,* Part I, *Report, 1902,* p. 470 and p. 472.

18. Ibid.: 1972.

6

Relation of Agriculture to Industry in the Context of South Asia*[1]

The relative positions of the South Asian economy and the world economy, of the Indian capitalist classes to the capitalist classes of advanced countries, and of the various strata of the South Asian societies have altered very significantly between, say, 1793 and today. In discussing the possibilities open to the various countries, and to the various classes in society, it is forgotten that it is often the relative strength of the economy or of the class in relation to the other economies of the world, and of the classes under consideration in relation to the other classes of the same society or to the class formations in other societies that is more important than the absolute size of these economies or classes. For example, the domination of the pattern of world trade by Britain in, say, 1851 (the year of the Crystal Palace exhibition) was made possible because Britain was the only industrialized country of the world. By the same token, once other capitalist economies had been set on the path of industrialization, the relative position of Britain was bound to decline, and furthermore, no other country was ever again to achieve the same degree of dominance in the network of world trade and payments. In the nineteenth century, first Great Britain and then the economies of Western Europe and the Overseas European offshoots (the USA, Canada, Australia, and New Zealand) industrialized partly by exploiting and expanding their own home markets but partly also by turning their formal and informal colonies into markets for their

*Reprinted from, 1975, *Frontier* (Calcutta), 8(22–4), pp. 12–27. In the present version some portions have been removed. For complete text see the original version.

manufactures and into sources of raw materials and cheap labour.[2] This pattern of development cannot be repeated, at least on the same scale, by the Third World countries, because they have few colonies in this sense. Again, the nineteenth century growth pattern is often held up as an ideal one from another point of view: it involved little inflationary pressure for the world as a whole. However, inflationary pressures were kept in check in the nineteenth century (a) because the working class in the advanced capitalist countries was not yet strong enough to erect rigid inflationary barriers against depression of their real wages, (b) because capitalist development in the colonies (including South Asia) was suppressed by colonialism and so the capitalist strata in the colonies could not compete for resources, and (c) because the pre-capitalist elements could be ruthlessly coerced, when necessary, by the colonial powers if they dared to oppose the expropriation of resources and labour by the rulers.

The 1960s

If we shift our attention to the 1960s, we can see that the situation has changed radically in this respect. The advanced capitalist countries are involved in a situation of inflationary recession. The rates of accumulation in some pace-setting countries like Japan and western Germany have been far higher after the Second World War than before and the other capitalist countries have also had to step up their rates of accumulation. This has, however, aggravated the inflationary pressures in the countries partly because of the successful struggle of the working class to defend their standards of living but also partly because of the markup pricing policies pursued by monopolistic and oligopolistic sellers. Furthermore, the advanced capitalist countries have to face competition from capitalist classes of the Third World for scarce resources. On the obverse side of this, the capitalist classes of the Third World cannot step up their rates of accumulation without running into inflationary, and balance of payments, difficulties, because among other things, they have to reckon with the formidable influence exerted on the world economy by the advanced capitalist classes. Moreover, since by the very nature of their development and their fear of the peasantry and the proletariat of their own countries in the epoch of the socialist revolution, the capitalist classes of the Third World have to adjust to the demands of the property-owning strata in control of sectors characterized by pre-capitalist relations; the resistance of the latter against a rapid rate of transfer of resources to capitalist accumulation aggravates the difficulties of the capitalist classes of the Third World. Furthermore, dependent as the capitalist classes of the Third World are on the advanced capitalist classes, they are unable to fully take advantage of any recession in the advanced capitalist countries: for (a) their exports are often crucially dependent on the fortunes of the capitalist countries, and (b) they lack an independent entrepreneurial and technical base for fully utilizing the resources that the advanced capitalist countries release. The contrast between the rates of accumulation attained in the 1930s by the USSR and Japan on the one hand and by countries like Argentina, Brazil, or India on the other is illuminating from this point of view.

These admittedly crude propositions will illustrate the importance of continually placing the relations between industry and agriculture in Third World countries, including India, Pakistan, and Bangladesh, in their scale, in relation to other capitalist countries, and assessing how they have evolved not only through their own dynamics but through the dynamics and dialectics of the evolution of capital and its successor, socialism.

Two Ways

There are at least two ways in which the evolution of agriculture-industry relations can be described, and their import for current developments assessed. The first line of enquiry would be to look at the change in the relative importance of agriculture or industry in the structure of occupations and in the structure of incomes. The second is to trace the evolution of the different types of production relations since the time of British conquest until today. We do not yet have full accounts of either of these two developments. But we do have some idea of how they have changed. In the next section, I summarize some of the evidence relating to the change in the structure of income and of occupations in India.

Changes in the Structure of Incomes and Occupations

Indian nationalists had complained for a long time that British rule had led to the de-industrialization of India. On the other side it had been claimed that while under the impact of 'one way free trade' in India, handicrafts had been destroyed, modern industries had grown up to take their place, and no de-industrialization had occurred.

Capitalist industrialization up to the phase of maturity is attended by at least three types of changes: (a) an increase in the proportion of the population engaged in secondary industry, (b) a sustained increase in per capita income and (c) a continual rise in the degree of mechanization in industry—and to a lesser extent perhaps, in agriculture. The reversal of any of these conditions over a long period of time can be characterized as de-industrialization. India experienced the reversal of the first two conditions from probably 1820 up to 1914.[3] We do not have detailed and reliable national income estimates before 1900: but some idea can be formed of the change in the proportion of population engaged in industry in the beginning and at the end of the period. This proportion would definitely indicate a decline. This decline was not offset by growth of employment or income in large-scale industries on a requisite scale. From 1900–01 onwards, we have the estimates of Sivasubramonian relating to national income and its composition, and the estimates of the Thorners, Kalra, and Krishnamurthy relating to occupational distribution. According to Sivasubramonian's estimate, the manufacturing output at constant (1938–9) prices for undivided India was Rs 387 million in 1900–01 and Rs 803 million in 1914–15 respectively, whereas the total secondary sector output was Rs 1,638 million and Rs 2,448 million in 1900–01 and 1914–15 respectively.[4] While Sivasubramonian's estimates of income from large-scale manufacturing and mining are based on reasonably firm data, his estimate of small-scale industry output is based on guesses supported by fragmentary evidence. In fact, the qualitative evidence we have contradicts the large increase (by Rs 394 million) between the two dates. Even accepting Sivasubramonian's estimate, the share of the secondary sector in national income at current prices was virtually stagnant between 1900–01 and 1914–15.[5] Since growth in modern manufacturing was substantial only from the last quarter of the nineteenth century onwards, whereas output of small-scale industry may well have been declining even between 1870 and 1900, this would indicate that in the period before 1900, the share of the secondary sector in national income would on balance have been declining.

The picture in respect of changes in occupational distribution is quite clear: there was a decline in the share of the secondary sector in the working force almost continuously from 1901 to 1931; the trend changed probably from the middle of the 1920s onwards, and there was a marginal increase in the proportion of the working force engaged in industry between 1931 and 1951 and between 1951 and 1961. Even in 1961 the proportion was no higher than what it was in 1901.[6]

In India as a whole, as we remarked earlier, the decline in the share of the secondary sector in employment was probably halted in the 1920s and a marginal rise in this share took place between 1931 and 1951, and under the stimulus of more active state patronage, the rise continued from 1951 to 1965. But after 1966 again the process of rise was halted and the share has at best remained stagnant since 1966. The only State of the subcontinent in which the share of the industrial sector in both national income and employment has gone up is Pakistan (former West Pakistan).[7] On the other side of the subcontinent, Bangladesh (former East Pakistan) witnessed a decline in the already low share of industry in the labour force between 1951 and 1961; the share probably went up in the 1960s, but very probably declined again. The share of industry in the total output may have increased in the 1950s and 1960s but it seems to have registered a decline again very recently.[8] It is interesting that the regional disparity in respect of the share of the industry in national income and employment predates the independence of the subcontinent. In 1931, East Bengal (which, with the addition of Sylhet formed East Pakistan in 1947) had 4.1 male workers in industry for every 100 male workers.[9] Punjab, on the other hand, in 1931 had the highest ratio of the occupied labour force engaged in industry (primarily small scale and cottage industries). However, the disparity between West Pakistan and East Pakistan was certainly aggravated by the following factors among others, (a) a much higher rate of public investment in West Pakistan than in East Pakistan, (b) the development of a capitalist class from among the immigrant communities investing heavily in West Pakistan which they came to regard as their homeland, (c) the more rapid development of agriculture in West Pakistan on the basis of the earlier stock of capital (in the form of irrigation works) built up under British rule and new large-scale investment by the State in agriculture, and (d) partly as a result of the operation of the earlier three factors and partly as a result of the creation of a common customs area in the two wings of Pakistan, a net transfer of resources from East to West Pakistan.

Bangladesh

Bangladesh exhibits, almost in a pure form, the results of the colonial capitalist mode of exploitation, which leaves its permanent mark on the structure of the economy and society and on the quantum and character of productive investment. Hence we shall spend a little more time on discussing the country's situation.

In undivided India and in India after independence, the share of the tertiary sector increased almost continuously. Most of the decline in the share of agriculture has been accounted for by expansion in the share of trade, commerce, banking, and services.[10] In Pakistan also, the tertiary sector has tended to expand over time at the cost of agriculture, even though industry also has expanded. The extreme is, however, reached in the case of Bangladesh where the share of the tertiary sector in GDP expanded from 44.7 per cent in 1969–70 to 48.9 per cent in 1972–3 at the cost of both industry and agriculture.[11]

South Asia is not peculiar among Third World countries in recording a faster rate of expansion of the tertiary sector than that of national income or total national employment. A full explanation for this phenomenon is, however, yet to be provided. Explanations in terms of a growing threat of unemployment or urbanization without adequate expansion of productive employment are not fully satisfactory, and in any case, do not explain much. Not only low-income employment but also high-income employment in the organized tertiary sector in India has expanded faster than total productive employment.[12]

The explanation, I believe, has to be sought in the mode of extraction of the surplus in South Asia and its utilization. To be more specific, before 1947 and particularly before 1914, most of the economy was geared towards the extraction of an exportable surplus; within this economy, however, eastern and northeastern (and to some extent southern) India was the part which was subjected to the most intense exploitation by the colonial power. Naturally, no major indigenous capitalist strata geared to the exploitation of the home market developed in this region. The colonial exploitation was made possible by the preservation or even creation of many pre-capitalist relations, particularly in rural areas. When an Indian capitalist class then took over from the British, it simply inherited the old colonial mode of exploitation based on trade, usury, and the export of primary products or crudely processed manufactures. This class had not developed on the basis of exploitation of home industry, as happened, for example, in western India. So when after independence, the home market was fully protected it found it difficult (because it would have been financially costly for it) to switch over to manufacturing on a large scale. On top of that, there were all the difficulties that a retarded capitalist class faced (such as the inability to generate innovations or borrow innovations cheaply, the inability to meet the resource needs for increasing degrees of economies of scale and for adapting to rapid changes in techniques and products) in embodying its profits in productive investment. So if a surplus occurred through the older methods of exploitation, and it could not be exported on the old scale because of a difference in the ethnic roots of the capitalists and because of changes in world market conditions, it took the shape of expansion of unproductive consumption. The latter took four main forms: increased consumption of luxury goods (insofar as they were produced at home, this would have some expansionary effect on industrial employment), increased employment of retainers in various guises, increased provision of 'jobs for the boys' (and girls) in unproductive sectors, and increased expenditure for the defence services.

In Bangladesh all these factors acted most intensely. Practically no indigenous capitalist class had developed, the State apparatus was primarily controlled by the West Pakistani ruling classes, most of the public investment was devoted to West Pakistan, and no major changes in class relations took place after independence: the removal of the Hindu zamindars did not lead to the freeing of agriculture from pre-capitalist relations. The observed rate of saving in an economy under dependent capitalism is almost always lower than the potential saving because of the severe constraints on investment. Taking the actual saving rate, we find that East Pakistani internal saving financed practically all of its domestic investment, whereas there was a large gap between the investment and saving rates in West Pakistan.[13] When Bangladesh became independent, while the new ruling classes inherited the surplus extracting mechanism, no new capitalist class automatically emerged to invest the surplus productively, nor of course, was there a party of the proletariat to reorient the economy. Naturally, the tendency was to utilize the surplus for the purpose of expanding the unproductive sector.

I have used Bangladesh to show in a dramatic form many of the tendencies at work in the whole subcontinent. As things are developing, the stagnation of the economy of eastern India may also be explained in terms of the inheritance of a colonial pattern of exploitation by a retarded capitalist class unable to develop industries on the basis of a home market, and given to export of capital to other regions and other countries when difficulties are faced in the home base.

I do not want to give the impression that political decolonization did not change anything. It did lead to the strengthening of the indigenous capitalist classes, a more purposive intervention of the state to develop the economy and the capitalist class, and an increase in the effective rate of accumulation in the economy. This is true of all the three States of the subcontinent. However, all these developments were not sufficient to free the growth of the economy from the constraints of a bastard social system whose most dynamic element—the capitalist class—is in a state of dependence on the world capitalist system.

Changes in Production Relations

Production relations in industry and agriculture in South Asia have been shaped both by the pre-British structure of relations and by the changes brought about under British rule. It will not be possible here to describe even schematically the evolution of all the forms prevalent in urban and rural areas. Instead, I shall present an extremely summary view of certain aspects of productive relations in agriculture, with only sketchy citations of evidence. The aspects we shall touch are the structure of the village and the relations between landlords and the agricultural labourers.

I have deliberately left the structure of landownership as such out of account. The researches of historians such as B.R. Grover, Irfan Habib, and Nurul Hasan, and of N.K. Sinha, lead to the conclusion that private property in land definitely predated British rule, but that the sale and purchase of land were limited both by the relative immobility of capital in an essentially non-capitalist economy and by various customary restrictions.[14] The British tried to introduce a more thorough-going private property in land, increase the revenue exacted by the State and at the same time minimize the cost of collection. Despite help from the work of an economy geared more and more to the working of the international market, the three objectives were often conflicting; this conflict was generally resolved by making the land revenue objectives paramount (subject to a minimum degree of stability of collection) and allowing private property rights of the actual cultivator to be quite overridden by the rights of intermediate level rent-collectors. There were very great regional differences in the structure of rights of superior right-holders, owing to differences in pre-British forms of land-ownership and to differences in the date of conquest of the territories by the British, but this is not the place to discuss them. From our point of view, perhaps the most important common denominator of all the changes was that the actual cultivator-tenant or the agricultural labourer was reduced to the subsistence level or below, and that the retarded industrialization process preserved the superior right holders in every region as a pure rantier class.

Layers of Control

How the efforts of the British to build up bourgeois property relations in land led to strange results and had mostly the effect of increasing the weight and the number of the pure rentiers can be illustrated with the case of eastern India. In eastern India after the decennial settlement (1790) and, more particularly, after the Permanent Settlement of

1793, several layers of control over land developed between the cultivator and the state. First, there was the zamindar who paid land revenue directly into the government treasury. He was generally called the *malik* or proprietor even though he might alienate the actual ownership of land to other intermediaries. The malik might lease out the land to somebody else 'in consideration of a money advance or mortgage on loan, for example, the *mukarari*, which was a lease from the malik at a fixed rental, after the payment of an installation fee called *nozarana*. This lease was either permanent, in which case it, was called *istimari* or *barfarzandan* (from generation to generation) or it was only granted for the life of the lease-holder, in which case it was called *hinhiyati*. In addition to the nozarana, the lease-holder had sometimes to pay an advance (*zar-i-peshgi*) as security for the payment of the rent. *Dar mukarari* is an exactly similar lease to the above, granted by the *mukararidar* to a third.'[15] Such a chain might be continued almost indefinitely until the actual cultivator is reached. The sub-lease might be of a temporary nature, in which case the term used was *thika*. There might be variations in the actual number and forms of sub-tenures from locality to locality, but both the chain of intermediary tenures and the difficulty of ascertaining the position about the actual ownership or control of the land would be constant.

First of all, there was a steady, legally recognized, process of subdivision of proprietary, that is, zamindari holdings going on from the time of the Permanent Settlement until the beginning of the twentieth century, and probably even later. In Gaya, for example, 'in 1789 the demand of land revenue ... was Rs 10,41,700, payable by 744 estates with 1,160 proprietors ...'[16] This district, which was formerly known as Bihar, lost a considerable part of its area to Patna, Palamau, and Monghyr before 1870. In the much smaller district of 1870–1, 'the total demand of land revenue was Rs 13,80,320, payable by 4,411 estates owned by 20,453 proprietors. In 1881–2 the current demand had risen to Rs 14,36,900 payable by 5,614 estates and 59,172 proprietors, and in 1900–01 to Rs 14,80,700 due from 7,514 estates owned by 72,404 proprietors. The average payment from each estate has thus fallen during the three decades ending in that year from Rs 313 to Rs 256 and Rs 197, and the payment from each proprietor from Rs 67–8 to Rs 24–4, and finally to Rs 20–8.'[17]

There were the results of legally registered partitions. 'Apart, moreover, from the partitions recognized by Government, private partition had gone to extreme lengths. In North Monghyr, for instance, (for which alone accurate statistics are available) though the total number of estates according to the Collector's registers, is 4,367, the Settlement Officers had to frame 9,730 separate records of proprietary interests. Also it was found that 901 estates had been privately partitioned into no less that 5,899 *patti*s or shares for each of which a separate sub-record had to be prepared.'[18] The smallest recorded subdivision of proprietary rights in the same district was

$$\frac{1}{2{,}480{,}000{,}000} \text{ of an anna or}$$

$$\frac{1}{39{,}680{,}000{,}000}$$

Most of the so-called proprietary interests had been alienated, but some of it had been brought under the maliks' control by other means. 'Out of the total area occupied by landlords in Monghyr, only 619 acres have been recorded as *zirat* or proprietor's private lands. Under *kâmat*, which is the term ordinarily used in this area instead of zirat, are locally included all lands in the landlord's cultivating possession, as well as lands which, though settled with tenants, have at any time been bought in by the landlord at sales of ryoti holdings for arrears of rent. Nearly 5 percent of the total number of tenancies, covering 10 percent of the occupied area, were recorded as *bakasht malik*, that is to say, as in the cultivating possession of the proprietor, but not proprietor's land.'[19] It can be easily seen that in this situation, it is very difficult to interpret data about so-called patterns of land ownership or land transfers before 1947 without detailed local information. There was the initial problem of deciding who was the actual owner of the land; then there was the problem of matching records with persons. A man might hold land in several different villages or districts. There was no method of figuring out how much land a particular person owned or controlled. This problem persisted in the post-independence period, and this was one of the rocks on which land reform measures came to grief.

Zamindars had legally been given almost unlimited powers by two laws passed in 1799 and 1812. Some of these powers were revoked by the laws of 1859 and 1885. But, as I shall have occasion to remark again, the benefits of the legal restrictions on the powers of zamindars were reaped mostly by occupancy ryots who were in a substantial fraction of the case not the cultivators of land at all. As it was, in spite of the sub-division of the 'proprietary estates' there continued to remain very large zamindaris in eastern India, and in spite of the legal restrictions, zamindars continued to oppress tenants almost with impunity. The District Magistrate of Bhagalpur district, for example, reported for the years 1907–08:

> Babu Rash Bihari Mandal (a big zamindar) not only forced all his tenants to accept the former cash rent which was 20 to 33 per cent in excess of what the survey fixed, but actually secured in addition in many villages a half share in 2 *cottahs* in every bigha, the produce of the bigha for the purpose of levying his rent being fixed at 12 maunds. The Maharaja of Sonbarsa similarly threw all the demands the settlement had cut down into "miscellaneous", and forced the tenants to accept them. I mention these names only, but I fear that many landlords not mentioned are in a similar category. The system worked was first to get back practically all rent receipts the tenants had, then to levy rent without giving receipts, then to demand the illegal high rate of rent, and if a man refuses, to sue him for four years' rental and use the decree as a threat to force him to accept.[20]

The total confusion in the field of land relations was perpetuated both by the processes of de-industrialization and by a legal machinery which would regulate the relations at the village level by remote control methods. Redress against 'injustice' defined within that system was extremely costly for a common man, who was often ignorant of his supposed 'rights'.[21] This latter aspect of the system persisted after independence. The Indian legal system obdurately refused to confer sole rights only on the cultivator and all attempts at land reforms aiming to give the land to the holder of the plough were successfully defeated.[22] But that is, of course, expected in a retarded capitalist economy dependent on the support of pre-capitalist holders of power.

Village Community

When we come to the structure of the village economy and society, we have an enormous amount of evidence pointing to a great deal of occupational and social differentiation among the rural people. The archetypal model is that of the village community; in its purest form, with little contact with the outside world except for payment of taxes: it certainly did not operate in the area where settled agriculture rather than pastoralism, hunting or shifting cultivation was the primary source of livelihood. But in an attenuated form, in which definite groups of artisans or other functionaries (generally organized into castes) served the village as a whole and received customary rewards, it may have operated in some parts of India up to, say, the early nineteenth century.[23]

Jajmani System

At the same time, it was observed, with much greater frequency, many villages operating the *jajmani* system: 'Briefly, the jajmani system is a system of distribution in Indian villages whereby high-caste land owing families called jajmans, are provided services and products by various lower castes such as carpenters, potters, blacksmiths, water carriers, sweepers and laundryman.'[24] Here every serving caste had its circle of *jajmans* or clients (who were really their patrons) and this circle generally did not include the village as a whole. The jajmani system was not confined to Hindus. In Bihar, for example, 'The exclusive right to employment by the people in the circle constituting a man's britis so well established, that it is regarded as hereditable property, and with Muhammadans, is often granted as dower.'[25] The jajmani system was to be found all over the country; however, in Bengal proper it is supposed to have decayed pretty completely by the beginning of the twentieth century, if it was ever strong there. The changes brought about by British rule led to the loosening of traditional, customary ties, but because of the massive process of de-industrialization and population growth, there was also a shrinkage of employment opportunities in relation to the people seeking employment. These contradictory tendencies, along with certain political changes, determined the speed with which the jajmani system decayed.

The relations between agricultural labourers and landlords have sometimes been sought to be fitted into the general scheme of the jajmani system. I think that such a specialization is in general inadmissible. There was widespread agrestic slavery, or rather serfdom, particularly in southern India, at the advent of British rule, and it survived legally until the Slavery Abolition Law, Act V, 1843.[26] Such a legal abolition can have had but a marginal effect within the short term, for the means of enforcing the law or making the relevant information available to the slaves or serfs were quite limited. Furthermore, because of the insecurity of the agricultural labourers and their dependence on loans from the masters, agrarian bondage survived on a large scale throughout India and persists even today. The British government itself largely nullified even the legal effects of the formal abolition of slavery by enacting a Workmen's Breach of Contract Act in 1859, and later on, enacting legislation that gave masters the right of arrest of absconding servants. This was done mainly in the interest of British tea planters in Assam. As is well known, Indian labourers were also indentured and transported to Mauritius, Fiji, Guyana, Jamaica, Trinidad, and Natal.

Thus pre-capitalist relations as such did not hinder labour mobility; they merely intensified the exploitation of labour.

In a recent study of the *hali* system in south Gujarat, Jan Breman has traced the disintegration of the formal system of tying of specified groups of labourers to specified families of masters (*dhaniamos*).[27] This has been attributed to the lessening of the need for bondage with the growth of the population of agricultural labourers, the change in the cropping system from labour-intensive crops to crops requiring less labour. But Breman places the greatest importance on the renewed growth of cities or towns like Surat, Navsari, and Baroda; this accords well with our emphasis on changes in the structure of occupations as strongly influencing production relations. However, with the emergence if a surplus population in agriculture, labour could not really be free: insecure labourers now entered into relations of random and casual bondage with landlords, the degree and duration of bondage varying from case to case. But in a situation in which traditional crafts vanished and employment in new industries did not expand and fast enough, agricultural labourers became just a residual, catch-all category. Hence it is illegitimate, apart from prior existence of agrestic bondage on a wide scale, to fit the master-attached servant relationship into the traditional jajmani framework.[28]

The relations between landlords and tenants under colonialism were also variegated. 'Tenants' were often superior right-holders and much of the movement for tenancy reform boiled down to a struggle of the nominal owners, leaving the real cultivator where he was. Share-cropping was prevalent on a wide scale in the late eighteenth and nineteenth centuries, and according to Colebrooke's estimate in 1794, sharecroppers were worse off than agricultural labourers and they often migrated from one district to another.[29] Instead of the so-called 'commercialization' of agriculture under British rule leading to the displacement of kind rents by cash rents, the next movement may well have been in the other direction. This movement has not been studied in sufficient detail yet. As far as Bihar in eastern India is concerned, the following factors seem to have been responsible for the prevalence and in some cases, growth, of the practice of leasing land for a share (generally 50 per cent) of the produce:

1. The indigenous system of irrigation on the basis of temporary embankments required the construction and maintenance of these works by large landowners; unless the landowners had an interest in the

exact size of the crop they would allow the system to decay. Hence a system of produce rents was necessary to keep their incentive alive.[30]

2. With closing of the opportunities of lucrative employment in the civil and military departments of the foreign governments and growth of population, a number of small landlords often came back to the villages where they owned land, and leased out land on a produce-rent basis, even for growing valuable crops such as tobacco and chillies.
3. The idea was generally prevalent, and it was also factually true, that 'occupancy rights do not accrue in lands held on produce rents'.[31] Since there were no records of rights of ordinary cultivators in the Permanent Settlement areas, it was easy to deprive the actual cultivator of even his legal rights generation after generation.
4. The tenancy reforms in Bengal—in the form of the Rent Act of 1859 and Tenancy Act of 1885—may well have paradoxically depressed the position of the actual cultivators and reduced many of them to the status of share-croppers.

Through these reforms many of the intermediary right holders managed to get themselves registered as occupancy tenants, and many landlords also became legally recognized as permanent tenants of the land for which they hand only collected the land revenue. The actual cultivators, who had very restricted access to a highly centralized legal machinery, were left out in the cold and had to accept the status of share-croppers.

Our discussion will already have indicated how difficult it is, before independence, to talk about a uniform growth of capitalist relations in Indian agriculture. Most European 'capitalist' planters (including the government as the cultivator of opium) used non-market coercion to exploit the labourers and the peasantry. When the cultivation of a plantation crop, say, indigo, became unprofitable many of them became zamindars in the Indian style; many (in fact, most) sugar factories found that it was more costly to cultivate sugar on their own on large-scale 'scientific' methods than to rent the land out to tenants on a share-cropping basis.

Even after independence, this continual interchange between capitalist and pre-capitalist relations has not ceased. This is caused partly by the low rate of capital accumulation and the existence of a permanent state of relative over-population in the countryside. But it is also caused by the fact that capitalist profit-making itself utilizes pre-capitalist methods, and that capitalist farmers (when such a category can be clearly identified) depend on other property-owing strata for maintaining their political and social power.[32] I do not know whether we gain much by characterizing the amalgam of usury, bondage, wage-labour, and tenancy prevailing in the Indian countryside as 'semi-feudalism', 'semi-capitalism', 'neither feudalism nor capitalism', 'both capitalism and feudalism'; I should be happy with any of the phrases so long as the basic laws of motion of such a society are correctly understood.

Perhaps this way of putting it would be regarded by some as shirking of the real issues. One major hindrance against a very sharp characterization of the amalgam of capitalist and pre-capitalist relations that we witness in South Asia and in many other underdeveloped countries is the immense gradation of the different types of relations that come into being. Two young Indian economists[33] make some very pertinent observations on the slowness of the speed of transition from the 'feudal' to the capitalist mode of production and on the 'phenomenal array of forms of organization and relations of production, ranging from pure capitalist relations on the one hand, to accredited feudal relations on the other'. They also point out the futility of the effort to discover capitalism or feudalism by verifying whether a certain arbitrary set of characteristics are satisfied at any given moment of time.

Then they go on to try find out how far capitalism has proceeded in the area under study. I find it difficult to follow them all the way with their robust faith in the laws of development of capitalism, (a) because, as I have argued, there is often a symbiotic relationship between pre-capitalist and capitalist modes of exploitation, so that the 'laws of development of capitalism' can hardly be applied without a very great deal of modification and (b) because I am not sure that the 'transition' to capitalism can ever be complete in the countries of South Asia. The difficulty of finding a scalar measure of the progress of capitalism and the difficulty of discovering the laws of motion of the complex amalgam of different relations of production, or of different modes of exploitation are not unrelated to each other. Pre-capitalist relations, almost by definition, are far more specific to a particular region and a particular moment of time than capitalist relations; it is not the least of the harmful legacies of colonialism that while it modified the pre-capitalist relations to alter its purpose, it also preserved them. Colonialism thus helped to impress upon the ex-colonies those peculiar shapes of retarded capitalism and modified pre-capitalism, and made them go in for three-legged races when the other competitors are free of similar encumbrances.

This gives us a convenient point of departure for linking up production relations in agriculture with those in industry. The British conquered India as a mercantile community, and the instruments they fashioned included those of a heavy land tax, concentration of control of the external trade, and a large part of the internal trade first in the hands of the East India Company and then in the hands of a very small number of European firms, the intensification of the exploitation of the interior through plantations and through the conversion of more and more land to the production of cash crops. At the base of this pyramid of exploitation were at first, the weaver of cotton goods and the spinner of silk yarn, the producers of salt and saltpetre, and finally, the peasant. After the landside of de-industrialization had got going, it was the peasant in India, the poorer consumers of salt in India and the consumer of opium in China who largely bore the brunt of exploitation. The machinery of exploitation was extremely hierarchical and had a more or less capillary effect on the surplus. The development of India as a market was achieved primarily by opening up the interior and destroying the handicrafts. India was never considered a suitable area for investment of capital on a large scale; she always exported a larger amount of capital in various forms than she received. Thus Britain's position as the first industrializing country did not in itself lead to a forward-looking revolution in the relations of agriculture and industry in India: most of the changes aggravated the forces of stagnation in both rural and industrial economies.[34]

Oligopolistic Structure

At the time of independence, India inherited a highly oligopolistic structure of control in industry, trade, and finance. Most of the big business houses had interests in all the three fields. Since a large part of profits in both agriculture and industry took the form of profit from alienation, and since lending to trade for various purposes was perhaps the most important form of bank-lending, major national conflicts between agricultural and industrial interests never had the chance to develop on a large scale. But inter-regional conflicts did develop. The heat generated by the controversy about the terms of trade is to be attributed to inter-regional differences in gains and losses from the Green Revolution. The Green Revolution was made possibly by a combination of imports of new technology and massive government investment in agriculture, and both the government investment and productivity growth in agriculture have been unevenly distributed. Hence a rise in the terms of trade of agriculture in relation to industry would tend to affect adversely the interests of the urban dwellers in States which have not gained much from the Green Revolution. Poor peasants and agricultural labourers who are net buyers of foodgrains and who do not gain at all from rationing and whose wages, particularly in the agriculturally stagnant States, have risen less than the retail price level, also lose, but it is not their plight which provides the political punch. However, it is doubtful whether the capitalist class as a whole has suffered much from changes in the terms of trade.

One could think of a 'healthier' pattern of relationship between property-owners in industry and in agriculture, where growth in agricultural productivity is fuelled by the enterprise of capitalist farmers, and industry is controlled by capitalists who specialize in production rather than in trade.

When capitalism develops in agriculture, trade, and small-scale industry, without any obvious control from big capitalists in metropolitan cities or ports, we can call it 'cellular capitalism' to distinguish if from what may be called 'siphoning capitalism', where the control over trade, industry, or agriculture even at the local levels is exercised by big capital in the port or metropolitan cities. Thus trade in jute and jute goods and the jute industry in eastern India would be an example of 'siphoning capitalism', whereas wheat production and wheat trade in today's Punjab might be an instance of cellular capitalism.[35] It is not the degree of pervasiveness of capital relations that is the distinguishing characteristic, but the structure of control over the surplus extracted. It is possible that in the ultimate analysis, the major distinction as far as agriculture in eastern India and agriculture in Punjab are concerned may turn out to be the difference in the rates of real capital formation in the two cases, and not the structure of control at all. However, we should remember that Punjab and Haryana have given rise to farmers' lobbies in a way in which eastern India has not generated them and these farmers' lobbies have agitated for government support not only in the field of prices but also in the field of investment in the form of more irrigation, more electric power, and subsidies for equipment and fertilizers. But, of course, the development of Punjabi capitalism is no more determined by only its own structure than that of Indian or Pakistani capitalism is determined by theirs. National and macroeconomic constraints determine how far any internal energy can carry a particular group of capitalists. On the Indian side, however, the enterprise of Punjabi capitalists with interests in industry, land, and trade has been severely limited by the enormous requirements of capital and managerial resources of modern large-scale industry, and by the fact that Punjabi capitalists have to compete with much longer established and bigger capitalist groups on an all-India basis. On the Pakistani side, the picture is very complex because the Punjabi elite dominated the Pakistani state which could do far more for the development of capitalism in the region, since it had not inherited any very large business groups. Even there, however, it appears that business houses with interests in trade came to dominate industry, and that capitalist farmers could rarely graduate to become big industrialists.

While it is fascinating to speculate on the regional differences in the patterns of growth in the subcontinent, the common constraints on growth must always be borne in mind. One constraint is the relative stagnation in the standards of living of ordinary people, caused both by the slow pace of capital accumulation and by the structure of exploitation built up over the centuries. Both in India and in Pakistan, for example, real wages of industrial labour have stagnated over the years,[36] and the share of wages in value added in industry has tended to decline. In agriculture also, real wages of labourers have tended to stagnate with some rise in pockets experiencing vigorous growth.

The constraints on the home market, the unevenness of capitalist development in different parts of the country, the existence of oligopolistic structures of control over different fields and the fear of domination by foreign firms if the latter are allowed free entry into the internal market—all these have led capitalists to generally rally behind various protectionist policies adopted by the government. Those who want relatively free trade and further liberalization of import export policies are largely talking to an empty audience hall.[37] Some capitalist groups—particularly the really big business houses—might chafe under government restrictions, but the capitalist class as a whole can hardly do without government controls in various fields. A dependent capitalist class, striving to retain its position, dare not hand over the levers of control to the forces of international capitalism. We have already, in the introduction, pointed to the constraints, imposed by the relative retardation of the Indian capitalist class and of the Indian economy in which they operate, and we need not elaborate the same point, all over again. Furthermore, controls—and their violation—provide various sources of untaxed income which the capitalist class would be extremely unwilling to give up. But the possibility of a more thorough-going alliance of this dependent bourgeoisie with international capitalism on, say, the

Brazilian pattern, when threatened with revolution or disorder inside, should always be kept in mind.

Notes

1. I am indebted to Nripendranath Bandyopadhyay, Amit Bhaduri, Asok Sen, and Partha Chatterjee for commenting on the preliminary ideas embodied in this essay.

2. For a summary of the evidence relating to capital transfers and labour migration in the nineteenth century, with special reference to South Asia, see Bagchi (1972b).

3. The evidence and the theoretical argument have been presented in two related articles: Bagchi (1976a) and (1976b).

4. Sivasubramonian (1965: Table 4.20).

5. Ibid.: Table 7.3.

6. See Krishnamurty (1970) and Chattopadhyay (1975).

7. See S.R. Lewis (1970: 19).

8. Cf. Griffin and Khan (1972a: 4) and UN (1973: Table II–2–4). There is an apparent discrepancy between the two estimates of the share of industry (and of agriculture) in national output in 1969–70. Khan and Griffin put it as high as 20.2 per cent whereas the UN publication puts it as 9.5 per cent. The discrepancy is due to the fact that Khan and Griffin's estimate includes construction and transport, along with mining and manufacturing. In fact, according to their estimate (p. 8) the share of manufacturing alone in national income is 8.4 per cent (5.4 per cent being the share of large-scale manufacturing and 3.0 per cent being that of small scale industry).

9. Thorner and Thorner (1964: 306).

10. See for data on the period before independence, Sivasubramonian (1965); and for the period since Independence, Government of India, *Economic Survey 1974–75*, 1975, New Delhi.

11. UN (1973: Table II–2–4).

12. See, for example, *Reserve Bank of India Bulletin* (1975: 129–39).

13. Griffin and Khan (1972b).

14. For example, in the Poona districts of Maharashtra, under Maratha rule, the purchaser of land, in a village had to have the consent of both the patil and all the kunbis (cultivators) who had a permanent stake in the village. See Kumar (1968: 26–7).

15. O'Malley (1906a: 179).

16. Ibid.: 177.

17. Ibid.

18. O'Malley (1909: 159).

19. Ibid.: 160.

20. Quoted in (Byrne 1911: 116). It was typical of the colonial method of rationalization that the result of a century and a half of colonial oppression was explained away by a characteristic piece of snobbery: '"This wholesale oppression could in my opinion only have existed owing to rent suits being decided" in the mufassil courts and "seeing the evil their orders bring about."'

21. The near impossibility of getting redress against a determined landlord is illustrated by the following instance cited by the same District Magistrate of Bhagalpur '… a Muhammadan landlord was anxious to oust some Sonthal tenants of his district. A creature was got up to sue them on a forged bond in Purnea, and the defendant was sold up.

> 'On being told of the case, I arranged for the plaintiff in the case to be made to identify the dependant in the presence of the Munsif, and it was found he could not. The whole proceedings had been fraudulent! Now, how is the Sontpal to get justice? He cannot get it by just asking the Munsif to sanction the prosecution of the plaintiff: the Munsif's decree, palpably gained by fraud bars the way. The Crown cannot move for the same reason, and can in fact do nothing unless the plaintiff agrees to be used as a pawn in the game, and pushed forward to ask for a review in one Court, to oppose an appeal in another, and if he secures the review, to give evidence. Then, if he gains the review, or if he has to bring title suit to declare the bond forged and wins that suit, still nothing can be done by the Crown unless the complainant will put in a final petition before the Munsif, asking for sanction to prosecute, and then move the Magistrate. Is it any wonder that the most impudent forgery is committed every day, and that a zamindar considers himself absolutely immune from any loss but that of his court-fees, if he attacks an enemy in the Civil Courts?' (Ibid.: 118)

22. For a graphic account, see Thorner (1954).

23. See, for example, Fukazawa (1972).

24. Kolenda (1967*:* 287).

25. Census (1901b: 473).

26. See Hjejle (1967: nos 1 and 2). Scattered accounts of agrestic slavery in eastern and northern India can be obtained from the various reports of Francis Buchanan Hamilton.

27. Breman (1974: part 2, Chapters 4 and 5).

28. The degree and forms of bondage varied from locality to locality, but farm servants in some forms were found practically all over eastern India.

> In Gaya the farm servant or Kamiya, takes loan from his employer and binds himself to work for him for 100 years, or until the loan is repaid …The same system is in force elsewhere, e.g., in the north of Chota-Nagpur. The farm servant is called Kamat in North Bengal and Krishan in Nadia… He receives less pay than temporary hands, but the fact is that he is kept on all the year round… (Census 1901b: 475).

The Collector of Monghyr wrote in the 1870s:

> The lands in this district are chiefly cultivated by Kamiyas, who are in point of fact bondmen to the landholder. They belong to the lowest castes, particularly Mushahars and Dosadhs. I doubt whether there is a single Musahar in the district who is not a bondman … The kamiyas are a lean race, and the wonder is how it is they manage to subsist with their food… I have on many occasions urged them to emigrate, but they pleaded that their masters will not let them go, and that they prefer the ills they have rather than fly to others they know not of.

So much for the paternalism of the masters, the freedom conferred by British law, or opportunities opened up by free markets. The situation was the same in 1909. See O'Malley (1909: 129–30). It was officially sound in India recently that bonded labour survived in most of the states. See *Statesman*, Calcutta), 30 May 1975, 'Move for abolition of bonded labour'. See Indian School of Social Sciences (1975).

29. Colebrooke (1804: Para 121).

30. See O'Malley (1906a: 137) and (1906b).

31. O'Malley (1909: 125).

32. For a perceptive analysis of the class structure in Pakistan and Bangladesh, see Chandra (1972a) and (1972b).

33. Saith and Tankha (1972: 707–23).

34. For details of the argument, see R.P. Dutt (1949); and Bagchi (1973b).

35. The reader may feel that I am indulging in the coinage of too many new terms. But in the context of the variegated world of today's underdeveloped countries, 'capitalism' as such seems to be much too inclusive a category.

36. See Khan (1972a); Sau (1973); A.K. Bagchi (1975a).

37. I analysed the logical and ideological basis of modern economic liberalism (as discussed by Little, Mirrlees, Bhagwati and their cohorts) in Bagchi (1971: 1669–76).

7

Indian Demography and Economy in the Long *Fin-de-siècle* 1876–1914*

The Presidency Banks and the Imperial Order in India

In 1876, the three quasi-government joint-stock banks in the three Presidencies of Bengal, Bombay, and Madras were brought within the purview of a uniform Presidency Banks Act.[1] By this law, the government withdrew as a shareholder of the Presidency banks, but retained strict control over the general manner of their functioning. The banks acted as government bankers in India (but not in Britain or any other foreign country), and had custody of public balances up to certain maximum limits, but were otherwise engaged in private commercial banking. The Presidency Banks Act of 1876 was supplemented by a series of agreements between the banks and the government. The agreements were renewed and changed in periodic intervals and the Act itself was amended several times between 1876 and 1914. However, the basic structure and functions of the three Presidency banks remained virtually unchanged for the whole period.

The imperial order within which the banks operated acquired a look of tested impregnability. Gone were the early days of British rule when many of the more perceptive members of the conquering race agonized over their right to rule India permanently or at least their ability to do so. Gone was also the shadow cast by the Indian Revolt (Mutiny) of 1857:

*Originally published as, 'The Demographic and Economic Developments 1876–1914' in 1989, *The Presidency Banks and the Indian Economy 1876–1914*. Calcutta: Oxford University Press.

after all, the British had come out triumphant and had done so with the help of loyal Indian troops and cowardly Indian princes. Lord Lytton and Lord Curzon embodied the imperial arrogance in its most assured form. Sporadic resistance in different parts of the country or even the emergence of nation-wide platforms for that resistance hardly shook the confidence and self-righteousness crystallized in Rudyard Kipling's phrase, 'white man's burden'.[2]

Under the imperial' order, the British parliament acted as a despotic ruler over the whole of British India and the Indian princely states which acted as the 'subsidiary allies' of the British. More immediately, the Secretary of State for India with the assistance of an advisory council and the bureaucrats of the India Office in London, and the British Governor-General and Viceroy in India, with the assistance of his own advisory council and a countrywide imperial bureaucracy, exercised the despotic authority on behalf of the British parliament. There were attempts to co-opt 'respectable' or 'responsible' public opinion in India by nominating non-official members to provincial and imperial legislative bodies and by allowing some of these members to be chosen by chambers of commerce, landholders' associations, and so on. The non-official members of these legislative bodies (and sometimes, even the official members) were able on occasion to voice their differences from the policies pursued by the government, but in case of any genuine conflict, almost without any exception, the official view prevailed, since the Governor-General or the provincial governor and their official advisors in charge of various portfolios, had a veto power. Similarly, sometimes there were dissensions among the official members of the Viceroy's council or the council of the Secretary of State for India in London, but in every case the will of the British parliament (enforced by the party forming a majority) ultimately prevailed. We will have occasion to advert to such dissensions in one or two cases, but it is well to bear in mind that for all the talk about constitutional government, British authority, as exercised on and through the Presidency banks and all civil organizations in India during this period, was fundamentally despotic, and the nature of that authority did not change in any fundamental way during the period we are considering.

The economic and demographic matrix on which the authority acted, however, changed over the period. Some of these changes were greatly influenced, if not directly caused, by measures initiated during this period or earlier by the imperial authorities, some were due to international developments which the authorities could not or did not want to alter, and some were due to causes which have a deeper origin or a longer periodicity than imperial measures or international developments. Despite being acted on by the fiscal apparatus of alien rule and the commercial forces of the international economy, most villagers continued to lead their own lives. While brave talk about sanitation and education was blared from public platforms, the lives of ordinary people remained nasty, brutish and short. Commerce and finance were activated not only by the penetration of new markets but also by exigencies of grain movements during famines, by the spoliation of virgin forests and by the forcible indenturing of labour in distant plantations. We turn now to an analysis of the forces that were recognized by the authorities and to those that were not. Only if we understand their bearing, shall we be able to perceive how the Presidency banks and other major financial institutions reacted on those forces and how their choices were in turn facilitated or constrained by them.

The Paradoxes of the Longue Durée in India

Fernand Braudel coined the concept of the *longue durée* in history, to distinguish the movements captured in it from mere events, or *conjunctures* of particular circumstances, or determinate lengths such as the short Kitchin cycles, that is, those caused essentially by changes in stocks, the Juglar cycles of eight to ten years, the object of analysis of classic economic cycle theories, the Kuznets cycles of perhaps twenty years' duration or the Kondratieff cycles that are alleged to have a forty- to fifty-year periodicity.[3] Orthodox economists are familiar with Alfred Marshall's 'long run', in which no costs of the competitive firm can be regarded as fixed any more, and any returns of the firm over and above its total costs can be competed away by the entry of new firms. Since the 1950s, numerous economists have built up life-cycle models of saving and investment in which the individual economic agent plans not for a day or a year but over his (her) whole lifespan.

In this [chapter], I want to borrow Braudel's phrase *longue durée* but use it mainly as a device for classifying the available information, partly because different movements in history do have different periodicities, but also because we have information of varying qualities about the different aspects of history.[4] Thereby we get away from a myopic concentration on month-to-month or year-to-year changes without claiming a very definite periodicity for the long-term movements, since different types of movements may have different patterns in the long run and we have not yet been able to determine those patterns exactly.

We shall illustrate the kind of problem we have in mind by tackling the question of changes in India's national income. Changes in national income are supposed to have an intimate relation to the use of money and credit in the economy either via changes in expenditures and their distribution (in the Keynesian variants of theories of national expenditure and money demand) or directly via changes in money stock required to support changes in real national income (in the 'monetarist' view of the nexus between money and national income). Moreover, if we want to find out the way the domestic demands for various commodities change over time, we need to have some idea of changes in national income and its distribution among the various income classes.

Indian National Income 1875–1914

Having set out this desideratum, we are faced with the problem that there is no acceptable national income series covering the whole period 1876–1914. S. Sivasubramonian made a careful estimate of the national income of undivided India (that is, the territory comprising today's India, Bangladesh, and Pakistan) for the period from 1900–01 to 1946–7.[5] Despite some criticisms that have been recently advanced against Sivasubramonian's estimates,[6] we can accept them as an approximation to whatever the true growth of income may be. For earlier periods, we generally have only point estimates for particular dates made by such political personalities as Dadabhai Naoroji, William Digby, Lord Curzon, and government officials such as Evelyn Baring (later Lord Cromer)[7] and F.J. Atkinson.[8] Of these persons, Atkinson was a senior official of the accounts department, and provided a virtually official reply to the criticisms of Dadabhai Naoroji, R.C. Dutt, and William Digby about the impoverishing effects of British rule in India. He tried to estimate the growth of national income in India between 1875 and 1895. All the later estimates[9] of nineteenth-century growth of income have been based on Atkinson's work, and some later students have even managed to inject their own fantasies into the fog created by Atkinson's methods.[10]

Atkinson estimated that the income per capita in India (but not necessarily of Indians, since the income-earning population included highly-paid British officials and British merchants amassing princely fortunes) had increased from Rs 30.5 in 1875 to Rs 39.5 in 1895 at current prices. If we deflate this figure by an index number of Indian prices with the average prices of a bundle of commodities for the years 1868–76 as the base,[11] the income per head in 1895 turns out to be only

4.95 per cent higher than in 1875 (the index numbers of prices in 1875 and 1895 were 94 and 116 respectively).

But even this figure is suspect. First of all, as F.H. Skrine, an ex-official of the British Indian government pointed out in the course of discussion on Atkinson's paper on national income,[12] Indian statistics related to production were fraught with a high degree of uncertainty. But Atkinson's statistics for the year 1875 were especially vulnerable. The *Estimates of Area and Yield of the Principal Crops in India* published annually by the Government of India and on which George Blyn based his study[13] of agricultural growth in India in the period from 1891–2 give comprehensive and comparable data only from 1891–2 onwards. Data relating to crop acreages, production of large-scale (mechanized) industries, artisanal industries, and so on *are* available for years earlier than 1891–2 but they are more fragmentary, and scattered in a large number of publications. Atkinson did not try to fit together such data and arrive at an estimate of the agricultural and non-agricultural production and national income for 1875. Instead he made certain *assumptions* about increases in the crop acreages and yields of crops, and in non-agricultural production, and extrapolated the figure for 1895 backward. Unfortunately, all these assumptions are, to put it mildly, questionable.[14]

Atkinson *assumed* that both the area under cultivation and the yield per acre of every single major crop increased between 1875 and 1895. While this assumption may have been valid in the case of such a 'superior' exportable grain as wheat, or a crop such as raw cotton, which benefited from expanding markets and extended irrigation, it was almost certainly invalid for such major crops as jowar, bajra, and ragi, which were mostly raised on non-irrigated land in dry areas, and for a rain-fed crop such as rice, which was the single most important field-crop in India, accounting for more than 25 per cent of the total acreage. As wheat acreage expanded, for example, in the Central Provinces, it did so at the expense of the millets which suffered a contraction in acreage or were driven on to more marginal lands.[15] Blyn's study for the period beginning in 1891–2 often reveals declining trends in yields per acre of many foodgrains such as rice, bajra, barley, and other crops such as jute, rape and mustard, and linseed, for major regions of India, and often for British India as a whole.[16]

The decline in yields was mostly caused by environmental deterioration such as deforestation, soil erosion, and soil exhaustion, with attempts at an extension of perennial cultivation in areas which had been under forests and grassland and had hitherto practised either shifting agriculture or agriculture punctuated by long fallows. There is no reason to believe that such factors had not acted before 1891–2. The only major deterrent against the decline in crop yields on farmers' fields was an extension of irrigation, which not only increased yields of existing crops but also allowed the introduction of higher-yielding varieties. New irrigation canals were being constructed in the last quarter of the nineteenth century. But generally speaking, such works had to meet the test of being 'productive', that is, they had to repay the expenditure made by the government with the full interest cost charged on it and show a profit. Even if an irrigation project met this test, it might not be undertaken because of the general financial stringency under which the Government of India laboured from the latter part of the 1870s. Moreover, a government canal often substituted for private works. For example, according to Atkinson's estimates (admittedly not entirely comparable over the years), while the area irrigated by government canals expanded from 5.032 million to 12.081 million acres between 1884–5 and 1899–1900, the total area irrigated by all sources expanded from 22.470 million acres to 30.745 million acres over the same period[17] (The omission of Bengal and Bombay from the figure for 1884–5, makes it an underestimate but not by more than 3 million acres or so.) Thus in estimating the growth in irrigated acreage, we must take care to adequately account for private sources of irrigation and for possible expansion of government-financed irrigation at the cost of private sources.

Irrigation works have often been taken as a major boon conferred by British rule in India. For example, the brothers John and Richard Strachey, who had served the Government of India in its highest echelon, wrote in 1882:[18]

> Whether as a means of increasing the necessary food supply of the people, or of stimulating the production of the agricultural staples of commerce, the extension of irrigation must be pronounced to be almost the greatest blessing that can be bestowed on the country, and the construction of the great works which have been carried out in conformity with the policy now under discussion, must unquestionably be classed among the most truly beneficial acts of the British government in India.

In assessing such claims, it should be remembered that many irrigation works served mainly rain-fed areas, and the increases in crop yields due to irrigation were often rather insignificant in normal years: taking good and bad years together, they rarely exceeded 20–5 per cent; that the government water rates were often excessive, eating up in some cases the whole of the expected increase in the value of the crop, so that force had to be used to compel the peasant to use the irrigation water;[19] and that badly planned irrigation works often caused long-term water-logging and salinity, thus leading to a decline rather than increase in yields.[20] Hence despite the apparently enormous amounts spent on irrigation, they did not necessarily lead to an improvement in the standard of living of ordinary peasants.

If the bases of estimates of changes in agricultural output made by Atkinson are rather infirm, the estimates made by him of changes in incomes and outputs of non-agricultural incomes are not more robust either. The major problem there is that, in the face of a large volume of evidence to the contrary,[21] Atkinson assumed that the population supported by non-agricultural occupations increased at least as fast as, if not faster than, that supported by agriculture. Since the incomes per head of the non-agricultural population were higher than that of the agricultural population in both years, and they were assumed to increase at least as fast as the income of those supported by agriculture, this lent a further upward bias to Atkinson's estimates of growth in income between 1875 and 1895.

Suppose we now leave the issue of income growth during the last quarter of the nineteenth century and turn to Sivasubramonian's estimates[22] of growth for the period from 1900–01 to 1913–14. At current prices, he estimated the income per head of an Indian to rise from Rs 42.1 in 1900–01 to Rs 62.1 in 1913–14; when converted to an index of 1938–9 prices, the per capita incomes were Rs 49.4 in 1900–01 and Rs 55.7 in 1913–14. The difference between the two rates of growth is a measure of the inflation between 1900–01 and 1913–14.

Can we even take this increase in per capita income as indicating that the income of the ordinary people and hence their power to purchase consumer goods from the market was increasing? In answering such a question we must remember that in the Indian economy only a fraction, perhaps no more than 40 per cent of the production, ever passed through the market. Thus it is theoretically possible that the market value of the output or services of ordinary people increased without an actual increase in the cash in their hands for buying consumer or essential producer goods. However, in an economy in which the use of money was expanding (and it was expanding fast in some periods), it is unlikely that the proportion of output mediated by the market should decline except sporadically. But the part of output used up outside the market is often underestimated. In that case, with a rise in the proportion of market-mediated output the *growth* of output may be overestimated, as monetization affects larger and larger shares of total output.

If we ignore this possibility, we have still to ask whether a major part of the income was earned by the very rich so that the income per head of ordinary people was substantially lower. We do not have any adequate study of the personal or class distribution of national income in India in the period before independence. But Atkinson did provide a break-up of the total national income as between the agricultural population, the common non-agricultural population, and the classes of 'sufficient or ample means'. From his calculations it turns out that in 1895, the last class, comprising 5.4 million out of a total British-India (including Burma) population of 222 million (or 2.04 per cent of the population) enjoyed an income of Rs 1,130.0 million out of the total national income of Rs 8,765.6 million (or rather more than 12 per cent of the total income). If we put it another way, while the income per head of the agricultural population was Rs 35.9, and that of the common non-agricultural population was Rs 34.1 per head, that of the classes of persons of ample means was Rs 208.2 or almost six times that of the income of an average Indian. Taking Atkinson's figures at their face value, this is an underestimate of the degree of inequality of incomes, for the landlords who earned their incomes from agriculture are clubbed together with ordinary peasants, so that the income per head of the latter was bound to be considerably lower than the Rs 36 derived by Atkinson. Furthermore, we must remember that a considerable part of the top incomes was earned, by expatriate Europeans who remitted a large part abroad, so that those expenditure flows were not available for financing Indian production. Moreover, a large part of the incomes of both Europeans and rich Indians would be spent on imported luxuries.

For an assessment of the relation of growth of incomes to current expenditures on consumer goods or investment expenditures, it is necessary to find out how the income distribution and the purchasing power were changing over time. During the period from about 1898 to the First World War, prices of agricultural goods tended to increase faster than those of industrial goods. At first blush, it would appear that since Indian producers were primarily sellers of agricultural commodities and buyers of industrial goods, by and large, most Indians would benefit as a result of these changes in the terms of trade.[23] But several caveats must be entered against any such unambiguously optimistic conclusion. First, a large part of the rise in agricultural prices consisted of a rise in prices of foodgrains. However, most small peasants and landless labourers were net buyers of foodgrains. So a rise in grain prices would, *ceteris paribus,* imply a fall in their real incomes. This would be true, *a fortiori,* for those workers in industry whose money incomes tended to lag behind rises in the cost of living. Most Indian industrial workers and artisans in the late nineteenth and early twentieth centuries would fit this category.

The second gross fact to remember is that big traders dealing wholesale in agricultural commodities would intercept a large part of the profits realizable from increases in their prices. In particular, exports in most parts of India (except for rice exports of southern India and cotton exports of western India) were handled almost exclusively by European merchants who pocketed the lion's share of most of the gains from enhanced prices and quantities of exports.

There were, almost certainly, some regions such as the western Jamuna *doab* of today's Uttar Pradesh, the canal colonies of western Punjab, or the irrigated regions of Sind, where large Indian farmers were gaining substantially from increased availability of irrigated land, realizing those gains through exports or sales of crops in the domestic market.[24] But where the supply of land could not be effectively increased through irrigation, or the opening up of new land, where peasants were at the mercy of moneylenders and traders, and where the export trade was effectively barred to even substantial Indian producers and traders, an increase in exports or their prices did not necessarily translate itself into increased standards of living of the ordinary people. This is clearly evinced by the case of Bengal and Bihar in the first three decades of the twentieth century. This region had been an exporter of rice in the nineteenth century. For example, in 1888–9, Bengal (including Bihar and Orissa) exported to foreign countries 9,045,993 maunds of rice and in the net, exported a total of 13,571,910 maunds of rice (or roughly 9.93 million cwts.).[25] Later, Bengal began to import rice from Burma, but continued to export a considerable amount of the fine rice produced domestically. This might be considered a profitable exchange, especially because Bengal proper (today's West Bengal and Bangladesh) was producing increasing quantities of jute, which displaced the relatively coarse *aus* or *bhadoi* paddy. However, what is tantalizing is that the net availability of foodgrains per head in Bengal, taking coarse and fine varieties together, decreased over the years from 1891–2 to 1920–1.[26] What is even more tantalizing is that the net availability of rice (which is the cereal consumed in Bengal) per head declined most steeply in those regions of Bengal which became the chief producers of the 'golden fibre', jute.[27] Thus it is not possible to deduce anything directly and simply about the condition of ordinary peasants or workers from the state of export trade or trade in general.

Can we perhaps shift the time-frame? Is it possible to say that during the period of the so-called Great Depression of 1873–96, when world agricultural prices tended to decline in relation to industrial prices[28] ordinary Indian peasants and workers were definitely doing better? Such a conclusion would certainly be hasty. There is evidence that many agricultural exports were expanding during the period. If such increases could be said to have always originated in extension of cultivation to land which did not produce valuable subsistence crops, or which was made more productive through public investment at a relatively low cost to the peasant, and if the gains were translated into increased earnings for the peasant rather more than into large profits for the trader, then it would be possible to say that such expansion would have benefited the peasants. Again, while this may have been true of substantial producers of exportable crops on land opened up through irrigation, it probably did not apply to the general run of peasant producers of exports. Expanding exports were not always translated into higher prices even in the case of crops in which international competition was weak or non-existent. If we take jute, a monopoly product of eastern India with booming exports, we find that the landed cost of jute in Calcutta from Narainganj (in the district of Dacca) and Serajganj (in the district of Pabna) behaved as in Table 7.1.

Table 7.1 Landed Cost of Jute per Maund in Calcutta, 1879–80 to 1882–3

Variety		1879–80			1880–1			1881–2			1882–3		
		R.	a.	p.	R.	a.	p.	R.	a.	p.	R.	a.	p.
Narainganj	Fine	5	2	9	5	0	3	4	15	10	3	7	6
	Medium	4	9	6	4	6	9	4	3	4	2	15	2
	Common	4	0	9	3	13	7	3	10	4	2	7	6
Serajganj	Fine	5	4	0	5	2	0	5	1	0	3	9	0
	Medium	4	11	0	4	8	0	4	4	0	3	1	0
	Common	4	2	0	3	15	0	3	12	0	2	9	0

Source: Watt (1972[1889]: 553).
Note: 12 pies = 1 anna; 16 annas = 1 rupee

The actual prices obtained by the peasant were much lower than indicated in Table 7.1, because the profit margins in the jute trade were high. Moreover, it is likely that in years of sagging prices, the proportion obtained by the peasant also declined. (One reason was that many of the small traders' margins were fixed by quantity and not according to value.) In order to appreciate the irony of the situation it has to be noted that the exports of both raw jute and jute manufactures from India increased steadily during these years.

To the extent that jute was grown on land, which would have otherwise been devoted to the production of aus rice, the interests of the consumers of the latter would have suffered as a result of higher production of jute. Apart from such indirect substitution effects, consumers of exportable food crops were more directly affected when such exports expanded fast. It was argued by British officials in the 1870s and 1880s and it continues to be argued even now that when expansion of infrastructure (such as railways) makes it possible to move grain from one point to the other, it benefits everybody by ironing out prices. Several arguments may be advanced against this view. In the first place, the effect of railway development in ironing out food prices in the late nineteenth century has generally been exaggerated,[29] since attention has been concentrated on the 'superior' and generally exportable grain crops, and not enough weightage has been given to the prices of millets which were the staple food of the poorer people in many parts of India. When the superior grains were exported to other regions or abroad, an upward movement in the prices of millets occurred. This effect would be more pronounced in local markets and would show up as a larger degree of seasonal fluctuations in the prices of the inferior foodgrains than at points of export and over the year as a whole, since the latter would be strongly affected by international movements in exports and prices. Table 7.2 briefly illustrates the greater volatility of the prices of millets than of wheat. If prices of localities mainly consuming millets were used, the swings would be much larger for the prices of dryland grains than for wheat. The poorer people would, of course, benefit from any increased employment generated by larger outputs of foodgrains, but under conditions of traditional cultivation of millets in unirrigated tracts, such effects would be marginal.

Independently of such substitution effects between superior and inferior foodgrains, the depletion of local stocks through exports of any grain would tend to push up the cost of living of the poorer peasants and workers and would, *ceteris paribus,* depress their real earnings.[30] This argument would be particularly strong if the money wages of agricultural labourers and artisans remained constant or even fell when

Table 7.2 Index Numbers of Retail Prices of Major Food Crops in India, 1880–1 to 1900–01 (base: 1873=100)

Year	Wheat	Jowar	Bajra
1880–1	96	91	98
1884–5	89	98	95
1888–9	118	118	126
1892–3	127	120	121
1896–7	206	211	204
1899–1900	176	207	196
1900–01	160	140	133

Source: Government of India, Department of Commercial Intelligence and Statistics: Index Numbers of Indian Prices 1861–1926, Calcutta, 1928, p. 3.
Note: Both 1896–7 and 1899–1900 were famine years.

food prices rose. This is what tended to happen for most of the last quarter of the nineteenth century, and even later.[31] Two of the main causes of this were the continual erosion of employment opportunities in artisanal occupations in most parts of India, and the failure to invest in agriculture and modern industry on a scale that would be adequate to counteract stagnation of opportunities in traditional pursuits.

Demographic Change 1871–1921

We now turn to perhaps the grossest index of changes in the conditions of living of the ordinary people, that is, rates of population growth—an index which economists tend strangely to neglect when trying to measure changes in per capita incomes or standards of living. During the period from 1871 to 1921, the population of the Indian subcontinent (excluding Baluchistan and North-Western Frontier Province) grew from 249.49 million to 299.63 million. This yields an annual rate of growth of 0.37 per cent only.[32] This was not the result of careful family planning, with low birth rates and low death rates, but the outcome of a precarious balance between high birth rates and high death rates yielding, say, a rate of growth of population of 1 per cent per annum being disastrously upset by virulent famines that wiped out net increases of population often years or more in district after district, even province after province. During the period from 1876–7 to 1899–1900 alone, the total number of deaths from famines was at least 16–17 million.[33] The effects of these deaths from famines, plagues, and excess mortality caused by malnutrition, and diseases aggravated by poor physique,[34] on intercensal population changes in some major provinces can be gauged from Table 7.3. (the figures in Table 7.3 are not strictly comparable because of changes in jurisdiction etc. but they are adequate for our purpose). It is clear that whole provinces with populations of 20 million and above as well as smaller areas suffered disastrous famines or epidemics not just in one decade but repeatedly, with only a few years of respite.

Table 7.3 Intercensal Percentage Changes in Population in Major Provinces and States in India, 1872–1921

Province or region	1872–81	1881–91	1891–1901	1901–11	1911–21(b)
British Territory					
Ajmer-Merwara	+16.2	+17.7	–12.1	+5.1	–12.5
Bengal	+6.4	+7.6	+7.8	+7.9	+3.2
Bihar and Orissa	+17.0	+6.1	+1.1	+3.8	–1.0
Bombay	+1.2	+14.5	–1.7	+6.0	–1.7
Central Provinces and Berar	+20.0	+9.3	–8.3	+16.2	+1.1
Coorg	+5.9	–2.9	+4.4	–3.1	–0.4
Madras	–1.2	+15.6	+7.3	+8.3	+2.7
Punjab	(a)	+10.0	+6.9	–1.7	+5.6
United Provinces	+5.1	+6.2	+1.7	–1.1	–2.7
Princely States					
Baroda State	+9.2	+10.7	–19.2	+4.1	+3.4
Bombay States	+2.1	+16.5	+14.5	+7.3	(c)
Central India Agency	N.A.	+9.4	–16.2	+10.1	–3.1(d)
Central Provinces States	+49.5	+23.4	–4.8	+29.8	(c)
Hyderabad State	N.A.	+17.2	–3.4	+20.0	–5.8

Source: Census of India, 1911, vol. I, India, part I—*Report* by E.A. Gait, 1913, Calcutta, Superintendent, Government Printing, Chapter 2, Subsidiary Table 1; Census of India, 1921, vol. I, India, part 1—*Report* by J.T. Marten, 1924, Calcutta, Superintendent, Government Printing, Chapter 1, Subsidiary Table IV.

Notes: N.A. = Not available

(a) The growth of the population of Punjab together with that of North-Western Frontier Province was +7.0 per cent over the period.

(b) Changes in natural population (excluding emigration and immigration).

(c) Not separately estimated.

(d) Estimated together with change in the population of Gwalior State.

The only decade in which the populations of all the provinces and regions enumerated had a positive growth was that of 1881–91 (Coorg is the only exception, but its population was rather small), and the only large province which had a positive growth in every decade was Bengal, but even Bengal suffered an unusually high death rate as a result of the influenza epidemic of 1918–19, so that the rate of growth over the decade of 1911–21 was only 3.2 per cent. Bombay Presidency seems to have suffered the worst, with a virtually zero rate of growth in the decade of the 1870s, a negative rate of growth in the 1890s, and again a negative rate of growth in the decade 1911–21. Madras Presidency did slightly better, but it had a negative rate of growth in the 1870s and virtually a zero rate of growth in the 1910s again. Most of the princely states fared no better than Bombay and Madras. What is even more striking is that United Provinces, which had a riverine terrain, with expanding government irrigation systems, suffered repeated reverses in its population growth, as did the neighbouring provinces of Bihar and Orissa.

Lest somebody imagine that a regrouping of the provinces and estimating the rates of population growth on a comparable basis would alter any of our conclusions about the patterns of population growth, let me point out that Visaria and Visaria[35] have carried out such a regrouping of all the Indian provinces (excluding Burma) and princely states, into five zones—East, West, Central, North, and South—and have estimated their annual rates of growth over the period 1871–1941. Their estimates confirm that only the East zone had a positive rate of growth for all the decades from 1871 to 1921, with the lowest rate of growth in the period 1911–21, the West zone had negative rates of growth in every alternate decade starting with 1871–81, the Central zone had negative rates of growth in the decades 1891–1901 and 1911–21, the North zone had very low rates of growth in the decades 1891–1901 and 1901–11 (0.09 and 0.11 respectively) and a negative rate of growth in the period 1911–21, and the South zone a strongly negative rate of growth in 1871–81; India as a whole had annual rates of growth varying between 0.09 per cent (in the decade of 1911–21) and 0.89 per cent (in the decade of 1881–91). It is worth noticing that the 'prosperous' province of Punjab was not spared the horrors of famines and pandemics.

Remittances of Imperial Tribute

It might be thought that these statistics of death tell a complete story: no further elaboration is needed on either their origins or their ends, their causes or their implications. But dreadful as it may sound, famines benefited quite a lot of people, and famines and epidemics were aggravated, if not actually caused by some specific policies. One way of averting periodic famines would have been to invest in agriculture and industry so as to increase the productivity and the employment potential of the Indian economy. Some investment, of course, took place, but not enough. A major constraint on output growth and domestic investment was the leakage of a significant fraction of the income of British India in the form of the so-called Home charges remitted to Britain for maintaining the apparatus of British rule in India. Some figures are only for the first five years of this century but their relationship to one another would probably be representative of the whole period from 1876 to 1914.

From Table 7.4 we see that disbursements in England regularly amounted to 3–4 per cent or an even larger fraction of the national income in India. It may be argued that not all of this was leakage; some part—say, one-third to one-fourth of the disbursements—consisted of expenditures for railway construction or irrigation canals. But against that we must balance the expenditure on British troops and civil servants in India, which was a pure leakage from the point of view of the Indian economy. Such expenditures certainly amounted to a much larger sum than that spent for productive purposes by the India Office in England.

Table 7.4 National Income and Foreign Disbursements, India, 1900–05

Year	National income of India (in Rs million)	Disbursements in England		(3) as percentage of (1)
	(1)	(2)	(3)	(4)
1900–01	11,972	34,869	523,035	4.37
1901–02	11,863	27,460	411,900	3.47
1902–03	12,164	25,730	385,950	3.17
1903–04	11,833	31,492	472,380	3.99
1904–05	12,971	31,168	467,520	3.60

Source: For col. (1), Sivasubramonian (1965: Table 5.1); for col. (2), Statistics of British India, Fourth Issue, for 1909–10 and preceding years, Part IV (a), Finance and Revenue (Calcutta, Superintendent, Government Printing, 1911), Table No. 1 of 'Ways and Means—Home Government'.

Note: Col. (3) has been derived from col. (1) by applying a multiplier of Rs 15 to the pound.

Thus India was made to spend 3–4 per cent of her national income for simply maintaining the apparatus of foreign rule in the country. Of even the amount that was spent on productive investment, a large part—one-third to half—was spent abroad for buying machinery and raw materials. The stimulus such expenditures could have provided—in the form of incomes to the producers of railway stores or machinery and millwork, and so on, and in the longer run, an incentive to invest in the facilities for producing the capital and intermediate goods—was lost to the Indian economy.

When we try to assess the extent of the depression in the short run caused by this kind of leakage ('drain' in the older parlance), we have to remember that in this period not more than half perhaps of the national income passed directly through the market mechanism. And while there was a considerable amount of private investment in land in kind, the major growth in the productive capital would be financed directly and indirectly by the incomes accruing to the people who operated in the market. Thus the leakage may have amounted to 6 per cent or even more of that portion of income which counted from the point of financing productive investment.

There is a further aspect of the leakage of incomes abroad which is not easily quantified. The extraction of the surplus from the Indian economy took place mainly through the fiscal mechanism of the state. The taxes were mostly indirect, imposed on items of necessary consumption, such as salt, and on land, and the mechanism of extraction involved a host of intermediaries, such as landlords, tax-gatherers, and moneylenders. Their operations not only impoverished the peasants and artisans but also impaired their efficiency because the levies were generally exacted at the wrong time and in the wrong shape.

We have also to remember that of the incomes remaining in Indian hands, a very large fraction accrued to a small section of the population, leaving the vast majority of the people extremely poor, and hence poor consumers of industrial goods.

In the later sections of the chapter, we consider factors that shaped the growth of modern manufacturing and mining or processing industries in India. While doing that, we have to keep in mind the fact that despite the demographic disasters, despite the impoverishment of large sections of artisans, workers, and peasants, some groups were definitely prospering in India in the late nineteenth and early twentieth centuries. These would be the merchants dealing in exportable commodities and those commodities which had a more or less assured market, landlords who could squeeze out more rents or illegal exactions from their tenants, small and large manufacturers who benefited from the further lowering of the cost of labour (provided that they could sell their goods), and farmers who profited from the extension of irrigation in newly opened up areas in Punjab, Sind, and some other pockets. Famines themselves provided opportunities for making money to traders and financiers involved in the moving of grain in their private capacity or as part of famine relief operations. So while the poorer consumers contracted their purchases of many commodities because they were unemployed or otherwise impoverished, or just died, the groups benefiting from either genuine productivity-rising investment or from the dreadful processes of famines or regressive redistribution of incomes provided new markets for manufactured and other goods. These in turn extended the field of operations of the apex banks.

The Global and Indian Political Environment: Expectations of Foreign Industrial Investors

The thirty-nine years from 1876 to 1914 are no more than the years from birth to maturity of a citizen in an affluent country today. But they were little short of two full generations as measured by the lifespan of an average Indian of those days.[36] For most other human beings of the time also a generation and a lifespan of an average person were synonymous.

Lifespans were about to be extended first in Europe and North America, and then elsewhere, through the discoveries of Louis Pasteur (1822–95), Robert Koch (1843–1910), Fritz Haber (1868–1934), and numerous other scientists and technologists, mostly in Europe but increasingly in other parts of the globe as well. Even in Calcutta, where the sewers and slums of the Black Town made every conception an obstacle race for survival of the mother and her child, Ronald Ross (1857–1932) discovered the carrier of the malarial parasite and thus made it possible to plan for the containment of the disease, if not its eradication.

Those scientific discoveries were accompanied by others, which provided more plentiful means to some human beings to kill other human beings. Alfred Nobel's (1833–96) explosives, which would provide the wherewithal for recognition of scientific and literary genius was only one in a series of increasingly powerful chemicals, materials, weapons, and engineering devices for destruction. Even if most scientists regarded such uses as only unforeseen by-products of their work, few of them could be unaware that the political levers of that world were in the hands of people for whom war was a trade and a passion.

Our book spans the period from the Congress of Berlin (held in 1878), which was a truce in imperialist rivalries till the outbreak of the First World War, the first armed conflict encompassing the whole world. Indeed, this was the period when imperialism took the specific form of repeated attempts to re-divide the world between imperial powers, and India as the largest British colony was inevitably dragged into the vortex.

The financial aspects of the global domination by imperialist powers must be at the heart of any attempt to find a meaning or a pattern in the senseless narrative that history can otherwise turn out to be. Even Indian banking is part of that pattern, and while we desist from any attempt to even provide a sketch of the global financial scene, our story must often assume as a background what was happening in London, Paris, Berlin, and New York.

What was happening in the corridors of power and the closets of bankers in those centres did not go entirely unchallenged in the world outside. The last quarter of the nineteenth century saw the emergence of Indian nationalism as a movement orchestrated by middle-class professionals and businessmen; in Europe it saw the rise of organized labour. While the October Revolution of 1917 saw the culmination of one part of the European struggle, 1919 and 1920 saw the ascent of Mahatma Gandhi to a position of virtually undisputed leadership of the nationalist movement in India.

If we change our vantage point slightly, we can see that the year 1900, which falls roughly in the middle of our period, was almost the midpoint of the careers of two men, Rabindranath Tagore (1861–1941) and Rudyard Kipling (1865–1936), who in their persons embodied the literary ethos of the two poles of the British empire in India: Tagore captured in his short stories and novels—but specially in his short stories—the texture of life of the ordinary people—middle-class men and women mostly—but also peasants and their visible oppressors. Kipling created a secular religion for the white man's imperialist activities.

That the spoken words of the book have behind them some awareness of the larger world that does not make a direct appearance has to be explicitly stated for two quite different sorts of reason. First the history of any human institution yields up its meaning most fully when it can be seen as part of the larger tapestry, of all the contradictory, all the jostling aspects of man's (or woman's) social and political existence. Secondly, to the extent that any explanation of the developments narrated in the book is at all possible, that explanation can be constructed only in terms of the lives lived and the deaths suffered by ordinary people as well as the instruments wielded by the functionaries of the institutions whose evolution is studied in this particular case. The pitiful nature of the earnings of an Indian peasant at the height of the British Raj is an extremely relevant piece of information for understanding why the Bank of Madras could not lend to the peasants but might have been anxious to see the birth of such institutions (for example, co-operatives) as would mediate profitably between itself and the peasants. If we have to explain why such hopes came to nought in most cases, we have to probe into the exact nature of the precariousness of the subsistence of a typical Indian peasant.

However we look at it, the years from 1876 to 1914 is a long period in terms of the history of colonial India. This was also a period in which many long-term changes were presaged but did not happen: the Indian people had to wait another thirty-three years for political independence to arrive. The works of J.J. Thomson and his students at Cambridge, and the work of Max Planck, Albert Einstein, and Niels Bohr would ultimately release the devil's offspring in the skies of Hiroshima and Nagasaki in August 1945. The promise offered by the Indian fields of stopping the famines and eventually allowing the poor people at least to live longer did not begin to be realized until after 1947. The struggle for giving the poor peasants and artisans access to reasonable credit facilities was not taken up in earnest until after 1947 either.

These long-term changes or the waiting or the struggling for them changed people's lives. But those lives were lived from day to day, from month to month, from year to year and then only from generation to generation. It will give a false idea of astonishing jumps in time if, for purposes of description and analysis, we only take the end points of changes that spanned a life-time or more. On the other hand, if we only narrate the day-to-day changes, we will miss out the way ordinary human beings try to plan their life cycles and the way groups or aggregates of human beings try to overcome long-standing obstacles. Expectations about the long-term and actual long-term changes do affect behaviour, not least of all, behaviour with regard to production, trade, and investment decisions.

To illustrate the problem of knitting myriad details of short-run behaviour to depict the texture of the *longue duàee*, let us ask in what ways the fact that India was a dependent colony of Britain influenced the behaviour of traders, and investors, who formed the major clientele of the Presidency banks.

In order the avoid misunderstanding, it is necessary to emphasize again that the British Government of India was a despotism. It was answerable to the British people, most of whom were thoroughly ignorant of Indian affairs, but not to the Indian people in its entirety or its representatives. The actual Government of India was carried on by a small and immensely powerful body of civil servants. They had to obey laws, whose implementation was largely in their own hands. Most of the decisions taken by the supreme government consisting of the British Viceroy and his council could not be appealed against. British rule in India and its absolutist character looked pretty permanent to most informed observers. By and large, those traders and investors did best who took this permanence for granted and adapted their behaviour accordingly.

The colonial state apparatus protected private property, and by and large, respected the sanctity of private contracts. But it was a state geared first of all to the preservation of British rule and authority in India; and its actual institutions and policies effectively created positions of privilege for British businessmen in India. It also facilitated the sale of British manufactured goods in India and Indian primary products abroad, and by extension, the sale of those few manufacturers that required only rudimentary industrial skills or involved practically no economies of scale in production in a static or dynamic sense. The Government of India practised a commercial policy which was tantamount to free trade for all foreign goods in India. But, of course, most foreign countries other than Britain to which Indian exports were sent did not practise free trade. We can characterize this policy, after R.P. Dutt, as 'one-way free trade'.[37]

In this period the Indian economy was heavily biased towards the production of agricultural goods with very few inputs except land, labour, and perhaps some organic manure and—in the few patches where it was available—water from anicuts, canals, tanks, and wells. The British Indian government was willing to promote the construction of railways and subsidize them, if necessary, especially if they were perceived to have military importance, or to build port facilities, but its promotional measures in other directions were extremely meagre. Irrigation was perceived to be necessary for ensuring a rise in the productivity of crops and in agricultural exports, which, it was thought, would pay for imports of British manufactures. But the government normally financed the construction of irrigation canals only if the water rates would fully pay for the cost of digging and maintenance of the irrigation works. The experience of repeated famines and expenditures incurred in ameliorating (rather than really relieving) the distress of the people probably modified the stance somewhat in the twentieth century but the First World War supervened before any such hypothesis could be tested on the ground. We can, therefore, treat most of the period as one of general official callousness with regard to promotional and developmental measures that did not yield quick commercial returns to the government.

But, of course, even in a poor country with old trading channels, commerce developed progressively as the means of communication and finance extended all over the world and the Indian railway network and port facilities also grew. Those traders and financiers generally came out on top and were in positions of vantage to utilize the evolving network in India and had connections with markets where demand was expanding or where new techniques for processing the goods were being perfected.

The European businessmen trading in India fitted this bill best. The channels of overseas trade had become virtually their monopoly in most parts of India by 1876. They retained control over them and extended their operations to new areas and commodities as bigger steamers plied the seas, powered by ever more powerful steam engines and backed by giant firms such as the Peninsular and Oriental, or the British Indian Steam Navigation Co.

The major areas of activity of the European businessmen remained trade—trade in imported manufactures and in exportable primary commodities—with a sprinkling of crudely processed agriculture-based manufactures such as jute gunnies and hessian and cotton yarn of low counts. When easy opportunities of making profit opened up in the latter class of goods they combined their trade with manufactures. Since manufactures carried out under the control of European and Indian firms using modern machinery also provided expanding avenues for the employment of banking capital, it is necessary to delineate the dynamics of such manufactures, sketchy though such delineation must be.

Jute Manufacturers 1870–1914

Let us take, for example, the case of jute manufactures and the way it was developed by European entrepreneurs from 1854 onwards.[38] Of what relevance is their political and social orientation to British colonialism in India and to the British empire in general in understanding the Europeans' manufacturing record with respect to jute?

Jute had been spun into yarn or ropes and woven into gunny bags by handicraft methods, long before it was taken up for making into gunnies or hessian by machinery. The pioneer in the processing of jute by machinery was Dundee in Scotland, which was a traditional centre of flax spinning and weaving. Processing jute by machine methods, and treating the fibre with suitable oils or chemicals for this purpose had stabilized in Dundee by the 1850s. The Crimean War of 1854–6 provided a strong stimulus to the machine manufacture of jute goods in Dundee, since the import of flax from Russia virtually ceased. A further stimulus was provided by the American Civil War, which expanded the market for jute goods, mainly for provisioning the warring armies. Dundee became and remained virtually the sole centre of machine manufacture of jute goods for three decades from the 1840s up to the beginning of the 1870s, since the Indian contribution to such manufacture was negligible till then, and so was the contribution of competing countries such as France and Germany. This was possible because Dundee was the centre of the flax and linen industry, located in the leading industrial nation of the day. But it was also helped by the fact that jute was the monopoly product of Bengal and jute exports were a monopoly of the British traders located in Calcutta or the eastern Bengal districts.

The entry of the Indian branch of machine manufacture of jute goods occurred not as a competitor of Dundee in the export markets but as a competitor of the products of the handicraft jute manufactures of Bengal. Characteristically, the first jute-spinning mill was set up at Rishra because it was near Serampore, which was a centre of spinning and weaving of jute and hemp.[39] But once jute mills came up in numbers, the occupation of the traditional weavers of jute-sacking, the *Kapalis* of Bengal,[40] was destroyed. Moreover, the jute mills increasingly turned to distant locations in Bihar and Uttar Pradesh (North-Western Provinces, or United Provinces of Agra and Oudh in British days) for recruiting their labour, which was cheaper. The Indian labourers served in positions where the very rudimentary skills required could be picked up on the job. Another case of absolute de-skilling of Indian labour had taken place through the advent of modern machine-operated industries in an atmosphere of colonialism and racialism.

The first jute mill set up by George Ackland, was, like the first cotton mill, a pure spinning concern. Soon handlooms were added to this mill and from the second mill onwards, all the jute mills were both spinning and weaving units. These pioneering ventures—the Rishra (Ishara) mill, the mill of the Borneo Company, which later became the Baranagore Jute Mills, and the mills at Shibpur and Gouripur—all displaced jute handloom products which were sold within India and used extensively in the coastal trade.

But from the 1870s onwards came mills which increasingly sought markets abroad and began competing with Dundee in foreign markets. The person credited with the pioneering work in finding markets abroad was Thomas Duff. He had close connections with both Dundee and Calcutta. He was a trader but had a family background in manufacture at Dundee, and he obviously combined the skills of both a production manager and marketing manager. He was a member of the Borneo mill staff in the 1860s, then went back to Britain, and, after successfully running a mill at Barking (near London), decided to float the Samnuggur jute mill in 1873 in association with three other Dundee men.[41]

The very profitable working of the five older jute mills (except the Rishra mill) during the years 1868–73 provided the stimulus for the launching of several new mills, which took the number of looms in the jute mills of Bengal from 1,250 in June 1873 to 3,858 in April 1877.[42] The flotations of mills in these early years came under three heads: the first was a speculation by adventurous men with little money or real experience in running business ventures but with a lot of gumption.

Such were men like George Ackland and Richard Macallister, the bus conductor from Philadelphia who took over the Fort Gloster Mill.[43] Most of these adventurers' speculations failed, and the concerns were either closed or taken over by others. The second were 'speculations' by men or firms with money who decided to take a hand in a promising new venture. Thus were floated the mills of the Borneo Company, and the mills of the two doctors, the Seebpore (Shibpur) and Gourepore (Gouripur) jute companies. Since they were controlled by hard-headed men of business with some idea of the trade they entered, most such ventures of Scotsmen or Englishmen seem to have turned out well.

Last came that group of men who had both money and a direct experience of handling jute or its manufactures when they floated new jute mills. Among the pioneers, Thomas Duff and his Dundee friends, A. and J. Nicol and J.J. Barrie, fitted this bill best. The mills managed by Thomas Duff and Co., and registered in the UK, did very well. But increasingly, such combinations of expertise and money were to be found in the Anglo-Indian managing agencies such as Andrew Yule & Co., Bird & Co., George Henderson & Co. (later Jardine Henderson & Co.) and the jute mill industry came to be dominated by these concerns.

Mill flotations and increases in the loomage of the jute industry came in pulses: large profits led to strong expansive movements, a decline in prices of final goods, and a fall in profits. This in turn slowed up expansion, and then the cyclical movement resumed its upward phase. Speculative movements in raw jute, jute manufactures, and loom expansion were an integral aspect of the growth of the jute industry. But the remarkable part of the story was that between 1880 and 1910 the jute mills showed hardly any slackening of growth on a decade to decade basis.[44] The sturdiness of long-term growth of the jute industry, despite the speculative behaviour of many of the relevant variables, loses its paradoxical nature once we grasp, both the specificity of the European control of the 'commanding heights' of the colonial economy and polity and the nature of the international competition faced by the industry.

The international market for jute manufactures was expanding rather strongly. Between 1880–1 and 1888–9, while the amount of raw jute exported from India expanded from 5,809,815 cwts. to 10,553,143 cwts., and its value from Rs 39.94 million to Rs 78.97 million, the value of jute manufactures exported from India rose from Rs 11.31 million to Rs 25.71 million. Since India was the sole producer of jute in the world, and the raw jute exported was made into sacks or cloth at Dundee, or the USA and Continental European centres of manufactures, this shows that the overseas market for jute manufactures was expanding, and that the fraction of jute processed overseas was much larger than that made into sacks and gunny cloth in the Calcutta mills. Thus, up to the end of the nineteenth century, the Calcutta jute mills were not yet taking away markets from Dundee or any other manufacturer but they were increasing their share in an ever-growing market. Secondly, jute manufactures were virtually a new industry at Dundee as in Calcutta, and the Dundee products had yet to become entrenched in most of the markets: those markets were yet to be formed in the 1880s and 1890s, through further expansion of grain production in the US prairie or the Argentine pampas.

That the political opposition from Dundee to the expansion of the Calcutta jute mills did not become very fierce is thus explained by a number of factors, such as the expanding nature of the international market, the relative newness of the industry at Dundee, the commonness of ties of many of the Dundee and the Calcutta entrepreneurs,[45] the countervailing interest of the machinery manufacturers at Dundee in supplying the Calcutta jute mills, and finally the relatively small dimensions of the industry and jute mill interests at Dundee (in contrast with the Lancashire cotton mills, which exerted a far more effective pressure on the Government of India in an attempt to slow down the growth of the Indian cotton mills).

Once the British businessmen found that it was much more economical to manufacture the simpler kinds of jute goods in Calcutta than in Scotland, they did not have too much to worry about the Dundee competition. In India, through their extensive commercial network, they had a firm hold of the wholesale trade in jute, at least up till the First World War, a labour force which was kept docile and cheap through the lack of alternative employment opportunities and the use of all the means of coercion available to members of the ruling race in a colonial setting, and privileged access to foreign markets through their agents and contacts in London and Scotland. To all this was added the consolidation of economic power by a few managing agency houses such as Bird & Co., Andrew Yule & Co., George Henderson & Co., Jardine Skinner, Gillanders Arbuthnot, Kettlewell Bullen, Ernsthausen, & Co., and F.W. Heilgers—a consolidation that was protected by privileged access to high finance and to any government patronage that was going, such as contracts for supplies of rice to fight famines, construction of port facilities, opening of branch railways, and so on. In the jute mill sector this control was further enhanced by the establishment (in 1884) of the Indian Jute Manufacturers' (later, Mills) Association, which operated something approaching a collective monopoly, especially when prices of jute manufactures fell, threatening profits. This setting gave the confidence to Ernest Cable who would write in 1903 (in a letter to C.S. Cox): 'In the prosperous times of a boom, we can "off our own bat" float a jute mill in three hours.'[46]

In the case of jute manufactures, we can take the growth of the major market as being exogenous to the Indian economy: the expansion of European overseas settlements and the growth of the grain trade propelled that market. A part of the market was in India. There, however, it was expansion of the railways and trade in grain and seeds—forces that were released by the colonial government or the international economy—which provided the chief impetus. We can also by and large ignore the handloom sector of the jute industry, for handicraft manufacture of jute very soon paled into insignificance in comparison with the mill output of jute goods, and never recovered the lost ground. For example, already in 1884–5, out of the total exports of 82,779,207 gunny bags, 77,841,776 were produced by powerlooms (all located in mills) and only 4,937,637,431 by handlooms.[47]

The jute industry in India continued to forge ahead, and the biggest managing agency houses of eastern India came to control a significant percentage of the productive capacity in the mills. Table 7.5 shows that there was hardly a slackening of the long-term rates of growth until the eve of the First World War. By 1909, the Indian mills had left Dundee far behind in their productive capacity.[48] From the first decade of this century, the exports of raw jute also began declining.[49]

Table 7.5 Indian Jute Mills, 1879–80 to 1909–10

Year or period	No. of persons employed	No. of looms	No. of spindles
1879–80	26,826	4,876	69,456
1889–90	58,830	7,629	155,318
1899–1900	101,630	14,021	293,218
1909–10	204,104	31,418	645,862
	Percentage growth in		
	No. of persons employed	No. of looms	No. of spindles
Between 1879–80 and 1889–90	119.3	60.6	123.6
Between 1889–90 and 1899–1900	72.8	83.8	88.8
Between 1899–1900 and 1909–10	100.8	124.1	120.3

Source: Government of India, Director-General (later, Department) of Commercial Intelligence and Statistics, *Financial and Commercial Statistics of British India*, and *Statistics of British India* and Bagchi (1972: Table 8.1).

Since there were other countries producing jute manufactures, and since these countries often imposed a higher tariff duty on imports of jute goods than on jute, Indian mills could not exercise a fully monopolistic control over prices or quantities of jute manufactures. But they could act as a local regulator of prices or quantities and as a quantity or price leader (depending on the prevailing situation, a quantity leader in the case of a shortage of jute and a price leader in the case of a glut of jute manufactures),[50] and this is what they became, probably from the 1890s onwards. The Indian Jute Mills Association helped organize short-time working agreements which formalized some aspects of the collective leadership exercised by the industry. (For exercising a collective local monopoly it was not necessary that prices of jute goods should be kept high permanently or that there should be insuperable barriers against the creation of new capacity.)[51]

Since the variations in the profitability of the mills were almost entirely governed by the price at which they bought jute and the price at which they sold their gunnies or hessian (since wages were stagnant, and techniques unchanging), what the mills sought to do through the short-time agreements was to drive a wedge between market arrivals of jute in Calcutta and their purchases, and between the sales of manufactures and their fabrication. On the other side, the short-time agreements forbade the extension of jute mill capacity beyond those already publicly admitted by the mills[52] and thus regulated the extension of the capacity within wide limits. The latter task became easier over time as a small group of European managing agencies came to control most of the mills.[53] The success of the short-time agreements is partly indicated by, and was in turn conditional upon, the fact that expansion of mill capacity and increase in mill consumption of jute kept in pace in the years up to the First World War.[54]

The continued growth of the jute industry the world over was made possible primarily through the expansion of production of grain and other bulky materials in countries such as the USA, Argentina, and Australia. The Indian mills were accounting for a larger and larger share in the world market for jute manufactures but that market was expanding fast enough to at least allow the other manufacturing centres to go on producing growing amounts (Table 7.6).

Table 7.6 Exports of Raw Jute and Jute Manufacturers from India, 1879–80 to 1909–10

Annual average for period	Exports of raw jute		Values of exports of jute manufacturers (Rs lakhs)
	Quantity (*cwts*)	Value (Rs lakhs)	
1882–3 to 1891–2	9,279,565	6,15	1,87
1892–3 to 1901–02	11,771,835	9,54	5,54
1902–03	13,036,486	11,13	9,02
1903–04	13,721,447	11,72	9,47
1904–05	12,875,312	11,97	9,94

Source: O'Conor (1908: Chapter 5, pp. 282, 287).

But as has been noted already, exports of raw jute from India and hence jute manufactures in foreign countries began to decline in the years immediately preceding the First World War. In the first decade of this century, as indeed in other periods, the price of raw jute fluctuated greatly, and fears were expressed that jute might be replaced by some cheaper fibre.[55] But no such fibre could be found, and the jute mill companies continued to promise about the best average returns over time among British-controlled enterprises.

Indeed, the prosperity of jute trade (apart from movement of grain for famine relief in 1899) was the only item explicitly mentioned in the reports of the Bank of Bengal, for the half-years ending in 31 December 1899, 31 December 1904, 31 December 1906, 31 December 1912, and 31 December 1913 as being responsible for creating an enhanced demand for money in those half-years. (The latter half of the year was, of course, normally the slack season for the Indian money market.)

The jute mill companies were a large absorber of working capital, and hence naturally major customers of banks. For example, for a group of six sterling companies, for the year 1908–09, the total stocks in hand at the end of the accounting year amounted to £1.54 million out of total assets of £4.20 million.[56] But there were other modern industries in eastern India, which were also large absorbers of working capital, and hence major users of bank finance. Tea and coal are the two other large 'industries' in eastern India, and they were almost as exclusively under European control before the First World War as the jute industry.

Tea Plantations 1870–1914

Indian tea could oust the China tea from the British market for several reasons: the Indian tea planters could reduce their cost of production and hence the price at which they sold their products as their cultivation practices improved, as the proportion of mature trees to immature plantations of tea increased over time and the size of cultivated areas or plantations under the control of a single managerial unit increased on an average.[57] But price changes were not the sole factor: for, Chinese tea prices in London also declined in response to Indian competition. While the price of Indian pekoe per lb. in Calcutta declined from Re 1-1-3 pies in 1871 to Re 0-I 5-3 pies in 1885, the price of China Souchong in London declined from Is. 8½d. in 1871 to Is. 4½d. in 1885.[58] Two factors, in addition to price reduction, seem to explain the advance of Indian tea in the London market: one was the continuous change in British taste from the green to the black varieties of tea, and the other was the inability of the Chinese peasant to match the responsiveness and the aggressiveness of the British tea planting and marketing companies.[59]

When the British planters in Ceylon (Sri Lanka) shifted from blighted coffee plants to the plantation of tea, tea plantations in India met a formidable competitor in the London market. The plantations in Ceylon were organized by basically the same class of people as controlled the plantations in India, and seem to have been more aggressive in increasing their output and marketing it abroad. During the late 1890s and early twentieth century, in response to the usual cyclical fluctuations and competition from Ceylonese tea, planters often raised a cry of 'overproduction', but most schemes of regulation of production fell through, and Indian acreage and output of tea continued to increase apace, as is shown by figures in Table 7.7. From this Table it is also seen that while cultivation in areas other than Assam and Bengal increased, eastern India retained its pre-eminence in the production of tea in India.

Table 7.7 Area under Tea and Average Annual Production of Tea in British India, 1886–1910

Period	Assam		Bengal		British India	
	Area (acres)	Output (1000 lbs)	Area (acres)	Output (1000 lbs)	Area (acres)	Output (1000 lbs)
1886–90	218,000	72,376	77,500	21,576	322,700	98,109
1891–5	258,100	92,656	99,300	31,151	389,800	131,246
1896–1900	319,200	119,154	124,500	41,457	488,600	169,388
1901–05	338,600	143,162	135,400	50,151	525,800	204,642
1906–10	345,100	168,613	141,300	61,325	547,400	251,072

Source: Misra (1985: Tables 2.2 and 2.7); these Tables are based on Government of India, Department of Statistics (later Department of Commercial Intelligence and Statistics), *Cultivation of Tea in India* (annual), *Production of Tea in India* (annual), and *Note on the Production of Tea in India*.

Before leaving the subject of tea in India, two structural characteristics of the industry must be considered, and for the relation of the tea industry to apex banking. First, tea gardens generally owned a considerable amount of land that was not used for cultivation.[60] Some of it was intended for new plantations in future, some of it was used as barriers against intrusion of wild animals (or as pathways for their passage without disturbing the plantation), and some was used to tie the workers down to plantations once their period of indenture was over. The tea gardens gave these workers small plots of land on which they could build cottages and grow vegetables. This way the workers' families provided a reservoir from which to draw labour in the peak plucking season. Over time, as workers became more settled in these areas, such policies were used to curb their discontent at the deplorable living conditions and ensure their subjection to the semi-servile discipline of the tea gardens.

The second characteristic to be noticed is that most large plantations were controlled by European companies or partnerships, and that

Indians were mostly owners of small gardens.[61] On the basis of data provided by *Thacker's Indian Directory* for the year 1910 it has been estimated that while the average size of estates controlled by Indians was 210 acres, that of estates controlled by the Europeans was 817 acres, the total area under the control of the former being only 28,311 acres as against 495,115 acres controlled by Europeans.[62] Moreover, a large fraction of the European gardens was controlled by big managing agency houses based in India and Britain.[63] Hence, besides the racial barriers that generally restricted the access of Indian businessmen to credit given by European-controlled banks, there were further structural factors limiting the access of Indian tea gardens to finance provided by the Bank of Bengal (and very probably other large joint-stock banks operating in eastern India). From the surviving correspondence of the head office of the Bank of Bengal with its Jalpaiguri branch (which was the first branch to be opened in 1894 in the tea-growing district, primarily to facilitate remittance of funds by the managing agents in Calcutta to the gardens under their control), it appears that in 1903 or 1904, the typical method of financing an Indian-owned tea garden (such as Anjuman Tea Co. Ltd., Chunia Jhora Tea Co. Ltd., or Gurjang Jhora Tea Co. Ltd.) or a small European garden (such as that of Preyer & Co. at Haldibari) was to get a demand promissory note from the company, guaranteed by a European tea broker in Calcutta (W.S. Creswell & Co., or A.W. Figgis & Co.) who handled their crop, and also get the crop in the plantation hypothecated as collateral security.[64] But the Bank of Bengal agent at Jalpaiguri claimed in October 1903 that he had got all the 'native' tea gardens in his district to do their 'financing through his branch', presumably, in the form of cash credit limits guaranteed by their tea brokers. This pattern of financing continued at least down to the 1920s. The Indian gardens borrowed directly from the Jalpaiguri Banking and Trading Corporation, Jotedars' Bank, and so on; later on, the Central Bank of India financed some Indian gardens.[65] By contrast, tea gardens controlled by large European managing agents had their finance arranged in Calcutta through those agents. This pattern of financing held throughout the period 1876–1914.

Coal Mining 1870–1914

The third branch of non-agricultural enterprise in India in which finance was required on a large scale was coal mining. As mentioned earlier, this industry can be traced back to early days of British rule.[66] However, down to 1879–80, the amount of coal mined annually in India fell short of one million tons: out of a total estimated Indian consumption of 1,455,873 tons in that year, imports amounted to 587,634 tons and Indian output to 868,239 tons.[67] There were many reasons for this slow growth. The first was the lack of industries which would use coal to run boilers or steam engines, or use it as an input for making dyes.[68] The second was the lack of acquaintance of ordinary Indians with mineral coal as a fuel and their continued use of wood or other vegetable and waste matter for cooking and heating purposes. The third reason was the wanton felling of forests not only by ordinary domestic users and businessmen for purposes of fuel, but also for use by railways which were the biggest potential consumers of coal at that time. To cite some figures at random, in 1887, Indian railways consumed 292,808 tons of wood as fuel;[69] in 1905 the consumption of wood (as fuel) was 253,159 tons, in 1914 it was down to 95,598 tons, and in 1917 it again increased to more than 243,450 tons.[70] The fourth factor behind the slow growth of the use of Indian coal was the prejudice against it harboured by European managers of railways and industrial enterprises. Coal raised from the Bengal mines had a typically higher ash content, and a lower carbon content than the imported English and Welsh coal, but it generally had a lower sulphur content.[71] In any case, Indian coal was much cheaper than imported coal, and if we go by the figures of ton-mile output per lb. of coal yielded on East Indian Railways by imported (Welsh) and Indian coal, and calculate the productivity per rupee of the two types of coal,[72] Bengal coal would come out as distinctly the superior input to use. However, almost certainly, the British equipment used on railways and in all industrial enterprises was not always adapted to handle the higher ash-content of the Indian coal, and the prejudices of European managers and engineers were slow to die.[73]

As the demand for coal in India increased, prejudices gave way to the attraction of lower prices, and the output of Indian coal increased, as is shown by Table 7.8. A major leap in output took place with the exploitation of the Jharia coalfields after 1894. This was made possible because a railway connection between the Jharia coalfields and the rest of the country (especially Calcutta, and through the trunk lines to Bombay) was built in 1894. But imports of foreign coal into India continued: part of the import was due to the low cost of sea carriage to the western coast of India compared with the cost of carrying coal from the Bengal coalfields, but part was also due to the continued consumption of foreign coal by Indian railways even in places which could have been supplied economically by the Bengal coalfields. As in

Table 7.8 Average Annual Production, Exports, and Imports of Coal in British India, 1886–1910

Year or period	Production of Indian coal	Net imports of foreign coal into India	Exports of Indian coal
1881–5	1,227	657	Negligible
1886–90	1,758	733	18[(b)]
1890–5	2,758	677[(a)]	41
1896–1900	4,750	333	305
1901–05	7,627	204	569
1906–10	11,523	344	775
1911	12,716	319	862
1912	14,736	561	899
1913	16,208	645	759
1914	16,464	419	580

Source: Misra (1985: Table 3.17); and *Investor's India Year-Book* (1919: 157).
Notes: (a) Four years' average.
(b) Three years' average.

the case of use iron rails,[74] the prejudice against Indian produce may have survived long in the hearts of some European railwaymen.

As Indian production increased, exports of coal to other countries, especially the Straits Settlements and Ceylon also increased. The generally slow growth of modern industry in India as a whole contributed to a slow growth of the coal industry. The operation of coal mines involved most of the large coal companies in Bengal and Bihar in the running of colliery zamindaris. The land from which the coal was mined was already permanently settled. The colliery companies either acquired the zamindari rights or leased them wholesale or piecemeal.[75] They used them to exploit the mines in any way they pleased, for there were few official guidelines regulating the operation of mines, and those few that were there were more often than not observed in the breach. These zamindari rights were also very powerful instruments for the control of labour. Mine-workers were generally recruited from the surrounding forest-dwellers or people belonging to the so-called tribal groups or scheduled castes. The conditions of work were bad, accident rates high, and naturally, labour sought many ways of evading this slavery. The coal mines tried to coerce people living on land controlled by them to go into the mines, or face being literally turned out of their hearth and home. On the other side, those mining companies which faced a shortage of labour at the going wages tried to entice workers by giving them tiny plots of land to live on and grow crops in. (The similarity with the practice in the plantations is obvious.) Thus the running of capitalist enterprise in coalfields involved a good deal of coercion by the colonial state and instruments to stop the unrestrained working of free markets in land and labour.[76] Some of the larger joint-stock companies such as the Bengal Coal Co. (controlled by Andrew Yule) and Burrakur Coal Co. (controlled by Bird & Co.) ruled their collieries virtually like feudal domains, and the racial superiority arrogated by the colliery controllers and the ruling race to which they belonged helped enormously in this mode of carrying on capitalist enterprise.

While there were several large collieries before 1914 raising and selling anywhere between Rs 1 million and Rs 10 million worth of coal,[77] most collieries were small; even many joint-stock coal companies raised and sold coal worth Rs 100,000 or less. Collieries mainly depended on cheap labour working under highly unscientific conditions to raise coal and make their profits: this was true of large as well as small companies. In fact, the coal mining operations of many large companies were leased out to raising contractors who invested as little as possible in modern mining equipment. Many managing agents had coal mines under their management, which they ran under very different systems of control. Some of the smallest or inconveniently located mines might be leased by them to private contractors or to other companies on payment of royalties (generally as so many rupees per ton of coal raised), in some mines the actual raising operations would be carried on by contractors, and only for the rest of the mines would the companies become direct employers of mining labour and conduct the raising operations themselves.

The coal mines under the management of large managing agencies were only a part of conglomerates consisting of jute mills, tea plantations, coal mines, mica mines, manganese mines, and perhaps an engineering works or two, and a paper mill or two.[78] Of course, these processing and mining enterprises would be linked together in a huge trading network covering say, imports of piece-goods, sales of shellac, oilseeds, raw jute, and any other products that might be profitably traded overseas or in the Indian market on a wholesale basis.

Patterns of Conglomerate Control

The horizontal or vertical patterns of integration between the different firms under their control were determined by the strategic goals of the particular conglomerate concerned.[79] The financial structures of the different companies within the conglomerate, and the use of the companies—as loss leaders or profit centres—would be determined by the strategic goals of the conglomerate as well as the histories of those particular companies. For example, where the companies were old and not particularly profitable, their equity capital would be large, because much of the windfall profit made by them would have already been realized at their moments, of glory in the form of sales or transfers of shares of the companies, and there would not be large profits to be alienated to shareholders unconnected with the managing agency house. But if a firm was expected to be outstandingly profitable, the equity capital base would be narrow, the company would be closely held, and the needed capital would be raised through debentures or preference shares. Such differences between company characteristics and expectations about their behaviour were there even within the same industry, but they could sometimes be seen emerging as a differential industry characteristic. Thus, for example, cotton mills in eastern India were not greatly profitable in the late nineteenth or early twentieth centuries, and sterling tea companies were generally highly capitalized through sales of shares at prices that reflected the expectations created by the promoters. This is why, for example, the values of paid-up capital for jute mill companies underestimated the total investment made in them and those of sterling or rupee tea companies or cotton mill companies in eastern India tended to give an exaggerated idea of the capital invested in them.[80]

The three industries we have so far taken up for a detailed examination formed the core of the group of modern industries in eastern India. For India as a whole also, apart from the cotton mill industry, which we take up in the next section, jute mills, tea gardens, and coal mines were the most important fields of investment of private capital on a large scale and employment of labour in relatively large units of organization. Besides these three fields, there were, of course, the railways, which might be regarded as the biggest field of employment of capital in India. But most railways had been promoted with public guarantees of profit, many were developed as state enterprises, and increasing mileages of the railway system were being bought up by the state. Their growth was far more influenced by the aims of the colonial state and the attitudes of European investors putting their money in the London money market for investment in Indian government securities than by the private profit motives of individual British or Indian investors in India. It is true that as the guarantee system was extended to promotion of railways by provincial governments and district boards, managing agency houses in India took a hand in running branch railway lines. Many such railway companies as well as port or municipal development authorities turned towards the Presidency banks to underwrite their bond flotations and subscribe to their paper. But all such activities belonged to the public domain of the colonial state and were not just outgrowths of the private commercial activities of British business, powered by the same sort of opportunities as actuated their investment in jute and tea companies. Besides the enterprises already mentioned, there grew up between 1876 and 1914, coffee plantations in southern India, a few sugar mills in northern India, a few paper mills scattered throughout India (the most important ones being located in eastern India), and a few engineering enterprises, the most important of which were again located in eastern India.

We have already noticed that Bengal alone, among all the major provinces of India, experienced a substantial growth of population throughout the four decades between the 1870s and 1914. Most of the growth of modern enterprises also came to be concentrated in the land and the abundant population of the eastern region. European managing agency houses drew not only on the labour force of the central, northern, and a part of the southern region, through the extensive network of recruitment maintained by the European managing agents in Calcutta.[81] The colonial state apparatus at its different levels, the particular land laws in operation in eastern India, and the system of indentured labour in the Assam tea plantations ensured the supply of cheap labour to all these enterprises without virtually any let or hindrance.

All these forces combined to give Bengal a lead in the expansion of exports. We have estimated five-yearly averages of figures of exports of merchandise from the three Presidency towns of Calcutta, Bombay, and Madras, and the hinterlands of their own ports and minor ports near them. We find that in comparison with the average annual merchandise exports of the five years from 1871–2 to 1875–6, the annual average merchandise exports of the five years from 1911–12 to 1915–16 expanded by 282.71 per cent in the case of Bengal, 162.53 per cent in the case of Bombay and 257.73 per cent in the case of Madras.[82] Since Bengal's exports were already in the first quinquennium Rs 241.5 million, as against Rs 221.0 million of Bombay, and Rs 67.2 million of Madras, by the beginning of the First World War, Bengal's total exports considerably exceeded those of Bombay and Madras combined. On the other hand, because of the definite retardation suffered by Bombay, the relative differential between the exports from Madras and Bombay was considerably narrowed over the period. That the rapid expansion of Bengal's exports failed to benefit the Indians of eastern India to any great extent had to do with the whole political economy of British rule in India, some aspects of which have already been touched.

The Development of Modern Industry and the Internal Market in India: The Case of the Cotton Textile Industry

The growth of the cotton mills in India was influenced more strongly by the state of the market for cotton cloth within India rather than abroad, thus providing a contrast with both jute mills and tea gardens. Moreover, unlike in the case of coal, which was an intermediate good, the current level of income rather than current investment had the major influence on the state of the market for cotton goods. Cotton mills contrasted with jute mills also in another respect: the interaction between the handicraft and the mill sectors of the industry had a far greater influence on the fortunes of the cotton mills than on those of the jute mills.

Down to the end of the nineteenth century, handlooms continued to produce the larger part of the total Indian output of cotton cloth. For example, in 1900–01, the output of cotton piece-goods of Indian mills was 420.6 million yards, that of Indian handlooms was 646.4 million yards and net imports of cotton piece-goods into India was 1,875 million yards.[83] Indian mill production of cotton piece-goods appears to have overtaken the handloom output only by 1909–10. But the two together fell short of the net imports of cotton piece-goods into India even in the years 1913–14 and 1914–15. We have already seen that despite lack of systematically estimated national income series before 1900, it is possible to say that by and large, in most regions of India ordinary people were poor, tended to die early and in large numbers; and they tended to fare no better in 1900 than they had done in 1870.

It is difficult to believe that the demand for consumer goods could grow fast among such a disease- and famine-ridden population. There were, of course, very rich landlords, princes, businessmen, and professionals, especially lawyers, among that population, but the demand coming from them would be mostly for luxuries and the better varieties of cloth, not for the coarse cloth which would be the major staple of the Indian cotton mill industry, once mills took up weaving in earnest.

When we turn from the consideration of the general economic background to the Indian market for mill-produced cotton twist and yarn, and cotton cloth, we have to bear in mind three factors tending to increase the demand for mill-produced cotton cloth and yarn even if the incomes of ordinary people were not increasing fast, or not increasing at all. First, the prices of ordinary cotton cloth and lower counts of yarn declined almost steadily from 1873 down to 1896 or so. The influences tending to this result had to do with the general slide in agricultural prices in international markets during the period,[84] and the intensification of competition in the international cotton textile industry. This would tend to increase the sales of cotton goods. Secondly, there was probably a change in tastes and fashions going on in India, so that those who could afford it wore more clothing than before and more mill-made cloth than before. Thirdly, during this period, the sales of mill-produced yarn continued to increase at the cost of handspun everywhere in India,[85] and the sales of mill cloth also tended to eat into the markets of hand loom cloth in many regions. But in some parts of India handlooms were able to expand by using mill-made yarn and displacing imported coarse cloth. However, the Indian and the Japanese mills proved to be much tougher competitors of Indian handlooms than the Lancashire mills had been in this range of fabrics.

If we ignore the Bowreah cotton mill (near Howrah)[86] in Bengal founded in 1817 or 1818 and the cotton mill established at Pondicherry some years later, which did not lead to any cumulative growth of the cotton mill industry, the real beginnings of that industry can be said to have taken place in western India. The first two factories, the one founded at Broach by James Landon in 1855, and the other by Cowasjee Nanabhoy Davar in Bombay in 1856 (these were the years when they began to function although they were conceived in 1854) were both spinning mills. The third mill, the Oriental, founded by Maneckjee Petit which began functioning in 1858 had a weaving shed housing 300 looms located in it.[87]

The Bombay mills constituted the predominant sector of the Indian cotton mill industry for a long time, and it is with their prospects that we must concern ourselves first. The Bombay mills suffered a setback after 1861, first with the cotton boom caused by the civil war in the USA and blockage of cotton exports from the southern states and then with the crash of 1866–7, which took a heavy toll of businesses in Bombay.[88] The cotton boom affected the expansion of the Bombay mills by raising the profitability of trading as against industrial investment, by increasing the price of cotton beyond all previous records, and probably also by making it scarce in the Indian market, since it was grabbed by exporting firms for sale in Britain. The last factor also adversely affected one major segment of the customers of the Bombay mills—the Indian handloom weavers. The crash caused further damage since many mills were saddled with stocks of cotton bought at fancy prices, and also of unsold finished goods and so were unable to clear the large loans taken in the years of inflated valuation of their security.

During most of the 1860s new mills came up, mostly in other parts of India than Bombay city. But between 1873 and 1875, Bombay witnessed a phenomenal amount of mill-building and when the Bombay Mill-owners' Association was established in 1875, the Bombay segment was the leader of the mill industry by a large margin.

The early mills specialized in the spinning of yam of an average count of 20s or even lower. Although some mills also had powerlooms for weaving, more than 50 per cent of all yarn spun was sold by them.[89] The Bombay merchants had close trading links with China, so yarn was exported to that country as well as to nearby Indian provinces such as the Madras Presidency from the late 1860s. But such exports, gathered momentum in the 1870s and 1880s (Table 7.9). What the mills in India were doing was to replace the lowest counts of yarn imported into India and China, and also, of course, displacing the work of spinners in both the countries.

Table 7.9 Annual Averages of Exports of Cotton Twist and Yarn to Foreign Countries from India, 1871–89

Quinquennium or year	Quantity (lbs)	Value (Rs)
1871–2 to 1875–6	4,370,329	20,96,007
1876–7 to 1880–1	19,524,665	86,55,305
1881–2 to 1885–6	54,035,981	2,06,16,340
1888–9	128,906,764	5,20,70,996

Source: Watt (1972[1890]: 169).

Despite competition from the Indian mills, the imports of twist and yarn into India continued to increase down to the end of the 1880s (Table 7.10). It can be seen that the prices of yarn, whether imported or exported, were declining all these years. Since the Indian mills were still mostly producing yarn of an average of count of 20s, their output was catering to the needs of the handloom weavers producing the coarser varieties of woven goods in India and China. However, the finer varieties of handloom cloth continued to be woven for a long time with imported yarn.

Table 7.10 Annual Averages of Imports of Cotton Twist and Yarn into India, 1871–9

Quinquennium or year	Quantity (lbs)	Value (Rs)
1871–2 to 1875–6	31,934,495	2,72,68,650
1876–7 to 1880–1	36,339,902	2,96,16,344
1881–2 to 1885–6	44,542,928	3,31,97,401
1888–9	52,587,181	3,74,67,969

Source: Watt (1972[1890]: 167).

The biggest segment of visible trade in cotton cloth in the 1870s was, however, the imports of mill-made cloth from abroad (Table 7.11).

Table 7.11 Annual Averages of Values of Imports of Cotton Manufacturers (other than twist and yarn) into India, 1866–89

Quinquennium or year	(in Rs)
1866–7 to 1870–1	14,78,63,641
1871–2 to 1875–6	15,55,54,760
1876–7 to 1880–1	17,45,54,086
1881–2 to 1885–6	21,23,08,636
1888–9	27,76,45,082

Source: Watt (1972[1890]: 170).

Indian mills found it far more difficult to substitute these imports than the imports of yarn or the production of coarse cloth by handlooms. An elaborate marketing network had been built up by the big British managing agency houses for servicing the imports of piece-goods—a network which involved organized banking, the flow of information, and infrastructure. The proportion of European and Indian piece-goods received by the different provinces in 1888–9 is indicated in Table 7.12.

As Table 7.12 indicates, in 1888–9 there was an enormous volume of interprovincial trade in cotton piece-goods. Bengal or rather Calcutta was the biggest import point of foreign piece-goods and it supplied North-West Provinces and Oudh (Uttar Pradesh), Assam, and even Punjab (Bihar and Orissa were included with Bengal). As the trade channels developed, the lines of supply changed: more and more of

Table 7.12 Net Imports of Cotton Piece-goods into Different Provinces of India in 1888–9

(*in Rs lakhs*)

	European manufacture	Indian manufacture	Total
North-West Provinces and Oudh	399	–17	382
Bengal	836	–2	834
Madras	138	–30	108
Punjab	281	11	292
Bombay	91	–37	54
Central Provinces	50.5	–10	40.5
Nizam's Territory	18	4	22
Rajputana and Central India	84	31	115
Berar	27.25	12	39.25
Mysore	26	10	36
Assam	64.25	2.25	66.25
Sind	43	34	77

Source: Watt (1972[1890]: 163–4).

Punjab would be supplied by Bombay and Karachi as the railway and trading network spread.

Since a large part of the piece-goods traded were of the finer varieties, these provincial import figures would not be taken as appropriate targets for the local, provincial cotton mill industries. This was especially the case where the province or centre concerned suffered from a comparative disadvantage vis-à-vis Bombay and Ahmedabad. It was otherwise with imports of twist and yarn, which were of a cruder variety. Here such provinces as Madras and North-West Provinces and Oudh, and even Bengal, would aspire to displace both imports of European yarn and yarn produced by the Bombay mills. In 1882–8, for example, of the total value of yarn (Rs 14,958,006) imported into Madras fully 84 per cent was of foreign origin.[90] Of the total import of European yarn worth Rs 14.96 million, Rs 10.35 million was directly imported from the UK, Rs 3.35 million from the Bombay Presidency and Rs 1.35 million from Bengal. The explanation of the latter figure was that besides the advantages conferred by the trading and financing networks of big Calcutta and Bombay firms, many places of the Madras Presidency were much more accessible from the ports of the Bengal and Bombay Presidencies than from ports of the Madras Presidency of 1888–9. The total imports of yarn from other provinces into Madras were Rs 11.7 million. Of this amount Rs 2.7 million was the product of Indian mills elsewhere (mostly in Bombay, but some in Bengal). Since these would be mostly coarse yarn, the Madras mills could try to substitute most of those imports. The provincial contours of the supply channels in 1888–9 are indicated in Table 7.13.

Table 7.13 Value of Imports of Cotton Twist and Yarn into Different Provinces of India, 1888–9

(*in Rs lakhs*)

	European manufacture	Indian manufacture	Total	Supplied from
Madras	90	27	117	Madras and Bombay
Bengal	85	31	116	Bombay
Bombay	83	8	91	Bombay
North-West Provinces and Oudh	32	12	44	Bengal
Punjab	28	3	31	NW Provinces and Bengal
Central Provinces	19	11	30	Bombay
Nizam's Territory	11	4	15	Bombay
Mysore	6	5	11	Bombay
Sind	8	1	9	Bombay
Assam	9	–	9	Bengal
Berar	16	1	17	Bombay
Rajputana and Central India	4	2	6	Bombay

Source: Watt (1972[1890]: p. 162).

Hence the proximate target for Indian mills would be to supply the coarse yarn (that is, yarn of low counts) consumed by weavers in local and nearby markets, to continue to supply coarse yarn to China from favourable locations in Bombay, Madras, and even Bengal and to take away the market for coarse cloth from handloom weavers and from the Lancashire mills. To Indian mills, the Indian market would not look like a vast undifferentiated plain to conquer in a massed campaign but as a variegated topography to be won by localized battles and positional warfare.

To the problem of the regional fragmentation of the market was to be added the heterogeneous nature of the product already alluded to.

Indian mills by and large would require better machinery and more skilled workmen than they had in the 1880s to produce finer counts of yarn and better qualities of cloth. The proposition that Indian cotton was almost exclusively of the short-staple and medium-staple variety and was hence an obstacle against the production of finer qualities is debatable. The fact of the matter is that Indian mills—especially at Bombay—seem to have suffered a decided setback in the 1890s and their rate of growth fell drastically in the 1890s and down to the First World War. The difficulty of conquering the markets for finer counts of yarn and better qualities of cloth cannot be blamed for this, for the Bombay mills suffered reverses in the market for coarse yarn in China, and their growth slowed down long before they had begun to wrest any significant part of the market for the finer varieties of cloth from the Lancashire mills.

Indian cotton mills produced both yarn and cloth. It would be difficult to construct composite indices of spindles and looms, or yarn and cloth, to represent the growth of cotton mills. We have instead used the total average employment to represent the size of the cotton industry and constructed the rates of growth accordingly (Table 7.14).

Table 7.14 Decadal Rates of Growth of Employment in Indian Provinces: Cotton Mills, 1879–1910

(*in percentage*)

Decade	Bengal	Madras	Bombay	North-Western Provinces (later United Provinces)	All India
Between 1879–80 and 1889–90	65.16	410.12	130.46	294.00	150.96
Between 1889–90 and 1899–1900	19.28	134.31	61.48	67.46	64.57
Between 1899–1900 and 1909–10	0.72	35.42	38.53	73.30	32.24

Source: Government of India, Department of Statistics, *Financial and Commercial Statistics of British India* and the Office of the Director-General of Commercial Intelligence: *Statistics of British India*, Government of India, Department of Statistics.

Note: The rates of growth are taken as the percentage difference between the beginning and the end year of the decade. There is no intention of claiming that such a crude measure represents the 'true' rate of growth of the cotton mills. It is only claimed that more sophisticated methods would not alter the major qualitative conclusions.

What comes out from Table 7.14 is the severe deceleration in the rate of growth of the Indian cotton mill industry over the three decades. It may be argued that in many centres such as Madras or the North-Western Provinces, the initial size of the industry was so small that the deceleration can be entirely explained by the meagreness of the base.

This is, however, not true in Bombay, where according to the *Reports of The Bombay Mill-owners' Association,* the numbers of spindles and looms were 1,154,184 and 12,396 respectively in 1879–80 and 2,350,728 and 17,735 respectively in 1889–90. It is the rate of growth of the Bombay mills which dominated the rate of growth of the all-India mill industry, as can be seen from Table 7.14. We can put it in another way: the Indian cotton mill industry suffered a major deceleration long before it had wrested the market even for the coarser varieties of goods from the Lancashire mills. While S.M. Rutnagur[91] and S.D. Mehta[92] both noted the phenomenon of slowing down of the growth of the Bombay cotton mills during this period, neither has tried to *explain* the slow-down properly. Mehta has implicitly placed all the blame on the tariff policy pursued by the Government of India. A recent analyst, Y. Kiyokawa, has fixed the blame for Indian failure to meet Japanese competition on technical and managerial retrogression of Indian mill-owners and managers without, however, putting his finger on what caused the retrogression.[93]

Roughly speaking, three clusters of factors can be identified as inhibiting the growth of the cotton textile industry in Bombay, and to a lesser extent in centres such as Madras and the North-Western Provinces, especially from the 1880s onwards. The first is a series of tariff changes, which individually affected the profitability of the cotton mills of the time, but more importantly, when seen as a sequence of policy packages, modified the long-term political expectations under which the investors in cotton mills operated.[94] The second is the more general regime of colonialism under which the mill managers and the shareholders or controllers of cotton mills operated. The third is the rise of Japanese competition. This affected the prospects of Indian cotton mills not only in third markets but also in India herself. Indian mills had to face a much more aggressive competitor than Lancashire, even before they were in a position to counter the financial, marketing, and political force of the Lancashire mills.

Tariffs as Imperial Instruments

The history of tariffs relating to imports of cotton yarn and cotton cloth into India,[95] reveals a persistent attempt on the part of the Lancashire interests to increase the sale of their products in India and to depress any increase in sales by Indian mills in the Indian market. The Government of India tried often' to block this pressure when this was in conflict with its revenue needs. In this resistance it was supported by major sections of British businessmen in India. But in the long run the Lancashire interests managed to impose the policies desired by them on the Government of India. Before we sketch the actual tariff changes affecting the growth of Indian cotton mills made by the government over the period 1876–1900, it is necessary to point out that the power of the Lancashire interests cannot be taken simply as the triumph of a section of metropolitan capital over the larger interests of the British imperial system. For, the import of British cotton yarn and cotton piece-goods accounted for between 40 and 50 per cent of the total Indian imports throughout the late nineteenth century. If these imports had vanished, it would have been far more difficult for Britain to balance her imperial accounts, even after taking into account the unrequited Indian exports Britain exacted as her political tribute. The import surplus India had with Britain, largely caused by the huge imports of cotton goods and yarn, along with the export surplus India had with most other countries helped Britain to square her accounts with the USA, and many other third countries with which she had persistent current account deficits.[96]

In 1871, the import duty on cotton twist and yarn was 3½ per cent, and that on cotton goods 5 per cent. In 1874, the Manchester Chamber of Commerce addressed a memorial to the secretary of state for India, in which it was argued that the duties were prohibitive as far as trade in low counts of yarn and coarse cloth was concerned especially since the custom valuations (the Chamber alleged) were too high. The Government of India promised to look into the valuations (which had already been revised in 1869). It appointed a committee consisting exclusively of British merchants and officials, and under the chairmanship of Alonzo Money (who had incidentally been president of the Bank of Bengal), to look into the tariff question. This committee unanimously rejected the demand of the Manchester Chamber for abolition of the tariff. The latter was not satisfied with the report of the committee and continued to pursue its real objective, which was to check the growth of cotton mill production in India.

A new tariff Act passed in 1875 retained the import duty on cotton twist and yarn and cotton goods, but reduced the valuation. It also imposed a 5 per cent duty on the import of long-staple cotton into India, which was a move openly made to obstruct the production of finer qualities of goods by Indian mills. The loss to the Indian exchequer caused by these changes was £388,000 or at least Rs 3.88 million. But Viceroy Lord Northbrook and his council were not willing to sacrifice the cotton duties which brought in a revenue of more than £800,000. Ultimately because of his differences with the Conservative secretary of state, Lord Salisbury, on this issue and on other matters, Lord Northbrook resigned, and Lord Lytton was appointed in his place.

Owing to the need to finance the famine relief operations and the warlike preparations set afoot by that jingoistic Viceroy, Lord Lytton, the reduction of the duties was deferred for a year. But the House of Commons passed a resolution on 11 July 1877 demanding the abolition of the cotton duties by the Government of India. In 1878, the latter exempted from duty certain coarser varieties of cloth with which Indian manufactures were supposed to compete.

The Manchester Chamber of Commerce was not satisfied with these exemptions, but wanted further concessions. In 1879, in opposition to the majority of the members of the council of India,[97] the Viceroy (and his finance member Sir John Strachey) exempted from duty 'all imported cotton goods containing no yarn finer than 30s'. Moreover, all cotton twist of no. 32 mule, and no. 20 water, and lower counts was exempted from duty.[98] In 1882, with Lord Ripon as the Viceroy (a Liberal appointee) and Major Evelyn Baring (later Lord Cromer) as the finance member, the remaining duties on cotton goods (along with all other import duties) were abolished. As far as the tariff regime affecting Indian cotton mills was concerned, the policy of the British government of India proved to be truly bipartisan!

In order to appreciate the trend of the policy with regard to cotton duties pursued by the British government, it is necessary to take a look at what happened in the 1880s. There were large increases of imports of yarn in 1879–80 but the competition of the Indian mills largely restricted the increased imports to varieties above 20s. After 1882, according to O'Conor's analysis, the same competition confined the increases in yarn imports to counts finer than 32. In the case of imports of cloth also, the tendency was for the better classes of goods to experience faster rates of increase.[99]

The two years of the major reduction of duties on cotton yarn and cotton goods (1879 and 1882) coincided with the beginning of an upturn in economic activity in England and the peaking of that activity.[100] From 1883–4 began a downturn of which the trough was reached in 1886. These were associated with fluctuations in the activity of the Lancashire mills and their exports to India. J.E. O'Conor, the official commentator on the foreign trade of India, observed in 1885 that in spite of the reduction of prices effected by the Lancashire mills (backed by reductions in the money wages of the workers), the consumption of imported cotton goods in India had not increased significantly over the preceding five years (from 1880–1 to 1884–5).[101] Lancashire mills had resorted to dumping,[102] and yet sales of coarse Indian mill-made cloth had been advancing because of locational advantages which were increasing with the extension of railways into the interior.

The glutting of the market with cotton cloth and the decline of prices, combined with other factors, such as a decline of yarn exports to China, depressed the profits of the Bombay mills very considerably in 1884–5 and in 1885–6.[103] However, official commentators made alarming predictions about the prospect of cessation of imports of grey cloth, and even some of the coloured varieties, and of yarn of both the lower counts and the medium ranges.[104] Yet the more sober observers noticed that most of the increases of cloth imported into India between, say, the 1860s and the late 1880s consisted not of the finer varieties of goods but of the despised grey goods, which were the only goods within reach of the majority of Indian consumers.[105] Given this background, it is not unreasonable to surmise that the Lancashire interests would fight tooth and nail any measure which promised an advantage to the Indian producers.

In December 1894, to meet dire financial needs, the Government of India imposed a 5 per cent *ad valorem* duty on cotton fabrics and yarn, and to propitiate Manchester, a countervailing excise duty of 5 per cent was imposed on yarn of counts above 20s (whether sold outside or woven in the mills) produced by Indian mills. But Manchester or the British parliament was not so easily appeased. The Secretary of State for India, Sir Henry Fowler, promised on 21 January 1895, to loyally obey the injunction of the House of Commons to avoid 'protective injustice'.[106]

Under pressure from British manufacturers, further enquiries were made into the composition of imports of yarns and cloth imported into India.[107] These revealed that there was very little overlapping as between imports and Indian production of yarn above 24s: the finer counts were almost exclusively imported, and the lower counts locally produced. In the case of cloth, there might be some overlapping in medium ranges because yarn of relatively low counts could be used as warp in such cloth. But the threat of Indian competition in the better classes of goods was still minimal. Such findings, and almost universal opposition to further revision of cotton tariffs, failed to overcome the Manchester lobby.[108] In 1896, the Government of India reduced the tariff on all woven cotton goods to 3½ per cent, exempted all yarn imports from duty and slapped an excise duty of 3½ per cent on all woven goods made by the Indian mills. This series of measures determined the political expectations of Indian cotton mills, which were given to understand that they would face very powerful political opposition if they aimed to take away the Indian market in cotton goods from Lancashire.

Colonial Blinkers

But the influence of colonialism was felt not just in a tariff policy which was inimical to the growth of the Indian cotton mill industry. It was felt in a much more general dependence on British methods and British advice in a period when the British were no longer the leaders in global industrial technology and when new leaders were changing the methods of production and organization in factories.[109] Indian mills clung, for example, much longer to mule spindles, installing them in large numbers in the 1880s and 1890s, even though ring spindles gave better results, especially in the lower counts of yarn. Indian mills also seemed to have accepted the idea prevalent in Britain that finer-quality cloth could be woven only out of long-staple cotton, while Germany, and other European continental countries were importing short-staple cotton (from India) and producing good-quality cloth by using machinery specially adapted for the purpose.[110] All this is not surprising, because the equipment used in Indian mills was bought from Lancashire manufacturers who generally sent out their men to set up the machinery. In the earlier years, they often trained the operatives or recruited weaving masters, engineers, and others in England to send out to India. The later weaving masters, engineers, and so on even when they were Indians had usually been trained in the Lancashire technology which bounded their horizon. (The Victoria Jubilee Technical Institute was established in Bombay in 1889 to train Indians in textile technology, but the methods were generally taken over entirely from Lancashire theory and practice.)[111]

Japanese Competition in Cotton Goods

Finally, the Japanese emerged as formidable competitors to the Indian cotton mills long before the latter were in a position to conquer the Indian market from the Lancashire firms. They bought Indian raw cotton and spun it more cheaply on the ring spindles they installed in their mills to sell the yarn first in Japan and then in China. They obtained a special footing in China after they had emerged victorious in the first Sino-Japanese war, and proceeded to acquire a thorough knowledge of the Chinese market in the interior, unlike the Indians who remained confined to the treaty ports or rather just to Hongkong and Shanghai (as shown by the figures of exports of Indian yarn to Chinese ports). The Japanese organized a cartel for the joint purchase of Indian raw cotton, and they naturally could bargain for good terms, especially since they were prepared to pay more for the Indian produce than most other importers of Indian raw cotton.[112]

Before we leave this subject, it should be pointed out that the short length of staple was not an absolute bar to the production of better-quality cloth.[113] But whether better-quality cotton cloth was made out of short- or long-staple cotton, a considerable additional investment in preparatory bleaching and finishing facilities would be needed. The long-term factors that damaged the profit prospects of the Bombay cotton mill industry also depressed the rate of investment in such facilities. Finally, a rapid advance towards production of finer quality cloth would have necessitated liberation from the power of Lancashire in at least two directions—overcoming the prejudices imbibed from the Lancashire managers and technicians with regard to the suitability of short-staple cotton for finer varieties, and the enormous market power of the Lancashire mills selling in India which was wielded with a greater degree of ruthlessness as Indian mills nibbled at their markets for lower counts of yarn and coarser varieties of cloth.

The short-staple cotton produced by the Indian growers survived because of both positive and negative factors. The emergence of Japan as a major consumer of Indian cotton and the pushing forward of Indian mills specializing in the coarse goods provided an expanding market for the short-staple cotton (local Indian mills and the Japanese generally paid better for Indian cotton than the European shippers). Most of the careful observers such as Henry St George Tucker (no other than the founder of the Bank of Bengal) and J. Forbes Royle,[114] all agreed that, on the negative side, the cultivator had little incentive for improving the staple length or producing clean cotton. While he lost in yield (in terms of lint) per acre by producing longer staple, he did not get enough as premium to compensate for the loss in yield and increase in expense. Hence many of the improved varieties deteriorated quickly in quality in the nineteenth century. Ginning in steam factories led further to a deterioration in quality since different varieties of cotton were mixed up in the ginning plants.[115]

However, as time went on, and indigenous cotton mills and the Japanese shippers gave a premium for better-quality cotton, the traders, and ultimately the cultivators, developed an incentive for acquiring and retaining the reputation of producing good-quality cotton. The Bombay Cotton Trade Association pointed this out to the Indian Cotton Committee in 1918:[116]

> We are of opinion that the substitution of short-staple cotton for long-staple varieties is, in a large measure, due to the fact that long-staple cottons have in the past not commanded a price corresponding with their intrinsic value whilst, on the other hand, short-staple varieties grown in districts otherwise known for the production of long-staple cotton have ... commanded prices considerably above their intrinsic value. As long as short-staple cotton is grown in these districts to such an extent only that it can be marketed mixed with the long-staple variety of the same district, the short-staple cotton passes off at approximately the same price as the long-staple cotton.

The staple of the Indian cotton really became longer once a sustained long-term growth in its demand emerged as a result of increase in the weaving of finer varieties of cloth in Indian mills[117] and as the irrigation facilities needed to grow the long-staple varieties expanded in Punjab and Sind. This growth of better varieties of cotton nicely illustrates the complex pattern of interaction of supply and demand factors at several different levels and in different epochs of competition.

The Bombay mills constituted the predominant section of the Indian cotton mill industry (see Table 7.15). In the 1890s and after, a combination of political factors, severe monetary stringency in Bombay after the closure of the mints, and famines and plague affected adversely both the demand for the products of the Bombay mills at home and conditions of their supply, and naturally the growth of the Bombay mills suffered badly. The whole export sector of the Indian cotton mill industry in Bombay and elsewhere was affected by all these factors and by ever-expanding Japanese competition. The growth of such centres as Ahmedabad and Madras was not enough to compensate for the severe slowdown elsewhere, and we obtain the results that have been summarized in Table 7.14.

Barring the cotton mills, tea and coffee plantations, a few sugar refineries and distilleries, the greater part of India outside the few centres of industry was agricultural and most of the financing was needed for trade. The dominance of trade over industry gave a noticeable seasonality to the demand for credit, especially from the apex banking system, as in the earlier part of the nineteenth century. At the annual general meeting of

Table 7.15 Progress of Cotton Mills in Bombay and India between 1880 and 1915

Year ending 30 June	Bombay Island				All India			
	No. of mills	No. of spindles	No. of looms	No. of hands employed daily	No. of mills	No. of spindles	No. of looms	No. of hands employed daily
1880	32	987,676	10,856	29,417	56	1,464,590	13,502	44,410
1885	49	11,347,390	12,011	41,545	87	2,145,646	16,537	67,186
1890	70	1,895,660	13,785	59,135	137	3,274,196	23,412	102,721
1895	69	2,123,892	20,217	75,740	148	3,809,929	35,338	138,669
1900	82	2,536,891	22,215	72,914	193	4,945,783	49,124	161,189
1905	81	2,560,916	28,073	92,924	197	5,163,486	50,139	195,277
1910	89	2,824,646	41,931	104,536	263	6,195,671	82,725	233,624
1915[(a)]	86	2,994,367	51,846	111,924	272	6,848,744	108,009	265,346

Source: *Report of the Bombay Mill Owners' Association for 1915.*
Note: (a) Year ending 31 August.

the Bank of Bombay held in July 1889, the chairman, the Honourable Frank Forbes Adam, had noticed that the demand for credit because of extension of industrial enterprise was mitigating the seasonality in the demand for credit, and he had judged that if the tendency continued, the capital of the Bank of Bombay would have to be enlarged soon.[118] But these expectations were not fulfilled, since industrial growth in Bombay faltered soon after. Even in the industrially more vibrant Bengal, industry remained the handmaiden of trade rather than becoming its mistress. We turn in the later chapters to a closer consideration of the movements of trade, finance, and credit in the forty-five years between the passing of the Presidency Banks Act and the coming of the First World War.

Notes

1. For details of the provisions of the Presidency Banks Act, see Bagchi (1987: Chapter 35 and Annexure 35.1).

2. For the history of India in its broad contours for most of the period, see Sumit Sarkar (1983: Chapters 2–4).

3. For Braudel's concepts of the *longue durée,* the event and the conjuncture, see Braudel (1980).

4. This is how Braudel (1972–4[1949]) had originally used the concept of *longue durée.*

5. Sivasubramonian (1965).

6. Maddison (1985: 201–10).

7. For a survey and critique of these estimates, see M. Mukherjee (1969: Chapter 2 and Appendix II).

8. F.J. Atkinson (1902).

9. See, for example, Mukherjee (1969: Chapter 2).

10. See, for example, Heston (1983).

11. F.J. Atkinson (1909).

12. *Journal of the Royal Statistical Society,* June 1902, pp. 277–8. The same charge has been made by many later economists and historians, but ironically enough, their criticism has primarily been meant to show that the agricultural statistics *underestimated* the rate of growth of output, thus detracting from the glory of *Raj Britannica* in India! On this issue see Mishra (1983); see also Mishra (1981: Chapter 3). Mishra, on the whole sides with Desai who showed that agricultural statistics in British India did not have any systematic bias one way or the other, and could be used to derive valid conclusions about trends.

13. Blyn (1966).

14. For a critique of Atkinson's (and Mukherjee's) methods, see A.K. Bagchi's review of Mukherjee, *National Income of India,* in *Science and Culture,* Calcutta), vol. 36, no. 10, October 1970.

15. Harnetty (1977); and Blyn (1966: Appendix Tables 3A and 4C).

16. Ibid.: Appendix Table 5A.

17. F.J. Atkinson (1902: Appendix Table IV).

18. Strachey and Strachey (1986 [1882]: 110).

19. See, in this connection, Chaudhury (1984: 60–73).

20. The best exposition and documentation of this last argument is given by Whitcombe (1972: Chapter 2).

21. There are problems in comparing the data on occupations for the Indian censuses of 1881, 1891, and 1901. But as R.E. Enthoven pointed out in his report on the census of the Bombay Presidency in 1901, the 1901 data on total numbers of workers in given occupations and dependents on those occupation (which were separately recorded in that census) can be compared with total numbers of persons (including dependents) supported by those occupations in 1891, or the numbers of actual workers in given occupations in 1901 can be compared with the figures of numbers of workers in those occupations, collected under the census of 1881. Making these comparisons for the Bombay Presidency (including the so-called 'Native States'), we find that the numbers supported by the textile industries were 969,000 in 1891 and 812,000 in 1901, while the actual numbers of workers in these industries were 702,000 in 1881 and only 445,000 in 1901. See Census (1901d: 220–2). We have cited the evidence for the Bombay Presidency, for during these years, the employment in modern cotton mills, presses, and so on, was probably expanding at a much faster rate in that region than anywhere else in India. Thus if the decline in employment in handicrafts was being compensated by increase in modern factory employment anywhere, it should have been in Bombay where such compensation should have been most evident. Yet the compensation was obviously not enough to cause an upturn in employment in secondary industry as a whole. For a discussion of the general issue of de-industrialization in the nineteenth century, see Bagchi (1976b); Chattopadhyay (1975); Vicziany (1979b); and Bagchi (1979a).

22. Sivasubramonian (1965: Tables 6.1 and 6.2).

23. For a discussion of the implications of price rises in India before the First World War, see Bagchi (1972a: 74–6).

24. See Mishra (1981), for the contrast between Maharashtra, where trader-moneylenders played a major part in controlling trade and indirectly, production of agricultural goods and Punjab, where production of agricultural commodities and regional, if not long-distance, trade in these commodities was dominated by large farmers, landlords, and landlord-moneylenders.

25. Watt (1972 [1891]: 526).

26. Blyn (1966: Appendix Table 5D). Blyn's Table shows a stagnation, with a slight tendency to decline in total net food grain availability over the period. Since the population was increasing over the period, this implied a fall in per capita availability of foodgrains.

27. Mukherji (1976).

28. For a study of the relevant issues in the context primarily of the British economy, see Saul (1969) and Perry (1973).

29. See, in this connection, A.K. Ghosh (1949).

30. This argument was strongly made by Connell (1885). It is interesting that Connell argued against the extension of railways under governmental guarantee and the subsidizing of wheat-carrying railway lines in the name of *laissez-faire*. He argued that local stocks were a better protection against famine than railways carrying grain in the event of a famine.

31. For evidence of stagnant or sagging real wages of agricultural and other workers in the late nineteenth century, see M. Mukherjee (1969: 87–90); Bagchi (1979b); and S. Krishnamurty (1987). In the last article is also given evidence of a fall in the proportion of the workforce engaged in industrial occupations. This would supplement the information given in the references cited in note 21.

32. Visaria and Visaria (1983: Table 5.8).

33. Estimated from Ibid.: Appendix 5.2.

34. See in this connection, Klein (1973) and (1984).

35. Visaria and Visaria (1983: Table 5.8).

36. According to the estimates made by census authorities and by later scholars, the life expectation of an average Indian at birth varied from 19.4 years to 25.7 years in the decades between 1871 and 1921. See Visaria and Visaria (1983: 502).

37. R.P. Dutt (1949: 118). Dutt had referred to the imposition of larger tariff rates on Indian goods in Britain than on British goods in India, but his phrase can be easily extended to cover a situation where Indian goods were imported into foreign countries only after paying a duty but foreign goods were imported virtually duty-free into India.

38. Our account is based mainly on the following, Wallace (1928); Buchanan (1966 [1934]: Chapter 2); Dasgupta (1965); Bagchi (1972a: Chapter 8); and Chakraborty (1989: Chapter 2).

39. Chakraborty (1989: 18).

40. Buchanan (1966 [1934]: 241–2).

41. Wallace (1928: 36).

42. Ibid.: 95.

43. Bagchi (1987: part II, pp. 85–6 [fn. 49]); S. Rungta (1985).

44. In our crude calculations we have tried not to identify the exact periodicity of the cycles but to capture some of the more robust aspects of long-term movements.

45. Birkmyre Bros., for example, had owned a small mill in Scotland (at Gourock, according to Wallace [1928: 38] and at Greenock according to Playne and Wright (1917: 85), which they had dismantled and brought over to establish their Hastings Jute Mills at Rishra.

46. Jacomb-Hood (1929: 198).

47. O'Conor (1885: 59).

48. Wallace (1928: 64).

49. For estimates of raw jute exports, exports of jute manufactures, total mill consumption of jute, see Mukherji (1982: Appendix Table 2.3).

50. The agreements often broke down because some mills found it to be against their interest to abide by them. Since the number of loom working-hours was generally fixed as a percentage of the total productive capacity, successful working-hour or selling price agreements often led to renewed expansions of capacity. But

these working-time agreements provided a cushion against severe losses in an otherwise highly profitable industry. For examples of starting and breaking down of selling price or working-time agreements, see Wallace (1928: 49–51 and 61–3).

51. A serious misunderstanding of the nature and objectives of the short-time agreements mars the analysis of Morris (1983: 571).

52. Chakraborty (1989: Chapter 2).

53. Cf. Bagchi (1972a: sections 6.8 and 8.1).

54. See, in this connection, Mukherji (1982: chart I).

55. Cf. *Investors' India Year-book 1921*, p. 142 for a Table of prices of raw jute (Naraingunge), corn-sacks and hessian between 1900 and 1919.

56. Bagchi (1972a: p. 275, footnote 38).

57. Misra (1985: Chapter 2).

58. O'Conor (1886: 84).

59. Cf. Watt: *Dictionary of Economic Products*, vol. VI, part III:

> The stronger teas from India and Ceylon have for many years been gradually displacing the weaker teas of China. Indian and Ceylon teas are capable of producing a far greater quantity of liquid tea, owing to their superior strength and quality. Thus, as the use of these stronger teas progressed, a given weight of tea would yield a larger volume of liquid.

60. Buchanan (1966 [1934]: Chapter 4); Griffiths (1967: Chapters 5–9, 20, and 32); Misra (1985: Chapter 2).

61. In 1891–2, out of the total area of 334,845 acres under tea in British India 108,277 acres were controlled by companies registered in London, 55,414 acres by companies registered in Calcutta, and fully 171,154 acres were controlled by private concerns (mostly European-owned, presumably). See Watt, *Dictionary of Economic Products*, vol. VI, part III, pp. 422–3. This example indicates why the paid-up capital of registered companies in this period cannot be taken as an index to the size of an industry or its components.

62. Misra (1985: Table 2.5).

63. For lists of managing agencies controlling rupee or sterling companies, in 1911 or 1914, see Bagchi (1972a: Tables 6.5 and 6.6).

64. This information is based on interviews with N.N. Bagchi, former managing director of Jalpaiguri Banking and Trading Corporation, B.C. Ghose and S.P. Roy, who both belonged to pioneer Indian families in the tea industry, and Dinesh Chandra Chakraborti, ex-employee of the Imperial Bank of India. For a list of the banks operating in the Jalpaiguri district in 1929–30, see the evidence of Digindranath Banerjee, director, Jalpaiguri Central Co-operative Bank Ltd., in *Report of the Bengal Provincial Banking Enquiry Committee 1929–30*, 1930, vol. II, Evidence-Part I, p. 504.

65. The relative insignificance of the Indian-controlled tea companies at least when seen from Calcutta, is also witnessed by the fact that virtually none of them were listed in the *Investor's India Year Books* (published by Place, Siddons, and Gough) of the years before the First World War.

66. For its history in colonial India, see Watt (1908: 333–5); and Buchanan (1966 [1934]: 254–7).

67. Ball (1881: 63).

68. Cf. Watt (1908: 341):

> ... the low price obtained (3s. 8d. per ton at the pit mouth in 1903) probably indicated that until the metallurgical industries have developed into important consumers of coal, present production may be viewed as approaching the limits of demand.

69. Watt 1972 [1889]: 392.

70. *The Investor's India Year Book 1919*, p. 157.

71. Watt, 1972 [1889]: 385–6.

72. Ibid. p. 387.

73. See Misra (1985: Chapter 3, section 4) for an exhaustive analysis of these issues.

74. Cf. Bagchi (1972a: Chapter 9, section 9.4).

75. Buchanan (1966 [1934]: Chapter 12); and D. Rothermund and Wadhwa (1978).

76. For a discussion of the theoretical framework which is suitable for an analysis of land–labour–capital relations in colonial India, see Bagchi (1988b).

77. These figures are based on the accounts of coal companies provided in the *Investor's India Year-Books* of the corresponding years.

78. Bagchi (1972a: Chapter 6).

79. See Papandieck (1978), for a case study of the vertical and horizontal links between coal companies under the control of Andrew Yule and Co.

80. This is the reason why Rungta's (1970: Chapter 9), gives a misleading idea of the absolute importance and relative rates of growth of the different industries in India in the late nineteenth century.

81. Bagchi (1972a: Chapter 5).

82. These rates of growth have been calculated on the basis of figures given in Table I of Bagchi (1976c).

83. The figures used in this paragraph have been taken from Bagchi (1972a: Table 7.1).

84. See for consideration of the various factors involved, Saul (1969:) and Perry (1973).

85. Cf. Raghavaiyangar (1893: Para 39).

86. Rungta (1985: 134–6).

87. S.D. Mehta (1954: Chapter 2, and p. 233).

88. Ibid.: Chapters 3 and 5; Bagchi (1987: Chapters 25–6).

89. S.D. Mehta (1954: 41). Mills outside Bombay sold nearly 70 per cent of their yarn output in the market in the 1870s.

90. *Administration Report of the Madras Presidency for 1882–83* (1883: 118).

91. Rutnagur (1927: 20–1).

92. S. D. Mehta (1954: Chapter 6).

93. Kiyokawa (1983).

94. For general accounts of the political developments in Britain and in India insofar as they affected the policies of the Indian government directly, see Gopal (1975); Moore (1966); and Thompson and Garratt (1934: Books VI and

VII). Thompson and Garratt remarked on p. 494, 'The removal of the duty [on manufactured cotton goods by Lord Lytton's administration] certainly too small to be protective according to modern standards seems to have had little effect on the development of Indian industry, which progressed steadily'. This is typical of the facile judgements on the issue made by many other historians.

95. The best account of these changes is still Dutt (1963b[1906]): Book II, Chapter 12, and Book III, Chapter 9). See also S.D. Mehta (1954: Chapters 4 and 6) and Bagchi (1972a: Chapters 2 and 7).

96. It is true that Britain's earnings from her stock of overseas capital were enough for most of this period to finance the large flows of investment going from Britain to other countries, and a smaller import surplus with Britain could have been sustained by simply lowering these flows. See Pollard (1985). But major adjustments would have been required in the British economy, and they might have been as painful as after the First World War, when many of those adjustments actually had to be made.

97. One of the objections raised by a dissenting member of the council, Whitby Stocks, is worth quoting for its irony,

> Indian newspapers will proclaim in every bazaar that the repeal was made 'solely in the interest of Manchester, and for the benefit of the Conservative Party, who are, it is alleged, anxious to obtain the Lancashire vote in the coming elections. Of course the people of India will be wrong: they always must be wrong when they impute selfish motives to the ruling race'. Quoted by Dutt (1963b[1906]: 301).

98. Watt (1972[1890]: 168).

99. Ibid.: 170.

100. Sayers (1967: 32).

101. O'Conor (1885: 31).

102. 'It may be added that the somewhat larger imports of last year were caused, not by a reviving demand, but by the necessity under which English manufacturers lay of diminishing stocks which had largely accumulated for which no other outlet was visible, and the existence of which brought about a fall of prices in Manchester, singularly depressing to the cotton industry.' (Ibid.: 31)

103. Ibid.: p. 57 and O'Conor (1886: 46–7).

104. See, for example, Watt (1972[1890]: 168 and 170).

105. Ibid.: 171. Watt's *Dictionary* or his later *Commercial Products* often speaks in several voices in different parts of the same entry. This is no doubt because the entries were jointly composed by several hands, even if Watt finally edited them.

106. Dutt (1963b[1906]: 394).

107. Findings of these enquiries are summarized in S.D. Mehta (1954: Chapter 6) and Bagchi (1972a: section 7.2).

108. Cf. also G. Watt (1908: 620): 'It was soon found... that this endeavour [that is, the Indian cotton tariff of 1894: A.B.] to equalize the burden of taxation on the two great competing sets of cotton manufacturers (Indian and foreign) was not a success.

109. For an elaboration of this part of the argument, see Bagchi (1988b).

110. Cf. Watt (1972[1890]: 166).

111. It is symptomatic that Platt Bros donated a complete set of machines to the Institute when it was established and that the first few principals and weaving masters etc., were all Englishmen (or Scotsmen) who had received their training in England. See Rutnagur (1927: 573–84). Cf. also comments by S.D. Mehta (1954: 103), on the supposed mechanical ineptness of the Indians, except, of course, the Parsis who happened to own most of the early mills! But Indians and Europeans in the Bombay mills were all in Lancashire blinkers, as far as textile technology was concerned. A description of the formal opening of the Institute to celebrate the year (1887) of the golden jubilee of Queen Victoria's accession to the throne is provided in Edwardes (1923: 76–8).

112. During the First World War, two representatives of the Japanese buyers of Indian cotton (who were organized in the Japanese Cotton Shippers' Association) were nominated along with two European shippers to serve on the board of directors of the Bombay Cotton Trade Association Ltd. See *Report of the Committee of the Bombay Millowners' Association* for 1915.

113. Cf. Watt (1908: 617):

> ... at the Delhi Durbar Exhibition of 1903 some remarkably fine muslins of Dacca were sold on behalf of the manufacturers ... the examples presently [*sic*] being turned out would measure 400's or 450's [counts: A.B.] while English power looms have been known to produce 600's.
>
> The point of interest in these Dacca muslins, however, lies in the fact that the hand spinners of Dacca *are* producing today yarns of fineness that no machinery in the world could spin from the inferior staple which they use. Dr Taylor wrote, in 1840, that the Dacca spinners failed to use the fine American cotton, and gave as their reason the fact that the English yarn swells on bleaching, while that of Dacca shrinks and becomes finer and stronger.

In spite of this example and the evidence of continental European and Japanese cotton mills utilizing short-staple cotton and mixing it with long-staple varieties where necessary, to produce better quality goods, Watt notes in another part of the same entry:

> One lesson alone seems to stand out through the past decades of the steam-power cotton industry of India as unwavering, viz. the conviction that when the time comes for India to assume once more the role of a producing and even exporting country in the finer cotton goods, it must either have improved its staple or discovered a country capable of meeting its necessities in suitable raw fibre (1908: 591).

114. For references see Ibid.: 590.

115. See in this connection, Bagchi (1988b), and the written statement (given on 28 January 1918) of the Bombay Cotton Trade Association submitted to the Indian Cotton Committee, in *Minutes of Evidence taken before the Indian Cotton Committee, 1920*, vol. IV, *Commercial*, part I, pp. 116–18. Difficulties were also faced initially in selling long-staple cotton growth with government patronage.

116. Ibid.: 117.

117. In addition to all the other evidence cited above, it may be mentioned that the Buckingham and Carnatic Mills of Madras offered to pay a premium for the so-called Cambodia cotton in the Madras presidency as soon as it was released in the market. Similarly, A. and F. Harvey promoted the Karungani strain of cotton in the deep south once it was introduced by the government department of agriculture (Baker 1984: 147–9).

118. *Bombay Gazette*, 1889, July.

8

Land Tax, Property Rights, and Peasant Insecurity in Colonial India*[1]

The question of private property in land in the eastern lands, including India, has been debated in Europe at least since the seventeenth century. It has been claimed that the British rulers had, for the first time, created private property in land and thereby conferred security on the owners. This claim is examined by analysing actually how land laws and land tax in the Bombay Deccan districts operated in the nineteenth century. The intimate relation between land tax and the nature of property rights in India under the British is brought out; and it is shown that British land laws tended to aggravate rather than mitigate the insecurity of peasants in the Bombay Deccan. The withdrawal of the State from public works or affordable loans to the peasants for land improvement was also a factor which exacerbated peasant insecurity and delivered peasants into the usurious net of the moneylenders. The debt process and the relation between ownership of tenure rights, the control over land, and insecure tenancy are examined to show how complex the process could be. Peasant adjustment included the repeated outbreaks of peasant resistance against the British rulers and their local collaborators. The epistemology of the recognition of the famine condition is examined, and the claim that population grew at a high rate in the Bombay Deccan in the first quarter of British rule is shown to be questionable. The reasons for failure of schemes for agricultural banking without state support are shown to lie in peasant insecurity associated with land policies followed by the rulers. The case of the Bombay Deccan throws light

*Reprinted from, 1992, *Journal of Peasant Studies*, 20(1), October, pp. 1–50.

on the wider issue of how peasant security is subverted in other areas of the world where the problem of a vulnerable ecology and uncertain peasant production is compounded by state policies regarding property rights and taxation.

Land Tax and Property Rights in British India

The control of land and its produce has been the *locus classicus* of most armed conflicts in recorded history. Its analysis has correspondingly been the *casus belli* in most accounts of social change, economic transformation, and political revolution. The lack of private property in land, the union in the person of the sovereign of both the public and private spheres of social life, and hence the lack of separation of the strictly political sphere from civil society have been regarded separately and jointly, as the characteristics and constitutive elements of 'Oriental' societies, and more specifically of Oriental despotism. This tradition, as is well known, goes back at least to Jean Bernier, writing in the seventeenth century, but was given its immense authority by the writings of G.W.F. Hegel.[2] With some modifications, this view also informed a very important group of officials and policy-makers in colonial India.[3] Paradoxically enough, the supposed lack of individual property as against mere possession in the village communities of Asia (including India) and their subjection to the sovereignty of the state provided the germ of the Asiatic mode of production as conceptualized by Karl Marx.

There was a rival tradition which considered Asian lands to have their share of private property in land. The implicit recognition of the presence of private property in land in the Mughal dominions goes back at least to Tavernier, a contemporary of Bernier. Among British officials and policy-makers, Philip Francis took the view that the zamindars or the landlords and not the state were the proprietors of the soil[4] and Mark Wilks was of the view that in the Mysore kingdom of the eighteenth century, land was owned by individual cultivators[5], and the same view was echoed in the writings of Mountstuart Elphinstone regarding the Maratha territory. However, the second view was drowned in the need that European writers of the eighteenth century felt to conceptualize the Orient as the changeless other to which European countries would also approximate if they failed to carry out the kinds of revolutions they were hoping for. Then, of course, with the spread of European colonialism, the Orient had to be seen as that passive corpse which European conquest would galvanize into life. Some of even Marx's writings could be interpreted along similar lines.[6]

Only a few writers were willing to recognize explicitly or implicitly that some forms of private property in land which existed before the onset of colonialism were fractured by the need of the colonial state to finance its operations—almost exclusively from land—a need that necessarily had to interfere, often arbitrarily, with pre-existing patterns of possession and ownership. Perhaps Richard Jones (1831), among the more famous political economists of the nineteenth century, came closest to this recognition. By the time Marx came to compose the materials that were published as *Capital*, vol. III, he had come round to the view that the property systems introduced by the British in their dominions in India were nothing but caricatures of their original models[7] (see also Marx on Jones).[8]

When Marx wrote in his final years his note on Phear (1880), it was clear to him that the system of property rights in land in Permanent Settlement Bengal was too complicated to be described in terms of either a village corporation or village republic, or in terms of allodial holdings of peasant proprietors, and that zamindars as rent-receivers and moneylenders as major appropriators of the surplus through advances to zamindars, other intermediary right-holders, and to the real cultivators of the soil were all participants in a system that defied description in terms of familiar European categories.[9] But a systematic analysis of the way in which the revenue systems introduced by the British fractured the possibility of creating a property-owning peasantry or initiating a process of accumulation based on improving productivity, remained still to be carried out for different regions in India. Such an analysis would also introduce a degree of concreteness into the notions of property rights, security of expectations, and other concepts beloved of jurists following the Benthamite tradition.

Despite all the caveats advanced by administrators and analysts from Wilks to Phear and Jones to the later Marx, the British rulers in India are still credited with the introduction of the concept of generalized private property into the Indian legal system and hence into Indian society. The locus par excellence of this generalized private property right was supposed to have been land. But since land taxes also financed colonial conquest and rule in India, a conflict was set up between an intended vesting of private persons with property rights and the need of the state to curb that property right wherever it came into conflict with the need to realize a secure, and growing revenue from land taxation. This produced the paradox that whereas in Britain the nature of property rights held by a person in land often determined the extent to which, and the form in which he was subject to taxation, in India it was the form of the land tax that determined the nature of property rights in land. It also determined the kind and the degree of security a person with such tax-determined property rights enjoyed in his property. In this essay, we will explore the kind of insecurity to which peasants were subjected in the British rulers' quest for a secure revenue from the land. This will also shed light on the question of freedom and unfreedom of the Indian peasant.

The British rulers, as is well known, instituted two main systems of land taxation in India. The first was the so-called Permanent Settlement or the Cornwallis system that was enforced in Bengal, Bihar, and Orissa, the first really large territory the British conquered in India. Under this system, the government authorized a small group of large revenue-payers to collect the land tax from the occupiers or cultivators of land and then pay most of it into the government coffers, after retaining a portion (initially authorized to be ten per cent of the revenue) as the reward for their trouble. This system is better styled as the zamindari, rather than the Permanent Settlement, because it was only in the case of these large revenue-payers (who were usually called zamindars in British documents) that the quantum of tax on a given piece of land was fixed permanently.

Under the second system, the government recognized the actual occupiers (but not necessarily the cultivators) of land as the persons required to pay the land tax directly to the government. The quantum of tax could vary from period to period: initially it varied from year to year but over time, the procedure was adopted of conducting periodic surveys of the tax-paying capacity of a particular region, and revising the taxes ('land revenues') accordingly. This system was called *raiyatwari* (or *raiyatwar*), because the occupiers of land were called *raiyat*s. Raiyatwari was born in the Baramahal region of the Madras Presidency under the administration of Alexander Read and Thomas Munro, but it was given a canonical formulation in the famous *Fifth Report* of the House of Commons on the Affairs of the East India Company of 1812–13.[10]

The distinguishing characteristic of the Cornwallis system was the recognition of a group of intermediaries as holders of property rights in land revenue; in contrast, under raiyatwari, no intermediary tax-payers, and hence holders of property rights in land, were in principle recognized: only the occupiers were recognized as holders of property in land. After its installation in Bengal, the Cornwallis system suffered in popularity among British policy-makers. Once the British had effectively attained paramountcy in the subcontinent, reasons of state did not require the recognition of big zamindars as revenue-payers; policy-makers did not see why they should hand over a substantial (and in the case of Permanent Settlement, a growing) fraction of the potential tax revenue to a group of idle landlords. Concern for peasant welfare also seemed to argue against the zamindari settlement: an enlightened British administration would take better care of the mass of the peasantry than a group of greedy tax farmers.

It should be stressed that raiyats in British legal terminology and actual cultivators of the land were not conterminous groups. In many regions, the raiyats were a privileged group such as the *mirasdar*s, *patidar*s, or the big sharers in *bhaiyachara* tenures. The British tried in some regions to settle with the so-called village communities which were dominated by such big men of the countryside.[11] Almost inevitably, they ultimately had to deal with the individual sharers in these village communities, even though particular village dignitaries were supposed to be responsible for the payment of the tax. More importantly, the mirasdars or other big men often became the intermediary right-holders since they did not cultivate or manage their lands directly. Moreover, in some parts of India, the British freshly recognized a group of intermediaries (the *taluqdar*s in Awadh, for example) as the group entitled to pay the land tax. Thus although outside the Bengal Presidency, and parts of the Madras Presidency, raiyatwari was the dominant system, in many regions of India, property rights in land were effectively held partly by actual cultivators and partly by groups of intermediary right-holders. (Between the cultivators and the zamindars or taluqdars who paid their taxes directly to the State, more than one layer of intermediaries grew up, claiming a share in the surplus produced by the peasants).

By and large, zamindari settlement was viewed unfavourably in the writings of contemporary British officials and opinion-makers such as Munro, Mountstuart Elphinstone, Charles (later, Lord) Metcalfe, James Mill, and John Stuart Mill, and in the analysis of later economists and historians.[12] In contrast, raiyatwari settlement has been taken to be equivalent to peasant proprietorship, and has been judged to be beneficial to the Indian peasantry. We shall take a closer look at the nature of property rights in land that raiyatwari conferred and at the conditions of existence enjoyed by the raiyats under this allegedly pro-peasant land tenure system. Although we will occasionally refer to the zamindari system, the latter will be brought in mainly for purposes of comparison.

It has come to be generally accepted that the British either introduced private rights in land where none existed or they consolidated such rights where they had a pre-British origin. What has been generally overlooked is how very contingent those property rights were in India under British rule. Private property in land in Britain assumed the form of freeholds where the proprietor held the land absolutely without making any regular payment to any higher authority, or the form of copyholds or long leaseholds, under which the proprietor made a fixed payment (often a nominal one) to a superior right-holder. The proprietors under freehold or copyhold tenure did not hold the land *under the condition* that they had to make regular annual payments to the Crown or to some superior landlord and would have to forfeit their property if they failed to make the payment punctually. In the eighteenth century, they paid a land tax. But they paid the tax because they were proprietors, and were not considered proprietors because they paid the tax.

By contrast, in British India, under both the zamindari and the raiyatwari tenures, it was the prompt payment of a tax to the government every year that allowed the so-called proprietors to hold the property in land.[13] The security of property was made subject to the superior requirement of security of public revenues from the land, which after all constituted the sinews of British colonial expansion, and almost the principal *raison d'être* for maintenance of the colonial state. In an era in which revenue needs grew both for making remittances to Britain (as 'dividends' on East India Company's stock, and as expenses of the British Indian establishment in Britain) and for defraying the costs of further conquest in Asia (and even in Africa), the requirement of the security of private property in land was to be subordinated to that of the security and size of the public revenue.

By stipulating that the designated revenue payers, whether they were zamindars, taluqdars or *jenmies* (in Malabar) or they were raiyats, must pay the land revenue promptly, or lose all their rights, the British made sure that the taxes would be paid, provided they had an adequate administrative and coercive machinery at their disposal to make the threat credible. By linking the revenue to be paid to the estimated average produce of the land with only minor adjustments for variation in harvests, and pitching the tax demands sufficiently high, they made it certain that a number of the designated revenue-payers would lose their titles every year. For an agrarian system that depended mainly on rainfall—in a subtropical climate it would necessarily yield varying amounts of produce. Moreover, the British policies added to the 'natural' risks in the system. First, by making all the land, including pastures and forests, subject to taxation or to monopolization by the State, the tax policies introduced ecological disturbances. The peasants could not keep cattle or other livestock as sources of manure or depend on forests as sources of timber or fuel and had to 'mine' the land on which they had engaged to pay taxes.[14]

Second, by depriving the zamindars and other superior right-holders or village *biradaris* (that is, the group of landowning families) of their local judicial or police powers and at the same time releasing them from their obligation to maintain roads, dams, or markets, they tended to depress the productive or profit-yielding capacity of the land, until new institutions evolved to repair the damage. Third, by compelling peasants and zamindars to pay their dues in money of a designated character, the system often glutted local markets with produce and depressed agricultural prices. In many parts of India, peasants and zamindars had been accustomed to pay their taxes or their tribute in kind (in grain, sugar, elephants, and so on) and even when money was used, it might be money of a low denomination such as cowries. The British demonetized vast stocks of such small denomination currencies; they went on effectively to demonetize gold coins for the purpose of payment of public dues.[15]

In a situation of demographic growth and a relatively low degree of uncertainty of produce, which approximated to the conditions in Bengal, the zamindaris changed hands rapidly, but remained saleable. A virtual revolution was effected in the ranks of the Bengal zamindars. Most of the old and big zamindaris disappeared or disintegrated into smaller fractions, and new men, often officials connected with the British land revenue administration, came to hold titles to these zamindaris. When the permanent settlement revenues were introduced in Bengal, the actual cultivators suffered a total loss of security of tenure, especially after the powers of the zamindars had been strengthened by Regulation VII (*haptam*) of 1799. Since the rights of the actual occupiers or cultivators were never registered at all, we have only the reports of the revenue collectors and other officials to go by in assessing the way in which their condition was affected by the British land tax system. Those reports are enough to convey the sense of utter turmoil in the conditions of the peasantry that the British innovations brought about.[16] Under the raiyatwari system, the revenue liability of the occupiers was assessed on the basis of periodic surveys. As we have noted earlier, the weight of British official opinion, starting with Alexander Read and Thomas Munro, tended to favour this style of settlement; a retrospective theoretical justification was sought to be provided by the Malthus-Ricardo-West theory of land rent.

We shall later scrutinize the theoretical basis of such rationalization. It is to be noticed, however, that the raiyatwari settlements had to be revised repeatedly, because the assessed revenues could not be realized and despite the official claim that the system provided security of property to the raiyats, in many areas no market in land could be conjured up in any shape or form. When the state failed to realize the assessed revenue from a raiyat, it auctioned the rights to the piece of land on which revenue was due. Again and again, it was found in southern and western India that there were no bidders for such rights.[17] Thus for a considerable length of time and in large parts of the country, the State failed to create even a minimal kind of private property.

Demographic growth and unlimited power of eviction granted to the zamindars made the permanent revenue settlement in Bengal a success in terms of raising revenues for the British. Bengal land revenues long provided the surplus for remitting tribute to England, for financing wars of conquest in and outside India, and for meeting the deficits of the Bombay and Madras Presidencies. We still do not know exactly how demographic factors and land revenue systems interacted in colonial India. Evidence has now accumulated of a demographic stagnation in southern India in the early part of the nineteenth century;[18] southern India was also badly affected from about 1825 down to around 1852 by a depression of prices of agricultural goods. Were these, at least partly, caused by the kind of insecurity we mentioned earlier? Or were they substantially exogenous to the land tax system? It is difficult to believe in such independent causation over such a long period. But in either case, demographic factors did not come to the aid of the raiyatwari system, until secular price rises had moderated the virulence of the fiscal demands of the colonial state.

One basic change the British introduced was to fix the tax on a piece of land in money, while earlier on, the tax generally varied with the seasons. This was supposed to give the peasants or the superior right-holders, such as the zamindars, a greater degree of security. Of course, the net income left in a given year to a peasant or a zamindar after paying the tax would depend not only on whether the tax was fixed in value but also on how high the tax rate was. If the tax rate was high enough, the peasants would be left with no surplus at all for investment or even for the working capital required for the next season; the zamindar would similarly find it impossible to pay his dues to the government without subjecting the subordinate right-holders to further exactions and thus depressing their condition further. In many raiyatwari areas it was admitted by the British officials that the initial rates were really high.[19] This was also true of the rates in Bengal under the Cornwallis system in the initial years.[20]

Apart from the effect of a rise in taxes, their fixity in the face of variability of the net produce of the land had the effect of increasing the degree of riskiness faced by the peasants (or the intermediary right holder). In order to see this, let us first assume that the price of the produce remains constant between good and bad years, so that we can ignore any variability of the return caused by price changes.

We adopt the following notation:

Y_t is the net income before tax received by the peasant (or the legally recognized occupier) in year t.

Z_t is the peasant's net income after tax in year t.

$E(Y)$ is the expected value of the net income of the peasant before tax. T is the total tax to be paid by the peasant: Let $KE(Y) = T$, where $0 < K < 1$

Under the pre-British system, the tax in any given year would be KY_t.

Under the British system, regardless of the size of Y_t in any year, a tax T is exacted.

Then $Z_t = Y_t - T$

and $Var(Z) = Var(Y)$ under the British system

Under the pre-British system,

net income in a given year t, is $Z_t = (1-K) Y_t$.

Denoting the variance of Z_t under the pre-British system as $Var(\hat{Z})$,

we have $Var(\hat{Z}) = (1-K)^2 Var(Y)$

$\therefore Var(\hat{Z}) < Var(Z)$ since $0 < K < 1$

Under the pre-British system, although the tax was calculated in money and on the average return from the land over a number of years, it was allowed to vary with the size of the actual crop harvested. Moreover, although calculated in money, it was often collected in kind. Under the British, not only was the payment fixed in money, it was also realized in money, exactly at harvest times. So the riskiness of prices was added to the risks inherent in the harvests and aggravated the peasant's burden.

The effects of price variations are far more complex than the effects of changes in output. If government taxes are fixed in money, and if prices of crops rise, then it would seem *a priori* that the peasants or intermediary right-holders would benefit because the real burden of taxes would go down. The validity of this conclusion could, however, be nullified by several factors. First, if price rises were due to famine conditions in general, and if the tax-payers had no stocks left in their granaries then they would become net buyers in general, and would be unable to pay their taxes unless they received credit from some source. In British Indian villages, this source would generally be village moneylenders. So if the tax-payers survived the famine, they would end up in debt; many of them would also lose their assets such as ploughs and cattle, and possibly land, if their land rights were considered worth acquiring. If price rises were due to a local famine, and if grain was imported into the region from outside, then the adverse effects on the tax-payers would be moderated through a fall in the cost of their net purchases—provided again that they had some means of making those purchases.

Second, if price rises were due to exogenous factors, but if the taxpayers were heavily indebted to moneylenders, then most of the gains of the peasants would be wiped out because their creditors would normally seize this opportunity of having some of their claims realized. In the long run, the peasants might be as badly off as before the price rise, if the debt to the moneylenders was large enough, and if the moneylenders could manipulate the size of the debt with impunity.

Third, in any normal year, some of the peasants would be net buyers of grain in the market, because their landholdings were too small. So while the bigger landholders gained by the price rise, the smaller peasants, and of course, the agricultural labourers would lose out in case of a secular (rather than seasonal) price rise compared with years of price stability.[21]

What happened in the case of a secular or even a temporary price fall? If the government tax dues had been fixed before the price fall, then the burden on the tax-payers would increase. If the surplus of the landholders was not large enough to pay the government dues with the reduced prices of their output, they would have to secure a fresh loan from the moneylenders and their indebtedness must go up. The net buyers of grain among the landholders would benefit provided they had any means left after paying the more burdensome government dues, and provided the next season was good enough for them to be more amply employed.

It would thus seem that for a large fraction of government tax-payers, a price rise or a price fall was equally bad. But over the long run, if price rises were accompanied by secular growth in output and population, then the fixity of land revenue in terms of money would benefit the more wealthy landholders or intermediary right-holders. This is what happened in Bengal for much of the nineteenth century. But in many of the raiyatwari areas, the depression in prices from the 1820s to the early 1850s spelled almost unmitigated disaster, and then the famines of the later part of the century nullified most of the benefits that would have accrued with a secular growth in output and population.

In order to study peasant insecurity caused by the British land taxation system, without the complication of the oppression of the intermediary right-holders as far as possible, we took the four Bombay Deccan districts of Ahmadnagar, Poona, Bijapur, and Sholapur over the period from the 1820s to the 1880s as our unit of study. Most of these areas were acquired by the British from the Marathas after the conclusion of the third Anglo-Maratha war, and some areas were acquired later from the Nizam of Hyderabad. They all had a raiyatwari tenure, and they were subjects of intensive investigation by the Deccan Riots Commissioners in 1875,[22] and by Harold Mann[23].

Insecurity, Penury, Deaths, and Stagnation in the Bombay Deccan during the First Century of British Rule

Many of the paradoxes created by British rule and by the conception the British administrators had of their role in Indian society had been noted by contemporary observers. For example, Captain Robertson, the first administrator of Poona after it had been seized from the Peshwa, noted that the *mirasi* tenant was 'in no way inferior on its original basis ... to the holder of the most undoubted freehold estate in England'.[24] He also noted that what the mirasi tenant paid was in the nature of a tax rather than a rent. Thus in making the rights of all raiyatwari tenants conditional on prompt payment of the government demand, the British abrogated pre-existing private property rights in land rather than introduce it *de novo* or strengthen it in any fashion. In the report that Mountstuart Elphinstone wrote after he had taken charge of the Peshwa's territories, he noted that with all the vices, which he naturally attributed to the rule of the defeated enemy, 'the Mahratta country flourished, and the people seem to have been exempt from some of the evils which exist under our more perfect Government.'[25]

These were initial reactions of the administrators in charge of the districts of the Bombay Deccan. Long after the so-called conservative or cautious policy of Elphinstone had been tried out, the radical assessments of Pringle had been tried out and rejected, and supposed better survey and settlement operations had been instituted in many districts and new assessments of land revenue had been made on that basis, a former Governor of Bombay, Sir George Clerk, giving his evidence before the House of Lords in 1852 asserted that the raiyatwari settlement was the most detrimental to the country and generally produced paupers.[26]

The main argument against the raiyatwari settlement advanced by its critics is that under it, generally speaking, the government jacked up its demands too high. In fact, some officials, such as Henry St George Tucker, recognized that it was precisely the absence of intermediaries to which the government might have to surrender part of its demand that made the system attractive to many administrators.[27]

Most of these judgements, sombrely echoed and consolidated by R.C. Dutt, seem to have been confirmed by later analysis. The Bombay Deccan and other territories of western India appear to have enjoyed a much greater degree of prosperity under Maratha rule than later British officials seem to have given them credit for.[28] The Maratha territories threw up significant pockets of commercial agriculture, big farmers, and improving landlords dominating the countryside;[29] under the British expediency and the desire to jack up rents as proof of the efficiency of the rent-collecting official seem to have played at least as large a role in the determination of the level of assessed government demands as any principles of utilitarianism or paternalistic conservatism did.[30] What has perhaps not been sufficiently stressed is that in many areas, including the Bombay Deccan districts (comprising Poona, Ahmadnagar, Sholapur, and Bijapur), all the experiments in revenue assessment failed to yield a solution to the peasants' problems of security of income or life, or to the British administrators' problem of ensuring a stable and growing revenue which would justify their rule in terms of the fullness of government treasury and hence a satisfactorily large remittable tribute, or in terms of the moral satisfaction of knowing that people were, 'happy and prosperous' under their 'guardianship'. The physical environment, land revenue policies, and price fluctuations all tended to make the attainment of the basic objectives of the rulers and the ruled equally elusive.

We have seen in the first section that even if the average land revenue realized from the cultivators by the British and the pre-British rulers were the same, the British system of keeping the land revenue fixed irrespective of the seasons would tend to increase the risks faced by the peasantry. These risks would extend to the risk of death. In a bad year, the peasant would be more likely to starve under the British system since he would be expected to pay his revenue even in that year if he wanted to retain his occupancy right (because that is all that the British land law guaranteed him), and this meant that for a poor or even a middling cultivator, the chance of retaining a subsistence after paying all his (her) dues could be slimmer in that year.

The British system increased the risks of the cultivator in yet another way. Earlier on, the title to a piece of land was not forfeited even if the owner failed to cultivate it and hence pay tax on it in one year or even for a number of years. Under the British dispensation, the holder of the occupancy title to a piece of land would lose it if he failed to pay the land revenue on it for a single year (unless he obtained explicit, official remission). So even in years of bad harvests or low prices (the latter were not generally considered grounds for remission of the government demand), he had to pay the full land revenue. Moreover, a poor peasant often did not have the wherewithal to cultivate a piece of land, especially if he had suffered a recent loss of cattle, or loss of his 'normal' income because of bad harvests or famines. But in the hope that he might be able to cultivate it some day, he held on to his occupancy title, thus incurring expenditure on an asset which remained under-utilized.[31] If he had incurred a debt because of bad seasons, this would, of course, add to his burdens. Since the majority of the cultivators of the Bombay Deccan were mired in debt in most years after British take-over of the region, this increase in risk was experienced by most peasants.

There is evidence that the British administrators not only radically changed the basis of land rights, and increased the rigour of payment of land tax which now became essentially a rent payable by tenants-at-will (except that the landlord of these tenants was the state itself); in the first few years, they also increased the tax burden on the general run of cultivators, that is, on both the recognized raiyats or 'state tenants', and on others who might be sharecroppers or tenants-at-will of the recognized state tenants.[32] So not only the variance, but the mean of the income left to the cultivators was diminished under British rule, at least initially.

How did the various fiscal and other economic factors tending to increase risk interact with the physical environment and what results did they produce? Data on output, population, or distribution of landholdings as between different groups of cultivators for the Bombay Deccan for the period from 1818 till the end of the 1870s are yet to be compiled. It is possible to compile figures of output from the 1880s on the basis of various published and unpublished reports of the government. Such calculations would be needed in order to separate out even approximately the roles played by different social and economic factors in making the typical Bombay peasants' life nasty, brutish, and short, and yet enabling a group of rich landholders and moneylenders to survive and even thrive in that environment.[33] But even without such detailed calculations, some of the gross risks faced by the ordinary run of cultivators can be illustrated by data on acreages and the history of reluctant remissions of land revenue granted by government administrators and the cultivators' defaults in revenue payment in spite of the penalties suffered by them for such default.

In order to give an idea of the degree of fluctuations in fortunes suffered by the cultivators, we will cite some data regarding the acreages in different parts of the Bombay Deccan from 1818 down to the 1880s. Most of the series do not cover the whole period, since the coverage of different administrative divisions changed over time. But even the fragmentary series are enough to give us a qualitative idea of the degree of fluctuation in fortune suffered by the peasants. Take Table 8.1, for example, relating to the *taluka* of Indapur in Poona district, an area which has become famous because of the assessments made by Pringle, who was supposed to have used the Ricardo-Malthus theory of rent for determining the land revenue and because of the frequent references made to it by later commentators.[34]

Table 8.1 shows that the tillage area varied from a low of 94,908 acres in 1825–6 to a high of 161,933 acres in the very beginning of the period. There is no easily discernible trend in these figures; they tended to move downward up to 1825–6, and generally stagnated around an average of about 130,000 acres during the next few years. The revenue collected also fluctuated between a low of Rs 6,305 and a high of Rs 129,057, and there is no easily discernible trend in these figures either, if we exclude the first four years of the series. Prices, on the other hand, moved distinctly downward, but fluctuated greatly from year to year: from a high of 12.50 *sher*s the rupee in the famine year of 1824–5 they moved to 64.00 shers in 1826–7, shot up to 32 shers per rupee in 1827–8 but plummeted to 80 shers the rupee in 1828–9.

All these fluctuations were reflected not only in the land revenues collected but also in the amounts of land revenue outstanding, in spite of remissions granted by government officials: the outstandings came down to a low of Rs 402 (after the suspension of the assessments made by Pringle from 1824 to 1828, and the revisions effected by Goldsmid and Wingate), but they far exceeded the actual revenues collected in 1822–3 and in 1830–4.

Table 8.1 Tillage, Land Revenue, and Prices, Indapur Taluka, 1818–37

Year	Tillage(a) in acres	Land revenue collected (Rs)	Land revenue outstanding (Rs)	Price of Juari (Indian millet) shers per Rupee (b)
1818–19	1,61,934	98,988	11,249	17.00
1819–20	1,57,899	1,21,593	6,834	19.50
1820–1	1,52,584	1,19,471	4,261	32.00
1821–2	1,58,226	1,29,057	4,593	32.00
1822–3	1,33,438	36,965	71,753	32.00
1823–4	1,30,422	19,332	13,049	36.75
1824–5	1,06,912	6,305	2,771	12.50
1825–6	94,908	38,937	4,920	44.00
1826–7	1,50,679	46,730	3,024	64.00
1827–8	1,19,455	8,746	6,154	32.00
1828–9	1,18,316	43,362	16,653	80.00
1829–30	1,26,050	48,020	44,358	46.00
1830–1	1,32,416	8,121	43,206	40.00
1831–2	1,30,671	11,344	558	60.00
1832–3	1,34,564	9,857	997	23.00
1833–4	1,50,604	35,635	23,933	46.00
1834–5	1,26,310	41,652	4,955	48.00
1835–6	1,31,707	45,478	1,327	38.00
1836–7	1,59,900	50,199	402	66.00

Source: *GBP* (1885b: 414).

Notes: (a) Up to 1828–9, the original figures were in bighas: they have been converted as one acre = four-thirds *bigha*, in accordance with the equivalence provided in *GBP* (1885b: 139J).

(b) The Indapur sher was bigger than the Poona sher, which in turn was more than twice the weight of the Bombay *sher*. So these prices may not be strictly comparable with those given later'.

Indapur was by no means exceptional in the immediate two decades after the British take-over. The tillage and revenue data for two revenue subdivisions of Karmala and Ropla of the district of Sholapur also reveal severe fluctuations (Tables 8.2 and 8.3). In these two cases also there is no discernible trend in areas tilled at least until the late 1830s. If there is an upward trend after that, the figures only indicate a recovery to the levels of the early 1820s. The British revenue officials had to struggle to extract revenues from a group of cultivators, most of whom were trying just to survive, and many of whom were not succeeding. The clearest evidence of the unequal struggle the officials waged to increase the revenue extracted comes from the Karmala revenue figures, where it is found that over the two decades ending in 1841–2 the amount of revenue extracted (Rs 823,109) fell short of the revenue remaining

Table 8.2 Dry-crop Tillage, Total Revenue Paid, Revenue Unpaid, and Prices in Karmala Group of Villages, Sholapur, 1822–42

Year	Dry crop tillage (in acres)	Revenue to be paid (a) (Rs)	Revenue unpaid (b) (Rs)	Amount paid (Rs)	Price of Juari at shers per Rupee (b)
1822–3	1,33,186	1,06,114	48,996	57,718	54
1823–4	1,13,934	1,00,852	37,457	63,395	32
1824–5	1,29,320	1,02,081	93,485	8,596	15
1825–6	1,17,661	95,143	36,940	58,203	32
1826–7	1,25,121	87,354	23,118	64,236	48
1827–8	92,188	69,992	37,998	31,994	33
1828–9	81,552	65,922	20,619	45,303	51
1829–30	1,10,848	69,751	56,199	13,552	2
1830–1	94,898	71,564	33,040	38,524	50
1831–2	1,00,853	76,268	30,978	45,290	40
1832–3	1,01,648	75,161	64,425	11,336	14
1833–4	98,334	77,159	23,711	53,448	24
1834–5	85,165	68,042	24,313	43,729	9
1835–6	83,720	65,409	33,154	32,255	48
1836–7	86,383	66,973	25,739	41,234	44
1837–8	1,00,444	72,691	33,281	39,410	48
1838–9	1,22,298	86,145	50,339	35,806	42
1839–0	1,31,829	88,845	56,228	32,617	45
1840–1	1,45,338	97,604	48,220	49,184	52
1841–2	1,43,196	1,03,963	46,684	57,279	–
Total		16,48,233	8,25,124	8,23,109	

Source: *GBP* (1884b: 326); price data are from *GBP* (1884b: 323).
Notes: (a) Includes land revenue and cesses.
(b) Compromises remissions and lease reductions.

unpaid (Rs 825,124). The Survey Superintendent, Lieutenant Nash, in submitting his report in 1843 considered the land revenue assessed for Karmala too high, but not for Ropla.[35] The difference between Karmala and Ropla was that the collections for the latter group came to 63 per cent of the assessed revenue instead of just about 50 per cent in the case of Karmala. However, Nash's conclusion was still not to revise the Karmala land revenues drastically, but effect only minor adjustments so as to diminish the chance of having to make remissions on a regular basis.

For different segments of the districts of Poona, Sholapur, and Bijapur (Table 8.4) it is clear then that the first twenty years after British rule witnessed severe fluctuations in the area tilled and land revenue realized. Moreover, even after the revision carried out by Goldsmid, Wingate,

Table 8.3 Tillage and Revenue in the Ropla Group of Villages, Sholapur 1822–41

Year	Tillage (acres)	Total revenue assessment (Rs)	Actual collection (Rs)	Juari (Jowar) Price (shers per rupee)
1821–2				64
1822–3	58,095	42,697	37,084	128
1823–4	54,897	40,219	34,765	44
1824–5	62,009	48,054	16,286	20
1825–6	63,455	47,106	34,451	42
1826–7	63,719	48,837	44,767	56
1827–8	50,340	43,219	18,890	58
1828–9	42,327	38,064	25,277	80
1829–30	47,220	38,996	10,637	48
1830–1	39,513	34,050	22,565	80
1831–2	46,467	40,219	28,489	64
1832–3	43,127	42,348	11,758	20
1833–4	47,759	46,973	36,474	48
1834–5	41,655	38,161	26,103	80
1835–6	42,391	35,955	24,466	57
1836–7	46,884	44,876	35,778	68
1837–8	51,830	44,230	31,942	80
1838–9	61,717	48,466	27,639	67
1839–40	65,835	56,676	28,129	52
1840–1	74,896	65,736	32,475	57
Total		844,876	527,975	

Source: *GBP* (1884b: 323).

and other survey officers to the draconian assessments of Pringle, the initial area of tillage was restored at best. With a longer series in the case of a major part of the Ahmadnagar district (Table 8.5), very similar conclusions are arrived at. It also appears that the third decade of British rule did not witness any improvement either in the condition of agriculture or in the predicament faced by revenue officers. It may be noticed that figures of tillage showed smaller fluctuations than figures of revenue collected. This underpins further the precarious conditions under which peasants cultivated their land: they undertook to cultivate more or less the same areas every year, but found that insufficient rains or other causes had destroyed a large proportion of their expected output. Then began pleadings with the officials, remissions, or outstanding payment by means of loans raised by the moneylenders. The same peasants might not be affected every year, but almost every year a substantial section of the peasants would find themselves in that predicament.

Table 8.4 Bijapur: Tillage and Land Revenue in the 475 Villages of Badami, Bagalkot, and Bijapur Segments, 1820–44

Year	Tillage (acres)	Land revenue (Rs)	
		For collection	Remissions
1820–1	–	3,19,959	11,948
1821–2	–	3,13,554	11,917
1822–3	–	3,15,458	52,952
1823–4	–	2,89,009	81,530
1824–5	–	2,72,569	1,18,532
1825–6	3,65,534	2,65,717	1,28,829
1826–7	3,81,103	2,76,932	1,18,716
1827–8	3,74,085	2,17,152	1,76,859
1828–9	3,82,701	2,60,545	1,33,105
1829–30	3,81,301	2,05,636	1,85,959
1830–1	3,73,259	2,35,420	1,46,921
1831–2	3,60,134	2,22,089	1,26,151
1832–3	3,40,969	1,53,852	1,75,243
1833–4	3,33,157	2,53,310	1,10,065
1834–5	3,37,772	2,64,250	70,396
1835–6	3,42,822	2,67,706	66,119
1836–7	3,47,467	2,65,926	65,081
1837–8	3,54,722	2,60,558	74,463
1838–9	3,58,044	2,07,208	1,28,301
1839–40	3,57,882	2,72,530	63,080
1840–1	3,61,653	2,54,694	80,444
1841–2	3,65,236	2,74,148	64,644
1842–3	3,51,725	2,68,198	55,674
1843–4	3,37,657	2,46,161	60,501

Source: *GBP* (1884c: 459–60).

The problems of the peasants in many parts of Bombay Deccan were further compounded by the poor development of infrastructure and transportation networks. A bumper harvest would depress prices all over the district, but the depression would be even more pronounced in those parts that had few roads and fewer market-places. Contrary to this, a scarcity would push up the prices even further in the more hilly and barren parts of the districts of Poona, Ahmadnagar, Sholapur, and Bijapur.[36]

While, as we have argued, in many parts of the Bombay Deccan districts, stagnation was the basic trend, even during the 1840s, there were some other parts which experienced a growth in tillage in the 1840s and in the seventeen years or thereabout from 1851 to 1868. This comes out from the aggregate data relating to the Poona district from 1839–40

Table 8.5 Tillage and Revenue, Ahmadnagar*, 1821–51

Year	Assessment on the basis of land given for cultivation (Rs)	Tillage (acres)	Assessment on the basis of tillage (Rs)	Remissions (Rs)	Actual Collection
1821–2	6,86,318	9,20,378	6,86,318	10,878	675,440
1822–3	6,65,376	7,66,911	5,99,567	50,748	5,48,819
1823–4	5,26,485	6,25,622	4,92,667	57,843	4,34,764
1824–5	5,58,318	6,75,714	5,44,164	2,86,302	2,57,862
1825–6	5,57,321	6,36,521	5,39,787	42,812	4,97,113
1826–7	5,72,085	6,61,987	5,64,062	32,130	5,31,794
1827–8	5,34,381	5,93,360	5,10,347	1,51,967	3,58,380
1828–9	5,15,909	5,97,199	4,96,296	95,698	4,00,000
1829–30	4,87,180	5,39,678	4,32,114	1,63,860	2,68,254
1830–1	4,78,458	6,15,137	4,57,420	58,085	3,99,335
1831–2	4,95,207	6,06,831	4,83,603	68,765	4,14,838
1832–3	4,93,864	5,43,343	4,41,229	2,41,725	1,99,504
1833–4	6,09,014	6,37,169	5,45,522	45,771	4,99,751
1834–5	5,07,346	6,14,348	4,89,354	82,436	4,06,918
1835–6	5,15,124	6,58,993	4,94,007	1,12,463	3,81,544
1836–7	5,27,337	7,38,582	4,99,455	1,02,947	3,96,508
1837–8	5,62,316	8,04,317	5,25,578	70,428	4,55,150
1838–9	6,04,510	8,69,020	5,70,732	1,16,615	4,54,117
1839–40	6,68,758	8,92,142	6,31,816	1,30,031	5,01,785
1840–1	7,08,012	9,23,244	6,95,638	1,34,143	5,62,495
1841–2	7,30,072	9,00,262	7,16,661	1,68,630	5,48,031
1842–3	7,11,993	9,94,937	7,10,445	17,836	6,31,609

Source: *GBP* (1884a: 483).

Note: *The area includes not the whole district but only the subdivisions of Nevasa Kharda, Ahmadnagar, Korti, Shevagon, and Jamkhed.

to 1882–3 (Table 8.6). The data reveal that there was rapid growth in tillage (by more than 33 per cent in eight years) in the district as a whole between 1839–40 and 1847–8, followed by several years of stagnation; growth resumed in 1851–2, was fairly rapid (at the rate of between 1 and 6 per cent) up to 1867–8, and then slowed down. Except for a brief spurt between 1872 and 1873, growth of tillage ceased altogether in the 1870s.

Of course, the apparent growth in tillage was not synonymous with growth in output, as the substantial remissions or outstandings of revenue in 1839–40, 1840–1, 1841–2, 1845–6, 1853–4, 1866–7 prove. But substantial growth took place in parts of the Bombay Deccan in the 1840s, 1850s, and 1860s. Officials attributed this to the lowering of land

Table 8.6 Tillage and Revenue in the Poona District, 1839–40 to 1882–3

Year	Tillage (acres)	Land revenue (Rs)		
		Remitted	Outstanding	Collected
1839–40	8,95,438	1,06,399	4,944	6,70,966
1840–1	9,47,840	99,262	17,503	6,82,792
1841–2	9,82,600	1,20,314	24,408	6,42,961
1842–3	10,00,881	26,937	9,635	7,69,580
1843–4	10,55,282	42,917	4,498	7,44,422
1844–5	10,63,127	92,395	33,321	6,89,399
1845–6	11,02,088	1,05,947	27,983	6,88,837
1846–7	11,48,755	19,283	22,473	8,15,606
1847–8	12,28,304	24,622	7,176	8,18,451
1848–9	12,27,898	40,610	11,838	7,75,355
1849–50	11,96,719	31,483	10,759	7,62,429
1850–1	12,15,015	51,961	4,168	7,20,324
1851–2	12,73,394	28,352	3,258	8,04,623
1852–3	13,16,767	7,278	452	8,00,721
1853–4	13,68,430	82,942	2,498	7,24,762
1854–5	13,95,080	6,123	244	8,14,863
1855–6	14,47,006	10,320	413	8,54,292
1856–7	15,34,473	16,489	351	8,79,282
1857–8	15,66,231	2,907	607	9,19,191
1858–9	15,98,898	2,427	93	9,33,046
1859–60	16,54,399	364	13	9,56,631
1860–1	16,64,802	238	47	9,66,183
1861–2	16,91,352	4	3,297	9,99,326
1862–3	16,96,097	422	423	9,96,991
1863–4	17,20,335	1,467	34,378	9,88,793
1864–5	17,36,582	228	15,357	10,06,414
1865–6	17,43,179	128	12,557	10,55,213
1866–7	17,84,390	80,038	71,766	9,37,296
1867–8	18,03,708	44,325	1,011	11,66,090
1868–9	18,14,896	48,592	429	11,55,784
1869–70	18,19,237	4,786	269	12,01,476
1870–1	18,31,953	4,756	2,553	11,11,378
1871–2	18,42,868	57,779	1,24,497	9,67,373
1872–3	18,48,831	5,468	45,521	11,26,729
1873–4	19,01,205	1,77,957	91,255	9,91,175
1874–5	18,84,679	40,615	7,203	11,83,328
1875–6	18,75,669	34,805	7,032	11,26,729
1876–7	18,64,475	1,736	4,56,828	7,03,213
1877–8	18,68,193	1,349	68,657	11,01,477
1878–9	18,61,631	250	1,08,644	10,40,305
1879–80	17,75,553	3970	24,446	11,07,763
1880–1	17,77,153	1,334	12,309	11,27,905
1881–2	17,86,064	3,392	2,882	11,50,687
1882–3	17,75,583	1,08,651	9,664	10,36,718

Source: *GBP* (1885b: 512).

revenue rates after the revisions suggested by Goldsmid and Wingate and other survey officials had been put into effect in the late 1830s, and after the rates had been fixed for ten-year or thirty-year periods.[37]

The growth in tillage from the 1850s was attributed by the district collectors and survey settlement officials to rise in prices from 1852[38]—which, incidentally, was an all-India phenomenon—to the construction of the Great Indian Peninsula Railway through the Poona district, bringing with it an injection of money into the local economy[39] and to the boom in cotton prices as a result of the breaking out of the American Civil War. However, this story of growth illustrated by Table 8.6 for Poona and by Table 8.7 for Indapur taluq within the same district, especially before the 1850s, has ever to be qualified by the endemic risk to crops and life suffered by the ordinary cultivators as a result of bad seasons, poor communications, severe fluctuations in grain prices, and arbitrary assessments. As the *Poona Gazetteer*, quoting reports of survey superintendents, revenue commissioners, and other officials put it:[40]

> The eighteen years ending 1854 was a period of little improvement. In Indapur and Bhimthadi, the people were few and poor. Over almost the whole of the district about half of the eighteen years, 1838, 1840, 1841, 1844, 1845, 1850, 1851, and 1853 were bad seasons and except when its price was raised by a general failure of crops, grain was ruinously cheap, the rupee price of Indian millet varying from 30 to 144 and averaging 104 pounds.

During all these years, new revenue survey and settlements were being carried out by government officials with expectations of higher and more stable revenues. But as Townsend, the revenue commissioner of Poona remarked in October 1849, 'every new assessment must be viewed as an experiment, the success of which could be estimated only by the experience of some years'.[41] Even if a low assessment were followed by an extension in tillage, and a rise in land revenue, this might not be sustainable even for a decade. According to Inverarity, the Collector of Poona in 1846, for example, the moderate settlement of Goldsmid had been by no means an unmixed blessing: the extension of tillage had led to the exhaustion of tillage from constant cropping. The more highly assessed lands had fallen waste because the unthrifty habits of the people led them to till for a few seasons the poorer waste fields rather than spend time and labour in renewing by artificial means the exhausted powers of the more valuable land.[42] We will analyse the significance of Inverarity's comment when we turn to the government policy regarding irrigation, roads, and so on.

Table 8.7 Indapur, Tillage, 1838–59

Year	Tillage (acres)
1838–9	2,12,407
1839–40	2,18,308
1840–1	2,24,695
1841–2	2,27,564
1842–3	2,28,551
1843–4	2,22,515
1844–5	2,27,089
1845–6	2,52,302
1846–7	2,54,972
1847–8	2,89,378
1848–9	2,91,165
1849–50	2,73,595
1850–1	2,71,007
1851–2	–
1852–3	–
1853–4	2,95,081
1854–5	2,97,106
1855–6	3,01,390
1856–7	3,04,743
1857–8	3,05,100
1858–9	3,00,003

Source: *GBP* (1885b: 425n., 433n., 435n., 439n., 440n., 441n., 442n., 448n., 451n., 465n., 466n., 467n).

As we have noted earlier, whatever growth might have taken place in the Bombay Deccan districts during the period 1840–70, it had ceased altogether by the middle of the 1870s. What happened after the 1880s? From Guha[43] we get figures of crop acreage in the Bombay Deccan (including the four districts covered by us plus the districts of Khandesh, Nasik, Satara, and Belgaum) for 1885–6 to 1940–1. Confining ourselves to the period 1885–1920, we find that the average area under crops was 21,162,000 acres during the quinquennium 1885–90 and 20,636,000 acres during the quinquennium 1915–20.

Of course, from this it does not follow that either the area under crops or the output in the four districts covered by us should have exhibited the stagnant pattern for the cropped area for the whole Deccan. But it is known that for the whole area, the output of cereals and pulses showed a stagnant or even a declining trend from 1885–6 to 1919–20 and the only major crop that showed a trend increase in output was cotton.[44] We also know that in 1881–2 or 1882–3, grain crops (mainly *jowar*, *bajra*, maize, or wheat) occupied 84 per cent of the cropped area in Ahmadnagar,[45] 86 per cent of the cropped area in Poona,[46] 79 per cent of the cropped area in Sholapur,[47] and 75 per cent of the cropped area in Bijapur.[48] Only in Bijapur was cotton responsible for more than 5 per cent of the cropped area. But we know from Mishra[49] that even in Bijapur the acreage under non-foodgrains in relation to the gross cropped area remained constant over the period from 1885–6 to 1897–8. In Ahmadnagar, Poona, and Sholapur, cotton occupied a very small fraction of the total acreage, and the proportion of cotton or of non-foodgrains to the gross cropped area virtually did not change between 1885–6 and 1897–8.

George Blyn[50] has computed the acreage and outputs of the major crops in India from 1891 to 1947. The two main grain crops of the Bombay Deccan districts were jowar (juari) and bajra, which normally accounted for 75 to 84 per cent of the area under crops in the four districts.

For the Bombay–Sind region, according to Blyn, the area under jowar was 8,757,000 acres in 1891–2 and 8,810,000 acres in 1920–1; the outputs of jowar in the two terminal years were 1,437,000 tons and 1,210,0009 tons respectively. The area under bajra in the Bombay–Sind region was 5,534,000 acres in 1891–2 and 3,764,000 in 1920–1; the output of bajra was 569,000 tons in 1891–2 and 497,000 tons in 1920–1. The last year of the series was a bad year. But even if we took the other years into account, and tried to fit a trend line, it would be difficult to find a positive trend for the whole period.

Finally, we turn to a gross measure of the risks faced by the population of the Bombay Deccan districts as a group, namely, the chance of life and death itself. We do not have readily constructed life tables for these districts. But for half the total period, that is, from 1872 to 1921, we have reasonably good census data. These data are reproduced in Table 8.8.

From Table 8.8, we see that the population of each district increased and decreased alternately in the intercensal decades between 1872 and 1921, and this was also true in the aggregate. Moreover for the districts of Poona, Sholapur, and the region as a whole we find that the population increased only marginally over the forty-nine years, 1872–1921, and the populations of Ahmadnagar and Bijapur actually declined over the period.

If we find that the latter half of half a century of stagnation in output and acreage is also associated with demographic stagnation—a stagnation which was the result of spurts of increase in population

Table 8.8 Population of the Four Bombay Deccan Districts, 1872–1921

District	1872	1881	1891	1901	1911	1921
Ahmadnagar	778,337	751,228	888,755	837,695	945,305	731,552
Birjapur	816,273	638,493	796,339	735,435	862,973	796,876
Poona	921,353	900,621	1,067,800	995,330	1,071,512	1,009,033
Sholapur	719,375	582,487	750,689	720,977	768,330	742,010
Total	3,235,338	2,872,829	3,503,583	3,289,437	3,648,120	3,279,471

Source: *GBP* (1884a: 46–7); *GBP* (1884b: 23–5); *GBP* (1884c: 71–2); *GBP* (1885a: 94–8); Census (1901d: 43); Census (1911: 36); and Census (1921: 25).

punctuated by disastrous famines—then it would be natural to expect that the earlier period of stagnation in tillage would also be associated with demographic stagnation. However, it has been claimed on the basis of the earlier population estimates that population in fact grew at rapid rates in the Deccan as a whole—from 2.4 per cent per annum over the period 1826–46, and between 1.2 per cent and 1.6 per cent per annum between the years 1846–72.[51]

At least for the four districts covered by us, the figure of population growth for the 1826–1846 period is plainly incredible, in view of the stagnation in tillage, the frequent harvest failures, and abject poverty of the average cultivator noted by Collectors, revenue commissioners, and survey and settlement officers. In view of the apparent growth in tillage observed from the 1840s down to the 1860s, the estimated figure of population growth appears to be more credible. The degree of credibility of the figures is assessed here on the basis of the record of these same districts during the period when population censuses were conducted systematically, namely, 1872–1921, the fact that figures of natural rates of the growth of population exceeding 2 per cent per annum were not reached in any large region in India for a decade-long period until the 1950s, and our information that no good reasons existed for assuming that land accreage or productivity had grown positively between the 1820s and 1840s.

Stagnation and the Burden of Land Revenue, Ecological Damage, and Moneylender Power

We have used a fairly informal method for describing the phenomenon of stagnation and fluctuations in cultivators' fortunes as a group. Sometimes ordinary least square methods of regression or graphical methods have been used in order to test the peasant's 'rationality', and usually the inference has been that the peasants were rational, and that the spread of money economy and better transport was associated with improvement in cultivators' fortunes.[52] Before the 1880s, yearwise data of acreage under different crops and their outputs were not available. Therefore, it is not possible to find out the ways in which peasants might have reallocated their resources so as to minimize the damage caused by crop failure. McCloskey has argued in favour of the risk-minimizing rationality of the English peasants' practices in the early modern period.[53] Many of the Indian peasants' practices may, on closer scrutiny, also turn out to have such damage-minimizing properties.

We face several difficulties in applying simple-minded statistical methods to data on agricultural outputs and yields, especially in areas subject to frequent harvest failures and famines, and characterized by a large degree of peasant differentiation as well. First, what are the relevant prices to use as the regressors or independent variables in a situation where they vary widely between one year and the next, or between one season and the next? (Prices also varied greatly as between different localities within the same district). Second, famines and harvest failures produce effects over several periods. For example, even by 1882–3, the district of Sholapur had not recovered from the effects of the 1876 and 1877 famines.[54] The cattle of many cultivators had died, their houses were in ruins, and they did not have resources even to cultivate all the land on which they had undertaken to pay revenue. So after being exposed to such severe external shocks, the dependent series—the area tilled—would itself be serially correlated.

Third, in the presence of a high degree of peasant differentiation, the aggregate outcome cannot be taken as simply the sum of the reactions of the 'average' peasant. A poor peasant facing prices had to find out the wherewithal for survival. In any plausible utility maximization exercise he will end up at a corner solution, with survival not being guaranteed every year. He may end up being unable to cultivate not only a larger plot next year (in response to a higher price), but being unable to cultivate any plot at all. Even if he is able to cultivate the same acreage, he may do a much worse job of tilling it than in a year of 'normal' harvest because he is enfeebled, or his draught animals are enfeebled, or he has no animals or no implements of his own left after meeting the subsistence needs of himself and his family. On the other hand, a cultivator with a large marketable surplus in his granary and facing high prices, will normally have an incentive to cultivate more land, or to cultivate it a little better. Of course, under the 'rational expectations' hypothesis, such a cultivator will try to separate out the noise from the information in the signal of a sudden price rise,[55] but I for one would not have known how to carry out the filtering operation for such a cultivator.

It remains to note that, there was a high degree of inequality in the distribution of holdings with occupancy rights in the Bombay Deccan districts. In Poona, in 1882–3, while the average size of a holding was about nine acres, more than 57 per cent of the holdings were below 10 acres, and about 1.2 per cent of the holdings were above 50 acres accounting for at least 10 per cent of the total area *taken for* cultivation.[56] In Ahmadnagar in 1882–3, the average size of a holding was about 15 acres, 73 per cent of the holdings were below 20 acres in size, and holdings above 50 acres accounted for about 2.5 per cent of the number of holdings and more than a sixth of the area taken for cultivation.[57] In Bijapur and Sholapur, the average sizes of holdings were larger at 38 acres and 48 acres respectively. But in each case, on the plausible assumption that the distribution of holdings within any size-class was skewed, more than half of the holdings were below the average size and the amount of land in holdings of the top size-classes numbering not more than 1 to 2 per cent of the total number accounted for more than 10 per cent of the land taken for cultivation.[58] Whether the differentiation among the peasantry had increased over the period from 1821 in any sense is a question we will not try to answer in this essay.

A favourite explanation of the British officials for the low productivity of land and frequent harvest failures in the Bombay Deccan was that peasants, because of increase in population, were forced on to marginal lands. However, the British land revenue system itself compelled the peasants to cultivate marginal lands, and also forced them to mine their land in a situation where most of them had few investable resources left to improve its productivity. Moreover, the British rulers took a long time to take up the provision of public irrigation, and even longer to provide agricultural loans to the peasants at low rates for effecting improvements. (The granting of such loans was a regular practice under the Mughal and the Maratha administrations.) When they did, the peasants had little incentive at first to take advantage of the public irrigation facilities or the official *taqavi* loans on terms which the government offered. These problems are all related to the basic subversion of private property rights and common property resources that the British land revenue policy was responsible for.

Under either the so-called 'utilitarian' or the Ricardo-Malthus rent doctrine, the landlord was supposed to be able to appropriate all the net rent after meeting the necessary expenses of cultivation. From a positive theory explaining the size of the rent, this was converted into a normative theory of the determination of land revenue demands by many British Indian officials. The latter regarded the state as the landlord and considered the net rent to be the appropriate size of the land revenue to be extracted by the state. There were several difficulties with this procedure, even if their construction of the role of the state in pre-British India were accepted. First, an environment in which neither labour nor capital was fully mobile, and where a very large fraction of the economic activities was conducted by family members with their own resources, it was difficult to determine what the appropriate wages for family labour or the 'normal' rate of profit on capital would be. Besides these microeconomic difficulties, there was the other conceptual difficulty: what was the competitive rent, or competitive wage or profit when the state constituted itself the absolute monopolist in control of the land? Besides these conceptual difficulties, which would arise even in a situation characterized by fully certain outputs and prices, little attention was paid to the appropriate concept of net rent in the presence of severe fluctuations in harvests and prices.[59]

The so-called Ricardo-Malthus theory of rent also justified the extraction of a higher rate of taxation from the better class of lands. With large fluctuations in harvests, and with high rates of interest charged by moneylenders, however, the peasants discounted the yield of all lands heavily. If the discount rate applied was high enough, the difference between, say, the expected values of the better class of land and the marginal lands might easily be less than the difference between the rates of land revenue on the better class of lands and the inferior plots. In such a situation, the phenomenon observed by Inverarity which we referred to earlier, namely, that peasants would take up the worse lands for cultivation and leave the better class alone could easily come about as a result of the peasants behaving 'rationally'.[60]

The British land revenue assessments also compelled the peasants to use as much land as possible for crop production rather than for the maintenance of livestock. This meant not only that crop production encroached on pastures that were generally less suitable for grain crops but also that peasants or shepherds had fewer resources to maintain cattle or other livestock. Since the latter were the main source of fertilizers, this meant that the normal productivity of land could not be maintained.[61]

A final aspect of the British land revenue system, which damaged the productivity of the land and increased the insecurity of the peasantry, was the virtual discontinuance of public expenditure on irrigation during the first 25 years of British rule. In the Poona district, in fact, the government spent very little on irrigation before the 1860s. In 1863–4 a survey of the potential for small reservoirs was made by Captain Fife, but the latter recommended the construction of waterworks only where flowing water from the Sahyadri was available.[62] Accordingly, Lake Fife and the Mutha canal works were constructed in Poona. In other districts of the Bombay Deccan also, public irrigation works were generally constructed only in the 1850s and 1860s. The irrigation potential of many of the public irrigation works remained under-utilized for a long time. For example, in the district of Sholapur, the Ekrur Lake was sanctioned in 1866, completed in 1881–2, and had a command area of 15,320 acres. In 1882–3, only 1,306 acres were irrigated with the water from the lake.[63] Apart from the fact that it often takes a considerable period for cultivators to get used to a new mode of irrigation, the water rates charged were also a deterrent. In the case of Ekrur Lake, for example, Rs 5,240 were collected as water rates in 1882–3; that is, the charge for use of the lake water came to more than Rs 4 per acre.

The tillage in the district of Sholapur in the same year was 1,906,235 acres and the land revenue collected was Rs 303,954 so that the land revenue per acre came to a little more than one-fourth of a rupee. Thus the water rate came to more than 16 times the land revenue rate. In view of the general uncertainty of prices, the stagnation in technology and the general scarcity of fertilizers, it is not surprising that peasants should have discounted anticipated earnings quite heavily, and that they should not have rushed to utilize highly priced irrigation facilities constructed by the government.

As we have noted earlier, the Maratha administration had advanced *taqavi* or *tagai* loans to cultivators for crop production and land improvement in the shape of livestock, wells, small irrigation reservoirs, and so on. The British were slow to resume the practice, and when they did, the amounts offered were meagre. Peasants were reported to be reluctant to take these advances, for, generally speaking, they involved a considerable degree of formality, and they were often not available when they were wanted. The local *vani*, on the other hand, was willing to lend money on the spot at exactly the time it was wanted. On the other side, of course, the resident vani could control the production or marketing activities of the debtor in a way that the officials could not. This phenomenon can be put in the language of 'information impactedness'[64], the interlinkage of markets, or the structural conditions for debt bondage, but the underlying reality would be the same.

As the British deepened their penetration into the rural economy, so did the moneylenders. Three factors contributed to this development. One was that the supply of capital to farmers and cultivators declined as a result of British conquest and the decline of Poona from the seat of an imperial government to a mere district headquarters.[65] According to the compiler of the *Poona Gazetteer*, who based himself on the Deccan Riots Commission (DRC) (1878) and the report of the Poona Collector, Captain H.D. Robertson in 1821, before the British conquest,

> Poona bankers had their agents in the districts and the ramification of the money trade in loans to the people and to the renters of villages created a wide circulation of specie, which returned to the coffers of the Poona bankers with an abundant accumulation of interest. Loans of this nature were usually repaid in grain which was received at a price much below the market rate, and this brought great returns to the lenders. Under the British revenue system all these advantages to the capitalists disappeared. The trade in moneylending was still further hindered by the substitution of suits in courts instead of the former private methods of dealing with debtors. The merchants were forced to be more cautious in their speculations and to look more to individual character and collateral security. A few bankers failed from bad debts contracted by broken-down nobles and officials. By about 1821, business was very dull in Poona; many rich bankers had fallen into poverty.[66]

The second factor helping the moneylender tighten his grip on the landholder was the inflexibility of the revenue demand in money in a situation of enormous uncertainty in harvests and prices—the sagging tendency of prices up to the beginning of the 1850s did not help matters.

The third factor weakening the position of the ordinary, illiterate cultivator vis-à-vis the moneylender was the location and the procedure of the civil courts. The courts were generally at a considerable distance from the typical village, and the latter usually had poor communications with the outside world. In these courts the evidence that counted most was a document, and documents, especially relating to loans, could be manufactured or forged by the typical moneylender since the ordinary peasant was mostly illiterate and ill-informed about the new-fangled procedures. These factors removed most means of redress against miscarriage of justice from his reach.

The British administrators, however much they might complain about the rapacity of the Gujarat or Marwari vani, knew that they were dependent on the moneylenders for realizing their land revenue demands from the peasantry. In Ahmadnagar district, this dependence was formally recognized by realizing the revenue not from the cultivators directly, but from moneylenders acting as *hawalas*, or sureties, for their clients. This practice was stopped in 1833. But soon after this, the land revenue demands were lowered and the value of the land offered as collateral increased. This improvement, and the stoppage of the hawala system led almost immediately to a surge in the number of civil suits filed against landholders from 2,922 in 1835 to 5,991 in 1839.[67]

The introduction of the Civil Court Procedure into the Bombay Presidency in 1827 resulted everywhere in increasing the power of the moneylender. This power, however, was exercised in seizing the occupancy right of the cultivators only in years when prices were high, or land revenue assessments were lowered officially. In general, therefore, the number of civil suits or seizures of land by creditors fluctuated as between different periods. The inflation in prices from the 1850s had the effect of increasing the creditors' interest in acquiring titles to occupancy rights of the indebted peasants. But it also allowed the more substantial cultivators at least to resist such demands.

Long before the passing of the Deccan Agriculturists' Relief Act, many Collectors or survey and settlement officers had been pleading for limiting the liability of the cultivators for debts contracted to moneylenders. For instance, Spooner, the Collector of Ahmadnagar in 1848 described how a small loan can, through the operation of a high rate of interest, compounded every year, and the signing of fresh bonds incorporating the interest charges together with the original principal, as a new loan, can gobble up all the movable assets of the cultivators together with his land, as a result of a decree passed by the Civil Court. Spooner then proposed that 'no court should be allowed to issue a decree in a lender's favour without inquiring into the debt and into the borrowers' means of paying the debt. ... In no case should a debtor's bullocks or other means of earning a living be liable to sale for debt'.[68] But the law moved exactly in the opposite direction. The anti-usury law limiting the legal rate of interest to 12 per cent was abolished soon after, and in 1859 a new judicial procedure was introduced requiring 'the punctual conduct' of duties by the subordinate courts. 'At the same time the landholders' credit was enhanced by adding his land and field tools to the security which was liable for his debts'.[69]

The fall in prices of a major cash crop, namely, cotton, in the late 1860s, and the sagging of prices in general in the early 1870s aggravated the problem of indebtedness of the more substantial landholders. These developments triggered the disturbances in Ahmadnagar and Poona which acquired fame as the Deccan riots of 1875. But increase in the power of the moneylenders over the peasantry, the increased likelihood of the latter to lose their occupancy rights, and peasant resistance were not phenomena that can be said to be immediately precedent to the Deccan riots but were virtually coeval with the British conquest of the territory of the Deccan.

The introduction of land revenue demand to be paid promptly in cash, the abolition of the hereditary rights of the mirasdars or *vatandar*s and the new power given to moneylenders to acquire occupancy rights of the indebted peasants may also have been responsible for the widespread supplanting of the Maratha vanis or kunbis by the footloose Marwari and Gujarati vanis as moneylenders in the villages, and contributed to the breaking out of the Deccan riots. Once the land rights became fully transferable, the moneylender did not have to depend on the village network and on the continuous monitoring of the peasant's activities in order to make the latter pay up. He could simply sell up the peasant's assets, get the land cultivated himself or retain the peasant as his sharecropper. But the readiness of the moneylender to sell up the peasant depended on the value of the occupancy right which in turn depended on the price of the produce and on the ease with which the peasant's assets could be seized either by resort to civil courts or through a settlement.

The supplanting of village—or region-level arbitration procedures by civil court procedures, and the virtual setting aside of the older village government network under the British—lessened the moneylender's dependence on the consent of the village for realizing his principal and interest. Moreover, the necessity of settling land revenue and debts in cash even in years in which harvests had failed or local or regional level prices were low meant that the moneylender needed large cash balances or an easy access to supraregional credit networks. The immigrant moneylender who was part of a large network of banking had a decided advantage over local kunbi or Brahmin moneylenders, and progressively supplanted them as British rule extended in time and space.

How did the peasants adjust or respond to all these changes? We have already referred to some of the adjustments in terms of extension of cultivation to inferior lands, turning of pasture into arable land, and reluctance to invest in land-improving capital works. The ultimate adjustment in the case of a peasant who suffered a disastrous harvest failure or lost his occupancy right was, of course, death. We have not tried to catalogue the number of years in which in particular regions peasants suffered loss of harvests. What the government reported as a famine was chosen on extremely arbitrary and changeable criteria. To give an illustration of the frequency with which harvests failed in the district as a whole, or in major parts of the district, I counted the number of such failures in the Poona district between 1821–2 and 1853–4.[70]

Of these the following crop seasons were considered to be either 'unusually bad', 'on the whole unfavourable', 'peculiarly unfavourable', 'bad on the whole', or a season of, 'failure of rain', of 'scanty rain', or a season of 'failure in east', or 'failure in east and centre': 1823–4, 1824–5, 1827–8, 1829–30, 1830–1, 1832–3, 1837–8, 1838--9, 1841–2, 1844–5, 1845–6, 1850–1, and 1853–4. So in thirteen out of thirty-three years, a substantial fraction of peasants experienced starvation or worse. Besides these, there were a number of years, in which the peasants suffered because of disastrously low prices. Sometimes low prices coincided with local harvest failures. Only a few of these years were described officially as years of 'famine'. So the prevalent idea that famines in the Bombay Deccan were concentrated only in the last quarter century must be seriously questioned.

One method of 'adjustment' which probably had pre-British roots, but which may have become more frequent after the formal abolition of slavery,[71] and the insecurity and loss of assets brought by the British land laws, was the practice of what was euphemistically described in the *Gazetteers of the Bombay Presidency* as 'mortgage of labour' or service mortgage. In the words of the *Ahmednagar Gazeteer*:

> A husbandman, who has fallen hopelessly in debt, has lost his land, and still owes money, as his last resource, will mortgage his labour for a term of years. It also sometimes happens that a family of three or four brothers, wishing to borrow money to buy cattle, will agree among themselves to work off the loan by one of their number serving the lender. ... Moneylenders are the only class in Ahmadnagar to whom labour is mortgaged. The services of a bondsman, or one who has mortgaged his labour, are rated at Rs 18–24 a year, exclusive of food and clothing. An ordinary grown workman takes four or five years to work off a debt of Rs 100. One case is recorded in which four persons, two brothers, and their wives, mortgaged their joint labour against an outstanding debt of Rs 900.[72]

The peasants, of course, adjusted to changing seasons and prices by altering the composition of crops under cultivation. However, in the absence of detailed data for the period before the 1880s, it is not possible even to begin the exercise of finding out the relative importance of rains (and their distribution), prices, and land revenue assessments in the allocation of land and other resources by the peasants. Harold Mann,[73] in a highly interesting exercise, tried to find out exactly how the total rainfall or its distribution as between different months or seasons influenced the outputs of crops in the four districts of Poona, Ahmadnagar, Sholapur, and Bijapur over the period 1871–1939.

The most important of his findings is that 'in the less precarious areas, the variability of the corps seems to be greater than that of the rainfall; in the tracts more liable to famine, the opposite is the case'.[74] This would be consistent with the hypothesis that the peasants in famine-prone areas try to ensure their survival by sticking to a rule that minimizes the probability of a total failure of crops. They would thus go in for the most drought-resistant crops which also were generally their chief means of subsistence (namely, jowar and bajra). In the areas less prone to famine, variations in crop composition could be broken down into at least two components. The bigger peasants would put more of their acreage under commercially more profitable crops. Secondly, even some of the smaller cultivators, either voluntarily or through debt-induced compulsion, would put some acreage under crops which are meant to be sold in a regional market—rather than consumed or sold in a local market.

Peasants' modes of adjustment to the compounding of insecurity effected by the British land revenue system were not always passive or non-violent. The British administrators reported numerous disturbances and rebellious outbreaks throughout the period covered by us: the Deccan riots should be counted among the milder disturbances. In 1826 the Ramoshis[75] of southern Poona revolted, 'partly owing to the scarcity of 1825'.[76] 'Under the leading [*sic*] of one Umaji they were so enterprising and successful that, in 1827, as they could not be put down, their crimes were pardoned, they were taken into pay, employed as hill police, and enriched with land giants'.[77] In 1828, the Kolis of Ahmadnagar rose under the leadership of Ramji Bhangria, who had been a police officer under the Marathas and then under the British, and Govindrau Khari, himself a Koli, who had earlier been the commandant of Ratangad fort under the Marathas. Govindrau had refused employment under the British government. Although the chief rebels were arrested by the British in 1829, the Koli uprising in the Sahyadris continued, under the leadership of Rama Kirva, a Koli. In 1830 he was joined by the Bhils.

But ultimately the British troops sent against the rebellious Kolis and Bhils prevailed and Kirva was captured and executed.[78]

Although Kolis, Ramoshis, and Bhils are the only groups which the *Gazetteers* mention as having broken out into open revolt, I do not believe that they had no support from other ethnic groups, communities, or castes: for example, the Brahmin Kulkarnis are supposed to have abetted the Koli risings of 1828–30 and deliberately misled the British counter-insurgency forces.[79] Nor do I assume that the uprisings took place only because of economic factors. However, economic factors played a role in either triggering a revolt or sustaining it by enlisting the support of other people suffering from a similar sense of injustice. The Kolis who had taken to agriculture tended to suffer from the exactions of the moneylenders even more than the Kunbis (the dominant peasant caste), some of whom were landlords and moneylenders. Thus in 1836, Captain Mackintosh, writing in *Transactions of Bombay Geographical Society*, vol. I,[80] found that the Kolis of Rajur in north Ahmadnagar complained bitterly against moneylenders from Gujarat:

> The moneylenders of Rajur were foreigners from Gujarat, visited their homes at intervals, and retired to their homes, when they made a competency. There were four headmen who had agents in different villages to buy up the grain. The moneylenders had induced the district hereditary officers to take shares in their shops as when people of local rank were mixed with them the Kolis were afraid to complain against the lenders. The Kolis keenly felt the injustice of which they were victims, and were eager to engage in any undertaking which gave them a chance of revenge.

In addition to charging excessive rates of interest, keeping fictitious accounts and compelling the debtors to settle the accounts at a time which suited the lender, the moneylenders also acted as monopsonist buyers of the Kolis' produce. The Kolis, apart from resorting to courts, sometimes attacked the Vanis' houses and burnt their books. They occasionally held naked swords at the Vanis' throats or slightly wounded them.[81]

The naked swords of the Kolis in Poona were again turned against the sovereign protectors of 'law and order' in the Sahyadris in 1839:

> Early in 1839 bands of Kolis appeared in various parts of the Sahyadris and attacked and robbed several villages. All castes joined them and their numbers soon rose to three or four hundred, under the leading of three Brahmans Bhau Khare, Chimnaji Jadhav, and Nana Darbare. The rising took a political character, the leaders declared that they were acting for the Peshwa, and assumed charge of the government in his name.[82]

No sooner had this revolt been crushed and two persons, a Brahmin and a Koli, had been hanged, and a number of others sent to prison or transportation for long terms (including life) than there was another uprising among the people of the hills. The uprising of Kolis, which began in 1844, was led by Raghu (Raghoji) Bhangria and Bapu Bhangria, both Kolis, but they were joined by persons belonging to other castes.[83] The revolt was finally crushed only after the capture and execution of Raghoji Bhangria in 1847.

There was a major uprising of the Bhils of Ahmadnagar and Poona in 1857; in this case the triggering event was the mutiny of the British Indian troops in May 1857 (which is often styled as the first Indian war of independence). The Bhils, who were led by Bhagoji Nai, Patharji Naik, and Harji Naik, were not finally quelled until Bhagoji Naik was killed in an engagement on 11 November 1859.[84]

In 1873 Honya Bhagoji Kanglia, a Koli, gathered a group of followers in the western hills of Poona and Ahmadnagar, and began attacking moneylenders.[85] Many moneylenders suffered a loss of property and some had their noses cut off. In 1875 the open violence against moneylenders, especially against those of Marwari origin, spread among the majority Kunbi cultivators, and it is the diffusion of that revolt, most of it taking the form of violence against property rather than violence against persons, that has come down in history as the Deccan riots. While the government appointed the Deccan riots commissioners to investigate the riots among the Kunbis, purely police methods were used against Honya Kanglia, who was arrested on 15 August 1876, and condemned to transportation for life.[86]

Apart from the general sense of grievance from which the cultivators suffered, specific developments in the profiles of land tax and produce prices contributed to the worsening of relations between the peasants and the moneylenders. One major element was an increase in land revenue demands effected after 1867, when in most parts of Poona the settlements made thirty years before had come to an end, and the government effected new revisions. The increases in government demand effected through the survey and settlement operations between 1869 and 1872 in five revenue subdivisions of Poona, namely, Indapur, Bhimthadi, Haveli, Pabal, and Supa ranged from 31.47 per cent (in the case of Supa) to 65.48 per cent (in the case of Haveli).[87] The second factor aggravating peasant insecurity and hardship was the fall in prices of produce between 1871–2 and 1873–4. The joint effect of these two developments was, in the words of the *Poona Gazetteer*, 'first to reduce the landholder's power of paying, secondly to make creditors seek by all means in their power to recover their debts or to enhance their security by turning personal debt into land mortgage, and lastly to check further advances to husbandmen'.[88]

The third factor which may have precipitated the violent action of the more substantial landholders was an order passed by the Revenue Department of the Government of Bombay on 5 February 1875. According to this order, if there were land revenue arrears, they should first be recovered by selling the movable property, and only when that was exhausted should the officials proceed to sell up the land of the defaulting cultivator. According to the *Poona Gazetteer*:

> This order the moneylenders turned to their own advantage at the expense of the landholders. In February and March 1875 the lenders refused to pay the second instalment of revenue on land whose produce they had received from their debtors. Landholders who found their movable property attached, after they had handed their creditors the produce of the land on the understanding that they would pay the rents, naturally felt that they were the victims of deliberate fraud.[89]

The riots had been preceded in many areas by the social and economic boycott of the moneylenders, often led by cultivators belonging to the upper castes.[90] When such measures failed to remove the incubus of moneylender power, it was then that villagers of Supa and Kedgaon invaded (on 12 and 13 May 1875, respectively) the houses of the moneylenders, and took away or destroyed their property. This was the official beginning of the Deccan riots.

The Debt Process and the Failure of Agricultural Banking for the Poor Peasant

The investigation conducted by the Deccan riots commissioners[91] and the search for a solution to peasant indebtedness through an agricultural bank, proposed in the 1880s by J.W. Wedderburn and M.G. Ranade, revealed that the debt process for the peasant could not be understood simply in terms of the rate of interest charged by the moneylender or the market value of the collateral offered by the peasant. The latter was caught in a web of a lack of freedom as soon as he was compelled to enter the debt process, a compulsion which was a regular feature of his life cycle.

According to the *DRC*'s findings, in the twelve villages of Poona and Ahmadnagar specially selected for detailed study, about one-third of those peasants and landholders who paid their land revenue directly to the government were in debt.[92] The total debt of these twelve villages was found to be Rs 194,242 and the land revenue assessment of the indebted peasants was Rs 10,603. The DRC took the value of dry crop land to be worth about seven years' assessment and irrigated land to be worth from fifteen to twenty years' assessment. Taking an average of the two types of land, the DRC concluded that the purchase price would not exceed ten years' assessment. Thus the total debt was twice the value of the land of the indebted peasantry.[93]

Most of these peasants were very poor with assessments of less than Rs 20. Their non-land assets generally had very little value. Thus it could hardly be claimed that the indebted peasantry had offered valuable collateral.[94]

The question then should be asked why did the moneylenders lend sums of money, which were far larger than the values of any assets the peasants could pledge? One answer is that the nominal amount of debt had little relation to the actual amount of money lent. At the very moment of lending a sum, very often, the interest that would accrue on the loan in the first year was deducted from it. And since the rate of interest was exorbitantly high, failure to repay any part of the principal or interest would soon make the loan assume astronomical proportions. A particular case was cited by Cockerell, introducing the Bombay Indebted Agriculturists' Bill (which eventually became the Deccan Agriculturists' Relief Act of 1879) in the Governor-General's Council on 20 June 1878.

A ryot had borrowed Rs 10 and at the end of ten years from the date of the loan, his account with his creditor stood thus: he had paid Rs 110 and still owed Rs 220 so that in the short space of ten years, through the process of repeated renewal of bonds in which compound interest at high rates was added to the principal, his debt had been made to mount up to thirty-three times the sum actually borrowed by him.[95]

The creditor often foreclosed on the mortgage, and even without civil suits, the right of occupancy was transferred to the creditor. But the transactions between the creditor and the debtor did not end there. Even after the right of occupancy had been transferred, the Ahmadnagar ryot often continued to pay the land revenue due from the mortgage.[96] The mortgagee in fact converted the ryot into a tenant-at-will on his (the ryot's) own land even before the right of occupancy had been transferred or the land had been sold up by instituting a civil suit (in which the *sowkar*, generally obtained an *ex parte* decree since the ryot failed to put in an appearance to contest the case).

Thus the creditor–debtor relationship was easily transformed into one in which the debtor delivered up whatever surplus produce he had to the creditor. The creditor became his landlord, and *de facto* the master of his whole family. Sons, wives, and daughters of the tenant became the sowkar's virtual serfs because of the debt obligations of the tenant. It is not really correct to say that the tenant had become a sharecropper on his own land because (a) the tenant continued to cultivate the land only at the creditor's and now the landlord's pleasure and (b) the share of the crop he had to deliver could be anything, depending on how the creditor chose to calculate the arrears on the debt for which the peasant had lost his hand.

Under these conditions, it is not surprising that the sowkars were often found not to foreclose on the mortgages even after the nominal debt had grown to be several times the value of the land; it was not the net value of the land but the present value of the gross earnings of the indebted peasant's family minus whatever minimum subsistence the sowcar chose to allow them that became the security for the loan. The seriously embarrassed peasant's family entered into a compact for enserfment when the peasant took a loan from the sowcar.

Under these circumstances it becomes very difficult to produce a convincing *economic* model of the course of indebtedness of the peasant and its outcome. That the seriously embarrassed peasant would, with only a little kick from Dame Luck, lose control over his land and his labour was virtually certain. But exactly when the *de facto* loss of land would be registered into *de jure* transfer of occupancy right or forced sale of land become an open-ended issue.

According to the *DRC*, the incidence of actual transfer of occupancy right and of forced sales through civil suits was higher in Ahmadnagar than in Poona. The reasons for this difference, as cited in official reports, are all related to variations in the debt process: (a) paradoxically, the lighter burden of land revenue in Ahmadnagar made land rights in that district a more attractive proposition for the moneylender or the rich landholder; (b) the greater degree of ignorance and helplessness of the Ahmadnagar ryot made him an easy victim in the law courts. Lastly, the virtual monopoly of moneylending enjoyed by the immigrant Marwari sowcars of the Ahmadnagar district had its impact. The moneylenders of Poona had among them a larger number of vanis with traditional ties to the village and may have, therefore, been restrained in their operations to some extent.

The open-endedness of the exact timing of transfer of land suggests that the statistics of the transfers of land as obtained through deeds of sales were poor indexes of the actual loss of land by the peasants. The DRC enquiries revealed that many peasants had lost their land to the sowcars. But the deeds of sale may have recorded a fact which had been accomplished long before a sale was registered. On the other side, registration of transfer of occupancy may indicate the beginning of a condition of serfdom of the tenant rather than his reduction to the position of a free, propertyless labourer.

Indeed, in many cases loans need not have been made at all against the security of land. The sowcar's dealings with a typical indebted peasant included the following transactions: 'the debtor delivers his produce, or as much of it as he is obliged to deliver, to his creditor, and the creditor supplies his needs, clothing, assessment, seeds, food, and cash for miscellaneous expenses'.[97]

The question naturally arises: how did the sowcar, turned into the effective landlord, subject always to the ultimate overlordship of the state, maintain his control over the debtor and his family?

In the case of the peasant who still had not legally lost possession of his land, the threat of dispossession and its opposite, the hope of recovering the land if the sowcar's demands were met, must have acted as a powerful means of control. But in the case of the debtor whose land had already been transferred to the landlord, the means of control would have taken diverse forms. First, there would be the use of the quasi-religious belief that an indebted man does not attain *moksha*, unless he or his descendants pay up the debts. These beliefs were also embedded in local customs which held the indebted man to be a thrall to the creditor even after the debtor had no more worldly assets to deliver. Secondly, there would be the whole coercive apparatus of the state working down to the village which almost automatically favoured the wealthy, in the name of preserving law and order. It was assumed that it was the poor who would breach the conditions of peace and not the rich. Thirdly, in a society where agriculture had come to be virtually the exclusive means of livelihood, and where unemployment was endemic, the mere threat of eviction of even a bonded sharecropper would be enough of a deterrent.[98]

The relations between the sowcar and his debtor were affected not only by the microeconomic and microsocial factors working at the level of the village but also by the structural constraints of a colonial, tributary economy. The DRC and later enquirers such as the Famine

Commission of 1901 were aware of most of these factors but, with a few notable exceptions, they tended to concentrate on excessive population growth, peasant irrationality, or peasant ignorance as the dominating issues. Many modern analysts who regard population growth or the working of the primeval peasant mentality rather than the framework of imperial rule and the fragile ecology of the tract, aggravated by that rule, as the basic reasons for the crisis of Deccan agriculture in the 1870s are repeating the arguments of the DRC and the Famine Commissions.

The DRC, the Famine Commission of 1880, and the Famine Commission of 1901 were all unanimous in concluding that the revenue system introduced into the Bombay Presidency was a major cause of the indebtedness of the ryot, and his impoverishment. The Famine Commission of 1901 expressed the gap between the intention of the makers of the Bombay revenue system and its outcome pithily:

> We desire to guard ourselves against the supposition that we impute want of care or solicitude for the people's interest to the authors of the Bombay revenue system. ... What we wish to point out is that their intentions have not been fulfilled. They expected the accumulation of agricultural capital: but their plans did not promote thrift, nor did they conduce to the independence of the *ryot*. They looked for the capitalist cultivator; and we find the *sowkar's* serf.[99]

As formulated by the same Commission, the salient features of the Bombay system were:

1. the creation of a territorial unit of land revenue assessment, which is called the 'field';
2. the assessment of land revenue on each 'field' independently, each thus becoming a separate holding;
3. the recognition of the recorded occupant of the 'field' as possessing complete proprietory rights over it, subject only to the payment of the revenue or tax from the recorded occupant in bad years as in good.[100]

The DRC commented extensively on the British laws which abolished ceilings on rates of interest to be charged, made civil procedures dependent on nothing but written evidence, and tilted the balance decisively against the small peasant without literacy or effective access to the civil courts.[101]

Despite official denials, force and torture were often used as late as the 1890s[102] to realize the arrears of revenue from tenants. The presumed increase in the value of the land as a result of the general rise in prices failed to improve the bargaining position of the ryot as against the moneylender. The recurrence of famines did not help matters. With the cattle often gone, the soil productivity further depleted because of lack of fertilizers, and with the peasant himself being emaciated as a result of months of starvation, his value to the moneylender was less than before. The moneylender's own surplus was also diminished because of the mass default of his borrowers. So while the demand for credit went up, its supply remained below normal in post-famine years.[103]

The DRC report also suggested that indebtedness of the peasantry discouraged their enterprise; it further discouraged them from making use of whatever public irrigation facilities were available because the increased yield would merely enrich the sowcar (or the government but the DRC were reluctant to adopt that position).[104] Moreover, the DRC pointed out that the transfer of land from the peasant to the sowcar might also have an important employment effect: 'Such holdings as pass into the hands of the *sowkar* will not, under hired labour, support as many persons as lands cultivated by proprietors, and these holdings are yearly increasing'.[105] Here we have an early formulation of the proposition that lands cultivated by family labour would display a higher degree of labour intensity than those cultivated by wage labour. But if our earlier argument is valid that many indebted peasants remained as virtual serfs on the land and their whole family labour was mobilized by the sowcar, then there should not be a great deal of difference in the intensity of labour use.[106] Obviously, the DRC formulation would require that the land is no longer cultivated by a sharecropper but by wage labour: or else it requires that the sharecropper effectively puts in less labour on the alienated land than on land he can call his own.

The British land revenue system rendered land, and especially the land of the small peasant, a very poor asset for banking purposes. This was fully grasped by those Poona capitalists who had offered to help Wedderburn to start an agricultural bank. This was also grasped by many of the British officials and other Englishmen or Scotsmen who interested themselves in these questions. Wedderburn in his speech at the meeting (of 4 July 1883) held in London to consider his proposal for an agricultural bank for India stated:

As to special disadvantages attaching to such an enterprise in India, from a banking point of view, there is no real and serious difficulty except that arising from the poverty of the individual ryot and the want of solidity in the security he is able to offer. He is, indeed, the absolute proprietor of his holding, subject to the payment of the government assessment; and if this assessment were either fixed or limited in a definite way, the security would be good but this is not the case; the demand being liable after 30 years to an enhancement which may swallow up the margin of profit on which the mortgages depend. The Poona Committee [of Indian bankers—A.B.] have asked that in the area of experiment the existing rates should not be disturbed for a period of 20 years from the present date.[107]

Sir James Caird, who had been a member of the Indian Famine Commission of 1878–80, and was considered an authority on agricultural subjects, reiterated the same point at the same meeting and reminded the listeners of the further complication of intermediary right-holders.

The danger of the failure of such an experiment as that proposed (namely, an agricultural bank for India) was the risk of such an enhancement of rent by the government, or the zamindar, as would swallow up the growing profit of the cultivator.[108]

Wedderburn and the Poona capitalists wanted the debt servicing charges of the agricultural banks due from the peasants to be put on the same basis as land revenue dues and realized by the same process. They also wanted an assurance that the government would not raise the land revenue demand, for a definite period of time. The former demand the government rejected as being politically inexpedient; it would in any case have been ineffective, because it is doubtful if peasants would have rushed from the comfortable, if smothering embrace of the sowcar who would theoretically meet all his needs and with a considerable degree of flexibility, to the cold embrace of a bank which would be niggardly, if just, in its supply of credit needs, but would be absolutely rigid in its demands.

The would-be bankers wanted to soften the rigidity of their terms if the government would also agree to soften its demands in case of a crop failure. Either a definite promise to grant remissions in case of a crop failure or a promise not to raise land revenue demands for a fixed term would have led to some loss of prospective revenue for the government, which might or might not be recovered through more productive lands and higher land revenue yields later in the day. This last possibility the government refused to contemplate, and so the Poona-Wedderburn scheme for agricultural banks came to nought.

Conclusion

The separation of the private and public spheres of law, and the emergence of a civil society have been prime concerns in the conceptualization of a bourgeois political system from Montesquieu to Gramsci.[109] The security of property and the stability of expectations have figured in the writings of all protagonists of the bourgeoisie from James Harrington down to Jeremy Bentham.[110] The same issues have surfaced in our own time again in discussions of the foundations of civil society, the possibility of a socialist democracy, and the virtue of disengagement of the State from society in post-colonial societies. Our analysis of the operation of the British land revenue in the Deccan should make it clear that contrary to some recent analysts such as Washbrook,[111] there is little evidence that the British authorities wanted to separate the domains of public from private law, at least as far as property in land was concerned. There were many British administrators who recognized the over-determining character of the state demand for revenue in shaping the land tenure system in British India.[112]

The issue of civil liberty is also connected with the question of the degree of security of life provided by the land tenure arrangements in British India. Can civil liberty be secure when life is not? The access of moneylender power and the institution of informal or legal bondage under British rule are not phenomena confined to the Bombay Deccan alone, as Elizabeth Whitcombe[113] had demonstrated in the case of Uttar Pradesh. What is ironical is that peasant insecurity and peasant unfreedom were as endemic in raiyatwari Deccan as in taluqdari Awadh. The enormous degree of imperfection in credit markets arising out of differences in values of collateral offered by different borrowers and the adverse selection process faced by borrowers in the presence of incompleteness and asymmetry of information in credit markets have been stressed in recent literature.[114] The peasants of the Bombay Deccan under colonial rule paid for such imperfections in the credit markets with their lives and their freedom, and not all the good intentions of the Poona bankers or Judge Wedderburn could rescue them from that condition of insecurity and potential bondage so long as the basic ingredients of colonial public finance endured.

The linkages of the majority of peasants living on an insecure margin of subsistence and the failure of private accumulation are too obvious to be stressed again. What needs to be emphasized, however, is that as I had noted earlier,[115] the transfer of thousands of workers in declining handicrafts to agriculture could not be effected without impoverishing the workers further if accumulation in agriculture was also sluggish.

Whether we look at issues of civil liberty or economic transformation, if colonialism was a process of 'creative destruction' (to lift a phrase from Schumpeter), the creativity was well hidden from the eyes of the vast majority of peasants in colonial India.

Notes

1. I am indebted to Sudhir Anand and Siddiq Osmani for detailed comments on an earlier version of this article. I am also indebted to Partha Chatterjee for directing my attention to Lawrence Krader's work. They are all absolved of any liability for any remaining errors in the article.

2. Krader (1975: Chapter 1).

3. Stokes (1959), (1976).

4. R. Guha (1963: Chapter 4).

5. Krader (1975: 62–4).

6. Avineri (ed.) (1969: 'Introduction').

7. Marx (1966: 331–2).

8. Marx (1971: 399–449).

9. Krader (1974: 243–84).

10. Firminger (ed.) (1917–18); Stein (1989: Chapters 2–4).

11. Nanavati and Anjaria (1951: 29–30).

12. For a representative sample, see Mill (1818: vol. I, Book II, Chapter 5, and vol. V, Book VI, Chapters 5 and 6); Jones (1831: Chapter 4) and (1857: Book II, Chapters 7 and12). Marx in the 1850s had obviously been greatly influenced by the *Fifth Report* of the House of Commons (Firminger [ed.] 1917–18). The evolution of Marx's thinking from his articles on India to a critical assessment of the views of Phear and Maine in the last years of his life has been traced in Krader (1974). Some major landmarks in the evolution of Marx's thinking in this area are to be found in Marx (1979 [1857–9]: 83–136); Marx (n.d.), (1966) and (1971).

13. The only exception to this was constituted by the lands given in fee simple, virtually free of cost, to mainly European planters in Assam and other areas where tea and coffee plantations were to be promoted A. Guha (1977: Chapter 1).

14. Bagchi (1976c); Baker (1984: Chapter 3).

15. Bagchi (1987: Chapters 1–3).

16. Ascoli (1917); Firminger (1917–18); Sinha (1962), (1965) and (1970); Chowdhury (1958).

17. Dutt (1963a[1906]: Chapters 8 and 20–1); Kumar (1968); Sarada Raju (1941); and Baker (1984: Chapters 3 and 6).

18. Lardinois (1989).

19. Dutt (1963b[1906]: Chapter 4); Klein (1965); Kumar (1968: Chapters 3 and 4).

20. S. Islam (1979); Gupta (1984: Chapters 1–3).

21. Cf. Mitra (1979); de Janvry and Subbarao (1986).

22. *DRC* (1878).

23. Mann (1955).

24. Robertson's *Report* dated 10 October 1821, as quoted by Dutt (1963b[1906]: 247). For accounts of land rights in the Maratha territories before British conquest, see Fukazawa (1965a), reprinted in Fukazawa (1991: 148–98); Fukazawa (1972), reprinted in Fukazawa (1991: 199–244); Fukazawa (1982: 193–203); Perlin (1978: 172–237); Wink (1986).

25. M. Elphinstone, Report on the Territories conquered from the Peshwas, dated 25 October 1819, as quoted by Dutt (1963a[1906]: 243).

26. Clerk's evidence is quoted by Dutt (1963b[1906]: 40–1).

27. Tucker (1853: 250).

28. Klein (1965) and Kumar (1968).

29. Perlin (1978).

30. Rabitoy (1975); Stokes (1976); Ambirajan (1978: 167–71).

31. *GBP* (1884c: 217); Bagchi (1976c).

32. *GBP* (1884b: 467); Dutt (1963b[1906]: 45). We shall use the word *raiyat*s or *ryot*s to designate the state tenants rather than those whose rights were dependent on the will of the *raiyat*s.

33. There has been a controversy on the question of whether a new class of rich peasants was making their presence felt in the countryside of western India in the nineteenth century. See in this connection, Charlesworth (1978: 97–113) and Mishra (1982: 3–51).

34. Kumar (1968: Chapter III); S. Guha (1985: Chapters 2–3).

35. *GBP* (1884c: 323–7).

36. *GBP* (1884b: 483–4, 529).

37. *GBP* (1885b: 414–19).

38. Ibid.: 464, 470.

39. Ibid.: 108–9, 471.

40. Ibid.: 464.

41. Ibid.: 445.

42. Ibid.: 439.

43. S. Guha (1985: 86).

44. Ibid.: 88–9

45. *GBP* (1884b: 245–6).

46. *GBP* (1885b: 7).

47. *GBP* (1884c: 229).

48. *GBP* (1884d: 319).

49. Mishra (1982: 14).

50. Blyn (1966: Appendix Table 3A).

51. S. Guha (1985: 162–8).

52. See, for example, McAlpin (1983).

53. McCloskey (1976) and (1989).

54. *GBP* (1884c: 217).

55. See, for example, Lucas (1973).

56. *GBP* (1885b: 6).

57. *GBP* (1884b: 244).

58. *GBP* (1884c: 218); *GBP* (1884d: 310).

59. Many of the conceptual difficulties were clear to the more reflective British officials. Pringle had been a thorough-going follower of the Ricardo-Malthus theory of rent and wanted to assess land revenue on the basis of the so-called net produce rather than on that of the gross produce. The latter was accepted as the basis of assessment by the survey settlement officers, Lieutenants Wingate and Nash, and Mills, the principal Collector of Poona in the late 1830s.

However, Williamson, the revenue commissioner in 1838, argued that if the government were the principal landlord, then 'it would undoubtedly be unjust to leave one man a greater proportionate share of the fruits of his labour than another. But if the object of an assessment was to impose a land-tax, the plan of taking a certain share of net produce was the only means by which any interest could be created in the land stronger than that local attachment which the Kunbi had for his fields; nor was the comparatively higher assessment of inferior soils, which was caused by such a system, to be deprecated' (*GBP* 1885b: 409n).

According to Williamson, it was 'natural and most profitable for the cultivator that the best soils should be first cultivated' as those in proportion to the capital and labour employed on them yield the best return, 'and when the fiscal arrangements of Government invert this natural order of things', it was a clear proof that there was something radically wrong in the system (ibid.). The officials in the headquarters however objected that Williamson's principle 'carried to extremity would seem to end in the abolition of all difference of rate or classification, and the settlement of one uniform rate for land of all qualities' (ibid.).

60. For this proposition to be true it is not necessary that the peasants should maximize expected net returns. It could be valid under a number of other rules of decision-making in the presence of uncertainty. For a discussion of a number of alternative decision procedures under uncertainty see Luce and Raiffa (1957: Chapter 13).

61. Bagchi (1976c).

62. *GBP* (1885b: 15).

63. *GBP* (1884c: 225).

64. Williamson (1975).

65. *GBP* (1885b: 97–8).

66. Ibid.: 98.

67. *GBP* (1884b: 473–4).

68. Ibid.: 483.

69. *GBP* (1885b: 115).

70. As reported in Ibid.: 369–461.

71. The main form of slavery in Poona at the time of British take-over seems to have been domestic slavery, although it was reported that some of the men slaves worked in the fields. A person could be enslaved for failure to pay a debt but this was rarely done (*GBP* 1885b: 133–4). Slavery generally resulted from the sale of kidnapped children or the sale of children during a famine. They were kept by Brahmins or wealthy Muslim families, and rarely by the major cultivating caste members, namely Kunbis (*GBP* 1884b: 320–1).

72. *GBP* (1884b: 304).

73. Mann (1955).

74. Ibid.: 38.

75. The Poona Ramoshis were classed by the compiler of the *Gazetteer* among 'the unsettled tribes'. The Poona Ramoshis seem to be 'the outlying northern remains of the great Kanarese ... group of tribes which are included under the general names of Bedars or Byadarus—hunters and woodsmen' (*GBP*, 1885a: 409).

76. *GBP* (1885b: 306).
77. *GBP* (1885a: 307).
78. *GBP* (1884b: 416–17).
79. Ibid.: 417.
80. As quoted in Ibid.: 307.
81. Ibid.
82. *GBP* (1885b: 307).
83. The account is based on *GBP* (1884a: 417–18) and GBP (1885b: 307–8). But there are discrepancies about the date of the outbreak, and the triggering event. According to the first account, Raghu and Bapu Bhangria were sons of a jamadar of Ahmadnagar whom the Kolis forced to join the rebels. According to the second account, Raghoji made a raid on some Marwaris who applied to the police. Raghoji's mother was tortured by the police conducting the investigation. At that point Raghoji revolted. Perhaps both the accounts are true. Although Raghoji might have been forced to join the rebels, his loyalty to the cause of the revolting peasants might have been cemented because of the outrage committed against his mother.
84. *GBP* (1884b: 418–20).
85. Ibid.: 420; *GBP* (1885b: 119–309).
86. *GBP* (1882: 526).
87. *GBP* (1885b: 118n).
88. Ibid.: 188. The qualification should be made that for the poorer peasants, personal debt and land mortgage were close kin to each other, if not at the time of contracting the debt, then definitely when it came to servicing it. This will be made clearer in the next section.
89. *GBP* (1885b: 119).
90. Ibid.: 119–20.
91. *DRC* (1878).
92. Ibid.: Para 75.
93. Ibid.: Para 77.
94. On the importance of the collateral in judging the 'price' or cost of credit, and in equilibrating well-behaved loan markets, while providing the rationale for rationing of credit, see Jaffee and Russell (1976: 651–66); Azzi and Cox (1976: 911–17). On the importance of asymmetric information in adversely selecting out the worse-off borrowers from the normal banking operations of credit institutions, see Stiglitz and Weiss (1981: 393–410). For an account of attempts to organize co-operative rural credit, with the help of the government, see Catanach (1970) and Laud (1983).
95. S.C. Ray (1915: 129).
96. *DRC* (1878: Chapter 3, Para 79).
97. Ibid.: Chapter 3, Para 78.
98. cf. Bagchi (1973a) and Breman (1974).
99. FC (1901: Para 333).
100. Ibid.: Para 327.
101. *DRC* (1878: Chapter 3).
102. Laud (1983: 5).

103. *GBP* (1884d: 347).

104. This is the converse of the case analysed by Bhaduri (1973) and (1984), in which the landlord discourages the introduction of technical change because the expected decrease in his interest income (from the decline in the money borrowed by the sharecropper because of increase in his income) more than offsets the increase in the share of the landlords' crop resulting from higher land productivity. For a general analysis of the constraints imposed on the poor peasant because of the interlinkages of the markets for his labour, the credit obtained by him and the output sold by him, see Bharadwaj (1974).

105. *DRC* (1878: Para 61).

106. Bagchi (1982a: Chapter 6).

107. *The Times* (1883).

108. Ibid.

109. Montesquieu (1989 [1748]: 20–76).

110. Macpherson (1962); Halevy (1972: part I); Long (1979); and Parekh (ed.) (1973).

111. Washbrook (1981).

112. Rabitoy (1975: especially, pp. 91–2).

113. Whitcombe (1972: Chapters 4 and 5).

114. Azzi and Cox (1976); Stiglitz and Weiss (1981).

115. Bagchi (1976b).

9

Markets, Market Failures, and the Transformation of Authority, Property, and Bondage in Colonial India*[1]

Pure Competition and Market Failures

Economists working in the tradition of Leon Walras and Vilfredo Pareto have derived a theorem about the dual correspondence between a purely competitive equilibrium and a Pareto-optimal state. This means roughly that every such equilibrium displays the zero-sum properties of Pareto optimality (that is, nobody can be made better off through a reallocation of activities without making somebody else worse off) and that every Pareto-efficient state can be supported by a set of prices such that every economic agent seeking to maximize utility or profits (which in equilibrium must be zero) with the prices as given ends up with the trades prescribed by the purely competitive equilibrium. Once the stringent conditions of such correspondence became clear,[2] some of the more perceptive economists began to worry about the numerous ways in which markets failed. Market failure may mean at least two different kinds of outcome. The first is that the given market may fail to produce an equilibrium in positive prices and quantities, as when a large supply of fish suddenly arrives in a market, and there are no takers even at zero prices, so that the sellers (or more often, public authorities) have to dispose of the surplus at a positive cost. The second is that there is an equilibrium, but that equilibrium is sustainable only if either the seller

*Reprinted from, 1996, Burton Stein and Sanjay Subrahmanyam (eds), *Institutions and Economic Change in South Asia*, Delhi, Oxford University Press, pp. 48–70.

or the buyer (and sometimes both parties) has a determinate influence on the price at which the commodity or service is traded. The rise of Keynesian macro-economics has been seen by many economists as the emergence of the study of market failure on a grand scale. The endemic unemployment in rural areas of Third World countries and the failure of even subsistence wages to bring about full employment is another example of market failure. The second type of market failure was long recognized in the literature as the case of industries with decreasing costs at the point of equilibrium.

Traditional neoclassical theory dealt with situations in which all features of the commodities were fully known to everybody. This theory was extended to situations in which states of nature were uncertain, but all the agents had full information about the possible state of nature and the probability of each of them occurring.[3] But Radner showed that when the agents had incomplete information about states of nature and about each other's behaviour, problems arose about the existence of competitive equilibrium; when the equilibria existed they could not be proved to be Pareto-efficient either.[4] Radner further demonstrated that if agents did not have unlimited computational ability (and unlimited time for carrying out the computations), the well-behaved competitive equilibria would vanish. In the case of both uncertainty about the agents' behaviour and limited computational ability, money would be needed to tide over the uncertainty and the limits of computational ability; thus the existence of competitive equilibria in any economy using money becomes a hazardous affair.

While neoclassical economics has something to say about the local conditions of market success (to coin a phrase) or even the varieties of market failure, it has virtually no light to shed on the conditions for sustainability of market success, or the reasons for persistent market failure. For the former, we have to turn to the followers of Keynes and Kalecki, and, of course, to the followers of classical political economy from Adam Smith to Karl Marx. For the latter we have to turn to discourses going far beyond the boundaries of traditional economics or traditional political economy as taught in academic institutions. The core of classical political economy has been claimed to be the investigation of the conditions for promoting the wealth of nations primarily through the instrumentality of capital accumulation, and of the determinants of income distribution between landlords, capitalists, and workers.[5] The latter in its turn was thought greatly to influence the speed of: accumulation and its quality through its influence on the distribution of workforce between productive and unproductive labour. In pre-Marxian classical political economy, very roughly speaking, the shifting of the income distribution from landlords to capitalists was supposed to promote economic growth by promoting accumulation and helping to shift labour from unproductive to productive uses (since landlords' consumption was regarded as the source of employment of unproductive labour).

I have argued elsewhere that Malthus overestimated the significance of effective demand failure in the British economy of his time and came to decidedly wrong conclusions regarding the remedial measures needed.[6] I would now argue, *pace* Eltis, that Malthus confused issues of short-run demand failure with those of long-term sluggishness of investment, and failed to see that abolition of landlordism was necessary in order finally to release the long-run propensity to invest from the shackles of pre-capitalist, non-market power, and pre-capitalist incentives.[7] That the British, with the advantage of the first start and global dominance in manufactures, were able to make landlordism wither away rather than abolish it formally, is another matter.

Political Economy as the Rhetoric of British Imperialism in India

It is this corpus of political economy that the more theoretically minded British policy-makers in India turned to when trying to rationalize their policies. That the justification was couched in terms of political economy has been eloquently argued by Ranajit Guha and Eric Stokes.[8] But that the justification was often no more than a cloak for expediency in many contexts has been argued by Rabitoy and Stokes in his later work.[9] On the balance of the evidence, my sympathies lie more with the latter view than with the former.[10] I have argued this in some more detail in a recent paper.[11]

I find the view that land tenure arrangements in India were modelled either on the experience in Britain or on the tenets of Ricardian political economy untenable for the following reasons. First, the British never created a set of landlords with freehold rights in India, except in the region of tea plantations where they gave most of the land away to European planters on a nominal payment. Correspondingly, they never created a set of capitalist tenant farmers with a secure tenure or long leaseholds. Secondly, for most of the period of British rule in India, there were severe constraints on mobility of labour and capital. So this idea of an economic rent to be calculated on the basis of a given market wage and a uniform rate of profit was mostly a fantasy. Both these reasons for the non-applicability of the British model and of the Ricardo-Malthus theory of rent were known to Richard Jones (1831), but their significance for conducting any discourse on land markets, commodity markets, or peasant rights has not been grasped by most analysts in the field.

Economic theorists love to indulge in fantasies of the first weaver meeting the first agriculturist to exchange each other's products in a completely spontaneous manner. But anthropologists and historians have long known that the actual functioning of markets has generally required them to be connected with social networks, political authority, and the organization of merchants and financiers transcending the borders of states.[12] In pre-British India one of the ways in which the rulers sought to establish their legitimacy and extend their authority was by licensing markets, augmenting the facilities for merchants to bring their wares to their realms, and making tax concessions to attract trade from neighbouring kingdoms or chiefdoms.[13] Of course, rapacious rulers sought also to treat merchants and bankers as lambs to be fleeced, but unless this was only a short-term expedient, the rule of such chiefs and princes did not generally endure. British rule greatly disrupted this network of markets, most of which were oriented towards domestic exchange, and the extension of overseas trade failed often to compensate for this disruption. Secondly, in pre-British India the successor states of the Mughals had to nurse their core domains in order to survive or gather the resources for further aggression. In proto-capitalist Europe poor laws, guild regulations, and state patronage of the economy were designed to ward off the shocks of famines, wars, and foreign competition. The British never treated such policies as part of their agenda of rule over India. Naturally, the incursion of unregulated international influences often led to uncompensated income losses and to the spread of monopolistic power of local controllers of money and authority over markets for goods, credit, labour, and land—to the point at which it became meaningless to talk about the working of a self-regulating market.

Market-places and Long-distance Trade: Creation and Destruction

At the time of the British conquest of Bengal and other major provinces, there were commodity markets for most consumer goods, there was long-distance trade in many staples, and there were money and credit markets linking the major centres of trade and government. The direction of trade and the location of markets were greatly influenced by the pre-British structures of regional power and the pre-British style of governance. As we have mentioned already, the market-places were themselves often created through the specific political act of a local ruler, a regional power or the supraregional authorities.[14] Colebrooke commented in 1795 on the decline of market-places in Bengal after the customs and other commercial duties (*sa'ars*) levied by the zamindars or the local rulers on the traders were abolished. The abolition of these tolls was part of the Cornwallis reforms turning the decennial settlement into the Permanent Settlement, and clipping the power of the big revenue farmers.[15] On the other hand, the British effort to 'rationalize' the internal tolls of the country made them much more burdensome than before, and especially damaged those manufactures which depended on long-distance supply of raw materials such as cotton, since the reforms had a cascading effect on costs.[16] Moreover, imported goods came to enjoy a tariff preference in the Indian market over the produce of Indian industry, varying between 2.5 and 10 per cent *ad valorem*,[17] as the British conquest of the country opened up the whole of the conquered territory to the influences of transoceanic trade. Of course, these influences had to negotiate all the real transport barriers, and other physical barriers to easy communication posed by the land mass of India, breached by the flow of the great rivers and their tributaries and deltaic offshoots. Then there was the fragmentation of the territory with internal tolls and custom duties which were survivals of pre-British times, though transformed by British diktat and practices. Finally, the rapid expansion of India's import and export trade was checked repeatedly by the recessionary force generated by the British conquest. This story of the survival and transformation of pre-British structures melding with market failures as an accompaniment of the impact of British rule, or even of institutional changes effected through international economic pressures, would repeat itself in different regions and different phases of the two centuries of British rule.

The recessionary impact of British rule was felt in the late 1760s in Bengal. This was the immediate occasion for the East India Company's appeal to the British parliament for financial help and led to the first Act passed by the parliament to regulate the Company's rule in India. This was also the occasion for the Company's decision to commission Sir James Steuart to examine the scarcity of money in Bengal and suggest possible remedies, which resulted eventually in the introduction of a

Scottish system of banking and note-issue in the Company's territories.[18] In many cases of British conquest, unrequited transfers and consequent impoverishment of the territory occurred long before the formal assumption of power by the British. Such was, for example, the case of the territories of the Nawabs of Arcot and of Awadh. However, a more dramatic displacement of authority could be followed, as in the case of Bengal, by a noticeable recession and widespread failures of markets, such that producers of crops were unable to sell them except at ruinously low prices. This monetary stringency led to widespread shortfalls in revenue, which is how the phenomenon came to the attention of the authorities, just as it was the failure to finance the Company's 'investment' with its normal territorial revenues that had provoked the enquiry into the problems of shortage of specie in Bengal. The fall in demand as a result of the fall in money incomes ensuing from the dismissal of the Peshwa's soldiers and effective dissolution of his court at Poona was cited as a major reason for the disastrous fall in price of grain in the erstwhile Peshwa territories.[19] This recession also was one of the causes of the decline of handicrafts in the Bombay Deccan.[20] The latter in turn fed the forces of recession and merged with the general phenomenon of depression in prices and economic activity in most parts of northern, western, and southern India from the middle of the 1820s down to the beginning of the 1850s.[21] Almost certainly this led, in many cases, to a contraction of the sphere of circulation of money. Symptomatic of the stagnation in demand for credit was the fact that although directors of the Bank of Bengal proposed to raise its capital from Rs 5 million to Rs 20 million, these limits of capital and note-issue were not reached until the abolition of the banks' right of note-issue from 1861.[22]

Land Tenures and Market Failures in Bundles and Fractions of Claims

The most contentious area in the historiography of the British Indian economy has been the subject of land tenures. It is not only the intentions or the ideologies of the policy-makers which have been under debate, but also the nature of land rights. One of the hardiest perennials in colonial India's historiography has been the contention that British colonial administrators introduced, or intended to introduce, capitalist farming of the type they were familiar with in Britain. The foundation of the prosperity of the agrarian bourgeoisie which ruled England from the Commonwealth period down to the eighteenth century was an absolute property in land, which was considered to be more or less inviolate.[23]

The land tax which this bourgeoisie imposed upon itself was light, and was neither the first charge nor the essential condition for the landlords to retain their land. In India, both in the Permanent Settlement and in the raiyatwari areas, the payment of the tax to the treasury became the first charge and the essential condition for the landlord's (zamindar's) or the smallholder's (raiyat's) right to the fruits of the land, a share of the rent in one case, and a share of the value of the produce in the other. What was sought to be commoditized was not the full present value of the land as a productive asset, but only certain shares or bundles of claims to the produce or the rent of the land, these claims being threatened with extinction every time the revenue payment (*kist*) became due. Such commoditization itself was confronted repeatedly with problems of market failure—during the first thirty years or so, in the case of the Permanent Settlement in Bengal, and during an even longer period in the case of the raiyatwari settlements in the Bombay Deccan and in Tamil Nadu.[24] Zamindars often failed to meet the undertaking for rent payment they had entered into with the government, and when their claims (their so-called 'estates') were disposed of, they often had to be sold at no more than the value of two or three years' revenue demand. Even then, often there were no purchasers at all at these auction sales. Some of the purchasers withheld their bids fraudulently, but 'fraud' was the counterpart of extortion by agents who had very little information about ground-level reality. Even then, a very large fraction of the zamindari rights changed hands between the institution of the Bengal Settlement of 1793 and the close of the second decade of the nineteenth century.[25]

Market failures in the zamindari areas might have occurred on an even more extensive scale, but for two reasons. In some cases, at the time of the settlement itself, the British administrators recognized the structures of local power in which the prospective revenue-payers could be expected to realize that rent out of which they would pay the government's demand. Additionally, the British either legalized, or deliberately averted their eyes from, that exercise of power without responsibility which became the style of rural governance by the local magnates recognized by the British. The explicit recognition of the local structures of lineage and local political structures, while settling land revenues, comes out clearest in the case of Banaras when Jonathan Duncan as British Resident at the court of the Raja of Banaras introduced Permanent Settlement there.[26] Duncan recognized that 'corporate groups as well as individuals had landed rights' in these territories.[27] According to Cohn:

Duncan wanted to collect the revenue from and to grant zamindari rights to what he termed the 'village zamindars' by which he meant those men in lineage territories or taluks who stood forward as leaders of the corporate body, or those individuals who could establish their rights to parts of villages or whole villages, either as grants from previous government or through tradition.[28]

Viewed from the standpoint of individual and exclusive property rights, a great deal of confusion resulted. Claims to shares were often based not on the rights alleged to be enjoyed by immediate ancestors, but on the bases of those enjoyed by the ancestors of ancestors.[29] There were claims and counter-claims that had to be arbitrated by the British officers in charge or by a recognized leader of the locality, often on the basis of oral tradition only. These modes of settlement built into the power structure of superior land right-holders a bias towards traditional, pre-commercial, and rather arbitrary modes of decision-making. They also led to the effective abrogation of the rights of inferior right-holders:

No record of rights of subordinate members of proprietary groups was recorded. Internal division of the revenue obligation was left to be recorded by members themselves. No record of rights of permanent tenants and other tenants was kept, so that subordinate cultivators had no legal protection.[30]

Cohn has shown how some new groups acquired zamindari rights in the Banaras division–groups which were connected with Banaras rajas, or other influential Indian chiefs of the region, with some of the early British Residents and other British officers and, increasingly, with the British apparatus of revenue collection. In the process, one caste, namely the Rajputs, declined decisively as landholders. However, after the initial upheavals caused by British take-over, it is remarkable how stable the structure of landownership became and how effective banking, trade, and subordinate offices under the British still remained as routes to acquisition of zamindaris and power until the beginning of the twentieth century.[31]

In the case of Bengal, the Regulation of 1790 was the real beginning of the Permanent Settlement and it required the revenue farmers to issue written undertakings (*pattah*) to tenants. However, in many cases, tenants, following earlier usage, claimed hereditary rights of occupancy, which the pattahs would deny to them. The pattahs also restricted their rights in other ways by increasing even their legal dues to extortionate levels. Intermediaries below the revenue-payers to the government used pattahs fraudulently to deprive the hereditary occupiers of their rights by entering their own or their family members' names in the pattahs. For all these reasons, probably the vast majority of the hereditary occupiers and cultivators failed to secure true records of rights and became mere tenants-at-will.[32] Under the new legal process instituted by the British, a single written document could overturn the information and judgement of a whole community, and these tenants-at-will had to fight for more than a century-and-a-half to get even a modicum of security of tenure.

The Permanent Settlement story of failure of markets and institutions that act as operative vehicles of markets did not end there. By Regulation VII of 1799, the government armed the zamindars with powers that bypassed legal process, and allowed them to realize whatever they considered to be their dues from cultivators. As the Collector of Midnapore wrote in 1801, the demand for Regulation VII came from the zamindars who could now transmit the coercion exercised by the Company's officers down to the lowest level, that is, to the cultivator or the actual occupier of the land.[33] The Bengal zamindars had already started creating various subordinate intermediate rights in order to facilitate the collection of the revenue. After the passing of Regulation VII, this process, and naturally the exploitative pressure on the tenant, were accentuated. Soon Bengal ended up with the score of layers of intermediaries and the hundreds of sharers in both the originally recognized zamindari rights, and the intermediary rights of later creation with which we are familiar.[34]

Thus the state in this case, in order to take care of a market failure, privatized part of the coercive powers that it claimed to monopolize. Such private coercive rights were also usurped by the European planters. In the districts dominated by the planters it was not always clear whether the District Collector or the big planters were the real rulers of a particular district. All this did nothing to unshackle the market in the countryside. In the meantime, the de-industrialization process, the failure of private accumulation and the decay of pre-British irrigation works in the Permanent Settlement areas enormously increased the pressure of a burgeoning population on the land.[35] But these same forces created a thriving market in various intermediary rights in land. That did not mean that 'land' became a free asset, because what were sold were bundles and fractions of claims to the produce of the land. Moreover, land remained the sole productive asset in many villages and the major anchor of social and political power, and in some cases, the sole instrument against the threat of pauperization, bondage, or exile. All kinds of non-market methods were used to obstruct transactions in claims to the rent or the produce of the land. Extremely unequal relations between creditors and debtors, and between the big buyers of produce and the peasant sellers prevailed. Thus pervasive dominance by a few big players allowed them to force the peasants to make their transactions in labour, produce, credit, and land rights in an interlinked manner.[36] Not surprisingly, the Permanent Settlement areas were characterized by endemic market failure. Although there were some respects in which the raiyatwari areas differed from the zamindari or taluqdari areas, market failure was as characteristic of the former as of the latter.[37]

Uncertainty, Market Failure, and Interlinkages of the Credit, Land, and Labour Markets

In a society in which the majority of the people derive their livelihood from agriculture, the uncertainty faced by peasants plays a very important role in determining their relations with the rest of the society and the state, and in determining the form which market success or market failure takes. Conversely, the relations of peasants to landlords, to traders and moneylenders, and to the state greatly influence the nature and degree of uncertainty faced by the peasant.

Except under highly unusual conditions, all cultivators face uncertainty in production, an uncertainty created by nature in the form of uncertain distribution of rainfall, uncertain levels and timing of inundation of rivers, uncertain incidence of floods, and of pests. In the market for agricultural produce, peasants face uncertainty in prices: this uncertainty can in turn take the form of seasonal variations or annual changes. For poor peasants, the distinction between seasonal and longer-term changes often becomes meaningless, but for more substantial cultivators and landlords this distinction makes sense. In addition to price and production uncertainty, there is the influence of the land tenure system in determining the shape of things for the peasant. Does the peasant pay his tax in kind or in money? Does the payment depend on the state of the harvest or is it a fixed payment? If it is fixed, is it fixed in terms of produce or in terms of money? Does the payment become due at fixed times of the year? If it does, then the peasant may face a liquidity crisis even if he may be judged solvent in the long run. Are there other claims on the peasant's produce than those of the state? Are they themselves fixed or variable?

A typical Indian peasant would face this complex of uncertainties under either a landlord system (zamindari or taluqdari) or a small-holder (raiyatwari) regime. But under the first perhaps the number of claimants to his produce other than the state would be larger. To simplify slightly, we will concentrate our attention entirely on the problems of a peasant ruled by raiyatwari tenure.

The introduction of the raiyatwari tenure in the Bombay Deccan, or in most parts of the Madras Presidency, did nothing to mitigate the risks faced by the peasant in respect of production. But by converting variable assessments into payments fixed in terms of money, the British regime enormously increased the variance of returns expected by the peasant.[38] When this was combined also with an increase in the mean share of produce claimed by the state, it led to a severe increase in the downside risk. In many areas the government had earlier granted production loans or advances (*taqavi*) to cultivators. The cessation or severe retrenchment of such advances under British rule led to a decline in supply of credit to the peasants exactly when the need for it increased.[39]

Borrowers and lenders in the market for credit to the peasantry, faced with such uncertain prospects, were caught up in problems of incomplete and asymmetric information, adverse selection, and unequal bargaining power. Because of the risk of bankruptcy, a higher rate of interest offered by a prospective debtor is not necessarily an indicator of his or her better credit-worthiness. Since the principal and the interest rate cannot be the only variables characterizing a loan, the quality and value of collateral acquire special significance in equilibrating the credit market.[40] Moreover, since the information about and assessment of risks faced by the debtor is bound to be different as between the debtor and the creditor, the equilibrium inevitably is characterized by credit rationing, the lender almost always extending a smaller loan than the debtor wants.[41] The creditor seeks to guard against loss through lack of information by extending his monitoring mechanism. This is one of the motivating factors behind the debt bondage so often observed in an extreme or a mild form in virtually all rural areas under British rule. This monitoring may extend to surveillance over all the activities of the debtor—including his operations in the labour, produce, and land markets. It is one of the structural bases of the interlinkages of markets we have already noted above. But the interlinkage of markets within these structural constraints is also an indication of the extreme inequality of economic and political power if, by political power, we denote all the relations of dominance in society which may have non-market coercion as their ultimate sanction.

Although this way of posing the problem has acquired academic currency only in recent years, the basic causes were known to many British administrators. Edward O'Brien, as Settlement Officer of

Muzaffargarh in Punjab in 1878–9, came to the conclusion that the moneylenders had stepped into the position of pre-British (Sikh) governments, which had minutely superintended agriculture in the area, whereas the British government had failed to remedy the deficiency of landowners as farmers and managers.[42] Market failure and institutional failure were the joint progenitors of interlinked markets.

In the raiyatwari areas of Bombay Deccan, the British revenue officials realized the importance of moneylenders, both for tiding the raiyats over from one season to another, and for enabling government officials to collect the land revenue demands. In fact for some years, the moneylenders had been recognized as sureties for realization of the revenue from the peasants. During the years of depressed prices, with high assessment rates, the value of land as collateral was so low that the moneylenders had little incentive to sell up the raiyats for unrealized dues. The local moneylenders, or sowkars, initially depended more on their personal relationship with the peasants than on courts of law to realize their dues. Even then, out of a desire to protect the rights of peasants, some officials in the 1840s suggested revision of civil court procedure and the restriction of the right to transfer land through sale or mortgage.

With a rise in prices and a decline in the proportion of produce realized as land tax, the value of the land increased, and local moneylenders were increasingly replaced by outsiders. Hence the problem of alienation of land in settlement of debts assumed major proportions and received increasing official attention. In fact, the peasant tended to be subject to the moneylender's will in respect of the allocation of his own and his family's resources long before the land became formally alienated. In many cases a combination of usufructuary mortgage and share-cropping yielded a better return to the creditor than the outright acquisition of the land would have done. As is well known, ultimately the dissatisfaction of the majority of peasants in Bombay exploded in the Deccan riots of 1875–6, and forced the government to pass the Deccan Agriculturists' Relief Act in 1879. The Act, *inter alia*, provided that the immovable property of the agriculturists should not be attached or sold in execution of a decree unless it had been specifically mortgaged and that even in such cases, the court might direct the lands to be cultivated by the debtor for a number of years on behalf of the creditor, after which the debt would be discharged.[43]

Many British administrators were dismayed alternately by the 'success' of markets, when the occupancy rights in land passed from less enterprising to more enterprising proprietors, and by market failures when the increased value of land as collateral merely strengthened the hold of the moneylender on the peasants without leading to agricultural improvement or peasant prosperity. This alternation led to interventions in the market process from the very beginning of conquest in at least one extensive territory, that is to say, the British Punjab (which comprised modern Punjab, Haryana, and Himachal Pradesh in India, and most of Punjab and the North-West Province in Pakistan today). In that larger Punjab, as in other regions, just after British conquest, prices fell drastically.[44] Partly in response to this fall, and partly because of a protective attitude towards village communities (whether they really existed on the ground or not), the Board of Administration in Punjab prescribed a rule of pre-emption in 1892. The Board pointed out that 'the land ... did not belong to the proprietor in an absolute sense, it was subject to land tax, and the Government had an undoubted right to prevent the deterioration of the revenue capacity of the village'. The Board had already prohibited the practice of subletting villages for the purpose of discharging[45] the revenue demand. In 1852, it was laid down that if, for any reason, land was alienated, it had first to be offered to a member of the village community at an equitable price according to a procedure outlined by the Board.[46] These protective rules were crystallized in the Punjab Civil Code of 1854. It empowered the courts to 'set aside unreasonable alienations (that is, alienations to spite heirs or relatives), if challenged by the aggrieved parties within the legal period';[47] it 'reiterated the rule of pre-emption in regard to permanent transfer of land'; and made it applicable to 'the sale of land for debt in execution of decrees'.

The Punjab case illustrates that the introduction of transferable property rights in land (however fragmented and conditional they might be) by the British had been from the very beginning hedged about with restrictions introduced for the sake of long-term stability of revenue demand and of social structure. Village communities were virtually invented, especially in the trans-Indus districts; restrictions on transferability were transferred from Hindu law into Muslim law which had not recognized such restrictions earlier.

After 1866, when the general Code of Civil Procedure was introduced into Punjab and the post of the Judicial Commissioner was replaced by the institution of the Chief Court, difficulties arose about the interpretation of the rule of pre-emption and the procedures to be followed in reviewing compulsory sales in satisfaction of land revenue demand or 'in execution of decrees for settlement debt. But these problems and the resulting debates did not overturn the rules of pre-emption.[48] There was a pause in government intervention in the land market between the 1870s and the 1890s. But during the pause opinion grew stronger, with the opponents of such opinion losing ground, for further restrictions on transfer of land rights. In particular, it came to be a matter of policy severely to constrain voluntary transfers of land. In the debates that sprawled across the reports of Settlement Officers, Deputy Commissioners, Revenue and Financial Commissioners, and Lieutenant-Governors, particular conceptions of the characteristics of castes and communities figure prominently. The fates of the 'improvident' Meo caste and the 'proud and unproductive' Rajputs (who could be either Hindus or Muslims), the sturdy Jats, 'the crafty' but enterprising Khatris were all sought to be weighed by a new all-embracing piece of legislation. Thus was born the Punjab Alienation of Land Act, which came into force in June 1901.

As Bhattacharya, Fox, and others have pointed out,[49] there were regional as well as local differences among the peasants and landowners in Punjab. Different communities had different attitudes to manual work in the fields, and average members of particular communities enjoyed different statuses: some were almost fated to be agricultural labourers, and some could not earn their living through honest sweat even if they were pauperized. However, members of 'respectable' peasant castes often joined the ranks of 'peasant proletarians',[50] that is, small peasants in the Lenin-Mao characterization of rural classes.[51] Some Khatri moneylenders or traders had become landlords even before the British advent, and many Muslim landlords themselves became moneylenders to their share-croppers and to other landowners. The British imposed a set of administrative interventions of their own or market failures that had been caused by the multiple sources of uncertainty faced by peasants, by pre-capitalist status rankings, and by the inequality of bargaining power caused by inequality of asset distribution. This administratively engineered interference in an imperfect market mechanism may or may not have arrested depeasantization. But arresting depeasantization was only a means to an end—that of finding a local political constituency among landowner and their dependent peasantry. It is possible that in soliciting a greater degree of loyalty among the landowners, the British might have exacerbated their brewing conflict with urban traders and bankers.[52] The political stance of the administrators of the British Punjab at the end of the nineteenth century showed that British officials had very largely shifted their expectation of a natural support base among the traders and bankers to that among the landlords and the dependent peasants. As the functioning of markets changed, so did the social basis of authority exercised by the British, although, of course, the shift was not uniform in all parts of the country.

In Punjab, the British went further than merely to bolster a landowning gentry and the upper stratum of peasant proprietors. In the canal colonies they effectively created a new class of landlords. That operation went hand in hand with the extraction of an ever larger revenue from the land, especially that which had the benefit of irrigation from government irrigation works.[53] It is difficult to maintain that unfettered operation of competitive market forces took precedence over either the extraction of a remittable surplus, or over the maintenance of a support base for imperium even in the high noon of empire in India, long after the phase of mercantile control had passed in the metropolis.

British Rule as an Awesome Theatre, and the Price of Distancing, Discrimination and Landlord Consolidation

All rule involves theatre, including democratic rule, as anybody who watched the performance of Ronald Reagan as President of the United States can vouch for. But some theatre is more awesome than others, and some theatre involves more pomp and circumstance than others. The theatre of rule also involves careful management of the distance between the watchers and the actors. The British administrators who came to India, habituated as they were to the ways of 'gentlemanly capitalism',[54] and as agents of a mercantile organization owing its birth to that same compromise that legitimized the landlord oligarchy of the eighteenth century, were well used to the nuances of the theatricality of public rule.[55] If Richard Wellesley, the 'glorious little man' inspired awe among his subordinates and naturally among the Indian subjects of the East India Company by his pomp, aggressiveness, and the hauteur of the local court he created (he was the builder of the first government palace in Calcutta), he was creature enough of his society to mind terribly when he was fobbed off with a mere Irish marquisate. (Of course he would be even more galled when his younger brother rose to the dignity of a ducal seat.)

We have fortunately a very clear account of the strategies used by the more far-seeing British conquerors and rulers for creating distance, but also instilling a sense of the British superiority in character (and hence in claims to the right to rule over Indians) in the instructions issued by John Malcolm to officers serving under him in 1821.[56] Malcolm appreciated that want of union among the Indians was 'one of the strongest foundations' of British power. He also foresaw that the reduction of Indians to the common yoke of British rule was likely to make them 'more accessible to common motives of action'.[57] According to him, while British power had so far 'owed much to a contrast with misrule and oppression', this strength was daily diminishing. Moreover, 'we have also been indebted to an indefinite impression of our resources, originating in ignorance of their real extent: knowledge will bring his feeling to a reduced standard'.[58] Malcolm wanted due respect to be paid to Indian perceptions of rank and authority:

> Though it is essential, in our intercourse with natives who are attached to and give value to ceremonies, to understand such perfectly, and to claim from all what is due to our station, that we may not sink the rank of the European superior in the estimation of those subject to his control it is now the duty of the former to be much more attentive to the respect which he gives them than what he receives, particularly in his intercourse with men of high rank. The princes and chiefs of India may, in different degrees, be said to be all dependent on the British government; many have little more than the name of that power they have enjoyed; but they seem, as they lose the substance, to cling to the forms of station. The pride of reason may smile at such a feeling; but it exists, and it would be alike opposite to the principles of humanity and policy to deny it gratification.[59]

The elements of oriental pomp and the style of the British landlord oligarchy were being mixed and remixed in different proportions throughout the period of British rule long before Lytton's apotheosis of Queen Victoria as the Empress of India, and long after the world had been treated to the spectacle of a 'naked fakir' sitting down at the same table as gentlemen who knew the proper attire for every hour of the day. But the maintenance of British power was not simply a matter of theatre. Might had to be demonstrated occasionally by blowing a score of Indian sepoys off the mouth of a cannon, by spectacularly finishing off the last mansion (*haveli*) of a recalcitrant chief, or publicly hanging the adult males of a whole hamlet when the need arose. There were other ways of demonstrating British might, as King Thibaw knew to his cost, and as Sayaji Rao II was made to realize through his humiliating treatment after an imagined slight to the 'durbared' Emperor of India.

The distancing, of course, had its material aspects: the high and mighty had to be maintained at a far higher cost than their servitors. This was emphasized as a principle during the Cornwallis reforms, and this became ingrained in every cell of the structure of British authority in all spheres of life. For instance, around 1795, whereas the 77 Indian employees in the Banaras district court together earned Rs 1,020 per month, the salary of the sole British judge presiding over the court was Rs 2,200 per month.[60] Again, when the Bank of Bengal started functioning in 1809, the salary of the British secretary and treasurer was Rs 800 per month, that of the highest paid Indian employee, the cash-keeper (*khazanchee*) (no less a person than Raja Ramachandra Roy, great-grandson of Clive's financier, Naku Dhar) was Rs 300, and the aggregate pay of the rest of the Indian staff together was Rs 500 per month.[61] The disparity in the salaries of Europeans and Indians did not change before the First World War. For example, in 1878, whereas the three principal European officers of the Bank of Bengal drew an aggregate salary of Rs 5,833 per month, the total wages of the Indian staff of the cash-keeper's department were Rs 4,224–8 per month. The secretary and treasurer alone drew Rs 2,600 per month; and if we exclude the salary of Rs 1,200 drawn by the khazanchee, the total of 112 employees in his department drew Rs 3,024–8 per month.[62] Keeping the Europeans in their noble positions had its economic effects. For example, down to 1878 (and I suspect, in many cases, even afterwards) European brokers were paid twice the fee paid to Indian brokers for government securities bought and sold. The 'taste for discrimination' exacted its toll by keeping technically and business wise better qualified people out of many occupations. Eventually, as Indian businessmen penetrated European preserves, the taste could no longer be so freely indulged in. The wonder is not that European dominance of Indian large-scale business crumbled in many sectors after the First World War; the surprising part is that it did not crumble much earlier.

The explanation for this delay would have to be sought in the enormous importance of government patronage, the interlocking nature of British domination of higher administration and large-scale business, the ideological hegemony imposed on Indian educated opinion by British imperium, and the sluggishness of accumulation produced by the haemorrhage of colonial remittance overseas. The last two factors had a major impact in shaping Indian society and technology, and hence their influence can be still traced in post-colonial India.

I have argued elsewhere that the imposition of the imperial view that Britain led the world in every sphere on educated Indian opinion and, of course, on British businessmen and technologists working in India, had harmful consequences for Indian technological development.[63] In the cotton textile industry, not only did the policy of 'one-way free trade' and the discriminatory treatment of Indian spinning and weaving mills hamper accumulation; by persuading mill managers to install obsolete and technologically inappropriate mule spindles in Indian mills long after they had been discarded in Japan, the USA, and most countries of continental Europe, the ideology of 'British is best' hobbled the Indian cotton mills more or less permanently in their competition with their new rivals from the early 1900s, namely the Japanese cotton textile industry.

The distancing and discrimination practised by members of the expatriate British community had discernible real costs for the economy as a whole. The virtual monopolization of the management of all jointstock banking by Europeans for most of the nineteenth century meant that most Indian business was denied credit on terms which were granted to large-scale European business, unless the particular Indian group had powerful European collaborators. For example, Nursey, Kessowjee & Co. was supported in their loan applications to the (New) Bank of Bombay by the direction of W. Nicol & Co. long after both the groups had become bankrupt.[64]

There was a double gap in the information flows between European-controlled banks and their Indian customers: the ordinary Indians, or even Indian businessmen, were badly informed about the business affairs of the powerful European constituents of, say, the Bank of Bengal, the Bank of Bombay, or Arbuthnot & Co., especially if the major part of the Europeans' business happened to be located abroad. Correspondingly, the bank managements were badly informed about the business affairs of Indians. The managements could generally pass on their losses to the Indian guarantors or collaborators of bankrupt firms. The Indians had no such remedy, and suffered very badly through the failures of the major agency houses in Bengal in the 1830s, the failures of the mushroom banks of the North-Western Provinces in the 1840s and 1850s, the failures of W. Nicol & Co. and Finlay Scott & Co. in 1878–9, and Arbuthnot & Co. in 1906. Only perhaps in the case of the failure of the Bank of Bombay in 1867 were the responsibilities and the losses of the Europeans and the Indians evenly distributed.

There is yet another area in which racially based discrimination probably had real effects on the economy. Practically all Indians were excluded from technical and supervisory positions in British firms and most public technical organizations. In modern parlance, no amount of signalling by Indians acquiring superior education could get them past the barriers manned by uninformed British management. All Indians were pushed below a threshold level, and a pooling equilibrium ruled, with all higher levels of technical and supervisory work being entrusted to often less qualified Europeans.[65]

Market failures of this kind were perhaps inevitable given the prevailing structure of unequal economic interdependence of the world economy and the structure of power implicit in colonial rule. But the colonial authorities adopted other measures directed at social and economic engineering even in the period since the 1870s, and these measures freshly clogged up the market mechanism in distinct ways, even as they created new channels for the market forces to flow into. One major illustration of this development is the social engineering practised by the British authorities in the canal colonies. The network of canals constructed by the British in Punjab and Sind from the 1880s added largely to the land revenue of the region (thus belying the claim that land revenue declined very significantly as a source of tribute for the empire). Moreover, the irrigation works were themselves, with the sole exception of Upper Jhelum Canal, enormously profitable, especially from the 1920s.[66] Instead, however, of settling the colonies with working peasants (on the pattern, say, of the settlements under the US Homestead Act of 1862), the British deliberately created a layer of landlords in the canal colonies, and these landlords were distinguished both by caste and by class from others. Whereas the peasant grantees belonged to such castes as Jat, Arain, Kamboh, Saini, the larger grantees (those with grants of 50 acres or above) were Rajputs, Qureshis, Sayyids, and Gujars.[67] Inevitably, this spawned a whole congeries of intermediary formations familiar in older, landlord-dominated regions—such as managers or lessees of absentee landlords, revenue farmers acting as agents of landlords and, of course, all types of dependent peasantry and workforce.[68] Thus, through all the changes in structures of authority during the two centuries of British rule, certain social formations continued to be reproduced through the very working of the colonial system—depressing accumulation and generating flows of distorted information—and through deliberate policy measures.

Capitalist colonialism works by introducing and exploiting markets. But the structure of colonial power is essentially political and not just a passive reflection of imperatives dictated by an impersonal market. Hence, market failures—deliberately engineered or systematically generated—are as much a component of the working of the system as market successes. Contradictions of capitalist colonialism expressed as market failures have been too little studied so far; hence I have concentrated on the failures rather than on the successes. A fuller account will have to deal with their interaction as a dynamic or dialectical process unfolding through history.

Notes

1. I am indebted to the participants of the international workshop on 'Meanings of Agriculture' and 'Production Units in Micro- and Macro-structural Perspective', held under the auspices of the Centre of South Asian Studies, School of Oriental and African Studies, University of London, in July 1992, for their comments on an earlier version. I alone, however, remain responsible for any errors in the paper.

2. Debreu (1959).

3. Arrow (1964 [1953]; Debreu (1959: Chapter 7).

4. Radner (1968).

5. Bharadwaj (1989: Chapters 1–5).

6. Bagchi (1988a).

7. Eltis (1984).

8. R. Guha (1963/1981); Stokes (1959).

9. Rabitoy (1975);Stokes (1976), reprinted in Stokes (1978: 90–119).

10. Bagchi (1982b).

11. Bagchi (1992).

12. Braudel (1982).

13. Naqvi (1972).

14. Cohn (1960), reprinted in Cohn (1987).

15. Colebrooke and Lambert (1795: 47–8). Colebrooke commented,

> Wanting the regulation, and protection received from officers of the sayer, markets have declined; and many have been totally disused, since the abolition of the sayers. This is undoubtedly an evil ... Numerous markets by promoting intercourse, contributed to general prosperity. The discontinuance of many markets in the short space of four years, and the decline of the existing marts is an alarming circumstance. (Ibid.: 48)

This passage was omitted when Colebrooke published a revised version of his part of the book in 1804 (Lambert, who wrote the part on the external commerce of Bengal, had died in the meantime).

16. Trevelyan (1835), reprinted (1976: 92–3) with an introduction by T. Banerjee.

17. Ibid.: 96.

18. Steuart (1772); Barber (1975: Chapter 4).

19. *GBP* (1884b: 433); *GBP* (1885b: 373).

20. S. Guha (1985: Chapter 2).

21. Raghavaiyangar (1893); Thomas and Pillai (1933); Siddiqi (1973).

22. Bagchi (1987: Part I, Chapter 10 and part II, Chapter 23).

23. See, for example, Beckett (1986); Rubinstein (1987); Stone and Fautier Stone (1984); F.M.L. Thompson (1963); E.P. Thompson (1991: 1696).

24. Baker (1984: Chapter 3); S. Guha (1985) and (1987).

25. S. Islam (1979: Chapters 5 and 6).

26. Cohn (1960) and (1969). Both reprinted in Cohn (1987).

27. Cohn (1969: 355).

28. Ibid.: 356.

29. See, for example, the case of the Raghubansi Rajputs of Dobhi taluk in Ibid.: 357.

30. Ibid.: 358–9.

31. See in this connection Nevill (1909: 113–23).

32. Chowdhury (1958: Chapter 3).

33. Ibid.: 125–7.

34. Bagchi (1975b).

35. Ibid.

36. Bharadwaj (1974: Chapter 1).

37. For a more detailed discussion of one particular raiyatwari area from the point of view of peasant insecurity, peasant dependence, and peasant resistance, see Bagchi (1992).

38. Ibid.

39. Whitcombe (1972: 161).

40. Azzi and Cox (1976); Jaffee and Russell (1976).

41. Stiglitz and Weiss (1981).

42. van den Dungen (1972: 126–7).

43. Dutt (1963b[1906]: 241).

44. B. Narain (1929/1984: Chapter 6).

45. van den Dungen (1972: 43).

46. Ibid.: 44.

47. Ibid.: 47.

48. Ibid.: Chapters 2 and 3.

49. N. Bhattacharya (1983) and (1985); Fox (1984).

50. N. Bhattacharya (1985: 120–4).

51. Bagchi (1982a: Chapter 6).

52. Cf. the critique of the Punjab Land Alienation Act by Hubert John Maynard, a high-ranking British official, before and soon after the Act was passed, as summarized by van den Dungen (1972: 287–95).

53. Ali (1989: Chapter 5).

54. Cain and Hopkins (1986).

55. For an analysis of oligarchic governance in eighteenth-century England as theatre, see E.P. Thompson (1991: 43–7).

56. 'Sir John Malcolm's Instruction and Orders to Officers: Instruction by Major-general Sir John Malcolm, G.C.B., KLS., to Officers acting under his Orders in Central India, in 1821', Appendix VIII, in Malcolm (1826), reprinted, 1970, in edition edited by K.N. Panikkar, New Delhi, pp. 307–407.

57. Ibid.: 378.

58. Ibid.: 377.

59. Ibid.: 389.

60. Cohn (1960: 330).

61. Bagchi (2006[1987]). The modal salary of an Indian employee was around Rs 10 per month.

62. Bagchi (1989: 23), and internal records of the Bank of Bengal.

63. Bagchi (1990b: 45–76).

64. Bagchi (1989: 190).

65. For a discussion of pooling equilibrium in markets characterized by asymmetric information, see Kreps (1989).

66. Ali (1989: 162–3, 67).

67. Ibid.: 73.

68. Ibid.: Chapters 2, 5, and 6.

Bibliography

Administration Report of the Madras Presidency for 1882–83. 1883. Madras: Superintendent Government Press.

Ahmed, R. 1981. *The Bengal Muslims 1871–1906: A Quest for Identity*. New Delhi: Oxford University Press.

Ahsan, Manzur. 2002. 'Reforming rural credit: Experience under the Fazlul Huq Ministry in Bengal', in A.K. Bagchi (ed.), *Money and Credit in Indian History since Early Medieval Times*. New Delhi: Tulika, pp. 170–85.

Ahuja, R. 1999. 'The origins of colonial labour policy in late eighteenth-century Madras', *International Review of Social History*, 44(2): 159–96.

__________. 2002. 'Labour relations in an early colonial context: Madras, c. 1750–1800', *Modern Asian Studies*, 36(4): 793–826.

Ali, Imran. 1989. *The Punjab under Imperialism, 1885–1947*. New Delhi: Oxford University Press.

Ambirajan, S. 1978. *Classical Political Economy and British Policy in India*. Cambridge: Cambridge University Press.

Amin, Samir. 1957. Les effets structurels de l'intégration internationale des économies précapitalistes. Une étude theoriquedu mécanisme qui a engendré les économies dites sous-développées. Doctoral thesis submitted to the University of Paris.

Appadurai, Arjun. 1981. *Worship and Conflict under Colonial Rule: A South Indian Case*. Cambridge: Cambridge University Press.

Armitage, David. 1998. 'Literature and empire', in Nicholas Canny (ed.), *The Oxford History of the British Empire*, vol. I, *The Origins of Empire: British Overseas Enterprise to the Close of the Seventeenth Century*. Oxford: Oxford University Press, pp. 99–123.

__________. 2000. *The Ideological Origins of the British Empire*. Cambridge: Cambridge University Press.

Arnold, David. 1999. 'Hunger in the garden of plenty: the Bengal famine of 1770', in Alessa Johns (ed.), *Dreadful Visitations: Confronting Natural Catastrophe in the Age of Enlightenment*. New York: Routledge, pp. 81–112.

Arrow, K.J. 1964. 'The role of securities in the optimal allocation of risk bearing', *Review of Economic Studies*, 31(2): 91–6. (Translated from 'Le rôle valeurs boursieres pour la repartition la meillure des risques', in *Econometrie* [1953]).

Arunima, G. 2003. *There Comes Papa: Colonialism and the Transformation of Matriliny in Kerala, Malabar, c. 1850–1940*. New Delhi: Orient Longman.

Ascoli, F.D. 1917. *Early Revenue History of Bengal and the Fifth Report 1812*. Oxford: Clarendon Press.

Atkinson, E.H. de V. and Tom S. Dawson. 1912. *Report on the Enquiry to bring Technical Institutions into Closer Touch and More Practical Relations with the Employers of Labour in India*, Calcutta.

Atkinson, E.T. (ed.). 1874. *Statistical, Descriptive and Historical Accounts of the North Western Provinces (NWP)*, Vol. I. *Bundelkhand*. Allahabad: Government Press.

_________. 1879. *Statistical, Descriptive and Historical Accounts of the North Western Provinces*, Vol. V, *Rohilkhand Division* [compiled by H.C. Conybeare]. Allahabad: Government Press.

Atkinson, F.J. 1902. 'A statistical review of income and wealth of British India', *Journal of the Royal Statistical Society*, 65(2): 209–83.

_________. 1909. 'Rupee prices in India, 1870 to 1908: With an examination of the causes leading to the present high level of prices', *Journal of the Royal Statistical Society*, 72(3): 496–573.

Avineri, S (ed.). 1969. *Karl Marx on Colonialism and Modernization*. New York: Anchor Books.

Azzi, C.F. and J.C. Cox. 1976. 'A Theory and Test of Credit Rationing: A Comment', *American Economic Review*, 66(5): 911–17.

Baak, Paul E. 1999. 'About enslaved ex-slaves, uncaptured contract coolies and unfree freedmen: Some notes about "free" and "unfree" labour in the context of plantation development in Southwest India, early sixteenth century-mid 1990s', *Modern Asian Studies*, 33(1): 121–57.

Bagchi, A.K. 1970. 'Long-term Constraints on India's Industrial Growth 1951–68', in E.A.G. Robinson and M. Kidron (eds), *Economic Development in South Asia*. London: Macmillan, pp. 170–92.

_________. 1971. 'The theory of efficient neocolonialism', *Economic and Political Weekly*, Special Number, VI (30–2): 1669–76.

_________. 1972a. *Private Investment in India 1900–1939*. Cambridge: Cambridge University Press (Indian edition, Madras: Orient Longman, 1975).

_________. 1972b. 'Some international foundations of capitalist growth and underdevelopment', *Economic and Political Weekly*, Special Number VII (31–3): 559–70.

_________. 1973a. 'Some implications of unemployment in rural areas', *Economic and Political Weekly*, VIII (31–3): 1501–10.

_________. 1973b. 'Foreign capital and economic development in India: A schematic view', in K. Gough and Hari P. Sharma (eds), *Imperialism and Revolution in South Asia*. New York: Monthly Review Press, pp. 43–76.

Bagchi, A.K. 1975a. 'Some Characteristics of Industrial Growth in India', *Economic and Political Weekly*, Annual Number.

_________. 1975b. 'Relation of agriculture to industry in the context of South Asia', Paper presented at the UN Conference on the Appraisal of the Relationship between Agricultural Development and Industrialization in Africa and Asia, Tananarive, Madagascar, July, *Frontier*, 8(22–4): 12–24.

_________. 1976a. 'De-industrialization in Gangetic Bihar: 1809–1901', in B. De *et al.*, *Essays in Honour of Professor S.C. Sarkar*. New Delhi: People's Publishing House.

_________. 1976b. 'Deindustrialization in India in the nineteenth century: Some theoretical implications', *Journal of Development Studies*, 12(2): 141–6.

_________. 1976c, 'Reflections on Patterns of Regional Growth in India Under British Rule,' *Bengal Past and Present*, XCV(1): 247–89.

_________. 1979a. 'A Reply', *IESHR*, 16(2): 147–61.

_________. 1979b. 'The Great Depression and the Third World with special reference to India', *Social Science Information*, 18(2).

_________. 1982a. *The Political Economy of Underdevelopment*. Cambridge: Cambridge University Press.

_________. 1982b. 'Ideas, ideologies and the other side of the moon', *Frontier*, 15(10–12): 15–20.

_________. 2006[1987]. *The Evolution of the State Bank of India, Vol. 1, The Roots 1806–1876*, part II, *Diversity and Regrouping 1860–1876*. Bombay: Oxford University Press (reprinted, Penguin Portfolio edition).

_________. 1988a. 'Problems of effective demand and contradictions of planning in India', in Amiya Bagchi (ed.), *Economy, Society and Polity: Essays in the Political Economy of Indian Planning*. Calcutta/Centre for Studies in Social Sciences: Oxford University Press, pp. 227–66.

_________. 1988b. 'Colonialism and the nature of "capitalist" enterprise in India', *Economic and Political Weekly*, XXIII (31) (reprinted in Bagchi [2002a: 99–136]).

_________. 1989. *The Presidency Banks and the Indian Economy 1870–1914*. Calcutta: Oxford University Press.

_________. 1990a. 'Wealth and work in Calcutta 1860-1921', in S. Chaudhuri (ed.), *Calcutta, The Living City*, Vol. I. Calcutta: Oxford University Press, pp. 212–23.

_________. 1990b. 'Colonialism and the nature of "capitalist" enterprise in India', in G. Shah (ed.), *Capitalist Development: Critical Essays*. Bombay: Popular Prakashan, pp. 45–76.

Bagchi, A.K. 1992. 'Land tax, property rights and peasant insecurity' (mimeo), Occasional Paper, Centre for Studies in Social Sciences, Calcutta.

_________. 1997. *The Evolution of the State Bank of India,* Vol. 2, *The Era of the Presidency Banks 1876–1920*. New Delhi: Sage Publications.

Bagchi, A.K. 1998. 'Studies on the Economy of West Bengal since Independence', *Economic and Political Weekly*, XXXIII (47–8): 2973–8.

_________. 1999. 'Dualism and dialectics in the historiography of labour', *Comparative Studies of South Asia, Africa and the Middle East*, 19(1): 106–21 (reprinted in Bagchi 2002a).

_________. 2000. 'Workers and the historians' burden', in T.J. Byres, K.N. Panikkar, and U. Patnaik (eds), *The Making of History: Essays Presented to Irfan Habib*. New Delhi: Tulika, pp. 276–327.

_________. 2002a. *Capital and Labour Redefined: India and the Third World*. New Delhi: Tulika.

_________. 2002b. 'The other side of foreign investment by imperial powers: transfer of surplus from colonies', *Economic and Political Weekly*, XXXVII(23): 2229–38.

_________. 2006[2005]. *Perilous Passage: Mankind and the Global Ascendancy of Capital*. Lanham, MD: Rowman & Littlefield; Indian edition, New Delhi, Oxford University Press.

_________. 2007. 'China India Russia: Moving out of backwardness', or, 'Cunning passages of history', Occasional Paper no. 10, Institute of Development Studies Kolkata.

_________. 2009. 'Nineteenth century imperialism and structural transformation in colonized countries', in A. Haroon Akram-Lodhi and Cristóbal Kay (eds), *Peasants and Globalization: Political Economy, Rural Transformation and the Agrarian Question*. London: Routledge, pp. 83–110.

Bagchi, Barnita. 2009. 'Ramabai, Rokeya, and the history of gendered social capital in India', in Jean Spence, Sarah Aiston, and Maureen Meikle (eds), *Women, Education and Agency, 1600–2000*. London: Routledge.

Bagchi, Jasodhara. 1990. 'Representing nationalism: Motherhood in colonial Bengal', *Economic and Political Weekly*, XXV(42–3), WS 65–72.

_________. 1996. 'Secularism as identity: the case of Tagore's *Gora*', in Madhusree Datta, Flavia Agnes, and Neera Adarkar (eds), *The Nation, the State and Indian Identity*. Calcutta: Samya, pp. 47–61.

Baker, C.J. 1984. *An Indian Rural Economy 1880–1955: The Tamilnad Countryside*. Oxford: Clarendon Press.

Ball, V. 1881. *A Manual of the Geology of India*, part III, *Economic Geology*. Calcutta: Office of the Geological Survey of India.

Bandopadhyay, Arun. 1992. *The Agrarian Economy of Tamilnadu 1820–1855*. Calcutta: K.P. Bagchi & Co.

Banerjea, Pramathanath. 1928. *Indian Finance in the Days of the Company*. London: Macmillan.

Bannerji, Himani. 2008. *Always Towards: Development and Nationalism in Rabindranath Tagore*, IDSK Special Lecture 2, Kolkata: Institute of Development Studies Kolkata.

Baran, P.A. 1957. *The Political Economy of Growth*. New York: Monthly Review Press.

Barber, W.J. 1975. *British Economic Thought and India 1600–1858: A Study in the History of Development Economics*. Oxford: Clarendon Press.

Bardhan, P. 1970a. 'Green Revolution and Agricultural Labourers', *Economic and Political Weekly*, Special number, V(29–31): 1239–46.

_________. 1970b. '"Green Revolution" and Agricultural Labourers: A Correction', *Economic and Political Weekly*, V(46): 1861.

Barrier, N.G. 1965. 'The Formulation and Enactment of the Punjab Alienation of Land Bill', *Indian Economic and Social History Review* (IESHR), 2(2): 144–5.

Bayly, C.A. 1989. *Imperial Meridian: The British Empire and the World 1780–1830*. London: Longman.

_________. 1990. *Indian Society and the Making of the British Empire*. Cambridge: Cambridge University Press.

Bayly, Susan. 1999. 'The evolution of colonial cultures: nineteenth-century Asia', in Andrew Porter (ed.), *The Oxford History of the British Empire*, vol. III, *The Nineteenth Century*. Oxford: Oxford University Press, pp. 446–69.

Beach, E.F. 1971. 'Hicks on Ricardo on Machinery', *Economic Journal*, 81(324): 916–22.

Beckett, J.V. 1986. *The Aristocracy in England 1660–1914*. Oxford: Blackwell.

Bergan, A. 1972. 'Personal income distribution and personal savings in East Pakistan', in Keith Griffin and A.R. Khan (eds), *Growth and Inequality in Pakistan*. London: Macmillan.

BH. 1809–10. *An Account of the District of Purnea in 1809–10 by* F. Buchanan, reprinted by the Bihar and Orissa research Society (BORS), Patna (1928).

_________. 1810–11. *An Account of the District of Bhagalpur in 1810–11* by F. Buchanan, reprinted by the BORS, Patna (1939).

_________. 1811–12. *An Account of the Districts of Bihar and Patna in 1811–12* (in two volumes) reprinted by the BORS, Patna (n.d.).

_________. 1812–13. *An Account of the District of Shahabad in 1812–13*. Reprinted by the BORS, Patna (1934).

Bhaduri, A. 1973. 'A Study in Agricultural Backwardness under Semi-Feudalism', *Economic Journal*, 83(329): 120–37.

_________. 1984. *The Economic Structure of Backward Agriculture*. Delhi: Macmillan.

Bharadwaj, K. 1974. *Production Conditions in Indian Agriculture: A Study Based on Farm Management Surveys*. Cambridge: Cambridge University Press.

_________. 1989. *Themes in Value and Distribution: Classical Theory Reappraised*. London: Unwin Hyman.

Bhattacharya, Durgaprasad (ed.). 1987. *Census of India 1961, Report of the Population Estimates of India, Vol. III, 1811–1820, Part B, India*. New Delhi: Ministry of Home Affairs, Office of the Registrar General, India.

Bhattacharya Durgaprasad and Bibhavati Bhattacharya (eds). 1963. *Census of India, 1961, Report on the Population Estimates of India (1820–1830)*. New Delhi: Office of the Registrar General, India.

Bhattacharya, N. 1983. 'The logic of tenancy cultivation: central and south-east Punjab', *IESHR*, XX(2): 121–50.

_________. 1985. 'Agricultural labour and production: central and south-east Punjab 1870–1940', in K.N. Raj, Neeladri Bhattacharya, Sumit Ganguly, and Sakti Padhi (eds), *Essays on the Commercialization of Indian Agriculture*. New Delhi: Oxford University Press, pp. 105–62.

Bihar and Orissa District Gazetteers. 1942. *Shahabad*, Patna.

Blyn, George. 1966. *Agricultural Trends in India 1891–1947: Output, Availability and Productivity*. Philadelphia: University of Pennsylvania Press.

Bose, Sugata. 1986. *Agrarian Bengal: Economy, Social Structure and Politics, 1919–1947*. Cambridge: Cambridge University Press.

_________. 1993. *Peasant Labour and Colonial Capital: Rural Bengal Since 1770*. Cambridge: Cambridge University Press.

Bose, Swadesh R. 1983. 'The Pakistan economy since independence (1947–1970)', in D. Kumar and M. Desai (eds), *The Cambridge Economic History of India*, vol. 2. Cambridge: Cambridge University Press, pp. 995–1026.

Boxer, C.R. 1973. *The Portuguese Seaborne Empire, 1415–1825*. Harmondsworth: Penguin.

Boyce, James. 1987. *Institutional Constraints to Technological Change*. Oxford: Oxford University Press.

Braudel, F. 1972–4 [1949]. *The Mediterranean and the Mediterranean World in the Age of Philip II* (translated by Sian Reynolds), in 2 vols. New York: Harper and Row.

_________. 1980. 'History and the social sciences: The *Longue Durée*', in Fernand Braudel (translated by Sarah Matthews) *On History*. London: Weidenfeld and Nicolson, pp. 25–54.

_________. 1982. *Civilization and Capitalism, 15th–18th Centuries*, vol. 2, *The Wheels of Commerce* (tr. S. Reynolds). London.

Breman, Jan. 1974. *Patronage and Exploitation: Changing Agrarian Relations in South Gujarat*. Berkeley, California: University of California Press.

Buchanan, D.H. 1966 [1934]. *The Development of Capitalistic Enterprise* in *India* (first edition, New York, Macmillan, 1934). London: Frank Cass.

Byrne, J. 1911. *Bengal District Gazetteers: Bhagalpur*. Calcutta: Bengal Secretariat Book Depot.

Cain, P.J. and A.G. Hopkins. 1986. 'Gentlemanly capitalism and British expansion overseas I. The old colonial system 1688–1850', *Economic History Review*, 39(4): 501–25.

Calvert, H.C. 1936. *The Wealth and Welfare of the Punjab*. Lahore: Civil and Military Gazette Office.

Canny, Nicholas (ed.). 1998. *The Oxford History of the British Empire*, vol. I, *The Origins of Empire: British Overseas Enterprise to the Close of the Seventeenth Century*. Oxford: Oxford University Press.

Catanach, I.J. 1970. *Rural Credit in Western India, 1875–1936*. Bombay: Oxford University Press.

Census. 1901a. *Census of India, 1901.* vol. I. *India,* Part I, *Report* by H.H. Risley and E.A. Gait. Calcutta: Office of the Superintendent of Government Printing, India, 1903.

_________. 1901b. vol. VI. *Bengal,* Part I, *Report* by E.A. Gait, 1902. Calcutta: Bengal Secretariat Press.

_________. 1901c. vol. VIA. *The Lower Provinces of Bengal and their Feudatories,* Part II, The Imperial Tables. Calcutta: Bengal Secretariat Press, 1902.

_________. 1901d. Vol. IX, *Bombay,* Part I, *Report* by R.E. Enthoven, 1902.

_________. 1911. *Census of India,* 1911, vol. VIII, *Bombay,* part I, *Report* by P.J. Mead and G. Laird Macgregor, Bombay: Government Central Press, 1912.

_________. 1921. *Census of India,* 1921, vol. VIII, *Bombay Presidency,* part I, *General Report* by L.J. Sedgwick, Bombay: Government Central Press, 1922.

_________. 1923. Vol. XV, *Punjab and Delhi,* Part I, *Report.* Lahore.

_________. 1931. Vol. XVII, *Punjab,* part I, *Report,* 1933, Lahore.

Chakrabarti, Manali. 2003. 'Industrialisation Process of Kanpur City 1914 to 1945'. Unpublished PhD thesis submitted to Jadavpur University, Calcutta.

Chakraborty, D. 1989. *Rethinking Working-Class History: Bengal 1890–1940.* Princeton, N.J.: Princeton University Press.

Chandra, N.K. 1972a. 'The class character of the Pakistani State', *Economic and Political Weekly,* VII (5–7): 275–92.

_________. 1972b. 'Agrarian clauses in East Pakistan (1949–70)', *Frontier,* Calcutta, 8 January, 15 January, and 22 January.

Charlesworth, N. 1978. 'Rich Peasants, and Poor Peasants in Late Nineteenth Century Maharashtra', in C. Dewey and A.G. Hopkins (eds), *The Imperial Impact: Studies in the Economic History of Africa and India.* London: Athlone Press, pp. 97–113.

Chattopadhyay, Raghabendra. 1975. 'De-industrialisation in India reconsidered', *Economic and Political Weekly,* X(12): 523–30.

Chaudhuri, B.B. 1969. 'Rural credit relations in Bengal, 1859–1885', *IESHR,* 6(3): 246–9.

_________. 1970a. 'Growth of commercial agriculture in Bengal', *IESHR,* VII(1): 25–60.

Chaudhuri, B.B. 1970b. 'Growth of Commercial Agriculture', *IESHR,* VII(2): 211–51.

_________. 1976. 'Agricultural growth in Bengal and Bihar, 1770–1860: Growth of cultivation since the famine of 1770', *Bengal Past and Present,* 95(1): 290–340.

_________. (ed.). 2005. *History of Science, Philosophy and Culture in Indian Civilization, Vol. VIII, Part 3, Economic History of India from Eighteenth to Twentieth Century.* New Delhi: Centre for Studies in Civilizations.

Chaudhuri, K.N. 1971. 'Introduction and Statistical Appendix', in K.N. Chaudhuri (ed.), *The Economic Development of India under the East India Company*. Cambridge: Cambridge University Press.

_________. 1972. 'Introduction and Statistical Appendix', in K.N. Chaudhuri (ed.), *The Economic Development of India under the East India Company, 1814–58*. London: Cambridge University Press.

_________. 1978. *The Trading World of Asia and the English East India Company 1660–1760*. London: Cambridge University Press.

Chaudhury, P.K. 1984. 'Commercialisation of Agriculture in Orissa 1900–1930', PhD thesis, Jawaharlal Nehru University, New Delhi.

Choksey, R.D. 1968. *Economic Life in the Bombay Presidency (1800–1939)*. Bombay: Asia Publishing House.

Chowdhury, B.B. 1958. 'Agrarian Relationship in Bengal after the Permanent Settlement 1793–1819', unpublished D Phil thesis, University of Calcutta.

Chung, Tan. 1973. 'The Triangular Trade between China and India (1771–1840): A Case of Commercial Imperialism'. Paper presented to the Indian History Congress, Chandigarh, December.

Clark, Colin. 1940. *The Conditions of Economic Progress*. London: Macmillan.

Clingingsmith, David and Jeffrey G. Williamson. 2004. *India's De-industrialization under British Rule: New Ideas, New Evidence*. NBER Working Paper 19586, Cambridge, MA: National Bureau of Economic Research.

_________. 2008. 'De-industrialization in 18th and 19th century India: Mughal decline, climate change and British industrial ascent', *Explorations in Economic History*, 45(3): 209–34.

Cohn, B.S. 1960. 'The initial British impact on India: a case study of the Benares region', *Journal of Asian Studies*, 19(4): 320–42.

_________. 1969. 'Structural change in Indian rural society 1596–1885', in R.E. Frykenberg (ed.), *Land Control and Social Structure in Indian History*. Madison: University of Wisconsin Press, pp. 343–421.

_________. 1987. *An Anthropologist among the Historians and Other Essays*. Delhi.

Colebrooke, H.T. 1804. *Remarks on the Husbandry and Internal Commerce of Bengal*, printed at Calcutta, (second edition, London).

Colebrooke, H.T. and A. Lambert. 1795. *Remarks on the Present State of Husbandry and Commerce of Bengal*. Calcutta.

_________. 1953 [1804]. 'Remarks on the Husbandry and Internal Commerce of Bengal', in A Mitra, *Census of India, 1951, vol. VI, West Bengal, Sikkim and Chandernagore, Part I c—Report*, pp. 180–231.

Connell, A.K. 1985. 'Indian railways and Indian wheat', *Journal of the Royal Statistical Society*, 48(2): 236–76.

Cuenca Esteban, Javier. 2001. 'The British balance of payments, 1772–1820: India transfers and war finance', *The Economic History Review*, New Series, 54(1): 58–86.

Cuenca Esteban, Javier. 2007. 'India's contribution to the British balance of payments, 1757–1812', *Explorations in Economic History,* 44(1): 154–76.

Darling, M.L. 1932. *The Punjab Peasant in Prosperity and Debt,* third edition, Calcutta: Oxford University Press.

Dasgupta, A. 1965. 'The jute industry', in V.B. Singh (ed.), *Economic History of India*. New Delhi: Allied Publishers, pp. 260–80.

Davenant, Charles. 1696/1771. *An Essay on the East-India Trade*. London.

Davis, Kingsley. 1951. *The Population of India and Pakistan*. Princeton, NJ: Princeton University Press.

Davis, Ralph. 1954. 'English Foreign Trade, 1660–1700', *The Economic History Review,* New Series, 7(2): 150–66.

De, B. *et al.* (eds). 1976. *Essays in Honour of Professor S.C. Sarkar*. New Delhi: People's Publishing House.

Dean, Genevieve. 1972. 'A note on the sources of technological innovation in the People's Republic of China', *The Journal of Development Studies,* 9(1): 187–99.

Deane, P. 1965. *The First Industrial Revolution*. Cambridge: Cambridge University Press.

Debreu, G. 1959. *Theory of Value*. New York: John Wiley & Sons.

De Cecco, Marcello. 1974. *Money and Empire: The International Gold Standard, 1890–1914*. Oxford: Basil Blackwell.

de Janvry, A. and K. Subbarao. 1986. *Agricultural Price Policy and Income Distribution in India*. New Delhi: Oxford University Press.

Desai, A.V. 1965. 'The Livestock Situation', *Economic Weekly*, Annual Number, pp. 329–38.

_________. 1968. 'Origins of Parsi Enterprise', *IESHR,* V(4): 307–17.

Desai, Meghnad. 1971. 'Demand for Cotton Textiles in Nineteenth Century India', *IESHR,* 8(4): 337–61.

Dhar, H. 1973. 'Agricultural servitude in Bengal Presidency around 1800', *Economic and Political Weekly,* VIII(30): 1349–56.

Dobb, M. 1946. *Studies in the Development of Capitalism*. London: Routledge & Kegan Paul.

Domar, Evsey D. 1970. 'The causes of slavery and serfdom', *Economic History Review,* 30(1): 18–32.

DRC (Deccan Riots Commission). 1878. *Report of the Deccan Riots Commissioners Appointed in India to Inquire into the causes of the Riots Which Took Place in 1875 in the Poona and Ahmadnagar Districts of the Bombay Presidency, 1875*. London: UK Parliamentary Papers, House of Commons, 2071 of 1878.

Drake, Michael (ed.). 1969. *Population in Industrialization*. London: Methuen.

Dutt, Romesh C. 1963a[1906]. *The Economic History of India,* vol. I, *Under Early British Rule 1757–1837,* second edition, London (reprinted, New Delhi: Publications Division, Ministry of Information and Broadcasting, Government of India).

Dutt, Romesh C. 1963b[1906]. *The Economic History of India*, vol. II, *In the Victorian Age*, second edition, London (reprinted New Delhi: Publications Division, Ministry of Information and Broadcasting, Government of India).

Dutt, R.P. 1949. *India Today*, Bombay, (second edn Calcutta: Manisha Granthalaya).

Edwardes, S.M. 1923. *Memoir of Sir Dinshaw Manockjee Petit, First Baronet (1823–1901)*. Oxford: Oxford University Press.

Eltis, W. 1984. *The Classical Theory of Economic Growth*. London: Macmillan.

Emmanuel, A. 1972. *Unequal Exchange: Study of the Imperialism of Trade*. London: New Left Books.

Encyclopaedia Britannica. 1906. Tenth edition. Edinburgh: Adam and Charles Black.

FC (Famine Commission). 1901. *Report of the Famine Commission, 1901*. Calcutta: Office of the Superintendent of Government Printing.

Felix, D. 1968. 'The Dilemma of Import Substitution—Argentina', in G.F. Papanek (ed.), *Development Policy—Theory and Practice*. Cambridge, MA: Harvard University Press.

Ferguson, Niall. 2004. *Empire: How Britain Made the Modern World*. Harmondsworth, Middlesex: Penguin.

Feuerwerker, A. 1968. 'The Chinese Economy 1912–1949', *Michigan Papers in Chinese Studies*, No. 1.

__________. 1970. 'Handicraft and Manufactured Cotton Textiles in China 1871–1910', *The Journal of Economic History*, 30(2): 338–78.

Final Report of the Royal Commission appointed to inquire into the Recent Changes in the Relative Values of the Precious Metals; with Minutes of Evidence and Appendixes, London: H.M.S.O.

Firminger, W.K. (ed.). 1917–18. *The Fifth Report from the Select Committee of the House of Commons on the Affairs of the East India Company dated 28th July 1813*, vols I–III. Calcutta: R. Cambray & Co.

Fisher, A.G.B. 1935. 'Economic Implications of National Progress', *International Labour Review*, Vol. 32, July, pp. 5–18.

__________. 1939. 'Primary, Secondary and Tertiary Production', *Economic Record*, June, pp. 24–38.

Fox, R.G. 1984. 'British colonialism and Punjabi labour', in C. Bergquist (ed.), *Labour in the Capitalist World Economy*. New Delhi: Sage Publications, pp. 107–34.

Frykenberg, R.E. (ed.). 1969. *Land Control and Social Structure in Indian History*. Madison and London: University of Wisconsin Press.

Frykenberg, R.E. and N. Mukherjee. 1969. 'The Ryotwari System and Social Organization in the Madras Presidency', in R.E. Frykenberg (ed.), *Land Control and Social Structure in Indian History*. Madison and London: University of Wisconsin Press, pp. 217–26.

Fukazawa, H. 1965a. 'Land and Peasants in the Eighteenth Century Maratha Kingdom', *Hitotsubashi Journal of Economics*, 6(1): 32–61.

Fukazawa, H. 1965b. 'The Cotton mill industry', in VB Singh (ed.), *The Economic History of India, 1857–1956*. Bombay: Asia Publishing House, pp. 223–59.

_________. 1972. 'Rural servants in the 18th century Maharashtrian village—demiurgic or Jajmani system?', *Hitotsubashi Journal of Economics*, 12(2): 14–40.

_________. 1974. 'Structure and change of the sharehold village (*Bhagdari* or *Narwadari* Village) in the Nineteenth Century British Gujarat', *Hitotsubashi Journal of Economics,* 14(2).

_________. 1982. 'Maharashtra and the Deccan: A Note', in T. Raychaudhuri and I. Habib (eds), *The Cambridge Economic History of India*, vol. I. Cambridge: Cambridge University Press, pp. 193–203.

_________. 1991. *The Medieval Deccan: Peasants, Social Systems and States: Sixteenth to Eighteenth Centuries*. New Delhi: Oxford University Press.

Furber, Holden. 1951. *John Company at Work*. Cambridge, MA: Harvard University Press.

GBP (*Gazetteer of the Bombay Presidency*). 1879a. Vol. III, *Kaira and Panch Mahals*. Bombay: Government Central Press.

_________. 1879b.Vol. IV, *Ahmedabad*. Bombay: Government Central Press,

_________. 1882, vol. XIII, *Thana*, part II, Bombay: Government Central Press.

_________. 1883. *Baroda*. Bombay: Government Central Press.

_________. 1884a. Vol. VIII, *Kathiawar*. Bombay: Government Central Press.

_________. 1884b. Vol. XVII, *Ahmadnagar*. Bombay: Government Central Press.

_________. 1884c. Vol. XX, *Sholapur*. Bombay: Government Central Press.

_________. 1884d. Vol. XXIII, *Bijapur*. Bombay: Government Central Press.

_________. 1885a. Vol. XVIII, part I, *Poona*. Bombay: Government Central Press.

_________. 1885b. Vol. XVIII, part II, *Poona*. Bombay: Government Central Press.

_________. 1887. Vol. II, *Surat and Broach*. Bombay: Government Central Press.

Geddes, J.C. 1874. *Administrative Experience Recorded in Former Famines*. Calcutta: Bengal Secretariat Press.

Ghosh, A.K. 1949. 'An Analysis of the Indian Price Structure since 1861', PhD dissertation, London School of Economics.

Ghosh, Parimal. 2000. *Colonialism , Class and a History of the Calcutta Jute Millhands, 1880–1930*. Hyderabad (India): Orient Longman.

_________. 2005. 'A history of a colonial working class, India: 1850–1946', in Binay Bhusan Chaudhuri (ed.), *History of Science, Philosophy and Culture in Indian Civilization*, pp. 525–698.

Gillion, K.L. 1968. *Ahmedabad: A Study in Indian Urban History*. Ahmedabad: New Order Book Co.

Gokhale, B.G. 1969. 'Ahmedabad in the Seventeenth Century', *Journal of the Economic and Social History of the Orient,* Vol. XII, pp. 187–97.

Gold and Silver Commission. 1888. *Final Report of the Royal Commission appointed to inquire into the Recent Changes in the Relative Values of the Precious Metals; with Minutes of Evidence and Appendixes*. London: Eyre and Spotiswoode for Her Majesty's Stationery Office.

Gopal, S. 1975. *British Policy in India 1858–1905*. Bombay: Orient Longman.

Gramsci, A. 1971. *Selections from the Prison Notebooks*, edited and translated by Quentin Hoare and Geoffrey Nowell-Smith, London: Lawrence & Wishart.

Greenberg, Michael. 1951. *British Trade and the Opening of China*. Cambridge: Cambridge University Press.

Griffin, Keith and A.R. Khan (eds). 1972a. *Growth and Inequality in Pakistan*. London: Macmillan.

_________. 1972b. 'A note on the degree of dependence on foreign assistance', in Keith Griffin and A.R. Khan (eds), *Growth and Inequality in Pakistan*. London: Macmillan.

Griffiths, P.J. 1967. *The History of the Indian Tea Industry*. London: Weidenfeld & Nicolson.

Gorrie, Maclagan, R. 1938. 'The Problem of Soil Erosion in the British Empire with Special Reference to India', *Journal of the Royal Society of Arts*, vol. 86.

_________. 1953. *Forestry Development and Soil Conservation in the Upper Damodar Valley–A 15-year Scheme*. Calcutta: Damodar Valley Corporation.

Guha, Amalendu. 1969. 'Regional Models for Entrepreneurship in Historical Perspective: A Case-study of Eastern India to 1857' (mimeographed paper presented at the Seminar on Historical Models in the Study of Tradition and Change in India, Simla, 19–26 October).

_________. 1970a. 'Parsi Seths as Entrepreneurs', *Economic and Political Weekly*, V(35): M 107–M 115.

_________. 1970b. 'The Comprador Role of Parsi Seths, 1750–1850', *Economic and Political Weekly*, V(48): 1933–6.

_________. 1977. *Planter Raj to Swaraj: Freedom Struggle and Electoral Politics in Assam. 1826–1947*. New Delhi: Indian Council of Historical Research.

Guha, R. 1963. *A Rule of Property for Bengal*. Paris: Mouton; new edition, Calcutta: Orient Longman, 1981.

Guha, Sumit. 1985. *The Agrarian Economy of the Bombay Deccan 1818–1941*. New Delhi: Oxford University Press.

_________. 1987. 'The Land Market in Upland Maharashtra c. 1820–1920', *IESHR*, 24(2): 117–44.

_________. (ed.). 1992a. *Growth, Stagnation or Decline? Agricultural Productivity in British India*. New Delhi: Oxford University Press.

Guha, Sumit. 1992b. 'Introduction', in Sumit Guha, *Growth, Stagnation or Decline? Agricultural Productivity in British India*, pp. 1–62.

Gupta, R.K. 1984. *The Economic Life of a Bengal District, Birbhum 1770–1857*. Burdwan: Burdwan University.

Gurley, J.G. 1971. 'Capitalist and Maoist Economic Development', *Monthly Review*, 22(9): 39–49.

Habib, Irfan. 1969. 'The potentialities of capitalistic development in the economy of Mughal India', *Journal of Economic History*, vol. XXIX (reprinted in Habib [1995: 180–232]).

__________. 1972. 'Indian Population, 1800–72: A Note', paper presented at the seminar on the colonization of the Indian economy held at the Centre of Advanced Study in History, Aligarh Muslim University, 10–12 March.

__________. 1975. 'Colonialization of the Indian economy', *Social Scientist*, 3(8), March, (reprinted in Habib [1995: 296–325]).

__________. 1995. *Essays in Indian History: Towards a Marxist Perspective*. New Delhi: Tulika.

__________. 2006. *A People's History of India 28, Indian Economy 1858–1914*. New Delhi: Tulika.

Halevy, E. 1972. *The Growth of Philosophic Radicalism*, translated from the French by Mary Morris and with a preface by J. Plamenatz. London: Faber.

Hamilton, Walter. 1815. *The East India Gazetteer*. London: John Murray.

Harnetty, P. 1977. 'Crop trends in the Central Provinces of India, 1861–1921', *Modern Asian Studies,* 11(3): 341–78.

Harvey, David. 2003. *The New Imperialism*, Oxford: Oxford University Press.

__________. 2005. 'From globalization to the new imperialism', pp. 91–100 in R.P. Appelbaum and W.I. Robinson (eds), *Critical Globalization Studies*. London: Routledge.

Hatekar, Neeraj and Ambarish Dongre. 2005. 'Structural breaks in Indian economic growth: Revisiting the debate with a longer perspective', *Economic and Political Weekly,* XL(10): 1432–41.

Hershlag, Z.Y. 1964. *Introduction to the Modern Economic History of the Middle East*. Leiden: E.J. Brill.

Heston, Alan. 1983. 'National Income', in D. Kumar and M. Desai (eds), *The Cambridge Economic History of India*, vol. 2. Cambridge: Cambridge University Press , pp. 376–462.

Hicks, J. 1969. *A Theory of Economic History*. Oxford: Clarendon Press.

__________. 1971. 'A Reply to Professor Beach', *Economic Journal*, 81(324): 922–25.

__________. 1973. *Capital and Time: A Neo-Austrian Theory*. Oxford: Clarendon Press.

Hjejle, Benedicte. 1967. 'Slavery and agricultural bondage in South India in the nineteenth century', *The Scandinavian Economic History Review*, XV (1 and 2): 71–126.

Hobsbawm, E.J. 1968. *Industry and Empire*. London: Weidenfeld and Nicolson.

Houthakker, Hendrik S. and Lester D. Taylor. 1966. *Consumer Demand in the United States 1929–1970*. Cambridge, MA: Harvard University Press.

Hunter, W.W (ed.). 1877a. *A Statistical Account of Bengal, Vol. XI, Patna and Saran*. London: Trübner & Co.

_________. 1877b. *A Statistical Account of Bengal*, XII, *Gaya and Shahabad*, compiled by D.B. Allen, A.W. Mackie, and H.H. Risley. London: Trubner & Co.

_________. 1877c. *A Statistical Account of Bengal*, XIV, *Bhagalpur and the Santal Parganas*, compiled by C.J. D'Donnell and H.H. Risley. London: Trubner & Co.

_________. 1877d. *A Statistical Account of Bengal*, vol. XV, *Monghyr and Purniah*, compiled by C.J. O'Donnell. London: Trubner & Co.

_________. 1881. 'India' in *Encyclopaedia Britannica*, ninth edition, Vol. XII. Edinburgh: Adam and Charles Black, pp. 731–812.

Husain, Iqbal (ed.). 2006. *Karl Marx on India*. New Delhi: Tulika.

Indian Livestock Census. 1966. New Delhi: Government of India, Ministry of Agriculture.

Indian School of Social Sciences. 1975. *Bonded Labour in India*. Calcutta: Indian School of Social Sciences.

Ishikawa, Shigeru. 1972. 'A note on the choice of technology in China', *The Journal of Development Studies*, 9(1): 161–85.

Islam, M.M. 1972. 'Agricultural Development of Bengal: A Quantitative Study', PhD thesis, School of Oriental and African Studies, London.

Islam, S. 1979. *The Permanent Settlement in Bengal: A Study of its Operation 1790–1819*. Dacca: Bangla Academy.

Issawi, C. (ed.). 1966. *The Economic History of the Middle East 1800–1914: A Book of Readings*. Chicago: The University of Chicago Press.

Investors' India Year-book 1921. Calcutta: Place, Siddons, and Gough.

Jackson, V.H. 1925. *Journal of Francis Buchanan (afterwards Hamilton) Kept during the Survey of the Districts of Patna and Gaya in 1811–1812*. Patna.

Jacomb-Hood, M.S. 1929. *A History of Bird & Co. 1864–1929*. Calcutta: Caledonian Printing Co.

Jaffee, D. and T. Russell. 1976. 'Imperfect Information, Uncertainty and Credit Rationing', *Quarterly Journal of Economics*, vol. 90, November, pp. 651–66.

Jones, R. 1831. *An Essay on the Distribution of Wealth and on the Sources of Taxation*, Part-I—*Rent*. London: John Murray.

Kalecki, M. 1971. *Selected Essays on the Dynamics of the Capitalist Economy*. Cambridge: Cambridge University Press.

Keatinge, G.F. 1913. 'Agricultural Progress in Western India', *Journal of the Royal Society of Arts*, LXI.

Kennedy, C., and A.P. Thirlwall. 1972. 'Technical progress: A Survey', *Economic Journal*, 82(325): 11–72.

Khan, A.R. 1972a. 'What has been happening to real wages in Pakistan?', in Keith Griffin and A.R. Khan (eds), *Growth and Inequality in Pakistan*. London: Macmillan.

_________. 1972b. *The Economy of Bangladesh*. London: Macmillan.

Khusro, A.M. 1962. *Economic Development with No Population Transfers*. Bombay: Asia Publishing House.

Kiyokawa, Y. 1983. 'Technical adaptations and managerial resources in India: A study of the experience of the cotton textile industry from a comparative view', *The Developing Economies*, 21(2): 97–133.

Klein, I. 1965. 'Utilitarianism and Agrarian Progress in Western India', *Economic History Review*, Second Series, vol. XVIII, pp. 576–97.

_________. 1972. 'Malaria and Mortality in Bengal', *IESHR*, IX(2): 132–60.

_________. 1973. 'Death in India', *Journal of Asian Studies*, 32(4): 639–59.

_________. 1974. 'Population and agriculture in northern India, 1872–1921', *Modern Asian Studies*, 8(2): 191–216.

_________. 1984. 'When the rains failed; famine, relief, and mortality in British India', *IESHR*, XXI(1).

_________. 2001. 'Development and death: Reinterpreting malaria, economics and ecology in British India', *IESHR*, 38(2): 147–79.

Kliuchevsky, V. 1960[1906]. *A History of Russia*, translated from the Russian by C.J. Hogarth, New York: Russell and Russell.

Kolenda, P.M. 1967. 'Toward a model of the Hindu Jajmani System', in G. Dalton (ed.), *Tribal and Peasant Economics*. Garden City, New York: National History Press, pp. 285–332.

Krader, L. (ed.), 1974, *The Ethnological Notebooks of Karl Marx* (*Studies of Morgan, Phear, Maine, Lubbock*), Assen (The Netherlands): Van Gorcum.

_________. 1975. *The Asiatic Mode of Production: Sources, Development and Critique* in *the Writings of Karl Marx*. Assen (The Netherlands): Van Gorcum.

Kreps, D.M. 1989. 'Out-of-equilibrium beliefs and out of-equilibrium behaviour', in F. Hahn (ed.), *The Economics of Missing Markets, Information, and Games*. Oxford: Oxford University Press, pp. 7–45.

Krishnamurty, J. 1970. 'Longterm changes in the industrial distribution of the working force in the Indian Union and the States: 1901–1961', *Report of the Committee of Experts on Unemployment Estimates*. New Delhi: Planning Commission, Government of India.

_________. 1983. 'The occupational structure', in D. Kumar and M. Desai (eds), *The Cambridge Economic History of India, Vol. 2: c. 1757–c. 1970*. Cambridge: Cambridge University Press, pp. 533–50.

_________. 1985. 'Deindustrialisation in Gangetic Bihar during the nineteenth century: Another look at the evidence', *IESHR*, 22(4): 399–416.

Krishnamurty, Sunanda. 1987. 'Real wages of agricultural labourers in the Bombay Deccan, 1874–1922', *IESHR,* 24(1): 81–98.

Kulke, Eckehard. 1974. *The Parsees in India.* Delhi: Vikas.

Kumar, D. and Meghnad Desai (eds). 1983. *The Cambridge Economic History of India, Vol. 2: c. 1757–c. 1970.* Cambridge: Cambridge University Press.

Kumar, Ravinder. 1968. *Western India in the Nineteenth Century.* London: Routledge & Kegan Paul.

Kuznets, S. 1966. *Modern Economic Growth.* New Haven: Yale University Press.

Lardinois, Roland. 1989. 'Deserted villages and depopulation in rural Tamil Nadu c. 1780–c. 1830', in T. Dyson (ed.), *India's Historical Demography: Studies in Famine, Disease and Society.* London: Curzon Press, pp. 16–48.

Laud, G.M. 1983. *Seven Decades of Co-operative Banking: History of the Maharashtra State Co-operative Bank, 1911–81.* Bombay: The Maharashtra State Co-operative Bank, Ltd.

Lefeber, L. 1974. 'On the paradigm for economic development', in A. Mitra (ed.), *Economic Theory and Planning: Essays in Honour of A.K. Das Gupta.* Calcutta: Oxford University Press, pp. 159–76.

Lewis, S.R. 1970. *Pakistan: Trade and Industrialisation Policies.* London: Oxford University Press.

Little, J.H. 1967. *The House of Jagat Seth* (with an introduction by N.K. Sinha). Calcutta: Calcutta Historical Society.

Long, D. 1979. 'Bentham on Property', in A. Parel and T. Flanagan (eds), *Theories of Property: Aristotle to the Present.* Ontario: Wilfred Laurier University, pp. 221–54.

Lovejoy, Paul E. and Jan S. Hogendorn. 1993. *Slow Death for Slavery: The Course of Abolition in Northern Nigeria.* Cambridge: Cambridge University Press.

Lucas, R.E. 1973. 'Some International Evidence on Output—Inflation Trade-offs', *American Economic Review,* 63(3): 326–34.

Luce, R.D. and H. Raiffa. 1957. *Games and Decisions.* New York: John Wiley.

Ludden, David (ed.). 1994. *Agricultural Production and Indian History.* New Delhi: Oxford University Press.

_________. 2005. 'The formation of modern agrarian economies in South India', in K.N. Chaudhuri (ed.), *History of Science, Philosophy and Culture in Indian Civilization, Vol. VIII, Part 3, Economic History of India from Eighteenth to Twentieth Century.* New Delhi: Centre for Studies in Civilizations, pp. 1–40.

Ludden, David (ed.). 2010. Rethinking 1905: Spatial Inequity, Uneven Development, and Nationalism (unpublished: personal communication).

Mackenzie, Compton. 1954. *Realms of Silver: One Hundred Years of Banking in the East.* London: Routledge.

Macpherson, C.B. 1962. *The Political Theory of Possessive Individualism: Hobbes to Locke.* Oxford: Oxford University Press.

Maddison, Angus. 1985. 'Alternative estimates of the real product of India, 1900–46', *IESHR*, 22(2): 201–10.

Maddison, Angus. 1995. *Monitoring the World Economy 1820–1922*. Paris: OECD.

_________. 2003. *The World Economy: A Millennial Perspective*. Paris: OECD.

Malcolm, John. 1826. *The Political History of India (1784–1823)*, vol. 2. London: John Murray.

Mann, H.H. 1955. *Rainfall and Famine: a Study of Rainfall in the Bombay Deccan*. Bombay: Indian Society of Agricultural Economics.

Mantoux, P. 1961. *The Industrial Development in the Nineteenth Century*. London: Jonathan Cape.

Marshall, A. 1923. *Money, Credit and Commerce*. London: Macmillan.

Marshall, P.J. 1998. 'The English in Asia to 1700', in Nicholas Canny (ed.), *The Oxford History of the British Empire*, vol. I, *The Origins of Empire: British Overseas Enterprise to the Close of the Seventeenth Century*. Oxford: Oxford University Press, pp. 264–85.

Martin (Martyn), Henry. 1701. *Considerations upon the East India Trade*, London: printed at Paternoster Row, A. and J. Churchill.

Martin, R. Montgomery. 1838. *History, Antiquities, Topography and Statistics of Eastern India*. London: W.H. Allen and Co.

_________. 1839. *Statistics of the Colonies of British Empire in the West Indies, South America, North America, Asia, Australasia, Africa and Europe*. London.

Marx, K. n.d. *Theories of Surplus Value*, vol. IV of *Capital*, part I, translated from the German by Emile Burns and edited by S. Ryazanskaya. Moscow: Foreign Languages Publishing House.

_________. 1853. 'The British rule in India', *New York Daily Tribune*, 25 June; (reprinted in Husain [2006]).

_________. 1886[1867]. *Capital*, vol.I, translated from the German by S. Moore and E. Aveling, (reprinted Moscow: Foreign Languages Publishing House, ca. 1957).

_________. 1966. *Capital*, vol. III, translated from the German edition of 1894, edited by F. Engels, Moscow: Progress Publishers.

_________. 1971. *Theories of Surplus Value*, vol. IV of *Capital*, translated by Jack Cohen and S.W. Ryazanskaya, part III. Moscow: Progress Publishers, Meek.

_________. 1976[1845]. 'Theses on Feuerbach', translated from the German and reprinted in K. Marx and F. Engels (eds), *The German Ideology*. Moscow: Progress Publishers, pp. 121–3.

_________. 1979 [1857–9]. 'Economic Manuscripts of 1857–1959,' in K. Marx and F. Engels, *Pre-Capitalist Socio-Economic Formations*. Moscow: Progress Publishers, pp. 83–136.

Masterman, Margaret. 1972. 'The Nature of a Paradigm', in I. Lakatos and A. Musgrave (eds), *Criticism and the Growth of Knowledge*. Cambridge: Cambridge University Press.

Mathias, P. 1972. *The First Industrial Nation: An Economic History of Britain 1700–1914*. London: Methuen.

Mayer, Peter. 1993. 'Inventing village tradition: The late 19th century origins of the North Indian "Jajmani System"', *Modem Asian Studies,* 27(2): 357–95.

McAlpin, M.B. 1983. *Subject to Famine: Food Crises and Economic Change in Western India 1860–1920*. Princeton, NJ: Princeton University Press.

McCloskey, D.N. 1976. 'English open fields as behaviour towards risk', *Research in Economic History*, vol. I, Fall, pp. 124–70.

_________. 1989. 'The Open Fields of England: Rents, Risk, and the Rate of Interest, 1300–1815', in D.W. Galenson (ed.), *Markets* in *History*: *Economic Studies of the Past*. Cambridge: Cambridge University Press, pp. 5–51.

Mehta, M.M. 1955. *Structure of Indian Industries*. Bombay: Popular Book Depot.

Mehta, S.D. 1954. *The Cotton Mills of India 1854 to 1954*. Bombay: Textile Association (India).

Metcalf, Barbara D. 2002. *Islamic Revival in British India: Deoband 1860–1900*. New Delhi: Oxford University Press.

Mill, J.S. 1857. *Principles of Political Economy with Some of their Applications to Social Philosophy*, fourth edition. London: John W. Parker & Son.

_________. 1858 [1818]. *The History of British India*, 5th edition with Notes and Continuation by Horace Hayman Wilson, 10 vols, London: James Madden, Piper, Stephenson and Spence.

_________. 1967. 'Profits and capital exports' in D.K. Fieldhouse (ed.), *The Theory of Capitalist Imperialism*. London: Longman.

Mishra, S.C. 1981. 'Patterns of Long-run Agrarian Change in Bombay and Punjab 1881–1972', PhD thesis, University of Cambridge.

_________. 1982. 'Commercialisation, peasant differentiation and merchant capital in late nineteenth-century Bombay and Punjab', *Journal of Peasant Studies*, 10(1): 3–51.

_________. 1983. 'On the reliability of pre-independence agricultural statistics in Bombay and Punjab', *IESHR*, XX(2): 171–90.

_________. 1985. 'Agricultural trends in Bombay Presidency 1900–1920: the illusion of growth', *Modern Asian Studies*, 19(4): 733–59.

Misra, B. 1985. 'The Growth of Industries in Eastern India, 1880–1910', PhD thesis submitted to the University of Calcutta.

Mitra, A. 1979. *Terms of Trade and Class Relations*. Calcutta: Rupa.

Montesquieu. 1989 [1748]. *The Spirit of the Laws*, translated and edited by Anne M. Cohler, Basia Carolyn Miller, and Harold Samuel Stone. Cambridge: Cambridge University Press.

Moore, R.J. 1966. *Liberalism and Indian Politics 1872–1922*. London: Edward Arnold.

Morris, M.D. 1963. 'Towards a re-interpretation of nineteenth century Indian economic history', *Journal of Economic History*, 23(4): 606–18.

Morris, M.D. 1983. 'Large scale industry', in D. Kumar and M. Desai (eds), *The Cambridge Economic History of India*, vol. 2. Cambridge: Cambridge University Press, pp. 553–676.

Mukherjee, Aditya. 1979. Agrarian conditions in Assam, 1880–1890: A case study of five districts of the Brahmaputra Valley, *IESHR*, XVI(2), 207–32.

_________. 2007. *The Return of the Colonial in Indian Economic History: The Last Phase of Colonialism in India*. Presidential Address (Modern India), Indian History Congress, Delhi, December 28–30.

Mukherjee, M. 1969. *National Income of India: Trends and Structure*. Calcutta: Statistical Publishing Society.

Mukherjee, N. 1962. *The Ryotwari System in Madras, 1792–1827*. Calcutta: Firma K.L. Mukhopadhyay.

Mukherjee, R.K. 2009[1938]. *The Changing Face of Bengal: A Study in Riverine Economy*, University of Calcutta (reprinted with an introduction by Arun Bandyopadhyay, Kolkata: Calcutta University).

Mukherji, Saugata. 1970. 'Trade in rice and jute in Bengal: Its effects on prices, cultivation and consumption of the two crops in early twentieth century (1900/01–1920–1), vol. I', Ph.D. thesis, Jadavpur University.

_________. 1976. 'Imperialism in action through a mercantilist function (a case study of the rural impoverishment in early 20th century Bengal as indicated by decline in per-capita consumption of foodgrains)', in B. De *et al., Essays in Honour of Professor S.C. Sarkar*. New Delhi: People's Publishing House.

_________. 1982. 'Some aspects of commercialization of agriculture in eastern India', in A. Sen, P. Chatterjee, and S. Mukherji (eds), *Three Studies on the Agrarian Structure in Bengal, 1850–1947*. Calcutta: Oxford University Press for Centre for Studies in Social Sciences, Calcutta.

_________. 2005. 'The evolution of the non-agrarian formal sector of the Indian economy through the eighteenth and nineteenth century', in K.N. Chaudhuri (ed.), *History of Science, Philosophy and Culture in Indian Civilization, Vol. VIII, Part 3, Economic History of India from Eighteenth to Twentieth Century*. New Delhi: Centre for Studies in Civilizations, pp. 355–436.

Myint, H. 1958. 'The "classical theory" of international trade and underdeveloped countries', *Economic Journal*, 68(2): 317–37.

Nanavati, M.B. and J.J. Anjaria. 1951. *The Indian Rural Problem*. Bombay: Vora & Co. for Indian Society of Agricultural Economics.

Naqvi, Hamida Khatoon. 1972. *Urbanisation and Urban Centres under the Great Mughals, 1556–1707*. Simla: Indian Institute of Advanced Study.

Narain, Brij. 1929/1984. *Indian Economic Life*, rpt, Delhi: Low Price Publications.

Narain, Dharm. 1965. *Impact of Price Movements on Areas under Selected Crops in India, 1900–39*. Cambridge: Cambridge University Press.

Narain, Dharm. 1967. 'Agricultural Change in India', *Economic and Political Weekly*, II (6).

Nevill, H.R. 1909. *Benares, a Gazetteer* (*District Gazetteers of the United Province of Agra and Oudh*), vol. xxvi, Allahabad, pp. 113–23.

Nightingale, Pamela. 1970. *Trade and Enterprise in Western India, 1784–1806*. Cambridge: Cambridge University Press.

O'Brien, Patrick K. 1982. 'Economic development: the contribution of the periphery', *Economic History Review*, second series, 35(1): 1–18.

_________. 1988. 'The costs and benefits of British imperialism 1846–1914, *Past & Present*, no. 120, pp. 163–200.

O'Conor, J.E. 1885. *Review of the Trade of India for 1884–1885*. Calcutta: Government Central Branch Press.

_________. 1886. *Review of the Trade of India in* 1885–86. Simla: Government Central Branch Press.

_________. 1908. *The Imperial Gazetteer of India: The Indian Empire*, Vol. III, *Economic*, new edition, Oxford: Clarendon Press.

O'Malley, L.S.S. 1906a. *Bengal District Gazetteers: Gaya*. Calcutta: Bengal Secretariat Book Depot.

_________. 1906b. *Shahabad*. Calcutta: Bengal Secretariat Book Depot.

_________. 1907. *Bengal District Gazetteers. Darbhanga*. Calcutta: Bengal Secretariat Book Depot.

_________. 1909. *Bengal District Gazetteers. Monghyr*. Calcutta: Bengal Secretariat Book Depot.

_________. 1911. *Bengal District Gazetteers, Purnea*. Calcutta: Bengal Secretariat Book Depot.

Oldham, C.E.A.W (ed.). 1930. *Journal of Francis Buchanan Kept during the Survey of the District of Bhagalpur in 1810–1811*. Superintendent, Government Printing, Bihar and Orissa, Patna.

Owen, W.F. 1966. 'The Double Developmental Squeeze on Agriculture', *American Economic Review*, 56(1): 43–70.

Pagden, Anthony. 1995. *Lords of All the World: Ideologies of Empire in Spain, Britain, and France, c. 1500–c. 1800*. New Haven, CT: Yale University Press.

Pandey, G. 2006. 'The bigoted Julaha', in G. Pandey, *The Construction of Communalism in Colonial North India*, second edition, New Delhi: Oxford University Press, pp. 66–108.

Papandieck, H. 1978. 'British managing agencies in the Indian coalfield', in D. Rothermund and D.C. Wadhwa (eds), *Zamindars, Mines and Peasants: Studies in the History of an Indian Coalfield and its Rural Hinterland*. Delhi: Manohar, pp. 166–227.

Parekh, B. (ed.). 1973. *Bentham's Political Thought*. London: Croom Helm.

Parkinson, Northcote, C. 1966 [1937]. *Trade in the Eastern Seas, 1793–1813*. London: Taylor and Francis.

Patnaik, Utsa. 2006. 'The free lunch: Transfers from the tropical colonies and their role in capital formation in Britain during the industrial revolution', in K.S. Jomo (ed.), *Globalization under Hegemony: The Changing World Economy*. New Delhi: Oxford University Press, pp. 30–70.

Paukert, F. 1968. 'Social security and income redistribution: Comparative study', *International Labour Review*, 98(5): 425–50.

Pavlov, V.I. 1964. *The Indian Capitalist Class*. New Delhi: People's Publishing House.

Perlin, F. 1978, 'Of White Whale and Countrymen in the Eighteenth Century Maratha Deccan: Extended class relations, rights and the problem of rural autonomy under the old regime', *Journal of Peasant Studies*, 5(2): 172–237.

Perry, P.J. (ed.). 1973. *British Agriculture 1875–1914*. London: Methuen & Co.

Peter, W.W. 1923. 'Observations on public health in the Orient', *American Journal of Public Health*, XIII(8): 627–35.

Phear, John Budd. 1880. *The Aryan Village in India and Ceylon*. London: Macmillan.

Phule, Jotirao. 2002. *Selected Writings of Jotirao Phule*, edited by G.P. Deshpande. New Delhi: Tulika.

Playne, S. and Arnold Wright (eds). 1917. *Bengal and Assam, Behar and Orissa*. London: Foreign and Colonial Compiling and Publishing Co.

Pollard, S.J. 1985. 'Capital exports, 1870–1914: Harmful or beneficial?' *Economic History Review*, second series, XXXVIII(4): 29–74.

Porter, Andrew (ed.). 1999. *The Oxford History of the British Empire*, vol. III, *The Nineteenth Century*. Oxford: Oxford University Press.

Prakash, Om. 1967. 'The Dutch East India Company and the Economy of Bengal, 1650–1717', unpublished PhD thesis, University of Delhi.

Prinsep, G.A. 1823. 'Appendix', in *Remarks on the External Commerce and Exchanges of Bengal, with Appendix of Accounts and Estimates* (reprinted in K.N. Chaudhuri [1971]).

Rabitoy, N. 1975. 'System vs. Expediency: The Reality of Land Revenue Administration in the Bombay Presidency, 1812–1820', *Modern Asian Studies*, 9(4): 529–46.

Radner, Roy. 1968. 'Competitive equilibrium under uncertainty', *Econometrica*, 36(1): 31–58.

Raghavaiyangar, S. Srinivasa. 1893. *Memorandum on the Progress of the Madras Presidency during the Last Forty Years of British Administration*. Madras: Superintendent Government Press.

Ramabai, P. 2000. *Ramabai Saraswati. Pandita Ramabai Through Her Own Words*. Edited and part-translated by Meera Kosambi. New Delhi: Oxford University Press.

Rao, G.N. 1999. *Agrarian Transition under Colonialism*. Thiruvananathapuram: Centre for Development Studies.

Ray, Indrajit. 2008. Bullion Movement and Its Impact on Money Supply in Bengal: Changing Scenario during the Early British Rule, (mimeo). Department of Commerce, University of North Bengal.

Ray, R.K. 1979. *Industrialization in India: Growth and Conflict in the Indian Corporate Sector, 1914–47*. New Delhi: Oxford University Press.

__________. 1998. 'Indian society and the establishment of of British supremacy, 1765–1818', in P.J. Marshall (ed.), *The Oxford History of the British Empire*, vol. II, *The Eighteenth Century*. Oxford: Oxford University Press, pp. 508–30.

Ray S.C. (compiler). 1915. *Agricultural Indebtedness in India and Its Remedies, being Selections from Official Documents*. Calcutta: Calcutta University.

Raychaudhuri, T. 1962. *Jan Company in Coromandel, 1605–1690: A study in the interrelation of European commerce and traditional economies*. 'S-Graven hage, Netherlands.

__________. 1969. 'Permanent Settlement in Operation: Bakarganj District, East Bengal', in R.E. Fryckenberg (ed.), *Land Control and Social Structure in Indian History*. Madison: University of Wisconsin Press.

RBI (Reserve Bank of India). 1954. *Banking and Monetary Statistics of India*. Bombay: Reserve Bank of India.

Report on the Marketing of Milk in India and Burma. 1941. Delhi: Manager of Publications.

Report of the Bengal Provincial Banking Enquiry Committee 1929–30, vol. II. 1930. Calcutta: Bengal Government Press.

Reserve Bank of India Bulletin. 1975. 'Employment in the organized sector, 1961–73'.

Resnick, S. 1970. 'The decline of rural industry under export expansion: A comparison among Burma, Phillippines, and Thailand, 1870–1938', *Journal of Economic History*, 30(1): 51–73.

Ricardo, David. 1966. 'On the principles of political economy and taxation', in P. Sraffa and M.H. Dobb (eds), *The Works and Correspondence of David Ricardo*, vol. I. Cambridge: Cambridge University Press.

Riskin, Carl. 1969. 'Local Industry and Choice of Techniques in Planning of Industrial Development in Mainland China', in United Nations Industrial Development Organization, *Planning for Advanced Skills and Technologies*. Vienna: United Nations, pp. 171–80.

Robinson, J. 1956. *The Accumulation of Capital*. London: Macmillan.

__________. 1959. 'Accumulation and the Production Function', *Economic Journal*, vol. 69, pp. 433–42.

Rosenberg, N (ed.). 1971. *The Rate and Direction of Technological Change*. Harmondsworth, Middlesex: Penguin Books.

Rostow, W.W. 1960. *The Stages of Economic Growth: A Non-Communist Manifesto*. London: Cambridge University Press.

Rothermund, D. 1992. *India in the Great Depression 1929–1939*. Delhi: Manohar.

Rothermund, D. and D.C. Wadhwa (eds). 1978. *Zamindars, Mines and Peasants: Studies in the HIstory of an Indian Coalfield and its Rural Hinterland*. Delhi: Manohar.

Roy, Tirthankar. 2000. *The Economic History of India 1857–1947*. New Delhi: Oxford University Press.

Rubinstein, W.D. 1987. *Elites and the Wealth in Modern British History: Essays in Social and Economic History*. Brighton: Harvester Press.

Rungta, R.S. 1970. *Rise of Business Corporations in India*. Cambridge: Cambridge University Press.

Rungta, S. 1985. 'Bowreah cotton and fort gloster jute mills, 1872–1900', *IESHR*, 22(2).

Rutnagur, S.M. 1927. 'Bombay industries: The cotton mills', *Indian Textile Journal*.

Saith, A. 1992. 'Long-term trends in per acre wheat yields in North India, 1827–1947: an evaluation of old controversies with some fresh evidence', in Sumit Guha (ed.), *Growth, Stagnation or Decline? Agricultural Productivity in British India*. New Delhi: Oxford University Press, pp. 207–58.

Saith, A. and A. Tankha. 1972. 'Agrarian transition and the differentiate of the peasantry; A study of a West U.P. village', *Economic and Political Weekly*, VII(14): 707–23.

Sanyal, M.K. 2004. *Peasant Paddy Production, Indebtedness: a study of Bengal districts 1901–1941*. Delhi: Manak.

Sanyal, M.K., P.K. Biswas, and S. Bardhan. 1998. 'Institutional change and output growth in West Bengal—end of impasse', *Economic and Political Weekly*, XXXIII(47–8): 2979–86.

Sarada Raju, A. 1941. *Economic Conditions in the Madras Presidency 1800–1850*. Madras: University of Madras.

Sarkar, Sumit. 1983. *Modern India 1885–1947*. Delhi: Macmillan.

Sarkar, Tanika. 1985. 'Bondage in the colonial text', in U. Patnaik and M. Dingwaney (eds), *Chains of Servitude: Bondage and Slavery in India*. New Delhi: Sangam Books, pp. 97–126.

Sastry, N.S.R. 1947. *A Statistical Study of India's Industrial Development*. Bombay: Thacker & Co.

Sau, R.K. 1973. *Indian Economic Growth: Constraints and Prospects*. Calcutta: Orient Longman.

Saul, S.B. 1960. *Studies in British Overseas Trade, 1870–1914*. Liverpool: Liverpool University Press.

__________. 1969. *The Myth of the Great Depression 1873–1896*. London: Macmillan.

__________. 1970. *Technological Change: The United States and Britain in the Nineteenth Century*. London: Methuen.

Sayers, R.S. 1967. *A History of Economic Change in England 1880–1939*. Oxford: Oxford University Press.

Schmookler, J. 1966. *Invention and Economic Growth*. Cambridge, MA: Harvard University Press.

Selections. 1864. *Selections from the Records of Government North Western Provinces*. Allahabad: Government Press.

Semmel, B. 1970. 'The philosophic radicals and colonialism', in A.G.L. Shaw (ed.), *Great Britain and the Colonies 1815–1865*. London: Methuen.

Sen, A. 1973. *Dimensions of Unemployment in India*. Calcutta: Indian Statistical Institute.

Sen, A. 1981. *Poverty and Famines: An Essay on Entitlement and Deprivation*. New York: Oxford University Press.

Sharma, T.R. 1946. *The Location of Industries in India*. Bombay: Hind Kitabs.

Shirras, Findlay, G. 1914. *Review of the Trade of India in 1913–14*. Department of Statistics, Government of India, p. 51.

Shklar, Judith N. 1987. *Montesquieu*. Oxford: Oxford University Press.

Siddiqi, Asiya. 1973. *Agrarian Change in a Northern Indian State: Uttar Pradesh 1819–1833*. Oxford: Clarendon Press.

Simmons, Colin. 1985. 'Deindustrialization, industrialization and the Indian economy, c. 1850–1947', *Modern Asian Studies*, vol. 19, pp. 593–622.

Singh, S.B. 1966. *European Agency Houses in Bengal*. Calcutta: Firma K.L. Mukhopadhyay.

Sinha, N.K. 1961. *Economic History of Bengal*, vol. I. Calcutta: Firma K.L. Mukhopadhyay.

_________. 1962. *The Economic History of Bengal*, vol. II. Calcutta: Firma K.L. Mukhopadhyay.

_________. 1965. *The Economic History of Bengal from Plassey to the Permanent Settlement*, vol. I, third edition. Calcutta: Firma KL Mukhopadhyay.

_________. 1970. *The Economic History of Bengal 1793–1848*, Vol. III. Calcutta: Firma K.L. Mukhopadhyay.

Sivasubramonian, S. 1965. National Income of India, 1900–01 to 1946–47 (mimeo), Delhi: Delhi School of Economics.

_________. 2000. *The National Income of India in the Twentieth Century*. New Delhi: Oxford University Press.

Soltow, L. 1965. *Toward Income Equality in Norway*. Madison and Milwaukee: The University of Wisconsin Press.

_________. 1968. 'Long-run Changes in British Income Inequality', *Economic History Review*, Second Series, 21(1): 17–29.

Spate, O.H.K. 1957. *India and Pakistan: A General and Regional Geography*, second edition. London: Methuen.

Spodek, Howard. 1965. 'The "Manchesterisation" of Ahmedabad', *Economic Weekly*, XVII(11): 483–90.

_________. 1969. 'Traditional culture and entrepreneurship: Case study of Ahmedabad', *Economic* and *Political Weekly*, IV(8): M27–M31.

Statistical Abstract of the Indian Union, 1967, 1968. Delhi.

Stein, B. 1989. *Thomas Munro: The Origins of the Colonial State and His Vision of Empire*. New Delhi: Oxford University Press.

Steuart, J. 1772. *The Principles of Money Applied to the Present State of the Coin in Bengal*. London.

Stewart, F. and Streeten, P. 1973. 'Conflicts between output and employment objectives', in R. Jolly, E. de Kadt, H. Singer, and F. Wilson (eds), *Third World Employment: Problems and Strategy*. Harmondsworth, Middlesex: Penguin Books.

Stiglitz, J.E. and A. Weiss. 1981. 'Credit Rationing in Markets with Imperfect Information', *American Economic Review*, LXXI(3): 393–410.

Stokes, E. 1959. *The English Utilitarians and India*. Oxford: Clarendon Press.

_________. 1976. 'The land tenure systems of the North-Western Provinces and Bombay Deccan 1830–1880: Ideology and the official mind', in C.H. Philips and M.D. Wainwright (eds), *Indian Society and the Beginnings of Modernization*. London: School of Oriental and African Studies.

_________. 1978. *The Peasants and the Raj*. Cambridge: Cambridge University Press.

Stone, L. and J.E. Fautier Stone. 1984. *An Open Elite? England 1540–1880*. New York: Oxford University Press.

Strachey, J. and R. Strachey. 1986 [1882]. *The Finances and Public Works of India 1869–1881*, reprinted by Delhi: Gian Publishing House.

Taban, Faruqi Anjum. 1995. 'Population of Lucknow in 1857: From records in contemporary Urdu newspapers', *Proceedings of the Indian History Congress, 55th Session, Aligarh, 1994,* Delhi, pp. 724–6.

The Investor's India Year Book 1919. Calcutta: Place, Siddons, and Gough.

The Statesman. 1975. 'Move for abolition of bonded labour', 30 May, Calcutta.

The Times. 1883. 'Land banks for India', 5 July, London.

Thomas, P.J. 1926. *Mercantilism and the East India Trade*. London: P.S. King.

Thomas, P.J. and B. Natarajan. 1936. 'Economic depression in the Madras Presidency (1825–54)', *Economic History Review*, VII(1): 67–75.

Thomas, P.J. and B.N. Pillai. 1933. *Economic Depression in the Madras Presidency 1820–1854*, Madras.

Thompson, E. and G.T. Garratt. 1934. *The Rise and Fulfilment of British Rule in India*. London: Macmillan.

Thompson, E.P. 1991. 'The patricians and the plebs', in E.P. Thompson, *Customs in Common*. London: Merlin Press.

Thompson, F.M.L. 1963. *English Landed Society in the Nineteenth Century*. London: Routledge.

Thorner, Alice and Daniel Thorner. 1964. 'The twentieth century trend in manufacture in India', in C.R. Rao, P.C. Mahalanobis, and D.B. Lahiri (eds), *Essays on Econometrics and Planning*. Calcutta: Statistical Publishing Society.

Thorner, Daniel. 1954. *Agrarian Prospect in India*. Delhi: Delhi School of Economics.

Thorner, Daniel. 2005 [1962]. '"De-industrialization" in India: 1881–1931', in Daniel and Alice Thorner, *Land and Labour in India,* rpt. New Delhi: Chronicle Books, pp. 85–95.

Tilly, Louise A. 1994. Connections, *American Historical Review*, 99(1): 1–17.

Tobin, J. 1973. 'The Economy of China: A Tourist's View', *Challenge*, reprinted in *Economic Impact* (Washington, D.C.), No. 3.

Townsend, R.M., 1988, 'Models as Economies,' *Economic Journal*, vol. 98, pp. 1–24.

Trevelyan, C.E. 1835. *Report upon the Inland Customs and Town Duties of the Bengal Presidency*, second edition, Calcutta, reprinted with an introduction by T. Banerjee, Calcutta, 1976, pp. 92–3.

Tripathi, Amalesh. 1956. *Trade and Finance in the Bengal Presidency: 1793–1833*. Calcutta: Orient Longman.

Tucker, H. St George. 1853. *Memorials of Indian Government*. London: Richard Bentley.

Turner, H.A. and D.A.S. Jackson. 1970. 'On the determination of the general wage level—a world analysis; or "Unlimited Labour Forever"', *Economic Journal*, 80(323): 827–49.

Turnham, D. 1970. *The Employment Problem in Less Development Countries*. Paris: OECD.

Tyabji, Nasir. 1995. *Colonialism, Chemical Technology and Industry in Southern India 1880–1937*. New Delhi: Oxford University Press.

UN (United Nations). 1973. *Economic Survey of Latin America 1971*. New York: United Nations.

__________. 1974. *Economic Survey of Asia and the Far East 1973*. Bangkok.

van den Dungen, P.H.M. 1972. *The Punjab Tradition: Influence and authority in nineteenth-century India*. London: Allen & Unwin.

Vicziany, Marika. 1979a. 'Bombay merchants and structural changes in the export community 1850 to 1880', in K.N. Chaudhuri and C.J. Dewey (eds), *Economy and Society: Essays in Indian Economic and Social History*. New Delhi: Oxford University Press, pp. 163–96.

__________. 1979b. 'The de-industrialization of India in the nineteenth century: A methodological critique of Amiya Kumar Bagchi', *IESHR*, 16(2): 105–43.

Visaria, P. and L. Visaria.1983. 'Population (1757–1947)', in D. Kumar and M. Desai (eds), *The Cambridge Economic History of India*, vol. 2. Cambridge: Cambridge University Press, pp. 463–572.

Wakefield, E.G. 1967. 'A Theory of Economic Imperialism', in D.K. Fieldhouse (ed.), *The Theory of Capitalist Imperialism*. London: Longman.

Wallace, D.R. 1928. *The Romance of Jute*. London: W. Thacker & Co.

Wallerstein, Immanuel. 1980. *The Modern World-System*, vol. 2, *Mercantilism and the Consolidation of the European World-Economy 1600–1750*. New York: Academic Press.

Warren, Bill. 1980. *Imperialism: Pioneer of Capitalism*. London: Verso.

Washbrook, D.A. 1973. 'Country politics: Madras 1880 to 1930', in J. Gallagher, G. Johnson, and A. Seal (eds), *Locality Province and Nation: Essays on Indian Politics, 1870 to 1940*. Cambridge: Cambridge University Press, pp. 155–212.

__________. 1981, 'Law, state and agrarian society in colonial India', *Modern Asian Studies*, 15(3): 649–721.

__________. 1993a. 'Land and labour in late eighteenth-century South India: the Golden age of the Pariah?', in Peter Robb (ed.), *Dalit Movements and the Meanings of Labour in India*. New Delhi: Oxford University Press, pp. 68–86.

Washbrook, D.A. 1993b. 'Economic depression and the making of "traditional" society in colonial South India 1820–1855', *Transactions of the Royal Historical Society*, sixth series, vol. 3, pp. 237–63.

__________. 1994. 'The commercialization of agriculture in colonial India: Production, subsistence and reproduction in the "Dry South", c. 1870–1930', *Modern Asian Studies*, 28(1): 129–64.

__________. 1999. 'India, 1818–1860: The two faces of colonialism', in Andrew Porter (ed.), *The Oxford History of the British Empire*, vol. III, *The Nineteenth Century*. Oxford: Oxford University Press, pp. 395–421.

__________. Forthcoming. 'The Indian economy and the British empire', in N. Gooptu and D. Peers (eds), *The Oxford History of the British Empire: India*.

Watt, G. 1908. *The Commercial Products of India*. London: John Murray.

__________. 1972 [1889]. *A Dictionary of the Economic Products of India, vol. II, Cabbage to Cyperus*, London (1889); (reprinted, Delhi: Cosmo).

__________. 1972 [1890]. *A Dictionary of the Economic Products of India, vol. IV, Gossypium to Linociera*, London (1890); (reprinted, Delhi: Cosmo).

__________. 1972 [1891]. *A Dictionary of the Economic Products of India, vol. V*, Delhi: Cosmo Publication.

Whitcombe, Elizabeth. 1972. *Agrarian Conditions in Northern India, Vol. 1, The United Provinces under British Rule 1860–1900*. Berkeley and London: University of California Press.

Williamson, O.E., 1975, *Markets and Hierarchies: Analysis and Anti-Trust Implications*. New York: Free Press.

Wilson, F. 1972. *Labour in the South African Gold Mines 1911–1969*. Cambridge: Cambridge University Press.

Wink, A., 1986, *Land and Sovereignty in India: Agrarian Society and Politics under the Eighteenth Century Maratha Swarajya*. Cambridge: Cambridge University Press.

Wong, R. Bin. 1997. *China Transformed: Historical Change and the Limits of European Experience*. Ithaca, NY: Cornell University Press.

Yule, Henry and A. C. Burnell. 1903. *Hobson-Jobson*. London: John Murray.

Zachariah, K.C. 1964. *A Historical Study of Internal Migration in the Indian Subcontinent, 1901–1931*. Bombay: Asia Publishing House.

Zuvekas, C., Jr. 1966. 'Economic growth and income distribution in postwar Argentina', *Inter-American Economic Affairs*, 20(3): 19–38.

Index